Terrorism and Exclusion from Refugee Status in the UK

Queen Mary Studies in International Law

Edited by

Malgosia Fitzmaurice
Phoebe Okowa
Sarah Singer

VOLUME 18

The titles published in this series are listed at *brill.com/qmil*

Terrorism and Exclusion from Refugee Status in the UK

Asylum Seekers Suspected of Serious Criminality

By

Sarah Singer

BRILL
NIJHOFF

LEIDEN | BOSTON

Library of Congress Cataloging-in-Publication Data

Singer, Sarah, (law teacher) author.
Terrorism and exclusion from refugee status in the UK : asylum seekers suspected of serious criminality / By Sarah Singer.
pages cm. -- (Queen mary studies in international law ; v. 18)
Includes bibliographical references and index.
ISBN 978-90-04-29207-9 (hardback : alk. paper) -- ISBN 978-90-04-29206-2 (e-book : alk. paper)
1. Terrorism--Great Britain. 2. Refugees--Legal status, laws, etc.--Great Britain. 3. Asylum, Right of I. Title.

KD8039.S56 2015
342.4108'3--dc23

2015004545

This publication has been typeset in the multilingual "Brill" typeface. With over 5,100 characters covering Latin, IPA, Greek, and Cyrillic, this typeface is especially suitable for use in the humanities. For more information, please see www.brill.com/brill-typeface.

ISSN 1877–4822
ISBN 978-90-04-29207-9 (hardback)
ISBN 978-90-04-29206-2 (e-book)

This book is printed on acid-free paper.

Contents

Acknowledgements

First and foremost I would like to express my gratitude to my PhD supervisors, Professor Malgosia Fitzmaurice and Dr Prakash Shah, for their invaluable support and guidance throughout the course of this research. I would also like to thank Queen Mary, University of London, for granting me a Research Studentship which materially supported my studies, and am grateful to the Modern Law Review for the financial assistance which enabled me to complete the final stages of this study.

I am also grateful to all those who participated in this research via interviews, questionnaires and submitting written comments. I thank all the judges, barristers, solicitors and Home Office staff that generously donated their time and experience in these ways. Unfortunately the confidentiality assured for the project means I am unable to name and thank them individually, but without their participation this book would be a shell of its current form, and I therefore express my unreserved gratitude to all those who were involved. I would also like to thank the Access to Justice Analytical Services team and the Presidents of the Upper Tribunal and the First-tier Tribunal of the Immigration & Asylum Chamber for granting permission for judicial participation in this research project and their help and assistance in co-ordinating these contributions. This research also owes a great deal to the participation of the Home Office's Special Cases Unit, and I am grateful to the individuals involved for their participation, help and advice. I also thank the Information Access Team at the Home Office's Migration Statistics Department for their patience in responding to my numerous Freedom of Information requests, and particularly Bill Gale of the Home Office's Operational Policy and Rules for his interest and support throughout this study.

I owe a great deal to Professor Kate Malleson, and thank her for her help and advice in formulating the application for judicial participation in this research and for all the support she has given me throughout the course of my doctoral studies. I would also like to thank Dr Josh Davis for his invaluable assistance in using statistical analysis software to analyse and display the results of the completed questionnaires, and for his comments on earlier drafts of these chapters.

Finally, I am grateful to my friends and family, and of course Tiago, for their moral support and encouragement. In particular, I would like to thank Matthew Gordon for his patience and helpful feedback during in the early stages of this research, Ana Alba Betancourt for her unwavering support and energy and Ellis Billowes for proof reading much of the first draft. I would also like to thank

Aleksandra Jordanoska for her assistance with technical editing and formatting.

I dedicate this book to my parents; my mum for her steadfast support and my dad for his indefatigable interest in my research topic and encouragement throughout the course of my academic studies, without which I would not have had the motivation to undertake this research at all.

Table of Cases

AA (Exclusion clause) Palestine [2005] UKIAT 00104.
AA-R (Iran) v Secretary of State for the Home Department [2013] EWCA Civ 835.
Abu Qatada v Secretary of State for the Home Department [2007] UKSIAC 15/2005.
Adimi, R (on the application of) v Uxbridge Magistrates Court & Anor [1999] EWHC Admin 765.
AH (Article 1F(b) – 'serious') Algeria [2013] UKUT 382.
AH (Algeria) v Secretary of State for the Home Department [2012] EWCA Civ 395.
Al-Sirri v Secretary of State for the Home Department [2012] UKSC 54.
Al-Sirri v Secretary of State for the Home Department & Anor [2009] EWCA Civ 222.
Amberber v Secretary of State for the Home Department (unreported; 00/TH/01570).
AS (s.55 'exclusion' certificate – process) Sri Lanka [2013] UKUT 571.
Asfaw, R v [2008] UKHL 31.
Attorney General v Tamil X [2010] NZSC 107; [2011] 1 NZLR 721.
Azimi-Rad (Art. 1F(a) – complicity – Arts 7 and 25 ICC Statute) Iran [2011] UKUT 339 (IAC).
Bankovic v Belgium, [2001] ECHR 890.
BB v Secretary of State for the Home Department [2006] UKSIAC 39/2005.
Bundesrepublik Deutschland (C-57/09) v B (C-101/09) and D [2010] ECR I–000.
Bundesrepublik Deutschland v B (C-57/09) and D (C-101/09) (Opinion of Mr Advocate General Mengozzi) [2010] ECR I-10979.
C v Secretary of State for the Home Department [2003] UKSIAC 7/2002.
Chahal v United Kingdom (1996) 23 EHRR 413.
CM (Article 1F(a) – superior orders) Zimbabwe [2012] UKUT 236 (IAC).
D.K.N. v A Decision of the Asylum & Immigration Tribunal [2009] ScotCS CSIH53.
DD & Anor v Secretary of State for the Home Department [2007] UKSIAC 42/2005.
Dispute regarding Navigational and Related Rights (Costa Rica v Nicaragua), ICJ Reports 133.
Engel and Others v The Netherlands [1976] ECHR 3.
European Roma Rights Centre & Ors, R (on the application of) v Immigration Officer at Prague Airport & Anor [2004] UKHL 55.
Ezokola v. Canada (Citizenship and Immigration), 2013 SCC 40.

F, R v [2007] EWCA Crim 243.

FTZK and the Min for Immigration and Citizenship [2012] AATA 312.

Garate (Gabriel Sequeiros) v Refugee Status Appeals Authority [1998] NZAR 241, 9 October 1997 (High Court of New Zealand).

Gul, R. v [2013] UKSC 64.

Gurung (Exclusion, Risk, Maoists) Nepal [2002] UKIAT 04870.

Immigration and Naturalization Service v Aguirre-Aguirre, 526 US 415 (1999) (US Supreme Court).

Interlocutory Decision on the Applicable Law: Terrorism, Conspiracy, Homicide, Perpetration, Cumulative Charging STL-11-01/1 (16 February 2011) (Special Tribunal for Lebanon).

Ireland v United Kingdom [1978] ECHR 1.

Islam v Secretary of State for the Home Department Immigration Appeal Tribunal and Another, Ex Parte Shah, R v [1999] UKHL 20; [1999] 2 AC 629; [1999] 2 All ER 545.

Island of Palmas Case (USA v the Netherlands) (1932) Scott Hague Court Rep.

Januzi v Secretary of State for the Home Department & Ors [2006] UKHL 5.

Jasarevski v Minister of Citizenship and Immigration [2012] FC 1145.

Jones, R v [2006] UKHL 16.

JS (Sri Lanka), R (on the application of) v Secretary of State for the Home Department [2010] UKSC 15.

JS (Sri Lanka), R (on the application of) v Secretary of State for the Home Department [2009] EWCA Civ 364.

Kasikili/Sedudu Island (Botswana/Namibia) [1999] ICJ Rep 1045.

KJ (Sri Lanka) v Secretary of State for the Home Department [2009] EWCA Civ 292.

KK (Article 1F(c), Turkey) [2004] UKIAT 00101.

Kuruparan et al [2012] FC 745.

Lai v Canada (Minister of Citizenship and Immigration) [2000] FCA 125.

Legal Consequences for States of the Continued Presence of South Africa in Namibia (South West Africa) notwithstanding Security Council Resolution 276 (Advisory Opinion) [1971] ICJ Rep 4.

Loizidou v Turkey (Preliminary Objections) [1995] ECHR 10.

MA (Palestinian Arabs – Occupied Territories – Risk) [2007] UKAIT 00017.

Maaouia v France [2000] ECHR, application 39652/98.

MH (Syria) v Secretary of State for the Home Department [2009] EWCA Civ 226.

MT (Algeria) & Ors v Secretary of State for the Home Department [2007] EWCA Civ 808.

MT (Article 1F (a) – aiding and abetting) Zimbabwe [2012] UKUT 15 (IAC).

Mugesera v Canada (Minister of Citizenship and Immigration) [2005] 2 S.C.R. 100, 2005 SCC 40 (Supreme Court of Canada).
Mukhtiar Singh v Secretary of State for the Home Department [2000] (unreported, SC 4/99).
North Sea Continental Shelf Cases (Federal Republic of Germany/Denmark; Federal Republic of Germany/Netherlands) (Merits) [1969] ICJ Rep 3.
PK (Sri Lanka, risk on return, exclusion clause) Sri Lanka [2004] UKIAT 00089.
PM and others (Kabul – Hizb-i-Islami) [2007] UKAIT 00089.
Prosecutor v Aleksovski (Appeal Judgment) ICTY-95-14/1-A (24 March 2000).
Prosecutor v. Blagoje Simic *et al.* (Trial Judgment) ICTY –95-9-T, (17 October 2003).
Prosecutor v Blaskic (Appeal Judgment) ICTY –95-14-A (29 July 2004).
Prosecutor v Brima (Appeal Judgment) SCSL-2004-16-A (20 June 2007) (Special Court for Sierra Leone).
Prosecutor v Fofana (Appeals Judgment) Case No. SCSL-04-14-A (May 28 2008).
Prosecutor v Furundzija (Trial Judgment) ICTY –95-17/1-T (10 December 1998).
Prosecutor v Kordic and Cerkez (Appeal Judgment) ICTY –95-14/2-A (17 December 2004).
Prosecutor v Krnojelac (Appeal Judgment) ICTY –97-25-A (17 September 2003).
Prosecutor v Kvocka *et al.* (Trial Judgment) ICTY –98-30/1-T (2 November 2001).
Prosecutor v. Milomir Stakic (Trial Judgment) ICTY –97-24-T, (31 July 2003).
Prosecutor v Milutinovic *et al.* (Appeal Judgment) ICTY –99-37-AR72, (21 May 2003).
Prosecutor v Perriera, Special Panels for Serious Crimes East Timor (27 April 2005).
Prosecutor v Simba (Trial Judgment) ICTR-01-76-T (13 December 2005).
Sylvestre Gacumbitsi v. The Prosecutor (Appeal Judgment) ICTR-2001-64-A, (7 July 2006).
Prosecutor v Tadic (Appeal Judgment) ICTY –94-1-A (15 July 1999).
Prosecutor v Tadic (Decision on the Defence Motion for Interlocutory Appeal on Jurisdiction) ICTY –94-1 (2 October 1995).
Prosecutor v Vasiljevic (Appeal Judgment) ICTY –98-32-A (25 February 2004).
Pushpanathan v Canada [1998] 1 SCR 982.
R (On the application of Hoxha) v Special Adjudicator [2005] 4 All ER 580.
Ramirez v Canada (Minister of Employment and Immigration) [1992] 2 FC 306 (Federal Court of Appeal).
RB (Algeria) v Secretary of State for the Home Department [2009] UKHL 10.
Reservations to the Convention on the Prevention and Punishment of the Crime of Genocide (Advisory Opinion) [1951] ICJ Rep 15.

Saadi v Italy (Application No. 37201/06).
Secretary of State for the Home Department v DD (Afghanistan) [2010] EWCA Civ 1407.
Secretary of State for the Home Department v K [2006] UKHL 46.
Secretary of State For The Home Department, Ex Parte Adan; R v Secretary of State For The Home Department Ex Parte Aitseguer, R v [2000] UKHL 67.
Sepet & Anor, R (on the application of) v Secretary of State for the Home Department [2003] UKHL 15.
Sivakumar [1994] 1 FC 433.
Sivakumuran, R (on the application of) v Secretary of State for the Home Department [1987] UKHL 1.
SK (Article 1F(a) exclusion) Zimbabwe [2010] UKUT 327 (IAC).
SK (Zimbabwe) v Secretary of State for the Home Department [2012] EWCA Civ 807.
Soering v United Kingdom [1989] 11 EHRR 439.
Sovereignty over Pulau Ligitan and Pulau Sipadan (Indonesia/Malaysia) [2002] ICJ Rep 645.
SS (Libya) v Secretary of State for the Home Department [2011] EWCA Civ 1547.
SS v Secretary of State for the Home Department [2010] UKSIAC 56/2009.
Stephen Hagan v Australia, Communication No. 26/2002, UN Doc CERD/C/62/D/26/2002 (20th March 2003) United Nations Committee on the Elimination of Racial Discrimination.
T v Secretary of State for the Home Department (Court of Appeal) [1995] 1 WLR 545; [1995] 2 All ER 1042; [1995] Imm AR 142.
T v Secretary of State for the Home Department [1996] UKHL 8; [1996] A C 742; [1996] 2 All ER 865; [1996] 2 WLR 766; [1996] Imm AR 443 (22 May 1996).
Tamil X v Refugee Status Appeals Authority; Attorney-General (Minister of Immigration) v Y [2009] NZCA 488, [2009] 2 NZLR 73.
Territorial Dispute (Libya Arab Jamahiririya/Chad) [1994] ICJ Rep 6.
Thangarasa, R. (on the application of) v Secretary of State for the Home Department [2002] UKHL 36.
The Effect of Reservations on the Entry Into Force of the American Convention on Human Rights (Arts. 74 and 75) (Advisory Opinion) OC-2/82 (1982) (Inter-American Court of Human Rights).
The Mayagna (Sumo) Awas Tingni Community v Nicaragua (Judgment) OC-79/01 (31 August 2001).
The Prosecutor v Nahimana, Barayagwiza, Ngeze (Appeal Judgment) ICTR-99-52-A (28 November 2007).
The Right to Information on Consular Assistance in the Framework of the Guarantees of the Due Process of Law (Advisory Opinion) OC-16/99 (1 October 1999) (Inter-American Court of Human Rights).

Tyrer v United Kingdom [1978] ECHR 2.
VXN and HN v Sweden (2 September 2000) UN Doc CAT/C/24/D/130/1999; CAT/C/24/D/131/1999 (UN Committee Against Torture).
Y v Secretary of State for the Home Department [2006] UKSIAC 36/2004.

Table of Treaties and Other Instruments

International Documents

Charter of the United Nations (24 October 1945) 1 UNTS XVI (UN Charter).

Convention Against Torture and Other Cruel, Inhuman or Degrading Treatment or Punishment (10 December 1984) 1465 UNTS 85.

Convention for the Suppression of Unlawful Seizure of Aircraft (16 December 1970) 860 UNTS 105.

Convention Relating to the Status of Refugees (28 July 1951) 189 UNTS 137 (Refugee Convention).

Council of Europe (CoE) European Convention for the Protection of Human Rights and Fundamental Freedoms (4 November 1950) ETS 5.

Geneva Convention for the Amelioration of the Condition of the Wounded and Sick in Armed Forces in the Field (12 August 1949) 75 UNTS 31 (Geneva Convention I).

Geneva Convention for the Amelioration of the Condition of Wounded, Sick and Shipwrecked Members of Armed Forces at Sea (12 August 1949) 75 UNTS 85 (Geneva Convention II).

Geneva Convention Relative to the Protection of Civilian Persons in Time of War (12 August 1949) 75 UNTS 287 (Geneva Convention IV).

Geneva Convention Relative to the Treatment of Prisoners of War (12 August 1949) 75 UNTS 135 (Geneva Convention III).

International Convention against the Taking of Hostages (17 December 1979) 1316 UNTS 20.

International Convention for the Suppression of Terrorist Bombings (15 December 1997) 2149 UNTS 284.

International Convention on the Suppression and Punishment of the Crime of Apartheid (30 November 1973) A/RES/3068(XXVIII), 1015 UNTS 243.

International Covenant on Civil and Political Rights (16 December 1966) 999 UNTS 171.

International Criminal Court Review, Resolution RC/Res.6 (11 June 2010).

League of Arab States, Arab Convention on Regulating Status of Refugees in the Arab Countries (1994) (not yet ratified).

Organization of African Unity 'Convention Governing the Specific Aspects of Refugee Problems in Africa' (10 September 1969) 1001 UNTS 1001.

Protocol Additional to the Geneva Conventions of 12 August 1949, and relating to the Protection of Victims of International Armed Conflicts (8 June 1977) 1125 UNTS 13 (Additional Protocol I).

Protocol Additional to the Geneva Conventions of 12 August 1949, and relating to the Protection of Victims of Non-International Armed Conflicts (8 June 1977) 1125 UNTS 609 (Additional Protocol II).

Protocol Relating to the Status of Refugees (31 January 1967) 606 UNTS 267 (the 1967 Protocol).

Rome Statute of the International Criminal Court (17 July 1998) 2187 UNTS 3 (Rome Statute).

UN Human Rights Committee 'General Comment No. 24: Issues Relating to Reservations Made upon Ratification or Accession to the Covenant or the Optional Protocols thereto, or in Relation to Declarations under Article 41 of the Covenant' (4 November 1994) UN Doc CCPR/C/21/Rev.1/Add.6.

United Nations 'Charter of the International Military Tribunal – Annex to the Agreement for the prosecution and punishment of the major war criminals of the European Axis' (8 August 1945).

United Nations 'Constitution of the International Refugee Organisation' (15 December 1946) 18 UNTS 3, Annex I Part II. Annex to UNGA Resolution 62 (I), UN Doc A/PV.67.

United Nations General Assembly 'Convention on the Prevention and Punishment of the Crime of Genocide' (9 December 1948) 78 UNTS 78.

United Nations General Assembly 'Declaration on Measures to Eliminate International Terrorism' (9 December 1994), annexed to United Nations General Assembly, Resolution 49/60 (17 February 1995) UN Doc A/Res/49/60.

United Nations General Assembly 'Declaration to Supplement the 1994 Declaration on Measures to Eliminate International Terrorism' (17 December 1996), annexed to United Nations General Assembly, Resolution 51/210 (16 January 1997) UN Doc A/Res/51/210.

United Nations General Assembly 'Final Act of Conference of Plenipotentiaries on the Establishment of an International Criminal Court' (17 July 1998) UN Doc A/CONF.183/10.

United Nations General Assembly 'Statute of the Office of the United Nations High Commissioner for Refugees' (14 December 1950) Annex to United Nations General Assembly Resolution 428 (V) A/RES/428(V) A/RES/428(V).

United Nations General Assembly 'Draft Comprehensive Convention on International Terrorism' (12 August 2005) UN Doc A/59/894.

United Nations General Assembly Resolution 3 (I) (13 February 1946) UN Doc A/PV.32.

United Nations General Assembly Resolution 3314 (XXIX) (14 December 1974) UN Doc A/Res/3314 (XXIX).

United Nations General Assembly Resolution 49/60 (17 February 1995) UN Doc A/Res/49/60.

United Nations General Assembly Resolution 51/210 (16 January 1997) UN Doc A/Res/51/210.

United Nations General Assembly Resolution 56/160 (13 February 2002) UN Doc A/Res/56/160.

United Nations General Assembly Resolution 59/195 (22 March 2005) UN Doc A/Res/59/195.

United Nations General Assembly Resolution 60/288 (20 September 2006) UN Doc A/Res/60/288.

United Nations General Assembly Resolution 62 (I) (15 December 1946) UN Doc A/PV.67.

United Nations Security Council 'Statute of the International Criminal Tribunal for the Former Yugoslavia (ICTY Statute)' (25 May 1993), established by Security Council Resolution 808/1993, 827/1993 and amended by Resolution 1166/1998, 1329/2000, 114/2002.

United Nations Security Council Res 1566 (8 October 2004) UN Doc S/RES/1566.

United Nations Security Council Resolution 1269 (19 October 1999) UN Doc S/RES/1269.

United Nations Security Council Resolution 1386 (20 December 2001) UN Doc S/RES/1386.

United Nations Security Council 'Statute of the International Criminal Tribunal for Rwanda (ICTR Statute)' (8 November 1994), established by Security Council Res 955 (8 November 1994) and last amended by Security Council Res 1717 (2006) (13 October 2006) UN Doc S/Res/955; 33 ILM 1598 (1994).

United Nations Security Council, Resolution 1373 (28 September 2001) UN Doc S/RES/1373.

United Nations Security Council, Resolution 1624 (14 September 2005) UN Doc S/RES/1624.

Universal Declaration of Human Rights, UNGA Res 217 A(III) (10 December 1948).

Vienna Convention on the Law of Treaties (23 May 1969) 1155 UNTS 331.

European Union Instruments

Council Common Position 2001/931/CFSP on the application of specific measures to combat terrorism. [2001] OJ L304/12.

Council Directive 2004/83/EC on the minimum standards for the qualification and status of third country nationals or stateless persons as refugees or as persons who otherwise need international protection and the content of the protection granted. [2004] OJ L304/12.

Council Directive 2005/85/EC of 1 December 2005 on Minimum Standards on Procedures in Member States for Granting and Withdrawing Refugee Status. [2006] OJ L326.

Council Framework Decision 2002/475/JHA on combating terrorism. [2002] OJ L164.

Directive 2011/95/EU of the European Parliament and of the Council on Standards for the qualification of third-country nationals or stateless persons as beneficiaries of international protection, for a uniform status for refugees or for persons eligible for subsidiary protection, and for the content of the protection granted (recast). [2011] OJL 337/9.

Directive 2013/32/EU of the European Parliament and of the Council on common procedures for granting and withdrawing international protection (recast). [2013] OJ L180/60.

United Kingdom

Anti-terrorism Crime and Security Act 2001.

Asylum and Immigration Appeals Act 1993.

Criminal Justice and Immigration Act 2008.

European Communities Act 1972.

Immigration Act 1971.

Immigration, Asylum and Nationality Act 2006.

Nationality, Immigration and Asylum Act 2002.

Special Immigration Appeals Commission Act 1997.

Terrorism Act 2000.

The Refugee or Person in Need of International Protection (Qualification) Regulations 2006, SI 2006/2525.

Tribunals, Courts and Enforcement Act 2007.

Table of Materials

International

Alain Pellet, Special Rapporteur 'Second Report on Reservations to Treaties' (13 June 1996) UN Doc A/CN.4/477/Add.i.

ECOSOC Social Committee '166th Meeting' (1950) UN Doc E/AC.7/SR.166.

ECOSOC Social Committee'160th Meeting'(1950) UN Doc E/AC.7/SR.160.

Institut de Driot International, 'Resolution adopted by the Institute of International Law at Wiesbaden on the Intertemporal Problems in Public International Law' [1975] Yearbook of the Institute of International Law 339.

International Law Commission 'Conclusions of the work of the Study Group on the Fragmentation of International Law: Difficulties arising from the Diversification and Expansion of International Law UN' (2006) Doc A/61/10.

International Law Commission 'The Charter and Judgment of the Nürnberg Tribunal: History and Analysis' (3 March 1949) UN Doc A/CN.4/5, Appendix II.

International Law Commission 'Draft Code of Crimes against the Peace and Security of Mankind' (1996) II Yearbook of the International Law Commission, Part Two.

Official Records of the Assembly of States Parties to the Rome Statute of the International Criminal Court, First session, New York (3–10 September 2002) UN Doc E.03.V.2.

Official Records of the Review Conference of the Rome Statute of the International Criminal Court, Kampala (31 May–11 June 2010) (International Criminal Court, RC/11).

UN Ad Hoc Committee on Refugees and Stateless Persons 'Ad Hoc Committee on Statelessness and Related Problems, France: Proposal for a Draft Convention Preamble' (17 January 1950) E/AC.32/L.3.

UN Ad Hoc Committee on Refugees and Stateless Persons, 'Ad Hoc Committee on Statelessness and Related Problems, First Session: Summary Record of the Twenty-fourth Meeting Held at Lake Success, New York, on Friday, 3 February 1950, at 2.30 p.m.' (27 Nov 1951) UN Doc E/AC.32/SR.24.

UN Ad Hoc Committee on Statelessness and Related Problems, 'Provisional Draft of Parts of the Definition Article of the Preliminary Draft Convention Relating to the Status of Refugees, Prepared by the Working Group on This Article' (23 January 1950) E/AC.32/L.6.

UN Conference of Plenipotentiaries on the Status of Refugees and Stateless Persons, Conference of Plenipotentiaries on the Status of Refugees and

Stateless Persons: Summary Record of the Thirty-fourth Meeting, 30 November 1951, A/CONF.2/SR.34.

UN Conference of Plenipotentiaries on the Status of Refugees and Stateless Persons, 'Draft Convention Relating to the Status of Refugees. Report of the Working Group Appointed to Study Section E of Article I of the Draft Convention Relating to the Status of Refugees' (19 July 1951) UN Doc A/CONF.2/92.

UN Conference of Plenipotentiaries on the Status of Refugees and Stateless Persons 'Conference of Plenipotentiaries on the Status of Refugees and Stateless Persons: Summary Record of the Twenty-ninth Meeting' (28 November 1951) A/CONF.2/SR.29.

UN Conference of Plenipotentiaries on the Status of Refugees and Stateless Persons 'Conference of Plenipotentiaries on the Status of Refugees and Stateless Persons: Summary Record of the Twenty-fourth Meeting' (27 November 1951) A/CONF.2/SR.24.

UN General Assembly 'Summary Record of the 11th Meeting' (4 October 1996) UN Doc A/C.6/51/SR.11.

United Nations 'Official Records of the United Nations Conference on the Law of Treaties, First and Second Sessions, Documents of the Conference' (1968–1969)UN Doc A/CONF.39/26.

United Nations Committee on the Elimination of Racial Discrimination, Stephen Hagan v Australia, Communication No. 26/2002, UN Doc CERD/C/62/D/26/2002 (20th March 2003).

United Nations Conference of Plenipotentiaries on the Status of Refugees and Stateless Persons, 'Draft Convention Relating to the Status of Refugees. Federal Republic of Germany: Amendment to Article 1' (13 July 1951) UN Doc A/CONF.2/76.

United Nations Conference of Plenipotentiaries on the Status of Refugees and Stateless Persons, 'Draft Convention Relating to the Status of Refugees. Report of the Working Group Appointed to Study Section E of Article I of the Draft Convention Relating to the Status of Refugees' (19 July 1951) UN Doc A/CONF.2/92.

United Nations Conference of Plenipotentiaries on the Status of Refugees and Stateless Persons 'Conference of Plenipotentiaries on the Status of Refugees and Stateless Persons: Summary Record of the Twenty-fourth Meeting' (27 November 1951) UN Doc A/CONF.2/SR.24.

United Nations General Assembly 'Principles of International Cooperation in the Detection, Arrest, Extradition and Punishment of Persons Guilty of War Crimes Against Humanity' (3 December 1973) A/RES/3020/(XXVII).

United Nations General Assembly 'Summary Record of the 10th Meeting' (3 October 1996) UN Doc A/C.6/51/SR.10.

United Nations High Commissioner for Refugees 'Beyond Proof, Credibility Assessment in EU Asylum Systems: Full Report' (May 2013).

United Nations High Commissioner for Refugees 'Note on the Exclusion Clauses' (30 May 1997).

United Nations High Commissioner for Refugees 'Addressing Security Concerns Without Undermining Refugee Protection – UNHCR's Perspective' (29 November 2001).

United Nations High Commissioner for Refugees 'Background Note on the Application of the Exclusion Clauses: Article 1F of the 1951 Convention relating to the Status of Refugees' (4 September 2003).

United Nations High Commissioner for Refugees 'Global Consultations on International Protection/Third Track: Asylum Processes' (31 May 2001) EC/GC/01/12.

United Nations High Commissioner for Refugees 'Guidelines on International Protection No. 5: Application of the Exclusion Clauses: Article 1F of the 1951 Convention relating to the Status of Refugees' (4 September 2003) HCR/GIP/03/05UNHCR.

United Nations High Commissioner for Refugees 'Improving Asylum Procedures: Comparative Analysis and Recommendations for Law and Practice – Key Findings and Recommendations' (March 2010).

United Nations High Commissioner for Refugees 'Roger Judge v Canada, Communication No. 829/1998' (13 August 2003) UN Doc CCPR/C/78/D/829/1998.

United Nations High Commissioner for Refugees 'Summary Conclusions on the Concept of "Effective Protection" in the Context of Secondary Movements of Refugees and Asylum-Seekers (Lisbon Expert Roundtable, 9–10 December 2002)' (February 2003).

United Nations High Commissioner for Refugees, 'Handbook on Procedures and Criteria for Determining Refugee Status under the 1951 Convention and the 1967 Protocol relating to the Status of Refugees' (January 1992) HCR/IP/4/Eng/REV.1.

United Nations High Commissioner for Refugees, 'The Exclusion Clauses: Guidelines on their Application' (2 December 1996).

United Nations Security Council '5261st Meeting' (14 September 2005) UN Doc S/PV.5261.

United Nations Security Council, Counter-Terrorism Committee Executive Directorate 'Technical Guide to Implementation of Security Council Resolution 1373' (2009) UN Doc S/2009/620.

United Nations 'Yearbook of the International Law Commission' (1966) UN Doc A/CN.4/SER.A/1966/Add. 1.

United Kingdom

Hansard, HC Deb 22 October 2005, vol 438, col 284.
Hansard, HC Deb 16 November 2005, vol 439, col 1055.
Home Office 'Immigration Statistics October–December 2012' (28th Feb 2013).
Home Office, Immigration Rules.
UK Border Agency 'Asylum Casework Instruction, Interim Asylum Instruction: Restricted Leave' (2012).
UK Border Agency 'Asylum Policy Instructions: Exclusion: Articles 1F and 33(2) of the Refugee Convention' (2008).
UK Border Agency 'Asylum Process Guidance, Considering Asylum Claims and Assessing Credibility' (2012).
UK Border Agency 'Asylum Process Guidance, Exclusion: Article 1F of the Refugee Convention' (2012).

List of Figures and Tables

Figures

Tables

List of Acronyms

AIT	Asylum and Immigration Tribunal
AJAS	Access to Justice Analytical Services
APG	Asylum Process Guidance
CAT	Convention Against Torture
CEAS	Common European Asylum System
CERD	Convention on the Elimination of Racial Discrimination
CJEU	Court of Justice of the European Union
CMR	Case Management Review
ECHR	European Convention on Human Rights
ECtHR	European Court of Human Rights
EIJ	Egyptian Islamic Jihad
EU	European Union
FOI	Freedom of Information
HOPO	Home Office Presenting Officer
HRC	Human Rights Committee
IAT	Immigration and Asylum Tribunal
ICC	International Criminal Court
ICCPR	International Covenant on Civil and Political Rights
ICJ	International Court of Justice
ICTR	International Criminal Tribunal for Rwanda
ICTY	International Criminal Tribunal for former Yugoslavia
ILC	International Law Commission
IMT	International Military Tribunal
IRO	International Refugee Organisation
ISAF	International Security Assistance Force
LIFG	Libyan Islamic Fighting Group
LTTE	Liberation Tigers of Tamil Eelam (Tamil Tigers)
MDC	Movement for Democratic Change (Zimbabwe)
OAU	Organization of African Unity
PKK	Kurdistan Workers' Party (Partiya Karkeren Kurdistan: PKK)
SCU	Special Cases Unit
SIAC	Special Immigration Appeals Commission
UDHR	Universal Declaration of Human Rights
UK	United Kingdom
UKBA	United Kingdom Border Agency
UN	United Nations

UNGA	United Nations General Assembly
UNHCR	United Nations High Commissioner for Refugees
UNRRA	United Nations Relief and Rehabilitation Administration
UNSC	United Nations Security Council

Introduction

In 2001, shortly after the 9/11 terrorist attacks on United States, the United Nations (UN) Security Council called on Member States to '[e]nsure…that refugee status is not abused by the perpetrators, organizers or facilitators of terrorist acts'.[1] This was not the first time the UN had called on States to exclude terrorists from refugee status, nor would it be the last.[2] The drive to deny the benefits of refugee status to suspected terrorists has led a number of states parties to the 1951 Convention relating to the Status of Refugees (the 1951 Convention) to interpret Article 1F, its 'exclusion clause', so as to bring terrorism within the scope of the provision.[3] However, although the UN Security Council has repeatedly called on Member States to exclude terrorists from refugee status, the Council did not define terrorism in these resolutions, nor did it refer to an existing definition of terrorism.[4] Indeed, whilst the international community has repeatedly condemned terrorist acts, at present there is

---

1 UN Security Council Resolution (UNSC Res) 1373 (28 September 2001) UN Doc S/RES/1373, para 3(g).

2 See also UNSC Res 1269 (19 October 1999) UN Doc S/RES/1269, para 4; UNSC Res 1624 (14 September 2005) UN Doc S/RES/1624, preamble para 7; Declaration on Measures to Eliminate International Terrorism (UNGA Dec 1994) (9 December 1994), annexed to UNGA Res 49/60 (17 February 1995) UN Doc A/Res/49/60, para 5(f); UNGA Declaration to Supplement the 1994 Declaration on Measures to Eliminate International Terrorism (UNGA Dec 1996) (17 December 1996), annexed to Res 51/210 (16 January 1997) UN Doc A/Res/51/210, preamble paras 6 and 3; UNGA Res 56/160 (13 February 2002) UN Doc A/Res/56/160, para 8; UNGA Res 59/195 (22 March 2005), UN Doc A/Res/59/195, para 10; UNGA Res 60/288 (20 September 2006), UN Doc A/Res/60/288, para 7.

3 Convention relating to the Status of Refugees (28 July 1951) 189 UNTS 137 (1951 Convention). Kidane W, 'The Terrorism Bar to Asylum in Australia, Canada, the United Kingdom, and the United States: Transporting Best Practices' (2010) 33 Fordham International Law Journal 300–371; Mathew P, 'Resolution 1373 – A Call to Pre-empt Asylum Seekers?' in Jane McAdam (ed) *Forced Migration, Human Rights and Security* (Portland, 2008) 19–61; Blake N, 'Exclusion from Refugee Protection: Serious Non-Political Crimes after 9/11' (2003) 4 European Journal of Migration and Law 425–447; Zard M, 'Exclusion, Terrorism and the Refugee Convention' (2002) 13 Forced Migration Review 32–34.

4 In its Technical Guide to Implementation of Security Council Resolution 1373 in 2009, the Counter-Terrorism Committee of the Security Council stated that 'there is no universally agreed definition of terrorism. Therefore, each state will approach this issue [i.e. the criminalisation of terrorist offences] on the basis of its own domestic legal framework'. UNSC Counter-Terrorism Committee Executive Directorate 'Technical Guide to Implementation of Security Council Resolution 1373' (2009) S/2009/620, 44.

 | DOI 10.1163/9789004292062_002

no universally agreed definition as to what in fact constitutes 'terrorism'. The repeated resolutions of the UN Security Council calling on states to deny refugee status to terrorists therefore grant Member States a broad discretion to determine what 'terrorism' is and who a 'terrorist' is. A number of commentators have expressed concern that this discretion leaves the 1951 Convention's exclusion clause open to abuse by Member States seeking to exclude genuine asylum seekers from refugee status.[5]

Over the past two decades there has indeed been an increased interest in the application of Article 1F globally, much of which appears to have stemmed from the UN resolutions outlined above.[6] In its early years, Article 1F was used rarely and attracted little legal or academic attention. However, exclusion from refugee status under Article 1F is an area which is rapidly growing in importance in the United Kingdom (UK) and other states parties to the 1951 Convention.[7] Despite the increased importance of Article 1F in UK asylum law, there is at present a lack of clear information on the application and interpretation of the provision in the UK. Unlike many other European States, the UK

---

5 Zanchettin M, Asylum and Refugee Protection After September 11: Towards Increasing Restrictionism? (Refugee Study Centre, 2003); Mathew P, 'Resolution 1373' (n 3) 19–61; Goodwin-Gill G, 'Forced Migration: Refugees, Rights and Security', in Jane McAdam (ed) *Forced Migration Human Rights and Security* (Portland, 2008) 1–17; Zard M, 'Exclusion, Terrorism and the Refugee Convention' (n 3) 32–34; Saul B, 'Protecting Refugees in the Global "War on Terror"' (2008) University of SydStudies Research Paper No. 08/130.

6 Gilbert G, 'Exclusion under Article 1F Since 2001: Two Steps Backwards, One Step Forward' (n 6). Turk V, 'Forced Migration and Security' (2003) 15(1) International Journal of Refugee Law 115. Brouwer also notes that UNSC Res 1373 was presented as the main justification of proposals or measures taken at EU level in the fight against terrorism, including in relation to EU and national measures relating to exclusion from refugee status. Brouwer E, 'Immigration, Asylum and Terrorism: A Changing Dynamic, Legal and Practical Developments in the EU in Response to the Terrorist Attacks of 11.09' (2003) 4 European Journal of Migration and Law 411–414. See also Guild E, and Garlick M, 'Refugee Protection, Counter-terrorism, and Exclusion in the European Union' (2010) 29(4) Refugee Survey Quarterly 63–82.

7 Kapferer notes that while exclusion decisions remain a fairly small percentage of the overall number of asylum decisions, there has been a considerable increase in attention being paid to the issue of exclusion in asylum policy, jurisprudence and academic commentary in the last ten years. Sibylle Kapferer, 'Revision of UNHCR's Guidelines on Exclusion: Update' (Nordic Asylum Seminar, Bergen June 2013) 3–4. Boccardi notes that during the first two decades following the adoption of the 1951 Convention Article 1F was very rarely invoked, and that its more frequent use is probably a direct result of the expansion of the purposes and principles of the UN through UN measures in the fields of human rights, drug trafficking and international crime. Boccardi I, *Europe and Refugees: Towards an EU Asylum Policy* (Kluwer Law International, 2002) 15.

does not at present publish comprehensive data on exclusion from refugee status under Article 1F.[8] Furthermore, although an important and highly politicised area of law, the use and interpretation of Article 1F in the UK is a little researched topic.

The purpose of this research is therefore to examine whether and in what ways 'terrorism' has featured in the UK's interpretation of Article 1F of the 1951 Convention, and how the provision has been applied in the practice of decision-makers in the UK. Although the term 'terrorism' does not appear in the text of Article 1F, terrorism has at least the potential to feature largely in the interpretation and application of the provision. A terrorist act could be considered to amount to a war crime or crime against humanity under Article 1F(a), a 'serious non-political crime' under Article 1F(b), or constitute 'acts contrary to the purposes and principles of the United Nations' under Article 1F(c). Those who participate in the activities of a terrorist organisation may also be considered responsible for the commission of such acts, and therefore fall within the scope of the provision.

This research draws on a number of sources, including data provided by the Home Office in response to a number of Freedom of Information (FOI) requests made by the present researcher, interviews and questionnaires conducted with immigration judges sitting in tribunals throughout the UK, and interviews conducted with legal representatives and the Home Office's exclusion unit. All reported UK cases concerning exclusion from refugee status under Article 1F were analysed, as were the Home Office's asylum guidance documents, primary and secondary UK legislation and legislative instruments and international legal sources pertaining to exclusion from refugee status. This research therefore provides, in an unprecedented way, a thorough analysis of whether and how terrorism is being employed in the UK's interpretation and application of each of the individual limbs of Article 1F.

The specific questions addressed in this research are:

- To what extent and in what ways does terrorism feature in the UK's interpretation of each of the limbs of Article 1F? How have these interpretations changed and developed over time?

8 See, for example, the reports of the UNHCR and European Council on Refugees and Exiles (ECRE), based in part on State information on the use of Article 1F. UNHCR 'Asylum in the European Union: A Study of the Implementation of the Qualification Directive' (November 2007): <www.unhcr.org/refworld/docid/473050632.html> accessed 12 December 2014; European Council on Refugees and Exiles (ECRE) 'The Impact of the EU Qualification Directive on International Protection' (October 2008): <www.unhcr.org/refworld/docid/4908758d2.html> accessed 12 December 2014.

- How often is Article 1F raised in the UK? On what grounds? Has there been a change in the frequency with which the provision has been raised in recent years? If so, why?
- What is the process by which an individual is excluded from refugee status in the UK? How does this apply to those suspected of involvement in terrorist activity?

This research began with the expectation that the past decade would have seen a dramatic increase in the number of instances in the UK where an individual was excluded from refugee status for their suspected role in terrorist activity. This expectation was based on a number of factors, including the prominent role played by the UK in the adoption of UN resolutions calling on Member States to exclude terrorists from refugee status, the introduction of primary legislation in the UK incorporating a broad definition of terrorism in the interpretation of Article 1F(c) and the concerns of a number of commentators that the absence of a universally accepted definition of terrorism could result in the abuse of Article 1F to exclude genuine refugees from the protection of the 1951 Convention. However, this research has revealed that, although there has certainly been an increase in the application of Article 1F in the UK in the last decade, this increase has predominantly been in relation to those suspected of committing international crimes under Article 1F(a) (war crimes and crimes against humanity) rather than involvement in terrorist activities. Exclusion from refugee status under Articles 1F(b) and (c), in which terrorism has featured, has remained truly exceptional.

Although there has been a clear (inter)governmental and political drive to ensure that refugee status is not granted to terrorists, the predominant practice of both courts and tribunals in the UK and the Home Office's exclusion unit has been to examine whether a particular act meets the definition of one or more of the crimes or acts enumerated in Article 1F, rather than rely on the characterisation of the act or individual as 'terrorist' in nature. Courts and tribunals in the UK have, on the whole, adopted a restrictive approach to the interpretation of the provision, an approach under which it has been stressed that Article 1F is not to be equated with a simple anti-terrorist measure. To this end, courts and tribunals have rejected domestic definitions of the crimes and acts listed in Article 1F, and rather looked to international legal sources to determine the 'autonomous' meaning of the provision as a matter of international law.

The practice of both courts and tribunals in the UK and the Home Office in relation to Article 1F(a) has been to look to sources of international criminal law to determine whether the act in question amounts to a war crime or crimes against humanity. A consequence of this approach is that individuals who could very readily be depicted as 'terrorists' or members of a terrorist organisation are not described as such. The predominant focus on Article 1F(a) and international criminal sources within the Home Office appears to be largely a result of the close relationship of these specialised units with the governmental policy of 'no safe haven for war criminals'. In common with the approach adopted in the interpretation of the crimes enumerated in Article 1F(a), courts and tribunals in the UK have recently begun to look towards international criminal sources in order to determine the standard of responsibility necessary for an individual to be excluded under Article 1F. In advocating an approach more closely aligned with international criminal law, the Supreme Court and Court of Appeal have disapproved the previous guidance on Article 1F responsibility which focused on the 'terrorist' nature of an organisation, and rather stressed that there had to be serious reasons for considering an individual had voluntarily contributed in a significant way to the commission of an Article 1F crime.[9]

The limb of Article 1F that has been traditionally relied on to exclude terrorists from refugee status, Article 1F(b) (serious non-political crime), appears to now be very rarely applied in the UK. This may be a result of the geographical and temporal limitations inherent in the provision and the requirement that a specific crime be identified in the exclusion decision.[10] The Court of Appeal appears to have furthermore recently moved away from the 'terrorist' focus of Article 1F(b) established in the earlier cases, and stressed that merely labelling an offence 'terrorist' is not adequate to determine that the offence is 'serious' for the purpose of the provision. Rather, the Court was of the opinion that the individual facts of each case must be considered in order to establish whether the crime in question is sufficiently serious to warrant exclusion from refugee status.[11]

The limb of Article 1F under which terrorism has featured most prominently in the UK is Article 1F(c), 'acts contrary to the purposes and principles of the United Nations'. That terrorism has featured largely in the UK's interpretation of this provision is unsurprising, as the UN in a number of resolutions has declared that 'acts, methods and practices of terrorism are contrary to the purposes and principles of the United Nations', recalling the wording of

---

9 *R JS (Sri Lanka), R (on the application of) v Secretary of State for the Home Department* [2010] UKSC 15, considered in Chapter 5.

10 Article 1F(b) is limited to acts committed outside the country of refuge prior to admission as a refugee.

11 *AH (Algeria) v Secretary of State for the Home Department* [2012] EWCA Civ 395, considered in Chapter 3.

Article 1F(c) and explicitly including terrorism in this ground of exclusion.[12] However, much like Article 1F(b), the application of Article 1F(c) in the UK appears to have remained truly exceptional. When examining the meaning of 'terrorism' for the purpose of this provision, courts and tribunals in the UK have generally chosen not to rely on the UK's broad domestic definition of terrorism, but rather looked to international and regional definitions of the term. Recently, the Supreme Court rejected the UK's domestic definition of terrorism entirely for the purpose of Article 1F(c), and instead stressed that, in order to fall within the scope of the provision, the terrorist activity in question must 'attack the very basis of the international community's coexistence', being assessed with regard to its gravity and impact on international peace and security.[13] Although courts and tribunals in the UK appear to have been increasingly strict in their interpretations of 'terrorism' in the context of Article 1F(c), a recent development has seen the provision expanded to apply to attacks directed at UN-mandated combatant forces.[14] It is suggested that the Supreme Court may have been misguided in this respect and that the decision be revisited.

While there has been an increase in the application of Article 1F in the UK over the last two decades, in practice the use of the provision has remained exceptional. The number of cases in which the Home Office has excluded individuals from refugee status for committing terrorist acts remains infrequent, and seems to have decreased in the last three years. In cases where terrorism is explicitly cited as a ground of exclusion it seems to be Article 1F(c) that is relied upon over and above the other limbs of Article 1F, and in a number of cases the Home Office has relied on this provision to revoke refugee status for acts committed in the UK or to exclude those who have participated in military activity that does not amount to an international crime under Article 1F(a).

A recurring theme raised by participants that took part in this research relates to the unfamiliarity of many Home Office interviewing officers, immigration judges and Home Office Presenting Officers with the issues raised by Article 1F cases. This research therefore concludes with a number of recommendations by which the exclusion process in the UK could be improved, to enable those involved to fully consider the complex legal and evidential issues involved, improve the quality of decision making and add a greater degree of fairness to the proceedings.

---

12 UNGA Dec 1994, para 2; UNGA Dec 1996, para 2; UNSC Res 1373, para 5; UNSC Res 1377, preamble para 5; UNSC Res 1624, preamble para 8.

13 *Al-Sirri v Secretary of State for the Home Department* [2012] UKSC 54, as explored in Chapter 4.

14 Ibid.

Terminology

This book is entitled 'Terrorism and Exclusion from Refugee Status in the UK: Asylum Seekers Suspected of Serious Criminality'.

The meaning of the term 'terrorism' is considered in Chapter 1 of this book. For the moment it is sufficient to note that 'terrorism' is an amorphous and ambiguous term. A multitude of definitions exist at present within international and domestic legal systems, none of which have achieved universal acceptance. The purpose of this research is not to provide a definition of terrorism, but to examine whether and in what ways 'terrorism' has featured in the UK's interpretation and application of Article 1F.

The research examines *the UK's* interpretation and application of Article 1F. The domestic legislation, immigration rules and legislative instruments referred to throughout this research apply to the UK in its entirety. Asylum applications in the UK fall within the remit of the Home Office, and were previously dealt with by the UK Border Agency (UKBA), a specialised border control agency of the Home Office. The Home Secretary Theresa May recently announced that she has decided to end the Executive Agency status of the UKBA and bring its functions back within the Home Office.[15] However, for all intents and purposes this has not affected the exclusion guidance and procedure adopted by the UKBA, and so these will be referred to throughout this analysis. Particularly relevant for exclusion issues are the UKBA's Asylum Process Guidance (APG) 'Asylum instruction exclusion: Article 1F of the refugee convention', which was most recently updated in May 2012.[16] A number of the sources referred to throughout this research therefore refer to the UKBA, and the terms 'Home Office' and 'Border Agency' are sometimes used interchangeably. The remit of the Home Office (and the UKBA) also extends throughout the UK to include England, Wales, Scotland and Northern Ireland.

Similarly, the tribunal system for dealing with asylum appeals extends throughout the UK. Appeals against a negative immigration decision (which do not involve national security issues) are heard within a two-tier tribunal system which consists of a First-tier Tribunal and Upper Tribunal, each of which has an Immigration and Asylum Chamber.[17] This new tribunal system

15 Home Office, 'Oral Statement' (26 March 2013): <https://www.gov.uk/government/speeches/home-secretary-uk-border-agency-oral-statement> accessed 12 December 2014.

16 Home Office, 'Asylum Instruction Exclusion: Article 1F of the Refugee Convention', 30 May 2012 (Home Office Exclusion APG) <https://www.gov.uk/government/uploads/system/uploads/attachment_data/file/257429/exclusion.pdf> accessed 4 December 2014.

17 Created by the Tribunals, Courts and Enforcement Act 2007.

replaced the single tier Asylum and Immigration Tribunal (AIT) in 2010. For ease of reference, both tribunal systems are referred to throughout this research as the 'immigration tribunal', except where differences between the two systems are materially relevant to the legal analysis. If the immigration decision was wholly or partly taken in reliance on information which should not be made public in the interests of national security, appeal lies to the Special Immigration Appeals Commission (SIAC) and not to the tribunal.[18]

Other domestic courts which are frequently referred to throughout this research are the Supreme Court and the Court of Appeal. Again, the remit of the Supreme Court extends throughout the UK, as did its predecessor the House of Lords. However, references to the Court of Appeal refer only to the Court of Appeal of England and Wales. Unfortunately, no decisions of the Court of Appeal of Northern Ireland or the Scottish Court of Session (regional equivalents of the Court of Appeal of England and Wales) concerning Article 1F were found throughout the course of this research.[19] References to the Court of Appeal throughout this research therefore refer to the Court of Appeal of England and Wales only.

This research concerns the UK's interpretation and application of Article 1F of the 1951 Convention. This provision should not be confused with Articles 1D and 1E, which exclude from the protection of the 1951 Convention those who are receiving protection or assistance from other UN agencies, or those whose legal status is largely assimilated to that of a national of the host country, respectively.[20] Article 1F must also not be confused with the exception to protection against *refoulement* contained in Article 33(2), or the exception to the

---

18 The Special Immigration Appeals Commission (SIAC) was set up by the Special Immigration Appeals Commission Act of 1997. The jurisdiction of SIAC is to hear immigration-related appeals where the Secretary of State has certified that the case involves national security issues.

19 Although a Scottish decision refusing leave to appeal to the Scottish Court of Session was *D.K.N. v A Decision of the Asylum & Immigration Tribunal* [2009] ScotCS CSIH53. This was not included in the case analysis, as decisions on leave to appeal or leave to seek judicial review were excluded from this sample.

20 These provisions provide:
Article 1D: 'This Convention shall not apply to persons who are at present receiving from organs or agencies of the United Nations other than the United Nations High Commissioner for Refugees protection or assistance'.
Article 1E: 'This Convention shall not apply to a person who is recognized by the competent authorities of the country in which he has taken residence as having the rights and obligations which are attached to the possession of the nationality of that country'.

prohibition on expulsion contained in Article 32 of the 1951 Convention.[21] These provisions relate not to exclusion from refugee status, but rather the expulsion of a refugee based on host state security or public order concerns. Whilst there have been concerns that a number of States have conflated these provisions in domestic legislation and jurisprudence,[22] this does not appear to have been the practice in the UK.[23] Articles 32 and 33(2) of the 1951 Convention are therefore only referred to incidentally in this research, where such reference is necessary to clarify the contours of Article 1F.

Structure of the Book

This book comprises this introduction, seven chapters and a conclusion. Chapter 1 gives an introduction to the topic of this research by exploring the meaning of terrorism in international law and how terrorist acts and actors may fall to be excluded from refugee status under Article 1F. The purpose and scope of this research is further outlined, as are the methodologies employed. This serves as a broader introduction to the examination of the UK's interpretation and application of the provision throughout the book.

---

21 Article 33 prohibits Contracting States, in absolute terms, from expelling a refugee 'to the frontiers of territories where his life or freedom would be threatened on account of his race, religion, nationality, membership of a particular social group or political opinion'. Paragraph 2 of Article 33, however, provides that protection against *refoulement* 'may not...be claimed by a refugee whom there are reasonable grounds for regarding as a danger to the security of the country in which he is, or who, having been convicted by a final judgment of a particularly serious crime, constitutes a danger to the community of that country'. Article 32 provides that 'Contracting States shall not expel a refugee lawfully on their territory save on ground of national security or public order', and specifies that such a decision shall only be reached in accordance with due process of law and refugees be given a reasonable period within which to seek admission into another country'.

22 Gilbert G, 'Exclusion and Evidentiary Evidence', in Gregor Noll, *Proof, Evidentiary Assessment and Credibility in Asylum Procedures* (Martinus Nijhoff, 2005) 161–178.

23 In response to a Freedom of Information request by the present researcher, the Home Office clarified: 'Article 1F should not be confused with Article 33(2) of the 1951 Convention... Unlike Article 1F which is concerned with persons who are not eligible for refugee status, Article 33(2) is directed to those who have already been determined to be refugees. Articles 1F and 33(2) are thus distinct legal provisions serving very different purposes'. FOI Response 22289. Kept on file with author this has also been the position of the immigration tribunal, which noted that there are 'substantial differences between Articles 32 and 33 on the one hand and Article 1F(b) on the other'. *KK* (*Article 1F(c), Turkey*) [2004] UKIAT 00101 [82].

Chapters 2, 3, 4 and 5 of this book comprise a primarily doctrinal analysis of the UK's interpretation of terrorism in the context of Article 1F, while Chapters 6 and 7 draw largely on the empirical aspects of this research and analyse the application of the provision in practice. Chapter 2 examines the overall approach taken by UK courts and tribunals to the interpretation of Article 1F, which is assessed with regard to the rule of treaty interpretation contained in the Vienna Convention on the Law of Treaties and the interpretive techniques developed by courts and treaty bodies when interpreting treaties of a human rights or humanitarian character.

Chapters 3 and 4 analyse whether and in what ways terrorism features in the UK's interpretation of the crimes and acts enumerated in Article 1F. Chapter 3 focuses on the UK's interpretations of Article 1F(a) and (b) crimes and Chapter 4 considers how the UK has interpreted terrorism in the context of Article 1F(c)'s reference to 'acts contrary to the purposes and principles of the United Nations'. In Chapter 5, the extent to which terrorism has featured in the UK's interpretation of the level of responsibility required to give rise to Article 1F exclusion is examined, with particular attention given to the issue of membership of a terrorist organisation. Reference is made throughout to international practice and guidance on the interpretation of these provisions and the principles of treaty interpretation explored in Chapter 2.

Chapters 6 and 7 of this book are drawn primarily from the empirical aspects of this study, including the results of case analyses, Home Office data and interviews and questionnaires conducted with the different stakeholder groups that participated in this research. Chapter 6 focuses on the application of Article 1F in the UK. The primary questions discussed are: When is Article 1F raised? Which limb of Article 1F is relied upon in exclusion decisions? How often is Article 1F raised and has this changed over time? Who is being excluded under Article 1F? Throughout this chapter particular attention is given to the application of the provision to suspected terrorists. Chapter 7 examines the exclusion process in the UK, in particular the process by which Article 1F decisions are made within the Home Office and the evidence relied upon to support such decisions; the treatment of evidence and legal issues on appeal before the immigration tribunal and the SIAC and; the practical and legal consequences of exclusion from refugee status in the UK.

Finally, the conclusion draws together the principal issues identified in previous chapters in order to evaluate and explain how terrorism features in the UK's practice of interpreting and applying of Article 1F.

CHAPTER 1

Introduction

The 1951 Convention was drafted in the aftermath of the Second World War, in an attempt to address the problems posed and faced by over 10 million people who had become refugees as a result of the events of the war.[1] The Convention grants a broad host of rights and benefits to those that fall within the definition of 'refugee' contained in its Article 1A.[2] That is, a person who is outside their country of origin, and unable or unwilling to return to that country due to a fear of individual persecution.[3] However, Article 1F provides that the Convention:

shall not apply to any person with respect to whom there are serious reasons for considering that:

(a) he has committed a crime against peace, a war crime, or a crime against humanity...
(b) he has committed a serious non-political crime...
(c) he has been guilty of acts contrary to the purposes and principles of the United Nations.

An individual who falls within the scope of Article 1F is excluded from the scope of the 1951 Convention *per se*, and all rights and privileges contained therein, notwithstanding a well-founded fear of persecution.[4]

The term terrorism does not appear in the text of Article 1F, nor was the issue raised during the debates surrounding the drafting of the provision.

1 Boccardi notes that the five years that followed the end of the Second World War were of pivotal importance for the development of the current international refugee regime. Boccardi I, 'Confronting a False Dilemma: EU Asylum Policy between "Protection" and "Securitisation"' (2007) 60 Current Legal Problems 208.

2 The 1951 Convention provides refugees with key civil and socio-economic rights. See James Hathaway, *The Rights of Refugees under International Law* (CUP, 2005).

3 The temporal limitation of the refugee definition to 'events occurring before 1 January 1951' was removed by the 1967 Protocol Relating to the Status of Refugees (31 January 1967) 606 UNTS 606 (the 1967 Protocol). Hereinafter all references to the 1951 Refugee Convention are taken to include the 1967 Protocol.

4 This does not mean, however, that an excluded individual will cease to benefit from the rights and benefits contained in other international instruments, human rights treaties in particular.

 | DOI 10.1163/9789004292062_003

However, the exclusion of terrorists from refugee protection is a theme which appears in a number of international instruments which both preceded and were adopted subsequent to the 1951 Convention. Prior to the Second World War, international instruments relating to the legal status of refugees did not contain exclusion provisions as such, as these instruments defined refugees in terms of discrete groups of persons considered in need of protection.[5] It was only with the move toward a more individualistic refugee definition, which focused more on the circumstances of the individual, rather than group membership, that the concept of exclusion emerged. The Constitution of the International Refugee Organisation (IRO Constitution) excluded large numbers of individuals from the IRO's mandate. These included: 'war criminals, quislings and traitors' and those who had, since the end of hostilities, participated in any organisation hostile to the government of a member of the United Nations or had participated in any terrorist organisation.[6]

Despite the reference to those who had participated in terrorist organisations in the exclusion clauses of the IRO Constitution, terrorism was not an issue debated during the drafting of Article 1F nor the equivalent provision (paragraph 7) contained in the Statute of the United Nations High Commissioner for Refugees (UNHCR Statute).[7] As both the UNHCR Statute and the 1951 Convention were drafted in the wake of the Second World War, considerable emphasis was rather placed on the need to exclude war criminals and associated persons from refugee protection. However, individuals who commit terrorist acts are explicitly excluded from the protection of a number of regional instruments adopted since the 1951 Convention came into force.

---

5 Early refugee instruments adopted under the auspices of the League of Nations applied to Russian and Armenian refugees, while later arrangements extended to Assyrians and other Christian minorities from the Ottoman Empire, and a small number of Turkish political refugees. Prior to the outbreak of World War II, a number of instruments also attempted to address the huge numbers of Jewish refugees fleeing Nazi Germany.

6 UN Constitution of the International Refugee Organisation, New York (15 December 1946) 18 UNTS 3, Annex I Part II. Annex to UNGA Resolution 62 (I) UN Doc A/PV.67 (IRO Constitution). The Constitution entered into force 20 August 1948. The Constitution of the IRO also made note of principles contained in Extradition and Punishment of War Criminals, UNGA Res 3(I) (13 February 1946) UN Doc A/PV.32 (later to become Annex III of IRO Constitution).

7 UNGA Statute of the Office of the United Nations High Commissioner for Refugees (14 December 1950) A/RES/428(V) (UNHCR Statute). Paragraph 7 provides: 'In respect of whom there are serious reasons for considering that he has committed a crime covered by the provisions of treaties of extradition or a crime mentioned in Article VI of the London Charter of the International Military Tribunal or by the provisions of Article 14, paragraph 2, of the Universal Declaration of Human Rights'.

The exclusion provision of the 1969 Convention Governing the Specific Aspects of Refugee Problems in Africa (OAU Refugee Convention) does not include a reference to terrorism.[8] Terrorism is, however, explicitly mentioned in the exclusion provisions contained in the 1994 Arab Convention on Regulating Status of Refugees in the Arab Countries (Arab Refugee Convention),[9] and the European Union's (EU) Qualification Directives which form part of the Common European Asylum System (CEAS).[10] Article 2(1) of the Arab Convention provides that the provisions of the Convention shall not apply to any person who '[h]as been convicted of having committed a war crime, a crime against humanity *or a terrorist crime* as defined in the international conventions and covenants'.[11] The Arab Convention has not, however, been ratified, and it is unlikely it will come into force. Terrorism also appears in the exclusion provisions of the EU's Qualification Directives.[12] In relation to Article 1F(c)'s reference to 'acts contrary to the purposes and principles of the United Nations', the preambles to the Qualification Directives provide:

> Acts contrary to the purposes and principles of the United Nations are set out in the Preamble and Articles 1 and 2 of the Charter of the United Nations and are, amongst others, embodied in the United Nations Resolutions relating to measures combating terrorism, which declare that 'acts, methods and practices of terrorism are contrary to the purposes and principles of the United Nations' and that 'knowingly financing, planning and inciting terrorist acts are also contrary to the purposes and principles of the United Nations'.[13]

8 Organization of African Unity (OAU) Convention Governing the Specific Aspects of Refugee Problems in Africa (10 September 1969) 1001 UNTS 45 (OAU Refugee Convention).

9 League of Arab States 'Arab Convention on Regulating Status of Refugees in the Arab Countries' (1994) (not yet ratified) (Arab Refugee Convention).

10 Council Directive 2004/83/EC on the minimum standards for the qualification and status of third country nationals or stateless persons as refugees or as persons who otherwise need international protection and the content of the protection granted. [2004] OJ L304/12 (2004 Qualification Directive); Council Directive 2011/95/EU of the European Parliament and of the Council on standards for the qualification of third-country nationals or stateless persons as beneficiaries of international protection, for a uniform status for refugees or for persons eligible for subsidiary protection, and for the content of the protection granted (recast). [2011] OJ L337/9 (2011 Qualification Directive). The 2004 Qualification Directive was recast in 2011. This did not, however, affect the provisions on exclusion from refugee status.

11 Emphasis added.

12 2004 Qualification Directive, Art. 12; 2011 Qualification Directive, Art. 12.

13 2004 Qualification Directive, Recital 22; 2011 Qualification Directive, Recital 31.

The EU Directives therefore refer directly to UN resolutions which refer to 'acts, methods and practices of terrorism' falling within the scope of Article 1F(c) of the 1951 Convention.[14]

These resolutions are those that have been adopted by the UN General Assembly and Security Council over the last two decades, beginning with the General Assembly's Declaration on Measures to Eliminate International Terrorism (the 1994 Declaration) and Declaration to Supplement the 1994 Declaration (the 1996 Declaration). These declarations contain several paragraphs that concern refugees and asylum seekers. Member States affirm that 'acts, methods and practices of terrorism are contrary to the purposes and principles of the United Nations' and also that 'knowingly financing, planning and inciting terrorist acts are also contrary to the purposes and principles of the United Nations'. States are also called on to 'take appropriate...before granting refugee status, for the purpose of ensuring that the asylum-seeker has not participated in terrorist acts'.[15] These provisions in the 1996 Declaration appear to have begun as a result of a UK proposal.[16]

The reference to asylum seekers and refugees in resolutions on terrorism first appeared in the UN Security Council in Resolution 1269 of 1999. This resolution 'Calls upon all States to...take appropriate measures...before granting refugee status, for the purpose of ensuring that the asylum seeker has not participated in terrorist acts'.[17] Two Security Council resolutions concerning terrorism which included reference to asylum seekers and refugees also followed the 9/11 attacks on the United States in 2001. Resolutions 1373 and 1377 again call on States to 'take appropriate measures...before granting refugee status, for the purpose of ensuring that the asylum seeker has not participated in terrorist acts', and further to '[e]nsure, in conformity with international law, that refugee status is not abused by the perpetrators, organizers or facilitators of terrorist acts'.[18] Both resolutions firmly declare that 'acts, methods, and practices of terrorism are contrary to the purposes and principles of the United Nations and that knowingly financing, planning and inciting terrorist acts are also contrary to the purposes and principles of the United Nations'.[19] This language also appears in Resolution 1624 of 2005, which again seems to be the result of a

14 See Boccardi for consideration of how Article 1F was included in previous EU measures, including the 1996 Joint Position of the Council (4 March 1996) OJ L63/2. Boccardi *Europe and Refugees: Towards an EU Asylum Policy* (n 7) 107–110.

15 UNGA Dec 1994, paras 2 and 5(f); UNGA Dec 1996, paras 2, 3 and 4.

16 United Nations General Assembly 'Summary Record of the 10th Meeting' (3 October 1996) UN Doc A/C.6/51/SR.10.

17 UNSC Res 1269, para 4.

18 UNSC Res 1373, paras 3(f) and (g).

19 UNSC Res 1373, para 5. UNSC Res 1377, preamble para 5.

UK initiative.[20] Indeed, during the drafting debates President Bush of the United States noted the Council was meeting just over two months after the 7/7 terror attacks in London.[21]

It is not clear why references to refugees and asylum seekers were included in these resolutions, since not one of the 9/11 hijackers was a refugee or seeking refugee status in the United States. Similarly, the 7/7 bombings in London were a classic case of 'home grown' terrorism: all the 7/7 bombers were born and bought up in the UK. Nevertheless, similar language concerning asylum seekers and refugees has also been included in a number of later UN General Assembly Resolutions, further entrenching the asylum-terrorism connection and stressing the need to exclude suspected terrorists from refugee status.[22]

In line with the increased international attention focused on the threat posed by international terrorism, there has been a clear inter-governmental desire on the part of States to ensure terrorists are excluded from refugee status. However, the Security Council did not define terrorism in these resolutions, nor did it refer to an existing definition of terrorism.[23] Indeed, whilst the international community has repeatedly condemned terrorist acts, at present there is no universally agreed definition as to what in fact constitutes 'terrorism'.

1 What is Terrorism?

Despite the great amount of legal and political attention within the UN that has focused on the threat posed by international terrorism, terrorism as a

20 UNSC, 5261st Meeting (14 September 2005) UN Doc S/PV.5261, p. 6.

21 UNSC Res 1624, preamble paras 7 and 8. SC, 5261st Meeting, UN Doc S/PV.5261 (14 September 2005), p. 5 (President Bush). The lack of debate surrounding the adoption of SC Resolutions 1373 and 1377 mean it is not possible to draw conclusions on the motivations underlying the inclusion of provisions relating to asylum seekers and refugees, although Tunisia, the UK and the US appear to have been the principle supporters. UNSC, 4413th Meeting, UN Doc S/PV.4413 (12 November 2001), p. 13 (Mr Ben Yahia); p. 15 (Mr Straw); pp. 16–17 (Mr Powell).

22 UNGA Res 56/160 (13 February 2002), paras 7 and 8; UNGA Res 59/195 (22 March 2005), paras 9 and 10; UNGA Res 60/288 (20 September 2006), para 7. The Call for States to 'take appropriate measures…before granting refugee status, with the purpose of ensuring that the asylum seeker has not planned, facilitated or participated in the commission of terrorist acts' has also been included in the UN High Commissioner for Human Rights' Res 2002/35 (22 April 2002), para 8; the European Union's Common Position on Terrorism of 2001 and a 2010 Statement by the President of the Security Council. Common Position on Terrorism, 2001/930/CFSP, see Articles 18 and 17; Statement by the President of the Security Council, S/PRST/2010/19 (27 September 2010), p. 3.

23 UNSC Counter-Terrorism Committee (n 4) 44.

concept has proved one the international community has struggled to define. At present, there is no universally agreed definition of 'terrorism'.

Recently, attempts were made to include terrorism as one of the core international crimes within the jurisdiction of the International Criminal Court. However, these attempts failed, as states were unable to agree on a definition of the crime.[24] There have also been attempts to draft a Comprehensive Convention on International Terrorism, but negotiations have fallen into deadlock, again because a definition of 'terrorism' cannot be agreed upon.[25] The primary problem that states encounter when attempting to agree upon a definition of terrorism concerns the question of whether an exception should be made for the activities of national liberation movements. Hence the old saying 'one person's terrorist is another's freedom fighter'. Was Nelson Mandela a terrorist or a freedom fighter? Is violence unjustified *per se*, or can exceptions sometimes be made, for example, for those fighting against repressive regimes?

Due to the difficulty agreeing upon a universal definition of 'terrorism', the international community has thus far preferred to adopt international conventions concerning certain categories of acts that are considered to be so heinous that they permit no exception for national liberation movements.[26] There are at present a host of international counter-terrorism conventions prohibiting acts such as hostage taking, hijacking, and the use of explosives.[27]

Nevertheless, some authors have argued that a definition of the crime of international terrorism has evolved as a matter of customary international law. Basing his analysis on the adoption of national laws, judgments of national courts, UN General Assembly resolutions and the ratification of international counter-terrorism conventions, Cassese argues that a consensus has emerged on the objective and subjective elements of a crime of international terrorism in times of peace, which includes three core elements:

---

24 UNGA 'Final Act of Conference of Plenipotentiaries on the Establishment of an International Criminal Court' (17 July 1998) UN Doc A/CONF.183/10 Resolution E. A definition of terrorism was also not included following the Review Conference in Kampala in 2010.

25 Ben Saul, *Defining Terrorism in International Law* (Oxford University Press, 2006) 184 *et seq*.

26 Anthony Aust, *Handbook of International Law* (2nd edn, CUP, 2010) 265.

27 For example, Convention for the Suppression of Unlawful Seizure of Aircraft (16 December 1970) 860 UNTS 105; International Convention against the Taking of Hostages (17 December 1979) 1316 UNTS 205; International Convention for the Suppression of Terrorist Bombings (15 December 1997) 2149 UNTS 284. For more see Saul, *Defining Terrorism* (n 50) 129–190.

(i) acts normally criminalised under national penal systems;
(ii) which are intended to provoke a state of terror in the population or coerce a state or international organisation to take (or abstain from) some sort of action;
(iii) are politically or ideologically motivated.[28]

Terrorism is therefore an umbrella term that can potentially cover a wide range of acts, provided Cassese's three cumulative conditions are met. These acts will generally already be crimes under domestic and/or international law. The classification of these crimes as 'terrorist' hinges on their underlying motivation, i.e. that the act be politically or ideologically motivated and intended to provoke a state of terror in the public or coerce a government or international organisation.

Despite the difficulties states have encountered in defining an international crime of terrorism, the Special Tribunal for Lebanon recently declared that a customary crime of terrorism in times of peace has crystallised at international law. Basing its decision on the adoption of national laws, judgments of national courts, international and regional treaties and UN resolutions, the Tribunal held that this definition of terrorism comprises three elements:

(a) The perpetration of a criminal act (such as murder, kidnapping, hostage-taking, arson, and so on), or threatening such an act;
(b) The intent to spread fear among the population (which would generally entail the creation of a public danger) or directly or indirectly coerce a national or international authority to take some action, or to refrain from taking it; and
(c) When the act involves a transnational element.[29]

This definition of terrorism essentially replicates Cassese's earlier formulations, with the added criteria that the act must involve some transnational

28 Antonio Cassese, 'The Multifaceted Criminal Notion of Terrorism in International Law' (2006) 4 Journal of International Criminal Justice 933, 937. See also Alex Conte, *Human Rights in the Prevention and Punishment of Terrorism* (Springer, 2010), who comes to a similar conclusion. However, the suggestion that a definition of terrorism has emerged as a matter of customary law is contentious, and Saul argues that no separate customary crime of terrorism exists. Saul, *Defining Terrorism* (n 50) 270.

29 *Interlocutory Decision on the Applicable Law: Terrorism, Conspiracy, Homicide, Perpetration, Cumulative Charging* STL-11-01/1 (16 February 2011) [85].

element.[30] Again, the definition permits a considerable range of acts that may constitute 'terrorism', and such acts will generally already be crimes under domestic or international law. The Tribunal's assessment of customary law in this decision is, however, highly controversial, and the validity of recognising a crime of terrorism under customary international law severely criticised.[31] It therefore remains to be seen whether the Tribunal's approach will be followed by courts and tribunals around the world, particularly as since the decision is not binding on courts other than the Tribunal itself.[32]

Whilst many definitions of terrorism exist, no one definition has achieved universal acceptance. The closest that the UN Security Council has come to defining the term was in Resolution 1566 of 2004, in which the Council offered a non-binding definition of the term, allowing States to adopt their own definitions.[33] The absence of a universally accepted definition of terrorism means that it is left to individual States, or regional organisations, to determine the range of acts (or crimes) that may be described as 'terrorist', and whether an exception is permitted for national liberation movements.

'Terrorism' is therefore an amorphous and ambiguous term. A multitude of definitions exist at present within international and domestic legal systems, none of which have achieved universal acceptance. The purpose of this research is not to provide a definition of terrorism; this topic has been examined extensively elsewhere.[34] Rather, this research examines whether and in what ways 'terrorism' has featured in the UK's interpretation and application of Article 1F. As will be considered below, although the term 'terrorism' does not appear in the text of Article 1F itself, those who commit terrorist acts may

---

30 Curiously, the definition does not include the requirement that the act be politically or ideologically motivated.

31 See, for example, Saul, B. 'The Special Tribunal for Lebanon and Terrorism as an International Crime: Reflections on the Judicial Function', in W.A. Schabas, Y. McDermott and N. Hayes (eds), *The Ashgate Research Companion to International Criminal Law: Critical Perspectives* (Ashgate Publishing, 2013), 79–99.

32 *Interlocutory Decision on the Applicable Law* (n 55) 142. While this decision was referred to by the UK Supreme Court in the criminal case *Gul, R. v* [2013] UKSC 64, [33]–[36], it is notable that the Supreme Court in *Al-Sirri* stated that 'there is as yet no internationally agreed definition of terrorism', as considered in Chapter 4. *Al-Sirri* [2012] (n 13) [37].

33 UNSC Res 1566 (8 October 2004) UN Doc S/RES/1566 (2004), para 3. As considered further in Chapter 4.

34 For example, Saul, *Defining Terrorism* (n 50); Conte (n 54). Klabbers J, 'Rebel with a Cause? Terrorists and Humanitarian Law' (2003) 14(2) European Journal of International Law 299–312. Singh S, 'Will Acceptance of a "Universally Approved Definition" of Terrorism Make Article 1F of the 1951 Refugee Convention More Effective in Excluding Terrorists?' (2006) 2(3) Journal of Migration & Refugee Issues 91–119.

fall to be excluded from refugee status under the provision, as the acts in question may fall within the definitions of the crimes enumerated therein. Similarly, those who participate in the activities of a terrorist organisation may be considered responsible for the commission of such acts and therefore fall within the scope of the provision.

2 Article 1F and Terrorism

Although the term 'terrorism' does not appear in the text of Article 1F, terrorism has at least the potential to feature largely in the interpretation of the provision. Many individuals suspected of committing terrorists acts will not qualify as refugees under Article 1A of the 1951 Convention at all, since they may not be fleeing persecution but legitimate *prosecution* in a third state.[35] Those that are fleeing persecution may nevertheless be excluded from refugee status under Article 1F. A terrorist act could be considered to amount to a war crime or crime against humanity under Article 1F(a). Provided they take place in the context of an armed conflict, the concept of 'war crime' includes many acts that would be considered terrorist in nature, such as intentionally directing attacks against civilians and civilian objects, using indiscriminate means of warfare, and taking hostages.[36] Massive attacks on a civilian population may also constitute a 'crime against humanity' under Article 1F(a). Attacks on a civilian population committed by a terrorist organisation, in the context of a widespread and systematic attack against it, may therefore

---

35 James Hathaway and Colin Harvey, 'Framing Refugee Protection in the New World Disorder' (2001) 34 Cornell International Law Journal 257, 284–285. However, illegitimate or irregular prosecution may amount to persecution where relevant forms of discrimination result in selective prosecution, denial of procedural or adjudicative fairness, or differential punishment.

36 Geneva Convention for the Amelioration of the Condition of the Wounded and Sick in Armed Forces in the Field (12 August 1949) 75 UNTS 31 (Geneva Convention I), Art. 50; Geneva Convention for the Amelioration of the Condition of Wounded, Sick and Shipwrecked Members of Armed Forces at Sea (12 August 1949) 75 UNTS 85 (Geneva Convention II), Art. 51; Geneva Convention Relative to the Treatment of Prisoners of War (12 August 1949) 75 UNTS 135 (Geneva Convention III), Art. 130; Geneva Convention Relative to the Protection of Civilian Persons in Time of War (12 August 1949) 75 UNTS 287 (Geneva Convention IV), Art. 147; Protocol Additional to the Geneva Conventions of 12 August 1949, and relating to the Protection of Victims of International Armed Conflicts (8 June 1977) 1125 UNTS 13 (Additional Protocol I), Articles 11 and 85; Rome Statute of the International Criminal Court (17 July 1998) 2187 UNTS 3 (Rome Statute), Art. 8.

fall within the definition of crimes against humanity as a matter of international law.[37]

Terrorist acts that do not meet the gravity of a war crime or crime against humanity may nevertheless fall within the scope of Article 1F(b) of the 1951 Convention, which excludes those that have committed 'a serious non-political crime'[38] from refugee status. Although Article 1F(b) refers to serious *non-political* crimes, terrorist acts may fall within the scope of this provision despite being committed with political objectives when the act in question is disproportionate to the alleged objective.[39] Many terrorist acts will also be considered sufficiently 'serious' to fall within the scope of the provision.

The final ground of exclusion under Article 1F is for those who are 'guilty of acts contrary to the purposes and principles of the United Nations'. As highlighted above, a number of UN resolutions call on states to exclude terrorists from refugee status and state that 'acts methods and practices of terrorism are contrary to the purposes and principles of the United Nations', specifically recalling the wording of Article 1F(c) of the 1951 Convention, and including terrorism within this ground of exclusion.[40] Terrorism has therefore explicitly been held to fall within the scope of Article 1F(c).[41] Those who participate in the activities of a terrorist organisation may also be considered responsible for the commission of such acts, and therefore fall within the scope of the Article 1F.

---

37 It has now been recognised that crimes against humanity can be committed during peacetime, and the application of crimes against humanity to non-state actors, in particular terrorist groups, has been confirmed. Statute of the International Criminal Tribunal for Rwanda (ICTR Statute) (8 November 1994), established by Security Council Res 955 (8 November 1994) and last amended by Security Council Res 1717 (2006) (13 October 2006) UN Doc S/Res/955, Art. 3; Rome Statute, Art. 7; *Prosecutor v Tadic* (Decision on the Defence Motion for Interlocutory Appeal on Jurisdiction) ICTY-94-1 (2 October 1995) [140]–[141].

38 '...outside the country of refuge prior to his admission as a refugee'.

39 UNHCR 'Guidelines on International Protection No. 5: Application of the Exclusion Clauses: Article 1F of the 1951 Convention Relating to the Status of Refugees (UNHCR Guidelines)' (4 September 2003) HCR/GIP/03/05UNHCR 5; UNHCR 'Handbook on Procedures and Criteria for Determining Refugee Status under the 1951 Convention and the 1967 Protocol relating to the Status of Refugees (UNHCR Handbook)' (January 1992) HCR/IP/4/Eng/REV.1, para 152.

40 UNGA Dec 1994, para 2; UNGA Dec 1996, para 2; UNSC Res 1373, para 5; UNSC Res 1377, preamble role 5; UNSC Res 1624, preamble role 8.

41 Goodwin-Gill however points out that a number of these resolutions also oblige Member States to act in accordance with international human rights and international refugee law implementing such measures. Goodwin-Gill G, 'Forced Migration: Refugees, Rights and Security' (n 5) 1–17.

Individuals who are suspected of committing terrorist acts may therefore be excluded from refugee status under Articles 1F(a), (b) and/or (c) of the 1951 Convention. However, in the absence of a universally agreed definition of terrorism, considerable discretion is left to Member States to determine what 'terrorism' is and who a 'terrorist' is. A number of commentators have expressed concern that this discretion leaves the 1951 Convention's exclusion clause open to abuse by Member States seeking to exclude genuine asylum seekers from refugee status.[42]

There has clearly been a strong political drive within the UK to ensure that terrorists are excluded from refugee status. As noted above, a number of the UN resolutions relating to terrorism and refugees began life as UK proposals. In addition, in 2006 the UK's Immigration Asylum and Nationality Act came into force, s 54 of which provides that '[i]n the construction and application of Article 1(F)(c) of the Refugee Convention the reference to acts contrary to the purposes and principles of the United Nations shall be taken as including... (a) acts of committing, preparing or instigating terrorism... and (b) acts of encouraging or inducing others to commit, prepare or instigate terrorism'. The meaning of 'terrorism' here is that given by the UK's broad domestic definition contained in the Terrorism Act 2000. Since the 1951 Convention has not been formally incorporated into the UK's domestic legal system, Article 1F represents one of the very few provisions of the 1951 Convention that are the subject of primary legislation in the UK. The increasing importance of Article 1F in the UK is furthermore highlighted by the fact that in the past few years the UK Supreme Court and the Court of Appeal have handed down an unprecedented number of decisions concerning the interpretation of the provision.[43]

---

42 Guy Goodwin-Gill and Jane McAdam, *The Refugee in International Law* (3rd edn, OUP, 2007) 191–197; Andreas Zimmermann and Philipp Wennholz, 'Article 1F 1951 Convention', in Andreas Zimmerman (ed.) *The 1951 Convention Relating to the Status of Refugees and Its 1967 Protocol: A Commentary* (OUP, 2011) 606–607. Zanchettin M, Asylum and Refugee Protection After September 11: Towards Increasing Restrictionism? (n 5); Mathew P, 'Resolution 1373 – A Call to Pre-empt Asylum Seekers?' (n 3) 19–61; Goodwin-Gill G, 'Forced Migration: Refugees, Rights and Security' (n 5); Zard M, 'Exclusion, Terrorism and the Refugee Convention' (n 3) 32–34; Saul B, 'Protecting Refugees in the Global "War on Terror"' (n 5).

43 *AA-R (Iran) v Secretary of State for the Home Department* [2013] EWCA Civ 835; *Al-Sirri v Secretary of State for the Home Department* [2012] UKSC 54; *SK (Zimbabwe) v Secretary of State for the Home Department* [2012] EWCA Civ 807; *AH (Algeria) v Secretary of State for the Home Department* [2012] EWCA Civ 395; *SS (Libya) v Secretary of State for the Home Department* [2011] EWCA Civ 1547; *Secretary of State for the Home Department v DD (Afghanistan)* [2010] EWCA Civ 1407; *JS (Sri Lanka), R (on the application of) v Secretary of State for the Home Department (Rev 1)* [2010] UKSC 15; *JS (Sri Lanka), R (on the application of)*

Despite the increased importance of Article 1F in UK asylum law, there is at present a lack of clear information on the application and interpretation of the provision in the UK. Unlike many other European States, the UK does not at present publish comprehensive data on exclusion from refugee status under Article 1F.[44] Furthermore, although an important and highly politicised area of law, the use and interpretation of Article 1F in the UK is a little researched topic. While there is a body of literature which focuses on terrorism and the interpretation of Article 1F of the 1951 Convention, this literature primarily examines the international UN measures outlined above.[45] Where the UK's domestic practice has been considered, this has principally been subsumed within comparative analyses with Canada, Australia, the United States and other European countries.[46] The wide scope of this research has restricted the depth of this examination and resulted in a rather limited analysis of the issue. Literature which has specifically considered the UK's domestic practice has been limited to examination of case law and not taken into account the UK's legislative framework,[47] and all this research fails to situate the UK's practice within the wider international legal context, with the result that there appears

---

v Secretary of State for the Home Department [2009] EWCA Civ 364; *KJ (Sri Lanka) v Secretary of State for the Home Department* [2009] EWCA Civ 292; *MH (Syria) v Secretary of State for the Home Department* [2009] EWCA Civ 226; *Al-Sirri v Secretary of State for the Home Department & Anor* [2009] EWCA Civ 222.

44 See for example UNHCR 'Asylum in the European Union' (n 8); ECRE 'The Impact of the EU Qualification Directive' (n 8).

45 Guy Goodwin-Gill, 'Forced Migration: Refugees, Rights and Security' (n 5); Penelope Mathew, 'Resolution 1373' (n 3); Matthew Gibney, 'Security and the Ethics of Asylum after 11 September' (2002) 13 Forced Migration Review 40.

46 Umut Turksen, *Protection Seekers, States and the New Security Agenda – A Comparative Analysis of the Impact of Anti-Terrorism Legislation on the Law Relating to Asylum Seekers in the United Kingdom, the United States of America and Australia* (DPhil, University of West of England, 2008); Won Kidane, 'The Terrorism Bar to Asylum' (n 3) 300; Evelien Brouwer, Petra Catz and Elspeth Guild (eds) *Immigration, Asylum and Terrorism: A Changing Dynamic in European Law* (Recht & Samenleving, 2003); Kapferer S, 'Exclusion Clauses in Europe – A Comparative Overview of State Practice in France, Belgium and the United Kingdom' (2000) 12 (Special Supplement) International Journal of Refugee Law 195–221; Guild E, and Garlick M, 'Refugee Protection, Counter-Terrorism, and Exclusion' (n 6) 63–82; Simeon JC, 'Complicity and Culpability and the Exclusion of Terrorists from Convention Refugee Status Post 9/11' 29(4) Refugee Survey Quarterly 104–137; Satvinder Juss, 'Complicity, Exclusion, and the "Unworthy" in Refugee Law' (2012) 31 Refugee Survey Quarterly 1; Rikhof J, *The Criminal Refugee: The Treatment of Asylum Seekers with a Criminal Background in International and Domestic Law* (Dordrecht, 2012).

47 Satvinder Juss, 'Terrorism and the Exclusion of Refugee Status in the UK' (2012) 17 Journal of Conflict and Security Law 465.

to be lack of sustained *legal* appraisal of the UK's practice in interpreting and applying Article 1F.

The purpose of this research is therefore to provide, in an unprecedented way, knowledge and understanding of the ways in which terrorism is being employed in the UK's interpretation and application of each of the individual limbs of Article 1F. The importance of this topic, and limited amount at present known about the use of Article 1F in the UK, was recognised by the Senior President's Office of the UK's immigration tribunal, which granted the present researcher permission to conduct research on Article 1F with immigration judges throughout the UK. The methodologies employed in this research are considered below.

3 Methodology

As noted above, the UK does not at present publish comprehensive data on exclusion from refugee status under Article 1F of the 1951 Convention. This means it is extremely difficult to establish what is happening in relation to the application of the provision in practice. As explained by a member of the Home Office's Special Cases Unit (SCU), which handles Article 1F cases:

> SCU 1: "But of course at the root of all this, which is for you, and for me and for the judiciary, is the lack of reliable data. It isn't recorded by them it isn't recorded by us, particularly at appeal."

A number of sources are therefore drawn on in this research in an attempt to provide an overview of the application of Article 1F in the UK.

Data concerning exclusion from refugee status in the UK under Article 1F was obtained from the Home Office in response to a number of Freedom of Information (FOI) requests made by the present researcher. This data relates to initial decisions made by the UK Border Agency (UKBA), and details the number of individuals excluded from refugee status under Article 1F of the 1951 Convention, the nationality of those excluded and the limb of Article 1F relied on in the exclusion decision. Due to the nature of the UKBA Case Information Database, this data does not concern decisions made prior to the last quarter of 2007 and relates only to initial decisions of the Agency.[48]

48 It therefore does not include instances where Article 1F is raised at a later stage, i.e. after asylum has been granted or upon appeal, or information on whether the initial decision was upheld or overturned upon appeal. Data was also not available for the number of

A quantitative analysis was also made of UK cases at tribunal and court level concerning exclusion from refugee status under Article 1F. These cases were compiled from searches of legal databases and the Upper Tribunal (Immigration and Asylum Chamber) Reported Determinations Database, in an attempt to capture all reported decisions. The method used in selecting cases for analysis involved a comprehensive survey, rather than selection of the most interesting or provocative cases. Decisions on leave to appeal or leave to seek judicial review were excluded from the sample of cases selected for analysis, as were cases in which Article 1F was briefly mentioned but considered irrelevant to the outcome of the case.[49] In total 33 cases were analysed. Two of these were conjoined cases, and it was decided to consider these as four separate cases, bringing the total to 35.[50] These cases were analysed and coded thematically, in order to draw out key information.

In order to triangulate and expand upon the data provided by the Home Office and the case analysis outlined above, a qualitative research study was undertaken that focused on the experiences of three stakeholder groups: immigration judges, legal representatives and Home Office staff with experience in Article 1F cases.

The primary method of data collection involving judicial participants was questionnaires. The sample of immigration judges was based on a convenience sampling technique, with the sole criteria of selection being individuals wishing to take part in the research project. Introductory letters and questionnaires prepared by the present researcher were electronically distributed to all full-time and part-time immigration judges sitting in both the First Tier and Upper Tribunal of the Immigration and Asylum Chambers in England, Scotland, Wales and Northern Ireland by the President's Office of the Immigration & Asylum Chamber in February 2013. In total 36 completed questionnaires were returned to the researcher in March 2013. The judicial participants that responded to questionnaires included

individuals excluded from subsidiary (humanitarian) protection, or granted protection but removed under Article 33(2) of the 1951 Convention.

49 For example, in a number of cases the asylum applicant was not considered credible and therefore found not in need of protection, but the tribunal made comments to the effect that if they had been found credible, they would fall to be excluded under Article 1F. *PM and others (Kabul – Hizb-i-Islami)* [2007] UKAIT 00089; *MA (Palestinian Arabs – Occupied Territories – Risk)* [2007] UKAIT 00017.

50 The sample included cases heard before the Supreme Court, the House of Lords, the Court of Appeal, the Upper Tribunal (Asylum and Immigration Chamber) and its predecessor the Immigration and Asylum Tribunal (IAT) and the Special Immigration Appeals Commission. Some of these cases are duplicated as they concern a case which rose through the higher courts.

experience at the First Tier and Upper Tier of the Asylum and Immigration Chambers (including the tribunals' previous incantations) and the Special Immigration Appeals Commission (SIAC). 21 judicial participants gave details of the specific tribunals they had experience sitting at. Experience included tribunals in England, Wales, Scotland and Northern Ireland.[51]

Interviews were also conducted with a number of immigration judges. These took place between April and July 2013. In total five interviews were conducted with judicial participants.[52] Interviewees included judges with experience sitting at the First-tier and Upper Tribunal of the Asylum and Immigration Chamber, the High Court and the SIAC. Interviews were also conducted with a number of legal representatives with experience in Article 1F cases. The sample included legal representatives that had acted both on behalf of asylum applicants and the Home Office. In total eight barristers were interviewed and one barrister responded in writing to questions provided by the present researcher. Three of the barristers that took part in this research had acted as counsel for the Home Office, and six had acted as counsel for asylum applicant(s), some also on behalf of interveners such as the UNHCR and Justice. A solicitor who had acted on behalf of asylum applicants in Article 1F cases was also interviewed via telephone. In June 2013 a member of the Home Office's Special Cases Unit (SCU) was also interviewed as part of this research. This interviewee had over ten years of experience working for both the War Crimes Unit and the SCU within the Home Office, and had personally handled and overseen scores of Article 1F cases.[53]

All these methodologies all involve relatively small sample sizes, which is reflective of the exceptional use of Article 1F in the UK and therefore the small number of people involved in the exclusion process. Viewed together, however, they provide a unique and compelling overview of the use and application of Article 1F in the UK.

---

51 The majority of participants had experience sitting at more than one immigration tribunal. Tribunals included: Belfast (1); Birmingham (1); Bradford (4); Croydon Magistrates Court (1); Field House (2); Glasgow (3) Harmondsworth (1); Hatton Cross (9); Havant (1); Manchester (3); Newport (1); North Shields (3) Nottingham (1); Stoke (1); Surbiton (2); Sutton (2); Taylor House (7). One participant also indicated London (unspecified).

52 Two judicial participants elected to be interviewed rather than complete the questionnaire.

53 For the purpose of this book, judicial participants who completed questionnaires are given anonymised numerical participant numbers (i.e. Judge 23). Participants who took part in interviews are assigned alphabetised participant labels (e.g. Judge C, Barrister E) in order to distinguish these from the comments and responses provided in the questionnaires. The Special Cases Unit team member who took part in this research is accorded the anonymised label SCU 1.

CHAPTER 2

Interpreting Article 1F

Although the term 'terrorism' does not appear in the text of Article 1F, and the issue was not raised during the debates surrounding the drafting of the provision, those for whom there are 'serious reasons for considering' have committed or been complicit in the commission of terrorist acts may indeed fall to be excluded from refugee status under Article 1F where these acts constitute war crimes, crimes against humanity, serious non-political crimes and/or acts contrary to the purposes and principles of the United Nations.[1] That acts of terrorism may potentially fall under any of the limbs of Article 1F is recognised in the UK Home Office's APG:

> Acts of terrorism are widely considered contrary to the purposes and principles of the United Nations, and may potentially fall within Article 1F(c). But they may also fall within Article 1F(b) because acts of terrorism are not necessarily political crimes, or even within Article 1F(a).[2]

However, it is equally clear that not every act classified as terrorism will necessarily fall within the scope of the provision, as not every terrorist act will automatically meet the definitions of the crimes or acts enumerated therein.[3] For example, under Article 1F(a) an act of terrorism may only be considered a war crime where it is committed in the context of an armed conflict. To fall within the scope of Article 1F(b), a terrorist act must be considered to be a 'serious' crime. Courts and tribunals in the UK have stressed that adjudicators should 'avoid equating Article 1F with a simple anti-terrorism provision'. Rather, it is necessary to 'make findings about the serious crime or act committed by the claimant and then explain how that fits within a particular sub-category

---

1 Article 1F(a) also refers to crime against peace. However, as considered in Chapter 3, it appears the commission of a crime against peace is limited to State action, rather than non-state irregular terrorist groups. In any case there very few UK cases where this ground of exclusion was considered.

2 Home Office Exclusion APG, s 2.5.

3 Indeed, the ECRE recommends that the focus on Article 1F be on the underlying offences rather than the question of whether or not they are 'terrorist', as '[t]his description is simply adjectival and adds no substantive value'. ECRE, 'Position on Exclusion from Refugee Status' (2004) 16(2) International Journal of Refugee Law paras 7 and 30.

 | DOI 10.1163/9789004292062_004

(or particular sub-categories) of Article 1F–1F(a), 1F(b) or 1F(c)'.[4] Whether and in what way(s) terrorist acts may fall within the scope of Article 1F therefore depends on the interpretation given to the provision.

Unlike many international treaties of a human rights or humanitarian character, the 1951 Convention does not have a designated treaty body that is mandated to provide authoritative interpretation of its provisions. Whilst the UNHCR has a supervisory role in overseeing the implementation and application of the Convention, this mandate does not extend to providing authoritative rulings or opinions on the meaning of particular treaty terms.[5] The absence of an international refugee court to act as final arbitrator on issues of interpretation means that there is no uniform international practice or single interpretation of the treaty.[6] Interpretation of the 1951 Convention has therefore developed in a piecemeal, *ad hoc* manner, through the domestic jurisprudence of Member States, advice and guidance provided by the UNHCR and its Executive Committee, and the opinions of academics and experts.

An examination of the UK's approach to interpreting Article 1F, and the 1951 Convention as a whole, is therefore of vital importance for understanding

4 *Gurung (Exclusion, Risk, Maoists) Nepal* [2002] UKIAT 04870 [151].

5 1951 Convention, Articles 35 and 36; Additional Protocol, Articles 2 and 3; UNHCR Statute, proverb 8. The UNHCR can therefore only issue guidance on the Convention's interpretation through its *Handbook*, guidelines, and its notes on international protection. Similarly, the UNHCR Executive Committee's *Conclusions on International Protection* may be instructive when interpreting and applying the Convention, but they are not binding on states. However, it has been suggested that in the absence of states' use of the International Court of Justice to resolve their differences on the interpretation or application of the 1951 Convention (as provided under Article 38 of the 1951 Refugee Convention) or the existence of any other mechanism among states at an international level to resolve such differences, UNHCR necessarily assumes a crucial role with respect to international refugee law. Corinne Lewis, 'UNHCR's Contribution to the Development of International Refugee Law: Its Foundations and Evolution' (2005) 17 International Journal of Refugee Law 69. However, it has been noted that the significance of UNHCR's advice is diminished by the fact that the 1951 Convention must now be applied in a context of parallel human rights treaty protections that the UNHCR lacks the authority to interpret. Tom Clark, 'Rights Based Refuge, the Potential of the 1951 Convention and the Need for Authoritative Interpretation' (2004) 16 International Journal of Refugee Law 593.

6 Although the International Court of Justice is the relevant international dispute-resolving forum, the Court has never been called upon to interpret the Refugee Convention. Boccardi notes that this absence of international control has led to widely differing interpretations of the 1951 Convention, and as such, it is difficult to outline a real international refugee regime. Boccardi I, 'Confronting a False Dilemma: EU Asylum Policy between "Protection" and "Securitisation"' (n 24) 208–210.

whether and how terrorism features in the UK's interpretation of the provision. The purpose of this chapter is therefore to examine the approach adopted in the interpretation of Article 1F in the UK, which will be critically assessed with regard to the rules and principles of treaty interpretation that exist in public international law. However, before the UK's interpretation of Article 1F is considered in detail a preliminary note must be made regarding the approaches to interpretation mandated by the rules on treaty interpretation contained in the Vienna Convention on the Law of Treaties, and the interpretive techniques developed by courts and treaty bodies when interpreting treaties of a human rights or humanitarian character.

1 The Vienna Rule and the Interpretation of Human Rights Treaties

When interpreting the 1951 Convention, and Article 1F in particular, courts and tribunals in the UK have made reference to the rules of treaty interpretation contained in the Vienna Convention on the Law of Treaties, and also appear to have been influenced to a large extent by the approaches to treaty interpretation developed particularly in the jurisprudence of the European Court of Human Rights (ECtHR) and other human rights treaty bodies. The following sections will therefore provide a brief examination of the aspects of these approaches to treaty interpretation that are pertinent to understanding the approach adopted by courts and tribunals in the UK to the interpretation of Article 1F.

1.1 *The Vienna Rule on Treaty Interpretation*

As the provision forms part of an international treaty, Article 1F must be interpreted in accordance with the rules and principles of treaty interpretation that exist as a matter of public international law. Any authoritative interpretation of the provision must therefore begin with the rules on treaty interpretation laid down in the 1969 Vienna Convention on the Law of Treaties (the Vienna rule).[7] The Vienna rule (contained in Articles 31–33 of the 1969 Vienna Convention) is generally considered to constitute a rule of customary

---

7 Vienna Convention on the Law of Treaties (23 May 1969) 1155 UNTS 331 (Vienna Convention). The Vienna Convention was intended to achieve a 'codification and progressive development of the law of treaties', and many of its provisions are declaratory of existing law, or constitute presumptive emergent rules of international law. Vienna Convention, preamble para 7. Ian Brownlie, *Principles of Public International Law* (7th edn, OUP, 2008) 608.

international law,[8] and therefore applies to the interpretation of all treaties concluded between States.[9] These provisions were largely a result of the International Law Commission's (ILC) draft rules on treaty interpretation.[10] The commentary provided by the ILC to supplement its draft rules on treaty interpretation is therefore very instructive and will be referred to throughout this section.

Article 31(1) of the Vienna Convention, entitled the 'General Rule of Interpretation', provides that '[a] treaty shall be interpreted in good faith in accordance with the ordinary meaning to be given to the terms of the treaty in their context and in the light of its object and purpose', whilst paragraph (2) goes on to define the meaning of context for the purposes of the provision. Paragraphs (3) and (4) of Article 31 require an interpreter to take into account subsequent agreements between, and the subsequent practice of, state parties to the treaty regarding the treaty's interpretation; relevant rules of international law; and any special meanings given to terms in the treaty. Article 32 goes on to define when recourse may be had to supplementary materials, such as the preparatory work of the treaty and the circumstances of its conclusion, and Article 33 concerns the interpretation of treaties authenticated in different languages. It must be noted that the Vienna rule of interpretation is not a rigid rule, but rather embodies techniques of interpretation that are a starting point for a treaty interpreter, and invariably offers more than one possible result.[11]

In formulating its draft articles, the ILC did not favour one doctrinal approach to treaty interpretation to the exclusion of others. The Vienna rule

---

8 *Sovereignty over Pulau Ligitan and Pulau Sipadan (Indonesia/Malaysia)* [2002] ICJ Rep 645 [37]. See also *Territorial Dispute (Libya Arab Jamahiririya/Chad)* [1994] ICJ Rep 6 [21]; *Kasikili/Sedudu Island (Botswana/Namibia)* [1999] ICJ Rep 1045 [18]. This position has been endorsed by international tribunals, states pleading before such courts and tribunals, and by many courts considering treaties within national legal systems. For more on the customary status of Articles 31–33 of the Vienna Convention see Richard Gardiner, *Treaty Interpretation* (OUP, 2008) 12–19.

9 Including treaties made before the Convention entered into force, whether or not those States are parties to the Vienna Convention itself. This is despite Article 4 of the Vienna Convention, which provides the Convention does not have retroactive effect.

10 The ILC's draft articles were adopted at the Conference with no substantive changes, apart from one addition to the provision on treaties authenticated in different languages.

11 Duncan French, 'Treaty Interpretation and the Incorporation of Extraneous Legal Rules' (2006) 55 International and Comparative Law Quarterly 281; Julian Arato 'Subsequent Practice and Evolutive Interpretation Techniques of Treaty Interpretation over Time and Their Diverse Consequences' (2010) 9 The Law and Practice of International Courts and Tribunals 452.

contains aspects of the 'textual', 'effective' and 'teleological' approaches to treaty interpretation. However, the ILC did emphasise 'the primacy of the text as the basis of interpretation'.[12] As the Commission explained:

> ...the text must be presumed to be an authentic expression of the intention of the parties...in consequence, the starting point of interpretation is the elucidation of the meaning of the text, not an investigation *ab initio* into the intention of the parties.[13]

This approach gives effect to the first of Sir Gerald Fitzmaurice's six principle of treaty interpretation, the 'Principle of actuality (or textuality)', which provides that '[t]reaties are to be interpreted primarily as they stand, and on the basis of their actual texts'.[14] The basic premise is that treaty obligations are embodied in the text of the treaty itself, and therefore this is the starting point for analysis. Under the Vienna rule, preparatory works and the circumstances surrounding the conclusion of the treaty are relegated to a lesser status than the text of the treaty itself.[15] Article 31(1) of the Vienna rule therefore directs an interpreter to the 'ordinary meaning' of the terms of the treaty.[16] Discerning

---

12 United Nations 'Yearbook of the International Law Commission' (1966) UN Doc A/CN.4/SER.A/1966/Add. 1, 218, para 4.

13 Ibid. 22, para 11.

14 Sir Gerald Fitzmaurice formulated six principles of treaty interpretation in his time as Special Rapportuer on the Law of Treaties for the ILC. The first three principles are: I. Principle of actuality (or textuality); II. Principle of the natural and ordinary meaning; III. Principle of integration. These principles are subject to: IV. Principle of effectiveness; V. Principle of subsequent practice; and VI. Principle of contemporaneity. Gerald Fitzmaurice 'The Law and Procedure of the International Court of Justice 1951–4: Treaty Interpretation and Other Treaty Points' (1957) 33 British Yearbook of International Law 210–212.

15 Article 32 of the Vienna Convention provides that, when interpreting a treaty '[r]ecourse may be had to supplementary means of interpretation, including the preparatory work of the treaty, and the circumstances of its conclusion in order to confirm the meaning resulting from the application of Article 31, or to determine the meaning when the interpretation according to Article 31: (a) leaves the meaning ambiguous or obscure; or (b) leads to a result which is manifestly absurd or unreasonable'. The ILC, in its commentary, explained: 'The word "supplementary" emphasizes that Article [32] does not provide for alternative, autonomous, means of interpretation but only for means to aid an interpretation governed by the principles contained in Article [31]'. UN 'Yearbook of the International Law Commission' (n 73) 223, para 19.

16 The text of the treaty is to be interpreted in accordance with the ordinary meaning of the terms, unless it is indicated a 'special meaning' is intended to apply (provided for in Article 31[4]).

the ordinary meaning of a treaty provision is not, however, intended to be an exercise in linguistics or dictionary definitions, but is intimately linked with the requirement that the text be interpreted in good faith in light of its context and object and purpose.[17]

The requirement that a treaty provision be interpreted in good faith, in light of its context and object and purpose allows a more generous interpretation of treaty obligations than a purely textual approach,[18] and is bound up with the notion of 'effectiveness'.[19] That is, 'the instrument as a whole and each of its provisions must be taken to have been intended to achieve some end, and that an interpretation that would make the text ineffective to achieve that object is...incorrect'.[20] Thus, the principle of effectiveness requires the provisions of a treaty to be interpreted in a manner which ensures their coherence and value. However, it is clear that a purposive approach to treaty interpretation should not depart from the terms of the text of the treaty itself. As explained by the ILC:

> Properly limited and applied, the maxim [effectiveness] does not call for an "extensive" or "liberal" interpretation in the sense of an interpretation going beyond what is expressed or necessarily to be implied in the terms of the treaty.[21]

The ILC has therefore cautioned that courts should not 'revise treaties or...read into them what they do not, expressly or by implication, contain... [as] ...an interpretation which ran counter to the clear meaning of the terms would not

17 This was emphasised by Sir Humphrey Waldock, Special Rapporteur to the ILC, at the Vienna Conference itself. United Nations 'Official Records of the United Nations Conference on the Law of Treaties, First and Second Sessions, Documents of the Conference' (1968–1969) UN Doc A/CONF.39/26 184, para 70.

18 Gardiner (n 89) 151; Anthony Aust, *Modern Treaty Law and Practice* (2nd edn, CUP, 2007) 234.

19 Malgosia Fitzmaurice, 'The Practical Working of the Law of Treaties', in Malcolm Evans, *International Law* (2nd edn, OUP, 2006) 202.

20 Ibid. 202. The principle of effectiveness was formulated by Sir Fitzmaurice as follows:

> Treaties are to be interpreted with reference to their declared or apparent objects and purposes; and particular provisions are to be interpreted so as to give them their fullest weight and effect consistent with the normal sense of the words and with other parts of the text, and in such a way that a reason and a meaning can be attributed to every part of the text.
>
> Fitzmaurice, 'The Law and Procedure of the International Court of Justice 1951–4: Treaty Interpretation and Other Treaty Points' (n 95) 210–212.

21 UN 'Yearbook of the International Law Commission' (n 73) 219, para 6.

be to interpret but to revise the treaty'.[22] The Vienna rule therefore reveals a distinct focus on the text of the treaty itself, although this textual approach is tempered somewhat by the requirement that the treaty be interpreted in a manner which makes its obligations effective.

The Vienna rule also requires that an interpreter look outside the text of a treaty. In particular, Article 31(3) states that, together with context, an interpreter must take into account:

(a) any subsequent agreement between the parties regarding the interpretation of the treaty or the application of its provisions;
(b) any subsequent practice in the application of the treaty which establishes the agreement of the parties regarding its interpretation;
(c) any relevant rules of international law applicable in the relations between the parties

The ILC made clear in its commentary that 'these three elements [of Article 31(3)] are all of an obligatory character and by their very nature could not be considered to be norms of interpretation in any way inferior to those which precede them'.[23] In particular, the ILC has advised that subsequent agreements and practice regarding the interpretation of a treaty constitute as significant an aspect of the Vienna rule as the text of the treaty itself, as it 'constitutes objective evidence of the understanding of the parties as to the meaning of the treaty'.[24] As state parties are in principle 'masters' of a treaty, subsequent agreement and/or practice can significantly alter the interpretation given to the text.[25] Subsequent agreements and practice of state parties may take a variety of forms;[26] it is crucial that the agreement or practice establishes 'the agreement of the parties'. However, in the context of multilateral treaties such as the 1951 Convention it is often difficult to establish the concordant *practice* of state

---

22 Ibid. 221.
23 Ibid. 221.
24 Ibid. 221, para 15.
25 Rudolph Bernhardt, 'Evolutive Interpretation, Especially of the European Convention on Human Rights' (1999) 42 German Yearbook of International Law 23. Although this should not amount to modification of the treaty. Modification or amendment of treaties should be undertaken through the proper procedures as set out in Part IV of the Vienna Convention.
26 For example, domestic legislation and case law, unilateral interpretive declarations, and the implementation of domestic practices and policies. Goodwin-Gill and McAdam (n 68) 8.

parties necessary to constitute 'the agreement of the parties'. That is 'that they have done essentially the same thing expressed in pursuance of the treaty, or, if the conduct is unilateral, that it reveals the agreement of the other party or parties'.[27] Indeed, the precise level of concordance required to bring a practice within the ambit of Article 31(3) is unclear.[28]

The Vienna rule further requires that an interpreter take into account 'relevant rules of international law' when interpreting a treaty. This aspect of the Vienna rule, contained in Article 31(3)(c), can be said to be based on the premise that no treaty exists in a legal vacuum, but instead has to be interpreted within the wider background of international law.[29] As explained by the ILC in its recent *Fragmentation Report*, this provision 'gives expression to the principle of "systemic integration" according to which, whatever their subject matter, treaties are a creation of the international legal system and their operation is predicated on that fact'.[30] Customary international law and general principles of law may be of particular relevance to the interpretation of a treaty where:

(a) The treaty rule is unclear or open-textured;
(b) The terms used in the treaty have a recognised meaning in customary international law or under general principles of law;
(c) The treaty is silent on the applicable law and it is necessary for the interpreter, to look for rules developed in another part of international law to resolve the point.[31]

Much dispute has surrounded the question of whether this reference to 'relevant rules of international law' applies to international law as it stood at the time of the treaty's adoption, or at the time of its interpretation or

27 Gardiner (n 89) 227.

28 For example, see the comments of Lord Browne in *R (On the application of Hoxha) v Special Adjudicator* [2005] 4 All ER 580 603–604 [72]–[74].

29 Malgosia Fitzmaurice, 'Interpretation of Human Rights Treaties', in Dinah Shelton (ed.) *The Oxford Handbook of International Human Rights Law* (OUP, 2013) 749.

30 International Law Commission (ILC), 'Conclusions of the Work of the Study Group on the Fragmentation of International Law: Difficulties Arising from the Diversification and Expansion of International Law' (2006) UN Doc A/61/10 (ILC Fragmentation Report, Summary Conclusions) para 17.

31 ILC Fragmentation Report, Summary Conclusions, para 20. Moreover, Article 31(3)(c) also requires the interpreter to consider other treaty-based rules so as to arrive at a consistent meaning.

application.[32] Determining which temporal legal regime is applicable may be dictated by the terms of the treaty itself. As explained by the ILC in its *Fragmentation Report*, '[a] treaty may convey whether in applying Article 31 (3) (c) the interpreter should refer only to rules of international law in force at the time of the conclusion of the treaty or may also take into account subsequent changes in the law'. However, to this statement the ILC added: '[m]oreover, the meaning of a treaty provision may also be affected by subsequent developments, especially where there are subsequent developments in customary law and general principles of law'.[33] Thus even when a treaty does not specifically provide that subsequent developments in international law should be taken into account in the treaty's interpretation these factors may remain relevant, particularly if the concepts used in a treaty are open or evolving in nature.

The relevance of current international law to the interpretation of treaty terms has been repeatedly emphasised by the International Court of Justice (ICJ).[34] In its *Advisory Opinion on Namibia*, the court noted that the interpretation of instruments:

> cannot remain unaffected by the subsequent developments of law, through the Charter of the United Nations and by way of customary law. Moreover, an international instrument has to be interpreted and applied within the framework of the entire legal system prevailing at the time of its interpretation.[35]

Similarly, the Institute of International law, in its 1975 Resolution on Intertemporal Problems in Public International Law, stated that '[a]ny

---

32 The former is commonly described as the 'principle of contemporaneity'. This aspect of the inter-temporal law was famously formulated by Judge Huber in *Island of Palmas Case* (*USA v the Netherlands*) (1932) Scott Hague Court Rep, 845. This doctrine also appears in as one of Fitzmaurice's six principles of treaty interpretation: 'VI. *Principle of contemporaneity*' Fitzmaurice, 'The Law and Procedure of the International Court of Justice 1951–4' (n 95) 210–212.

33 ILC Fragmentation Report, Summary Conclusions, para 22.

34 *Sovereignty over Pulau Ligitan and Pulau Sipadan* (n 89) [37]. In the Costa Rica v Nicaragua case, the ICJ stated that evolutive obligations 'must be understood to have the meaning they bear on each occasion on which the Treaty is to be applied, and not necessarily their original meaning'. *Dispute regarding Navigational and Related Rights* (*Costa Rica v. Nicaragua*) [2009] ICJ Reports 133 [70].

35 *Legal Consequences for States of the Continued Presence of South Africa in Namibia (South West Africa) notwithstanding Security Council Resolution 276* (Advisory Opinion) [1971] ICJ Rep 4 [21].

interpretation of a treaty must take into account all relevant rules of international law which apply between the Parties at the time of application'.[36]

This dynamic approach to treaty interpretation is very much still a developing concept and the legal features of the approach are not yet fully defined.[37] The ILC suggests that the concepts used in a treaty may be considered open or evolving particularly where: (a) the concept is one which implies taking into account subsequent technical, economic or legal developments; (b) the concept sets up an obligation for further progressive development for the parties; or (c) the concept has a very general nature or is expressed in such general terms that it must take into account changing circumstances.[38] The approach has indeed been adopted and developed particularly by bodies interpreting treaties which do not regulate fine detail, but set out broad, general principles that are intended to apply in a wide range of circumstances and over a long period of time, such as human rights treaties, as is the subject of the following section. It must be stressed, however, that there is not one but many theories of dynamic interpretation, which are still very much in development. The dynamic approach to treaty interpretation has proved itself controversial, particularly in Europe, as it has been viewed by some as resulting in unwarranted expansions of state obligations which were not agreed to or envisaged during the adoption of the original treaty text. Nevertheless, the approach has proven very popular with a number of international and national courts and tribunals, and appears to have influenced the approach taken to the interpretation of the 1951 Convention in the UK.

In sum, therefore, the Vienna rule mandates a primarily textual approach to treaty interpretation, although this is tempered somewhat by the requirement that a treaty be interpreted in context and in light of its object and purpose, so as to make its obligations effective. The Vienna rule also requires an interpreter to take into account the subsequent practice and agreement of state parties to a treaty, and rules of international law that are relevant to its interpretation. A dynamic approach to treaty interpretation may also be adopted in some cases, although the parameters of this approach are not yet clearly defined.

---

36 Institut de Driot International, 'Resolution Adopted by the Institute of International Law at Wiesbaden on the Intertemporal Problems in Public International Law' (1975) 399 Yearbook of the Institute of International Law para 4.

37 Fitzmaurice, 'Interpretation of Human Rights Treaties' (n 110) 752.

38 ILC Fragmentation Report, Summary Conclusions, para 23.

1.2 *The Interpretation of Human Rights Treaties*

The approach of human rights tribunals to the interpretation of human rights treaties has frequently been to assert the applicability of the Vienna rule to the treaties under consideration. However, it has been noted that, at the same time, these bodies have 'adopted positions concerning interpretation that are hard to reconcile with the provisions', developing approaches which expand upon or introduce interpretive techniques outside the Vienna rule.[39]

Perhaps the most important feature that is used to distinguish human rights treaties from other international treaties is the non-reciprocal character of the human rights obligations contained therein. The 'special nature' of human rights treaties has been repeatedly emphasised by international human rights treaty bodies. As explained by the Inter-American Court of Human Rights:

> Modern human rights treaties in general, and the American Convention in particular, are not multilateral treaties of the traditional type concluded to accomplish the reciprocal exchange of rights for the mutual benefit of the contracting States. Their objective and purpose is the protection of the basic rights of individual human beings irrespective of their nationality, both against the State of their nationality and all other contracting States. In concluding these human rights treaties, the States can be deemed to submit themselves to a legal order within which they, for the common good, assume various obligations, not in relation to other States, but towards all individuals within their jurisdiction.[40]

The UN Human Rights Committee has also emphasised that the International Covenant on Civil and Political Rights (ICCPR) is not a web of inter-state obligations, but designed to safeguard individual human beings.[41] The European Court of Human Rights (ECtHR) in particular has repeatedly stressed the European Convention's 'special character as a human rights treaty' and as an 'instrument of European public order'.[42] The Court has noted that:

---

39 Fitzmaurice, 'Interpretation of Human Rights Treaties' (n 110) 739–740.

40 *The Effect of Reservations on the Entry into Force of the American Convention on Human Rights (Articles 74 and 75)* (Advisory Opinion) OC-2/82 (24 September 1982) 568, [29].

41 UN Human Rights Committee (HRC) 'General Comment No. 24: Issues Relating to Reservations Made upon Ratification or Accession to the Covenant or the Optional Protocols thereto, or in Relation to Declarations under Article 41 of the Covenant' (4 November 1994) UN Doc CCPR/C/21/Rev.1/Add.6 para 17.

42 *Loizidou v Turkey* (Preliminary Objections) [1995] ECHR 10 [93]; *Bankovic v Belgium* [2001] ECHR 890 [80].

> [u]nlike international treaties of the classic kind, the [European] Convention comprises more than mere reciprocal engagements between contracting States. It creates, over and above a network of mutual, bilateral undertakings, objective obligations which, in the words of the Preamble, benefit from a 'collective enforcement'.[43]

The special nature of human rights treaties has also been recognised by other courts and tribunals, including the ICJ.[44]

However, Alain Pellet, during his work as Special Rapporteur on the ILC's 'Guide to State Practice on Reservations to Treaties', rejected the claim of distinctiveness in relation to human rights treaties, or treaties of a 'normative character' as a whole. Rather, Pellet took the view that no treaty contains only provisions of a normative unilateral character, as all treaties, including those governing the protection of human rights, also contain provisions of a reciprocal, contractual nature'.[45] Despite this view, however, the special status of human rights treaties has continued to be re-asserted by international human rights treaty bodies and tribunals, and the approach adopted by these bodies has had a dramatic effect on the interpretation of the treaties in question.

The approach of human rights tribunals to treaty interpretation has been to make substantial use of the concept of 'effectiveness', tied to the notion of the 'object and purpose' of the treaties in question.[46] It has been suggested that this aspect of interpretation is particularly significant for human rights treaties, 'since the status of specific human rights norms in general international law may be of importance in the process of interpreting their content, scope and effect as they are enshrined in a given convention'.[47] These bodies have therefore developed approaches to treaty interpretation which may be considered to in some ways expand upon, and in some ways depart from, the Vienna rule. These include the development of a 'pro homine' approach to interpretation, which emphasises that the source of human rights is not merely the texts

---

43 *Ireland v United Kingdom* [1978] ECHR 1, 291.

44 *Reservations to the Convention on the Prevention and Punishment of the Crime of Genocide* (Advisory Opinion) [1951] ICJ Rep 15 [23].

45 Alain Pellet, Special Rapporteur 'Second Report on Reservations to Treaties' (13 June 1996) UN Doc A/CN.4/477/Add.i, para 85.

46 Fitzmaurice, 'Interpretation of Human Rights Treaties' (n 110) 764.

47 Alexander Orakhelashvili 'Restrictive Interpretation of Human Rights Treaties in the Recent Jurisprudence of the European Court of Human Rights' (2003) 14 European Journal of International Law 536.

of the Conventions themselves, but the very nature of man.[48] Another approach is the doctrine of 'evolutive' interpretation, which requires an interpreter to take into account changing conditions in law and society when determining the scope of the obligations contained in a treaty.

Whilst evolutive interpretation is a developing concept whose contours are as yet quite unclear,[49] some observations may be made regarding the initial premise of the doctrine. The evolutive approach to treaty interpretation has been grounded in Article 31(1) of the Vienna rule, on interpreting a treaty in light of its object and purpose, and Article 31(3)(c), on interpretation in light of changing applicable rules of international law. A treaty or treaty provision may be determined to have an 'evolutive' character, which requires an interpreter to take into account changing conditions in state and society when determining the scope of the obligations contained in a treaty. In the ICJ's words, evolutive obligations 'must be understood to have the meaning they bear on each occasion on which the Treaty is to be applied, and not necessarily their original meaning'.[50] Indeed, it has been suggested that human rights treaties intend an effective and not only theoretical protection of the individual, and this aim can only be reached if an interpretation takes account of changing conditions in State and society.[51] Whilst this approach to treaty interpretation is still a developing concept, it has been suggested that the practice of evolutive interpretation may be 'tentatively' categorised into two discreet forms: evolutive interpretation based on terminology, and evolutive interpretation in light of object and purpose.[52] The former approach is grounded in the nature of the text itself.[53] The latter mode of evolutive interpretation takes the object and purpose as its starting point, and asks whether it is necessary to give the treaty an evolutive reading in order to make the agreement effective in terms of its object and purpose.[54]

---

48 Fitzmaurice, 'Interpretation of Human Rights Treaties' (n 110) 755–756. Indeed, Letsas argues that the moral principles embodied in the European Convention are universal and objective. He points out that the European Court's undue reliance on notions of consensus and state practice makes a mockery of this idea. George Letsas, *A Theory of Interpretation of the European Convention on Human Rights* (OUP, 2007) 124–126.

49 Fitzmaurice M, 'Dynamic (Evolutive) Interpretation of Treaties: Part I' (2008) 21 Hague Yearbook of International Law 752.

50 *Dispute Regarding Navigational and Related Rights* (n 115) [70].

51 Bernhardt, 'Evolutive Interpretation' (n 106) 23.

52 Arato 'Subsequent Practice and Evolutive Interpretation' (n 92) 467–468.

53 See text to n 119 for instances where the ILC considered terms may be considered evolutive in nature.

54 Arato 'Subsequent Practice and Evolutive Interpretation' (n 92) 473.

Both these approaches to treaty interpretation have been adopted and expanded upon by human rights treaty bodies and tribunals. The ECtHR for instance has repeatedly stated that the European Convention on Human Rights (ECHR) is a 'living instrument which…must be interpreted in the light of present-day conditions'.[55] The Human Rights Committee has also expressly stated that the International Covenant on Civil and Political Rights should be interpreted 'as a living instrument' and further that the rights protected under the Covenant 'should be applied in context and in the light of present-day conditions'.[56] The Committee on the Elimination of Racial Discrimination (CERD) and Committee against Torture (CAT) have made similar statements, and the Inter-American Court of Human Rights has followed the ECtHR's reasoning in adjudging the Charter of the Organization of American States as 'evolutive' on the basis of its similar object and purpose.[57] The doctrine of evolutive or dynamic treaty interpretation is not unique to the interpretation of human rights treaties, and has been endorsed and developed outside the context, particularly by the ICJ.[58] However, the concept is one which has primarily developed through the jurisprudence of these bodies based on the special statuses of the treaties in question. This approach to treaty interpretation appears to have had a marked affect on the approach of courts and tribunals in the UK to the interpretation of the 1951 Convention, and Article 1F in particular, as will be considered further below.

2 The Interpretation of Article 1F in the UK

Article 1F of the 1951 Convention is not formally incorporated into UK law by way of statute. However, s 2 of the 1993 Asylum and Immigration Appeals Act

---

55 *Tyrer v United Kingdom* [1978] ECHR 2 [15].

56 HRC, *'Roger Judge v Canada'*, Communication No. 829/1998 (13 August 2003) UN Doc CCPR/C/78/D/829/1998, para 10.3.

57 The CERD Committee made similar statements in *Hagan v Australia*, as did the CAT Committees in *VXN and HN v Sweden* and the IACtHR in *Information on Consular Assistance*. Stephen Hagan v Australia (20 March 2003) Communication No. 26/2002, UN Doc CERD/C/62/D/26/2002 (United Nations Committee on the Elimination of Racial Discrimination (CERD)); *VXN and HN v Sweden* (2 September 2000) UN Doc CAT/C/24/D/130/1999; CAT/C/24/D/131/1999 (UN Committee Against Torture) [73]; *The Right to Information on Consular Assistance in the Framework of the Guarantees of the Due Process of Law* (Advisory Opinion) OC-16/99 (1 October 1999) (Inter-American Court of Human Rights) [114].

58 *South West Africa* (n 116) [53]. The Court also adopted an evolutive approach to treaty interpretation in *Dispute regarding Navigational and Related Rights* (*Costa Rica v Nicaragua*) [2009] ICJ Rep 133.

prohibits the Immigration Rules from endorsing any practice that would be incompatible with rights under the Convention.[59] Immigration Rule 328 also confirms the applicability of the 1951 Convention to decisions on asylum, stating 'all asylum applications will be determined by the Secretary of State in accordance with the Geneva Convention'. Positive comments as to the effect of the 1951 Convention have been made by the judiciary,[60] and the House of Lords has confirmed that the Convention is for all effects and purposes incorporated into domestic law.[61] Article 1F is also incorporated into UK law by the 2006 Qualification Regulations, Regulation 7 of which provides:

> (1) A person is not a refugee, if he falls within the scope of Article 1D, 1E or 1F of the Geneva Convention.[62]

When interpreting the 1951 Convention, courts and tribunals in the UK appear to have been influenced to a large extent by the approaches to treaty interpretation adopted by human rights tribunals and treaty bodies. The UK judiciary has repeatedly stressed that the terms of the 1951 Convention are to be given an 'autonomous meaning', distinct from the domestic legal culture of any state parties to the 1951 Convention, and have repeatedly affirmed the 'humanitarian character' of the 1951 Convention and its special status as a 'living instrument'. When interpreting the 1951 Convention, and Article 1F in particular, courts and tribunals in the UK have therefore adopted a dynamic and purposive approach

---

59 Section 2 provides: "[n]othing in the immigration rules (within the meaning of the 1971 Act) shall lay down any practice which would be contrary to the Convention." Immigration Rules are subordinate legislation, made pursuant to the duty of the Secretary of State to do so under s 3(2) of the Immigration Act 1971.

60 In *Sivakumuran*, the House of Lords took the view that 'the UK having acceded to the Convention and Protocol, their provisions have for all practical purposes been incorporated into UK law'. In *Adimi*, the Divisional Court held that refugees had a legitimate expectation that the provisions of the Convention would be followed. *Sivakumuran, R (on the application of) v Secretary of State for the Home Department* [1987] UKHL 1 [16]; *Adimi, R (on the application of) v Uxbridge Magistrates Court & Anor* [1999] EWHC Admin 765.

61 *European Roma Rights Centre & Ors, R (on the application of) v Immigration Officer at Prague Airport & Anor* [2004] UKHL 55, [7] (Lord Binham) [41–42] (Lord Steyn) [50] (Lord Hope).

62 The Refugee or Person in Need of International Protection (Qualification) Regulations 2006, SI 2006/2525 (Qualification Regulations). Also see Immigration Rule 339A vii, whereby '[a] person's grant of asylum under paragraph 334 will be revoked or not renewed if the Secretary of State is satisfied that…he should have been or is excluded from being a refugee in accordance with regulation 7 of [the Qualification Regulations'.

to its interpretation, drawing on legal developments in many areas of international law to give meaning to the terms of the Convention, an approach reminiscent to that taken by the ECtHR and other human rights treaty bodies.[63]

2.1 *The Search for an Autonomous Meaning*

Courts and tribunals in the UK have repeatedly stressed that the terms of the 1951 Convention are to be given an 'autonomous meaning'. As famously stated by Lord Steyn in *ex parte Adan*:

> In principle therefore there can only be one true interpretation of a treaty… In practice it is left to national courts, faced with a material disagreement on an issue of interpretation, to resolve it. But in doing so it must search, untrammelled by nations of its national legal culture, for the true autonomous and international meaning of the treaty. And there can only be one true meaning.[64]

Lord Steyn here drew attention to the independent meaning of a provision of the 1951 Convention, derivable from international legal sources 'without taking colour from distinctive features of the legal system of any individual contracting state'. This seems to echo the approach to treaty interpretation adopted by human rights treaty bodies. For example, the European and Inter-American Courts of Human Rights have insisted that the terms of the European and Inter-American Conventions have their own meaning, an 'autonomous interpretation', regardless of national legislation concerning their interpretation.[65] This has indeed been the approach adopted by courts and tribunals in the UK to the interpretation of Article 1F, which have repeatedly stressed that 'there can be only one true interpretation of Article 1F…an autonomous meaning to be found in international rather than domestic law'.[66]

---

63 Gilbert notes that in the period after 2001 the scope of Article 1F seemed to be expanding, but more recent decisions of courts carrying out refugee status determination have shown a greater degree of nuanceing in their interpretation of Article 1F, in accordance with the humanitarian aim of the 1951 Convention. Gilbert G, 'Exclusion under Article 1F Since 2001' (n 6).

64 *Secretary of State For The Home Department, Ex Parte Adan; R v Secretary of State For The Home Department Ex Parte Aitseguer, R v* [2000] UKHL 67 [515–517] (Lord Steyn).

65 See e.g. *Engel and Others v The Netherlands* [1976] ECHR 3 and *The Mayagna (Sumo) Awas Tingni Community v Nicaragua* (Judgment) OC-79/01 (31 August 2001).

66 *JS* (*Sri Lanka*) (n 69) [18]. Lord Brown referring to Article 1F(a). See also comments made by the Court of Appeal in MT (Algeria): 'Like any provision of a convention, the language of Article 1F(c) of the Refugee Convention must be construed in accordance with the

Following this approach, the UK judiciary have repeatedly rejected attempts by the UK legislature to impose statutory interpretations on the terms of Article 1F, as will be considered throughout the course of the following chapters. The UK Supreme Court in *Al-Sirri* recently side-stepped the UK's statutory definition of 'terrorism' for the purpose of Article 1F(c), rather defining the term by looking to guidance from international sources. In doing so, the Supreme Court noted that Member States to the 1951 Convention are not free to adopt their own definitions of Article 1F(c), for 'it is clear that the phrase "acts contrary to the purposes and principles of the United Nations" must have an autonomous meaning'.[67] Similarly, the Court of Appeal in *AH* (*Algeria*) recently rejected the UK's statutory definition of 'particularly serious crime' in the context of Article 1F(b), noting:

> Being an international convention, it must be given an autonomous meaning. They are ordinary words and should be given their ordinary universal meaning.[68]

The Court was rather of the opinion that the determination of what constituted a 'serious' crime for the purpose of Article 1F(b) must be founded upon a 'common starting point'.[69]

In seeking to establish the 'autonomous meaning' of the terms of the 1951 Convention, courts and tribunals in the UK have made frequent reference to the rule of treaty interpretation contained in the Vienna Convention on the Law of Treaties (the Vienna rule). The applicability of this rule of treaty interpretation to the 1951 Convention was recognised by Lord Steyn in case *ex parte Adan*, noted above, in which he referred to 'an independent meaning derivable

---

ordinary meaning to be given to the terms of the convention in their context and in the light of its object and purpose: see Article 31(1) of the Vienna Convention on the Law of Treaties 1980, which codified pre-existing customary international law'. *MT* (*Algeria*) & *Ors v Secretary of State for the Home Department* [2007] EWCA Civ 808. Lord Steyn's famous quotation in *Adan*, 'there can be only one true interpretation of a treaty…' was referred to with approval by the Supreme Court in *Al-Sirri* [2012] (n 69). In KK the immigration tribunal similarly noted: 'We are searching for the international autonomous meaning of the relevant provisions of the Refugee Convention. It is not open to us to provide a purely national or local interpretation'. KK (*Article 1F(c), Turkey*) [2004] UKIAT 00101 [60].

67 *Al-Sirri* [2012] ((n 69) [36].

68 AH (*Algeria*) [2012] (n 69), [50].

69 Ibid. [31].

from the sources mentioned in Articles 31 and 32 [of the Vienna Convention]',[70] and has been referred to in a number of cases concerning the interpretation of the 1951 Convention.[71]

The Vienna rule has also been referred to by the immigration tribunal in a number of cases specifically concerning the interpretation of Article 1F.[72] However, reference to the Vienna Convention has been notably absent from a number of these decisions, particularly those of the Supreme Court and Court of Appeal.[73] Indeed, the approach adopted by courts and tribunals in the UK to the interpretation of Article 1F, and the 1951 Convention as a whole, appears to have been influenced largely by the concept of 'evolutive' interpretation based on the 1951 Convention's special status as a 'living instrument', as will be considered in the following section.

2.2 *Dynamic Interpretation*

Courts and tribunals in the UK have adopted a purposive approach to the interpretation of the 1951 Convention, and Article 1F in particular. This approach has been based largely on the object and purpose of the treaty, an aspect which forms part of the 'General Rule of Interpretation' under the Vienna rule. The object and purpose of the 1951 Convention, as stated in its preamble, is to 'assure refugees the widest possible exercise of…fundamental rights and freedoms'.[74] The 1951 Convention's primary purpose is therefore not the regulation of inter-state rights and obligations, but the protection of individual human beings. This has led courts and tribunals in the UK to draw attention to the humanitarian aims of the Convention, and as such the need to approach the Convention as a 'living instrument' bearing in mind the protective purpose of

---

70 *Ex parte Adan* (n 145) [515–517] (Lord Steyn).

71 *Sepet & Anor, R (on the application of) v Secretary of State for the Home Department* [2003] UKHL 15 [6] (Lord Bingham): 'The task of the House [of Lords] is to interpret the 1951 Convention and, having done so, apply it to the facts of the applicants' cases… In interpreting the Convention the House must respect Articles 31 and 32 of the Vienna Convention on the law of Treaties 1969…'. *Januzi v Secretary of State for the Home Department & Ors* [2006] UKHL 5 [4] (Lord Bingham): 'The [1951] Convention must be interpreted as an international instrument, not a domestic statue, in accordance with the rules prescribed in the Vienna Convention on the Law of Treaties'.

72 *MT (Algeria)* (n 147) [79]; *KK* (n 147) [61].

73 For example the Vienna rule was not mentioned in the recent cases: *Al-Sirri* [2012] (n 69); *AH (Algeria)* [2012] (n 69); *JS (Sri Lanka), R* (n 69) or *Al-Sirri* [2009] (n 69).

74 1951 Refugee Convention, preamble para 2. Goodwin-Gill and McAdam (n 68) 8. Hathaway similarly notes that the preamble of the Refugee Convention unequivocally establishes the human rights purposes of the treaty. James Hathaway, *The Rights of Refugees* (n 25) 53.

the Convention, in a similar manner to the approach taken by many human rights courts. The adoption of a purpose approach to the interpretation of the 1951 Convention has meant that courts and tribunals in the UK have tended to adopt a dynamic approach to the interpretation of Article 1F.

It will be recalled that in formulating the Vienna rule the ILC mandated a primarily textual approach to interpretation, albeit mitigated somewhat by the requirement that the terms of a treaty be interpreted in good faith in light of its object and purpose. The UK House of Lords has accordingly stressed that 'the starting point of the construction exercise must be the text of the Refugee Convention itself, because it expresses what the parties to it have agreed'.[75] However, it appears that courts in the UK have, overall, adopted a more flexible approach to the interpretation of the 1951 Convention rather than a purely textual one. As noted by Lord Lloyd in *Adan*, 'A broad approach is what is needed, rather than a narrow linguistic approach'.[76] Indeed, it seems that the approach to the interpretation of the 1951 Convention adopted by courts in the UK has been influenced largely by the approach taken by human rights treaty bodies. Thus courts in the UK have repeatedly stressed the 1951 Convention's special character as a treaty of humanitarian nature, a 'living instrument', and thus the need to adopt a purposive and evolutive approach to interpreting its provisions:

> the best guide is to be found in the evolutionary approach that ought to be taken to international humanitarian agreements. It has long been recognised that human rights treaties have a special character… Their object is to protect the rights and freedoms of individual human beings generally or falling within a particular description…[77]

That the 1951 Convention is a 'living instrument' means that 'while its meaning does not change over time its application will'.[78] The 1951 Convention has thus been recognised by courts in the UK to have a dynamic, 'evolutive' character, as a result of its special status as a treaty of humanitarian nature.

The 1951 Convention's special status as a living instrument has influenced the interpretation of Article 1F. In the seminal *Gurung* decision of the immigration tribunal, Judge Storey noted that:

---

75 *Secretary of State for the Home Department v K* [2006] UKHL 46 [10] (Lord Bingham).

76 *Ex parte Adan* (n 145), 305 (Lord Lloyd).

77 *Asfaw, R v* [2008] UKHL 31 [54].

78 *Sepet & Anor* (n 152) [6] (Lord Bingham). The ECRE also considers the 1951 Convention to be a 'living instrument'. ECRE, 'Position on Exclusion from Refugee Status' (n 84) para 14.

> in respect of the Exclusion Clauses it is particularly salient to recall the well-settled principle that the Refugee Convention is a living instrument whose interpretation requires a dynamic approach which bears in mind the objects and purposes set out in its Preamble, so as to ensure that it gives a contemporary response to contemporary realities.[79]

This sentiment has been echoed throughout the higher courts, which have adopted a purposive and dynamic approach to the interpretation of Article 1F. This dynamic approach to interpretation has manifested itself in two ways: firstly, by taking into account the subsequent practices and agreements of states parties to the 1951 Convention, and secondly, by referring to contemporary rules of international law.

2.2.1 Subsequent Agreement and Practice

As noted above, under the Vienna rule an interpreter is required to take into account the subsequent agreement and practice of states parties to a treaty when interpreting its terms. This aspect of the Vienna rule has proved particularly difficult in the context of multilateral treaties, such as the 1951 Convention. One particularly useful 'shortcut' that has been employed in the context of the 1951 Convention is resort to the UNHCR's Handbook on Procedures and Criteria for Determining Refugee Status.[80] The Handbook records the practice of state parties to the 1951 Convention, and also takes into account exchanges of views between the UNHCR and the authorities of state parties. As such, the Handbook has been considered by some commentators to provide 'coordinated evidence of the practice and an institutional input' of member states'.[81] It has also been suggested that many of the *Conclusions on International Protection* issued by the UNHCR's Executive Committee should also be taken into account as evidence of 'agreement between the parties', as these are generally adopted in dialogue with state parties to the Convention.[82] In the context of Article 1F, this would include the UNHCR's *Guidelines on*

79 *Gurung (Exclusion, Risk, Maoists)* (n 85) [35].

80 UNHCR Handbook (n 65).

81 Gardiner, *Treaty Interpretation* (n 89) 249, fn 138.

82 Hathaway, *The Rights of Refugees* (n 25) 54, fn 146. Jane McAdam also notes that, although not binding on States, ExCom Conclusions 'may…contribute to the formulation of *opinio juris* by setting out standards of treatment or approaches to interpretation which illustrate States' sense of legal obligation toward refugees and asylum seekers'. McAdam J, 'Interpretation of the 1951 Convention', in Andreas Zimmerman (ed.) *The 1951 Convention Relating to the Status of Refugees and its 1967 Protocol: A Commentary* (OUP, 2011) 112.

International Protection and the accompanying *Background Note on the Application of the Exclusion.*[83]

The UNHCR Handbook has been well received in a number of UK cases concerning interpretation of the 1951 Convention. As noted by Lord Steyn:

> While the Handbook is not by any means itself a source of law, many signatory states have accepted the guidance which on their behalf the UNHCR was asked to provide, and in those circumstances it constitutes in our judgment, good evidence of what has come to be international practice within Art. 31(3)(b) of the Vienna Convention.[84]

However, its reception in cases concerning the interpretation of Article 1F have been mixed. In the early case *T v Secretary of State*, the House of Lords endorsed the use of the UNHCR Handbook as 'a useful recourse on doubtful questions'.[85] However in a particularly scathing passage the immigration tribunal in *AA Palestine* stated:

> The UNHCR Handbook…is not necessarily a guide to state practice, because it may not relate to state practice in any particular paragraph but more to UNHCR's exhortations. Its exhortations may also reflect the humanitarian perspective, wider than the Refugee Convention, which UNHCR sometimes adopts. Interpretation or guidance from UNHCR is entitled to great respect but it may also be inaccurate or tendentious.[86]

The UNHCR's Guidelines have similarly received mixed reviews from courts and tribunals in the UK. In *KK*, the immigration tribunal noted that, although the views of the views of the UNHCR must be accorded 'the very greatest

83 UNHCR Background Note, UNHCR Guidelines (n 65). Nor should the previous guidance on Article 1F issued by the UNHCR be taken into account as evidence of State practice. UNHCR, The Exclusion Clauses: Guidelines on their Application (2 December 1996) and *Note on the Exclusion Clauses* (30 May 1997).

84 *Ex parte Adan* (n 145) [500]. See also *Asfaw, R v* [2008] (n 158) [13] (Lord Bingham) and *Adimi, R (on the application of) v Uxbridge Magistrates Court & Anor* [1999] EWHC Admin 765 [20], to the effect that views of the UNHCR must be accorded 'considerable weight' in light of supervisory role under Article 35 of 1951 Convention. See also *Secretary of State for the Home Department v K* (n 155) [15]: the guidelines 'clearly based on a careful reading of the international authorities, provide a very accurate and helpful distillation of their effect'.

85 *T v Secretary of State for the Home Department* [1996] UKHL 8 [768C] (Lord Mustill).

86 AA *(Exclusion clause) Palestine* [2005] UKIAT 00104 [67].

respect. Those views are not, however, binding on us and they do not necessarily reflect the correct interpretation of the Convention'.[87] The Supreme Court in *Al-Sirri*, however, recently reiterated that the guidance provided by the UNHCR, although not binding, 'should be accorded considerable weight' in light of the obligation, under Article 35 of the 1951 Convention, to supervise the application of the provisions of the Convention.[88] Indeed, in this case the Supreme Court chose to follow the UNHCR's Guidance on the interpretation of the term 'acts contrary to the purposes and principles of the United Nations' which appears in Article 1F(c) of the 1951 Convention.

The EU 2004 Qualification Directive, to which the UK is party, may also be seen as evidence of the subsequent practice of a number states parties to the 1951 Convention in interpreting the terms of the Convention. As noted in the Directive's preamble, its provisions are aimed at guiding Member States in the application of the 1951 Convention which is the 'cornerstone of the international legal regime for the protection of refugees'.[89] The Qualification Directive may also be considered to constitute 'relevant rules of international law' under the Vienna rule, as will be considered in Section 2.2.2 below.

When interpreting Article 1F, courts and tribunals in the UK have also drawn heavily on the jurisprudence of other states parties to the 1951 Convention. Case law emanating from Canada has been particularly influential in this respect, whilst jurisprudence of the Court of Justice of the European Union (CJEU) interpreting Article 12(2) of the European Qualification Directive has also been relied upon.[90] In turn, jurisprudence emanating from the UK has been very influential on other jurisdictions. In particular, the UK Supreme Court's recent decision in *JS* (*Sri Lanka*) has been followed by the Supreme Courts of New Zealand and Canada.[91]

Another manner in which courts and tribunals have taken a dynamic approach to the interpretation of Article 1F has been referring to other sources of international law, as considered in the next section.

---

87 *KK* (n 147) [68].

88 *Al-Sirri* [2012] (n 148) [36].

89 Qualification Directive 2004, preamble paras 3 and 16. See also preamble para 10.

90 For Canadian influence see particularly *Gurung* (*Exclusion, Risk, Maoists*) (n 85). Jurisprudence of the CJEU was referred to in *Al-Sirri* [2012] (n 148) and *SS* (*Libya*) (n 69).

91 *Attorney General v Tamil* X [2010] NZSC 107; [2011] 1 NZLR 721; *Ezokola v. Canada* (*Citizenship and Immigration*), 2013 SCC 40. As considered in Chapter 5. Indeed, it has been suggested that national courts and tribunals increasingly take account not only of national standards and advice from the UNHCR, but also of decisions rendered by tribunals and courts in other state parties. Roundtable of the Future of Refugee Convention Supervision, Summary Conclusions, Downing College, University of Cambridge, 28–29 September 2012, para 3.

2.2.2 Relevant Rules of International Law

When interpreting the 1951 Convention, courts and tribunals in the UK have made frequent reference to international rules and principles external to the 1951 Convention itself.[92] In doing so, these bodies have frequently made reference to the 1951 Convention's status as a 'living instrument' which must be interpreted dynamically in order that the protective object and purpose of the Convention remain effective. As such, courts and tribunals in the UK have made reference to many contemporary international legal standards, in an approach reminiscent to that adopted by human rights treaty bodies.

For example, when interpreting the 1951 Convention, courts in the UK have made frequent use of contemporary human rights standards. In *ex parte Yogathas* the House of Lords determined the scope of the obligation of non-*refoulement*, contained in Article 33 of the 1951 Convention through reference to the jurisprudence of the ECtHR, concluding that the obligation contained in the 1951 Convention was broadly similar to that contained in Article 3 ECHR.[93] Courts have also used international human rights standards to imply terms into the 1951 Convention. Although the text of the Convention itself does not prohibit persecution on the basis of gender or sex, in *K's Case* Baroness Hale argued that:

> State parties to the Refugee Convention, at least if they are also parties to the International Convention on Civil and Political Rights and to the Convention on the Elimination of All Forms of Discrimination against Women, are obliged to interpret and apply the Refugee Convention compatibly with the commitment to gender equality in those two instruments.[94]

Baroness Hale therefore held that gender was, by implication, included in the prohibited grounds of persecution contained in the 1951 Convention. The House of Lords has similarly recognised the status of the 1951 Convention as a living instrument, 'in the sense that while its meaning does not change over time its application will'.[95] In *ex parte Shah*, Lord Hope explained that it was important to take an 'evolutionary approach' to interpreting the meaning of

---

92 This practice may be considered to relate to the principle of systemic integration, which is given effect to by the Vienna rule's requirement that an interpreter take into account 'relevant rules of international law' when interpreting the terms of a treaty.

93 *Thangarasa, R. (on the application of) v Secretary of State for the Home Department* [2002] UKHL 36 [61] (Lord Hutton).

94 *Secretary of State for the Home Department v K* (n 155) [86] (Baroness Hale).

95 *Sepet & Anor* (n 152) [6] (Lord Bingham).

'particular social group' in the Refugee Convention, because this 'enables account to be taken of changed in society and discriminatory circumstances which may not have been obvious to the delegates when the Convention was being framed'.[96]

When interpreting Article 1F, courts and tribunals in the UK have also frequently relied upon sources external to the 1951 Convention. Each of the three limbs of Article 1F contains concepts which cannot be interpreted without reference to international rules and principles external to the 1951 Convention itself.[97] For example, Article 1F(a) refers to a crime against peace, war crime or crime against humanity 'as defined in the international instruments drawn up to make provision in respect of such crimes'.[98] Article 1F(c) furthermore excludes individuals who are guilty of 'acts contrary to the purposes and principles of the United Nations'. This phrase again cannot be interpreted without recourse to external legal rules and standards, and leads the interpreter directly to the terms of the Charter of the United Nations and practice of the UN General Assembly and Security Council.[99] Article 1F(b)'s reference to 'non-political crimes' is unclear, and in practice has been interpreted with reference to the political offence exception in extradition law.[100] Courts and tribunals in the UK have of course also made reference to the 2004 EU Qualification Directive, and associated jurisprudence of the CJEU.[101]

The 2004 Qualification Directive is given domestic legal force in the UK by the European Communities Act of 1972,[102] and was implemented by the Refugee or Person in Need of International Protection (Qualification) Regulation 2006 and Part 11 of the Immigration Rules,[103] both of which came

96 *Islam v Secretary of State for the Home Department Immigration Appeal Tribunal and Another, Ex Parte Shah, R v* [1999] UKHL 20; [1999] 2 AC 629; [1999] 2 All ER 545, 657 (Lord Hope).

97 Kaushal A and Dauvergne C, 'The Growing Culture of Exclusion: Trends in Canadian Refugee Exclusion' (2011) 23 International Journal of Refugee Law 57.

98 These terms may be considered to have 'special meanings' within the terms of Article 31(4) of the Vienna rule, and cannot therefore be authoritatively interpreted without consideration of the international legal instruments and jurisprudence that define them. Considered further in Chapter 3.

99 Charter of the United Nations (24 October 1945) 1 UNTS XVI (UN Charter).

100 *T* (n 166). For an in-depth analysis see Hathaway and Harvey, 'Framing Refugee Protection' (n 61) 257–320.

101 See n 171.

102 1972 European Communities Act, s 2(1).

103 Home Office, Immigration Rules: <http://www.ukba.homeoffice.gov.uk/policyandlaw/immigrationlaw/immigrationrules/part11/> accessed on 12 December 2014.

into effect on 9 October 2006. Regulation 7 of the Qualification Regulations provides '[a] person is not a refugee, if he falls within the scope of Article 1D, 1E or 1F of the Geneva Convention'. Courts and tribunals in the UK have referred extensively to the Directive and associated jurisprudence of the CJEU in cases concerning Article 1F. The Directive has been held by courts and tribunals in the UK to condition and qualify domestic legislation concerning Article 1F.[104] Similarly, judgments of the CJEU concerning Article 12(2) of the Qualification Directive have been recognised as binding on courts and tribunals in the UK, and therefore held to take prominence over guidance provided by the UK Supreme Court.

When referring to these external sources of law, courts and tribunals have made reference to the need to adopt a dynamic approach to the interpretation of Article 1F.[105] Thus in relation to Article 1F(a), the Supreme Court noted it was common ground that 'the international instruments referred to in the article are those existing when disqualification is being considered, not merely those extant at the date of the Convention'.[106] In line with the dynamic approach that has been taken to the interpretation of Article 1F, courts and tribunals do not appear to have resorted to the *travaux preparatoires*, finding them unhelpful.

2.3 *The Principle of Restrictive Interpretation*

The adoption of a purposive approach to the interpretation of Article 1F has also led courts and tribunals in the UK to advocate a restrictive approach to the interpretation of the provision, based on its object and purpose.

The rationale underlying Article 1F is twofold: to exclude those considered to be 'undeserving' of refugee protection and to ensure such persons do not misuse the institution of asylum to evade legitimate prosecution.[107] Article 1F

---

104 See *Al-Sirri v Secretary of State for the Home Department* (n 148) [2]; MT (*Article 1F (a) – aiding and abetting) Zimbabwe* [2012] UKUT 15 (IAC); SS (*Libya*) (n 69) [28–29].

105 *Gurung (Exclusion, Risk, Maoists)* (n 85) [35].

106 *JS (Sri Lanka), R* UKSC (n 69) [2].

107 UN Ad Hoc Committee on Refugees and Stateless Persons 'Ad Hoc Committee on Statelessness and Related Problems, First Session: Summary Record of the Twenty-fourth Meeting Held at Lake Success, New York, on Friday, 3 February 1950, at 2.30 P.M.' (27 November 1951) UN Doc E/AC.32/SR.24. (See particularly statements of Belgium and the UK). Gilbert, 'Current Issues in the Application of the Exclusion Clauses', (n 188) 427–428; Elspeth Guild and Madeline Garlick, 'Refugee Protection, Counter-Terrorism, and Exclusion in the European Union' (n 6) 73. The UNHCR Guidelines state:'[Article 1F's] primary purpose is to deprive those guilty of heinous acts, and serious common crimes, of international refugee protection and to ensure that such persons do not abuse the

therefore serves the important function of preserving the institution of asylum by excluding those considered to be undeserving of such protection. However, courts and tribunals in the UK have repeatedly affirmed that, because of the serious consequences of excluding a person who has a well-founded fear of persecution from the protection of the 1951 Convention, the provision 'should be interpreted restrictively and applied with caution'.[108] The Home Office's APG similarly provides that Article 1F 'is not a punitive measure and should always be applied responsibly, bearing in mind the humanitarian character of the Convention and the serious possible consequences of exclusion for the individual'.[109] The principle of restrictive interpretation entails that in the case of any ambiguity, the narrower, stricter sense which favours non-exclusion is to be preferred. This restrictive approach to the interpretation of Article 1F is widely argued to be in line with, if not mandated by, the protective function of the 1951 Convention.[110] The UNHCR in particular advises that '[c]onsidering the serious consequences of exclusion for the person concerned…the interpretation of these exclusion clauses must be restrictive'.[111]

Another aspect of the restrictive approach to interpreting Article 1F which has been recently emphasised by courts and tribunals in the UK is the requirement of individual consideration of each case to which the provision may apply. The Supreme Court has recently stressed the requirement of individualised assessment in Article 1F cases, and held that it is not justifiable to base a

institution of asylum in order to avoid being held legally accountable for their acts'. UNHCR Guidelines (n 65) 3. Hathaway states the exclusion clause is 'rooted in both a commitment to the promotion of an international morality and a pragmatic recognition that states are unlikely to agree to be bound by a regime which requires them to protect undesirable refugees'. Hathaway, *The Law of Refugee Status* (CUP, 1991) 214. The Home Office's APG similarly provides that: 'The purpose of Article 1F is firstly, to deny the benefits of refugee status to certain persons who could otherwise qualify as refugees but who are undeserving of protection, because there are "serious reasons for considering" that they committed war crimes, crimes against peace or humanity, serious non-political crimes or acts contrary to the purposes and principles of the UN, and secondly, to ensure that such persons do not misuse asylum in order to avoid being held to account for their acts'. Home Office Exclusion APG (n 16) s 2.1.

108 *Al-Sirri* [2012] (n 69) [16]; JS (*Sri Lanka*), *R* UKSC (n 69) [2]; *KK* (n 147) [64]; *Gurung (Exclusion, Risk, Maoists)* (n 85) [36], [151].

109 Home Office Exclusion APG s 2.1.

110 Gilbert, 'Current Issues' (n 188) 428; Michael Kingsley Nyinah, 'Exclusion under Article 1F: Some Reflections on Context, Principles and Practice' (2000) 12 International Journal of Refugee Law 296.

111 UNHCR Handbook (n 65) para 149. See also ECRE, 'Position on Exclusion from Refugee Status' (n 84) para 2.

decision to exclude an individual under Article 1F solely due to a person's membership of a group classified as a 'terrorist organisation'.[112] The Court of Appeal has similarly rejected attempts by the Secretary of State to impose generalised classifications of Article 1F crimes based on the length of sentence imposed, or likely to be imposed, upon conviction.[113] Again, this approach appears to be in line with academic commentary on the interpretation of Article 1F, in which it has been argued that any generalised approach to the application of Article 1F risks excluding *bona fide* refugees from the protection of the 1951 Convention,[114] an approach which would run counter to both the object and purpose of the 1951 Convention and the individual nature of refugee status determination under the Convention.

3 Conclusions

Whilst terrorism is not explicitly referred to in the text of Article 1F, those for whom there are 'serious reasons for considering' have committed or been complicit in the commission of a terrorist act may nevertheless be excluded from refugee status under the provision. However, this depends on the interpretation given to the crimes and acts enumerated therein. For this reason, an examination of the approaches taken by courts and tribunals in the UK to the interpretation of Article 1F is of vital importance for understanding whether and how terrorist acts might be considered to fall within the scope of the provision.

Whilst the practice of courts and tribunals in the UK has not been wholly consistent or clear, it appears that when interpreting the 1951 Convention and Article 1F in particular these bodies have drawn heavily on the 'evolutive' approach to treaty interpretation developed in the jurisprudence of the ECtHR. Courts and tribunals in the UK have therefore frequently referred to the 1951 Convention's humanitarian aims and its status as a 'living instrument'. As such, courts and tribunals have adopted a dynamic approach to the interpretation of the provision, drawing on contemporary sources of international law external to the text of the treaty itself, and making reference to the UNHCR's guidance and the practice of other state parties to the 1951 Convention. The focus on the protective object and purpose of the 1951 Convention has also led courts and

112 *JS* (*Sri Lanka*), *R* UKSC (n 69), approved in *Al-Sirri* [2012] (n 148) [15]. See Chapter 5 for further discussion.

113 *AH* (*Algeria*) (n 69) as considered in Chapter 3.

114 Zimmermann and Wennholz (n 68) 601; Gilbert, 'Current Issues' (n 188) 450.

tribunals in the UK to adopt a restrictive approach to the interpretation of Article 1F, one which merits individual assessment of each case to which the provision may apply and mandates against expansive interpretations of the crimes enumerated therein. The approach taken by the UK judiciary to the interpretation of Article 1F appears to be in line with academic commentary and the UNHCR's guidance on the interpretation of the provision, and has furthermore influenced the jurisprudence of other state parties to the 1951 Convention.

CHAPTER 3

Terrorism as a Crime against Peace, a War Crime, a Crime against Humanity or a Serious Non-political Crime

Under the first two limbs of Article 1F, an individual may be excluded from refugee status where there are 'serious reasons for considering' they have committed a crime against peace, a war crime or a crime against humanity (Article 1F(a)) or a serious non-political crime (Article 1F(b)). The purpose of this chapter is to examine whether and in what ways terrorism has featured in the UK's interpretations of these crimes, and is accordingly divided into two parts, with each of these limbs of Article 1F considered separately. The ways in which terrorism has featured in the UK's interpretation of 'acts contrary to the purposes and principles of the United Nations' under Article 1F(c) will be considered in the following chapter, while responsibility for the commission of a crime within the meaning of Article 1F will be considered in Chapter 5. The purpose of this chapter and of Chapter 4 is to examine the UK's interpretation of the crimes and acts listed in Article 1F, before attention is later turned to the issue of responsibility.

Part 1 of this chapter examines the UK's approach to interpreting the crimes listed in Article 1F(a), and the ways in which terrorism has (and has not) featured in the interpretation of 'crime against peace', 'war crime' and 'crime against humanity', while Part 2 considers how terrorism has featured in the UK's interpretation of 'serious non-political crime' under Article 1F(b).[1] Terrorism has the potential to feature largely in the interpretation of both these provisions, as a terrorist act may qualify as a war crime or crime against humanity under Article 1F(a) or a serious non-political crime under Article 1F(b). However, terrorism has not featured significantly in the UK's interpretation of Article 1F(a). The jurisprudence of courts and tribunals in the UK has rather focused primarily on the interpretations given to the crimes listed in Article 1F(a) as a matter of international law, as defined in the statutes and jurisprudence of international criminal courts and tribunals. The individuals that have been considered for exclusion under this provision have not

1 Part 2 of this chapter is drawn in part from Singer S, 'Exclusion from Refugee Status and Terrorist Related Offences: The Case of AH (Algeria)' (2012) 26(4) Journal of Immigration Asylum and Nationality Law 337–348.

 | DOI 10.1163/9789004292062_005

generally been defined as 'terrorists', nor have international or domestic definitions of terrorism been employed in the interpretations of the crimes listed in the provision. Terrorism has, however, featured largely in the UK's interpretation of Article 1F(b). Courts and tribunals have, on a number of occasions, excluded individuals under this provision for committing crimes defined as terrorist in nature. The Home Office's APG similarly notes that terrorist-related offences are likely to fall under this provision. However, the Court of Appeal has recently made clear that simply labelling an act 'terrorist' is not sufficient to raise it to the level of gravity required to constitute a 'serious' crime for the purpose of Article 1F(b). Rather, regard must be had to the individual facts of each case in order to determine that a particular terrorist offence constitutes a 'serious' crime, the definition of which must be based on a 'common starting point'.

1 Terrorism as a Crime against Peace, a War Crime or a Crime against Humanity

Article 1F(a) of the 1951 Convention provides:

> The provisions of this Convention shall not apply to any person with respect to whom there are serious reasons for considering that...he has committed a crime against peace, a war crime, or a crime against humanity, as defined in the international instruments drawn up to make provision in respect of such crimes.

An individual will therefore be excluded from refugee status under Article 1F(a) where there are serious reasons for considering they are responsible for the commission of a crime against peace, war crime or a crime against humanity.

A number of international instruments may be considered pre-runners of Article 1F(a). The 1948 Constitution of the International Refugee Organisation (IRO) excluded 'war criminals, quislings and traitors' from the organisations mandate. Reference was also made to those who had assisted enemy forces in the persecution of civilian populations or operations against the United Nations, and those who had, since the end of hostilities, participated in any organisation hostile to the government of a member of the United Nations, or had participated in any terrorist organisation.[2]

2 IRO Constitution, Annex I Part II.

Despite reference to terrorist organisations in the Constitution of the IRO, terrorism did not feature in early formulations of Article 1F(a), nor was the issue of terrorism raised during the debates surrounding the drafting of the provision. It must be remembered that the 1951 Convention was drafted in the wake of the Second World War. During the drafting of Article 1F, considerable emphasis was therefore placed on the need to exclude war criminals and associated persons from refugee protection. These debates did not centre on the issue of terrorism, but rather the most appropriate international instruments that should be referred to in the provision's definition of crime against peace, war crime and crime against humanity.[3] The issue was referred to in the Working Group of the Conference, which recommended the phrasing now found in Article 1F(a): 'he has committed a crime against peace, a war crime, or a crime against humanity, *as defined in the international instruments drawn up to make provision in respect of such crimes*'.[4]

Terrorism did not therefore feature in the drafting of Article 1F(a). The provision was shaped largely by the 1951 Convention's status as a post-World War II instrument, and the ensuing concern that those who had committed atrocities during the war should not benefit from refugee protection. Reference to terrorism was, however, included in Article 1F(a)'s equivalent provision in the Arab Refugee Convention, which refers to any person who '[h]as been convicted of having committed a war crime, a crime against humanity *or a terrorist crime* as defined in the international conventions and covenants'.[5]

---

3 The Federal Republic of Germany proposed an amendment to the exclusion provision, which replaced the reference to the London Charter with reference to the Geneva Conventions I to IV and the Convention on the Prevention and Punishment of the Crime of Genocide. UN Conference of Plenipotentiaries on the Status of Refugees and Stateless Persons 'Draft Convention Relating to the Status of Refugees. Federal Republic of Germany: Amendment to Article 1' (13 July 1951) A/CONF.2/76. However, the representative for Israel argued that the German amendment 'seemed to have been inspired by a fear of calling things by their right names'. UN Conference of Plenipotentiaries on the Status of Refugees and Stateless Persons 'Conference of Plenipotentiaries on the Status of Refugees and Stateless Persons: Summary Record of the Thirty-fourth Meeting' (30 November 1951) A/CONF.2/SR.34; Convention on the Prevention and Punishment of the Crime of Genocide (9 December 1948) 78 UNTS 227.

4 UN Conference of Plenipotentiaries on the Status of Refugees and Stateless Persons 'Draft Convention Relating to the Status of Refugees. Report of the Working Group Appointed to Study Section E of Article I of the Draft Convention Relating to the Status of Refugees' (19 July 1951) UN Doc A/CONF.2/92 (emphasis added). This formulation was adopted by twenty votes to one, with two abstentations.

5 Arab Refugee Convention, Article 2(1) emphasis added.

This reference to terrorist crimes was not included in the formulations of Article 1F(a) in the EU Qualification Directive or the OAU Refugee Convention however, which retain Article 1F(a)'s reference to crime against peace, war crime or crime against humanity 'as defined in international instruments drawn up to make provision in respect of such crimes'.[6]

The international instruments to which Article 1F(a) refers could include a number of possible sources. Earlier formulations of Article 1F made explicit reference to Article VI of the London Charter, which defines the crimes that fell within the jurisdiction of the International Military Tribunal at Nuremberg: 'crimes against peace', 'war crimes' and 'crimes against humanity'.[7] During the Conference of Plenipotentiaries, reference was also made to the Geneva Conventions I to IV, and the 1948 Convention on the Prevention and Punishment of the Crime of Genocide.[8] These instruments may therefore be relevant to the interpretation of the crimes enumerated in Article 1F(a). The most recent formulation of Article 1F(a) crimes appears in the 1998 Statute of the International Criminal Court (the Rome Statute).[9] Other recent definitions of these crimes appear in the statutes and jurisprudence of the International Criminal Tribunal for Rwanda (ICTR) and the International Criminal Tribunal for former Yugoslavia (ICTY)[10] and the 1977 Additional Protocols I and II to the 1949

6 OAU Refugee Convention, Article 1(5); Qualification Directives, Article 12(2)(a).

7 UN Charter of the International Military Tribunal – Annex to the Agreement for the Prosecution and Punishment of the Major War Criminals of the European Axis (8 August 1945) (London Charter). This document, commonly known as the Charter of the Nürnberg Tribunal (or Nuremberg Tribunal) formed an integral part of the Agreement for the establishment of an international military tribunal, which was signed in London on 8 August 1945. ILC 'The Charter and Judgment of the Nürnberg Tribunal: History and Analysis Appendix II' (3 March 1949) UN Doc A/CN.4/5.

8 Geneva Convention I; Geneva Convention II; Geneva Convention III; Geneva Convention IV; Convention on the Prevention and Punishment of the Crime of Genocide.

9 Rome Statute of the International Criminal Court (last amended 2010) (17 July 1998) 2187 UNTS 3. The Rome Statute established the International Criminal Court (ICC), the first permanent, treaty based, international court established to prosecute perpetrators of the most serious crimes of concern to the international community. Also relevant to the interpretation of the Rome Statute is the ICC's Elements of Crimes. Official Records of the Assembly of States Parties to the Rome Statute of the International Criminal Court, First session, New York (3–10 September 2002) UN Doc E.03.V.2; Official Records of the Review Conference of the Rome Statute of the International Criminal Court, Kampala (31 May–11 June 2010) (International Criminal Court, RC/11).

10 UNSC Statute of the International Criminal Tribunal for the Former Yugoslavia (25 May 1993) established by UNSC Res 808/1993, 827/1993 and amended by UNSC Res 1166/1998, 1329/2000, 114/2002 (ICTY Statute).

Geneva Conventions.[11] These sources may be relevant to a dynamic interpretation of the provision.[12]

Although terrorism is not specifically mentioned in the text of Article 1F(a), and the issue was not raised during the drafting of the provision, terrorism has the potential to feature largely in the interpretation of the provision since terrorist acts may qualify as a war crime or crime against humanity. However, terrorism has not featured significantly in the UK's interpretation of Article 1F(a) crimes. The jurisprudence of courts and tribunals in the UK has rather focused primarily on the interpretations given to the crimes listed in Article 1F(a) as a matter of international law, as defined in the statutes and jurisprudence of international criminal courts and tribunals. The Home Office's Asylum Process Guidance (APG) on exclusion similarly refers to international criminal instruments for the purpose of defining the crimes that fall within the scope of Article 1F(a). The individuals that have been considered for exclusion under this provision have not generally been defined as 'terrorists', nor have international or domestic definitions of terrorism been employed in the interpretations of the crimes listed in the provision. Although explicit reference to the Vienna rule has not been frequently made, courts and tribunals in the UK have tended to approach the definitions of Article 1F(a) crimes by reference to international legal instruments and the jurisprudence of international criminal courts and tribunals in order to arrive at the 'autonomous' meaning of the provision.

Courts and tribunals in the UK have furthermore adopted a dynamic approach to the interpretation of the crimes listed in Article 1F(a). In the

---

11 Additional Protocol I; Additional Protocol II. Other relevant legal instruments include the 1973 Apartheid Convention and the 1984 Convention Against Torture. International Convention on the Suppression and Punishment of the Crime of Apartheid (30 November 1973) A/RES/3068(XXVIII), 1015 UNTS 243; Convention Against Torture and Other Cruel, Inhuman or Degrading Treatment or Punishment (10 December 1984) 1465 UNTS 85. Relevant authoritative but non-binding sources include the 1950 Report of the International Law Commission (ILC) to the General Assembly, the 1973 Principles of International Cooperation, and the Draft Code of Crimes Against Peace and Security of Mankind which was provisionally adopted by the ILC in 1996. UNGA 'Principles of International Cooperation in the Detection, Arrest, Extradition and Punishment of Persons Guilty of War Crimes Against Humanity' (3 December 1973) A/RES/3020/(XXVII); ILC 'Draft Code of Crimes against the Peace and Security of Mankind' (1996) II Yearbook of the International Law Commission, Part Two.

12 For a comprehensive (although slightly dated) examination of the notion of the crimes enumerated in Article 1F(a) see Pejic Z, 'Article 1F(a): The Notion of International Crimes (2000) 12(Special Supplement) International Journal of Refugee Law 11–45.

seminal case *R* (*JS* (*Sri Lanka*)), Lord Brown, in his leading judgment for the UK Supreme Court, stated 'the international instruments referred to in the article are those existing when disqualification is being considered, not merely those extant at the date of the Convention'.[13] In particular, Lord Brown stated that the Rome Statute 'should now be the starting point for considering whether an applicant is disqualified from asylum by virtue of Article 1F(a)...ratified as it now is by more than a hundred States and standing as now surely it does as the most comprehensive and authoritative statement of international thinking on the principles that govern liability for the most serious international crimes'.[14] This reasoning has been followed in later decisions of the Court of Appeal and the immigration tribunals, which have consistently maintained the importance of the Rome Statute as the 'starting point' for the interpretation of the crimes that fall within the scope of Article 1F(a).[15] Jurisprudence in the UK has also referred to the International Criminal Court's (ICC) Elements of Crimes, the Statutes and jurisprudence of the ICTY and ICTR, and the London Charter. The Home Office's APG on exclusion similarly concedes that '[t]here is no one single set of definitions of what constitutes a war crime, crimes against humanity or genocide for the purposes of the Convention', but directs caseworkers to the detailed definitions provided in the Rome Statute of the ICC.[16] The definitions of Article 1F(a) crimes provided in the Home Office's APG are further drawn from the London Charter and the Statutes of the ICTY and ICTR. The UK's approach to interpreting each of the crimes listed in Article 1F(a) will now be considered in turn.

---

13 *JS* (*Sri Lanka*), *R* UKSC (n 69) [2]. As early as 2002 the tribunal stated: 'it is not just the world which has changed, so has the law dealing with such crimes...there is a need, in the interpretation and application of Article 1F, to draw on "developments in other areas of international law since 1951, in particular international criminal law and extradition law as well as international human rights law and international humanitarian law." Cases before the International Criminal Tribunal for the Former Yugoslavia (ICTY) and the International Criminal Tribunal for Rwanda (ICTR) have greatly advanced the jurisprudence. Basing interpretation of Article 1F on international law developments yields the same advantage as has accrued from doing the same in respect of key terms contained within Article 1A(2): it enables decision-makers to proceed on a more objective footing'. *Gurung* (*Exclusion, Risk, Maoists*) (n 85) [34].

14 *JS* (*Sri Lanka*), *R* UKSC (n 69) [8]–[9].

15 *SK* (*Article 1F (a) – exclusion*) *Zimbabwe* [2010] UKUT 327 (IAC) [10]; *Azimi-Rad* (*Art.1F(a) – complicity – Arts 7 and 25 ICC Statute*) *Iran* [2011] UKUT 339 (IAC) [16]; *MT* (*Article 1F (a) – aiding and abetting*) (n 185) [3]; *AA-R* (*Iran*) (n 69) [9]; *AS* (*s.55 "exclusion" certificate – process*) *Sri Lanka* [2013] UKUT 571 (IAC) [37].

16 Home Office Exclusion APG (n 16) s 4.1.

1.1 *Terrorism as a Crime against Peace*

The first international crime listed in Article 1F(a) is 'crime against peace'. Crime against peace was defined in Article VI(a) of the London Charter as:

> planning, preparation, initiation or waging of a war of aggression, or a war in violation of international treaties, agreements or assurances, or participation in a common plan or conspiracy for the accomplishment of any of the foregoing.[17]

This definition played a part in defining the 'crime of aggression' as a crime against peace in the UN General Assembly's 1974 Resolution on the Definition of Aggression (the General Assembly Definition) and the Rome Statute of the ICC.[18]

There have been very few asylum cases in which crime against peace has emerged as a ground of exclusion in the jurisprudence of states parties to the 1951 Convention.[19] Indeed, in international criminal law the concept has attracted much less international attention than the other crimes listed in Article 1F(a); unlike war crimes and crimes against humanity, a definition of the 'crime of aggression' as a crime against peace was not included in the Statutes of the ICTR and ICTY, and was only defined in the Rome Statute following a review conference in 2010.[20] It has therefore been suggested that it is 'most unlikely that this ground for exclusion will ever play a significant practical role' in refugee exclusion cases.[21]

---

17 Roscini points out that while aggression (including planning and preparation) is widely recognised as a crime under international law entailing individual responsibility, this does not appear to extend to the threat of aggression. Roscini M, 'Threats of Armed Force and Contemporary International Law' (2007) 54 Netherlands International Law Review 266 and 277.

18 UNGA Resolution on the Definition of Aggression, annexed to United Nations General Assembly Resolution 3314 (XXIX) (14 December 1974) UN Doc A/Res/3314 (XXIX) (General Assembly Definition); Rome Statute, Article 8*bis*.

19 Joseph Rikhof, *The Criminal Refugee* (n 72) 158–180.

20 The Review Conference of the Rome Statute, held in Kampala, Uganda, from 31 May to 11 June 2010 adopted the amendments on the crime of aggression on 11 June 2010 by Resolution RC/Res.6. Articles 8*bis* and 15*bis* of the Rome Statute now provide for both the definition of the crime of aggression and the role of the Security Council in this regard. These articles will not, however, enter into force before 1 January 2017, and one year after the ratification or acceptance of the amendment by 30 State Parties, whichever is later.

21 Zimmermann and Wennholz (n 68) 595.

The present author suggests that non-state terrorist actors cannot be excluded from refugee status for committing a crime against peace, since crime against peace, as defined in international criminal law, is limited to State action. Both the Rome Statute and General Assembly Definition define an 'act of aggression' as 'the use of armed force *by a State* against the sovereignty, territorial integrity or political independence of another State, or in any other manner inconsistent with the Charter of the United Nations'.[22] These definitions suggest that individual responsibility for a crime against peace is limited to leaders of a State, or high ranking State officials.[23] This conclusion is reinforced by the terms of the London Charter, which refer to 'a war of aggression' in the context of 'a war in violation of international treaties, agreements or assurances'. It would therefore appear that only individuals occupying a position of power within a state and therefore capable of breaching such international treaties and agreements, would be able to fall within the definition of crime against peace.[24]

It has been suggested, however, that in the context of Article 1F(a) a definition of a crime against peace might also include 'leaders of rebel groups in non-international armed conflicts which seek secession, but few if any others'.[25] The UNHCR also advises that 'a crime against peace can only be committed by individuals in a high position of authority representing a State *or State-like entity*'.[26] This approach could potentially include the acts of non-state

22 Rome Statute, Article 8(2)*bis*; General Assembly Definition, Article 1 [emphasis added]. The provisions contain an extensive list of acts which qualify as acts of aggression, including invasion or attack; bombardment by armed forces; blockade of ports or coasts; and the sending of armed bands, groups, irregulars or mercenaries. Article 4 of the General Assembly Definition states these acts are not exhaustive, and the Security Council may determine other acts constitute aggression under the provision of the Charter. In order to qualify as a crime of aggression under the Rome Statute, importantly, Article 8*bis* contains the threshold requirement that an act of aggression must, 'by its character, gravity and scale, constitute...a manifest violation of the Charter of the United Nations'. Article 2 of the General Assembly Definition also provides that the UN Security Council may conclude that aggression has not been committed in light of relevant circumstances, 'including the fact that the acts concerned or their consequences are not of sufficient gravity'.

23 See *R v Jones* [2006] UKHL 16, in which UK House of Lords held the crime of aggression exists as a matter of customary international law.

24 Indeed, those who were accused of committing crimes against peace during the Nuremburg trials were almost exclusively leading members of the governments of Axis States, principally policy makers.

25 Gilbert, 'Current Issues' (n 188) 435.

26 UNHCR Background Note (n 164) 11, para 28 [emphasis added]. Although it must be borne in mind this position was before the Rome Statute's definition of the crime of aggression was adopted.

terrorist rebel groups within the scope of the provision. However, the assertion that a crime against peace for the purpose of Article 1F(a) may include the actions of non-state actors does not appear to accord with the Rome Statute and General Assembly Definition, nor that of the London Charter. It is therefore suggested that acts of aggression by non-state terrorist groups, whether internal or international in character, do not fall within the scope of a crime against peace for the purpose of Article 1F(a).

There have been few exclusion cases involving crime against peace in the UK, but the approach taken by the immigration tribunal has been to confine 'wars of aggression' to waging wars across international boundaries, and not extend the concept to participation in internal attacks conducted by rebel groups.[27] The determination that rebel groups and low-ranking members of a State's armed forces do not fall within the terms of crime against peace appears to be consistent with the interpretation of the crime in international legal instruments. In particular, this approach excludes terrorist groups from the scope of crime against peace for the purpose of Article 1F(a).

1.2 *Terrorism as a War Crime*

War crimes are grave breaches of the laws or customs of war, which give rise to individual criminal responsibility. The London Charter included in this definition:

> murder, ill-treatment or deportation to slave labour…ill-treatment of prisoners of war or persons on the seas, killing of hostages, plunder of public or private property, wanton destruction of cities, towns or villages, or devastation not justified by military necessity.[28]

International law has since expanded upon and developed the definitions of acts that qualify as war crimes, not least through the Geneva Conventions I to IV and Additional Protocol I, the Statues and jurisprudence of the ICTR and the ICTY and the Rome Statute of the ICC.[29]

---

27 *Amberber v Secretary of State for the Home Department* (unreported; 00/TH/01570) concerned an Ethiopian accused of 'wars of aggression' for participation in internal attacks. Similarly, the mere participation of a soldier in a war of aggression has been held not to bring an individual within the scope of Article 1F(a). PK (*Sri Lanka, risk on return, exclusion clause*) *Sri Lanka* [2004] UKIAT 00089 [10].

28 UN Charter, art VI.

29 See common Article 3 of the four Geneva Conventions; Geneva Convention I, Article 50; Geneva Convention II, Article 51; Geneva Convention III, Article 130, and Geneva

Terrorism has the potential to feature largely in this category of Article 1F(a) crimes. Provided they take place in the context of an armed conflict, war crimes may include many acts that would be considered terrorist in nature, such as intentionally directing attacks against civilians and civilian objects, using indiscriminate means of warfare, and taking hostages.[30] Importantly, it has now been recognised that war crimes can be perpetrated during both international and non-international conflicts, and by non-state actors taking an active part in the hostilities.[31] In the ICTY Appeals Chamber case of *Galic* it was held that 'acts or threats of violence the primary purpose of which is to spread terror among the civilian population' is a war crime as part of customary international law, a finding which has been confirmed by the Special Court for Sierra Leone.[32] Therefore, the actions of non-state terrorist organisations engaged in an armed conflict may be caught by this provision.[33]

In the UK, however, terrorism has not featured greatly in decisions to exclude individuals from refugee status for committing war crimes. Rather, the focus of courts and tribunals in the UK has centred on whether the acts committed constitute war crimes as defined in the relevant international instruments. For example, in one case the initial asylum adjudicator had decided that the applicant's voluntary membership of a terrorist group in Sri Lanka meant that it was reasonably likely that he had committed a crime against peace, a war crime or a crime against humanity under the terms of Article 1F(a), and so was excluded from refugee status.[34] On appeal, the tribunal

Convention IV, Article 147; Additional Protocol I, Articles 11 and 85; Rome Statute, Article 8; see also the ICTY and ICTR Statutes.

30 In the context of international armed conflicts, grave breaches of Geneva Conventions I to IV of 1949 and Additional Protocol I. These grave breaches are codified in Article 8(2)(a) Rome Statute. In the context of non-international armed conflicts, individual criminal responsibility attaches to serious violations of common Article 3 of the four Geneva Conventions. This provision is codified in Article 8(2)(c) Rome Statute. Furthermore, following the ICTY's decision in *Tadic*, in the context of non-international armed conflicts, individual criminal responsibility may also attach to other serious violations of the laws of war that go beyond the scope of common Article 3GC. The approach of the ICTY has been followed in the Rome Statute, Article 8(2)(e) of which 'supplements' common Article 3 by providing an extensive list of 'Other serious violations of the laws and customs applicable in armed conflicts not of an international character', to which individual responsibility may attach'. *Prosecutor v Tadic* (n 63) [134].

31 Ibid. [89], [96], [234] (Tadic).

32 *Prosecutor v Galic* (Appeal Judgment) ICTY-98-29-A (30 November 2006) [86]; *Prosecutor v Fofana* (Appeals Judgment) Case No. SCSL-04-14-A (May 28 2008) [169].

33 See Simeon JC, 'Complicity and Culpability' (n 72) 1115–1118 for a more detailed examination of how terrorism can amount to war crimes and crimes against humanity.

34 *PK* (n 222) [5].

rightly held that activities carried out by the applicant in the course of combat, which did not constitute war crimes within the terms of international instruments such as the London Charter, could not bring him within the scope of Article 1F(a).[35] In this case, the asylum applicant was a Sri Lankan national who had fought for the Liberation Tigers of Tamil Eelam (LTTE) against Sri Lankan government forces. Although the LTTE could readily have been described as a terrorist organisation by the tribunal (and was indeed described as such by the initial adjudicator), terrorism was not referred to by the tribunal in their decision. Rather, the tribunal analysed whether the activities of the applicant could be considered to amount to war crimes, as defined by international legal instruments.

Similarly, the *JS* (*Sri Lanka*) case concerned a Sri Lankan national, who had been a member of the Intelligence Division of the LTTE for a number of years. The Court of Appeal however did not refer to the LTTE or its members as 'terrorist'. Rather, Toulson LJ, in his leading judgment, noted that the principal sources of reference for the definition of the crimes referred to in Article 1F(a) must be the international instruments drawn up to make provision in respect of them, and the jurisprudence of international criminal tribunals which had had to interpret and apply them.[36] The Supreme Court agreed with the reasoning of the Court of Appeal in this respect.[37] In his leading judgment, Lord Brown concluded that, based on the evidence provided by the Secretary of State, the LTTE in general, and the Intelligence Division in particular, were guilty of widespread acts and atrocities that constituted war crimes within the meaning of Article 8 of the Rome Statute, including suicide bombings, attacks upon civilians, assassinations, kidnappings and the forcible recruitment of children.[38] Although these activities could clearly have been described as terrorist in nature, the Supreme Court chose not to do so.

1.3 *Terrorism as a Crime against Humanity*

Crimes against humanity involve the fundamentally inhumane treatment of a population in the context of a widespread or systematic attack against it.[39] Article VI of the London Charter defined crimes against humanity as:

---

35 Ibid. [10]–[11].

36 *JS* (*Sri Lanka*), *R* EWCA (n 69) [95].

37 *JS* (*Sri Lanka*), *R* UKSC (n 69) [8]. The Supreme Court disagreed with the Court of Appeal as to the standard of responsibility that should be employed in Article 1F(a) cases, but agreed Rome Statute should be the starting point for the definition of international crimes.

38 Ibid. [10].

39 UNHCR Background Note (n 164) 13, para 33.

> murder, extermination, enslavement, deportation, and other inhumane acts committed against any civilian population, before or during the war, or persecutions on political, racial or religious grounds in execution of or in connection with any crime within the jurisdiction of the Tribunal, whether or not in violation of the domestic law of the country where perpetrated.

The definition of crimes against humanity has been further developed in the Statutes of the ICTY and ICTR, and the most recent codification is again contained in the Rome Statute of the ICC.[40]

Again, terrorism has the potential to feature largely in this category of Article 1F(a) crimes. The very definition of a crime against humanity is that it is an attack 'committed against any civilian population',[41] and many of the acts that may form part of this attack may be considered terrorist in nature. For example: murder; torture; persecution against a group or collectivity and enforced disappearance. In order to rise to the level of a crime against humanity, the Rome Statute provides that the act(s) must be committed 'as part of a widespread or systematic attack directed against any civilian population... pursuant or in furtherance of a State or organizational policy'.[42] This is commonly known as the 'chapeau requirement'. Given that under this definition crimes against humanity can be committed as part of an 'organizational policy', they could include not only actions directed by States, but also non-state groups. The application of crimes against humanity to non-state actors, in particular terrorist organisations, has been confirmed.[43] Furthermore, although Article 5 of the ICTY Statute refers to crimes against humanity 'committed in armed conflict', it is now generally accepted that crimes against humanity can occur during peacetime. This view is confirmed by the ICTR Statute, Rome Statute and the jurisprudence of the ICTY,[44] and has been recognised by the UK immigration tribunal.[45] As a consequence, terrorist attacks such as the 9/11 attacks on the United States in 2001 may be subsumed under the provision.[46]

---

40 ICTY, Article 5; ICTR, Article 3. Rome Statute, Article 7.

41 See London Charter definition above. See also Rome Statute, Article 7.

42 Rome Statute Articles 7(1) and 7(2)(a). See also ICTR Statute Article 3, which does not provide that the attack must be pursuant to a state or organisational policy.

43 *Prosecutor v Tadic* (n 63) [140]–[141]. Gilbert, 'Current Issues' (n 188) 437.

44 *Prosecutor v Tadic* (n 63) [140]–[141].

45 MT (*Article 1F(a) – aiding and abetting*) (n 185).

46 Zimmermann and Wennholz (n 68) 596.

In the UK, the term 'terrorism' has not featured in decisions to exclude individuals from refugee status for committing crimes against humanity under Article 1F(a). Much like the approach taken to the interpretation of war crimes, the approach taken by Courts and tribunals to the interpretation of crimes against humanity has focused on the definitions provided in international legal instruments. Although reference to 'terror' has been made in the jurisprudence, this has been in the context of definition of crimes against humanity contained in international instruments. For example, where the expelling of persons from their homes, accompanied by 'terror' and the burning of their homes was held to be a crime against humanity within the scope of Article 7(1)(k) of the Rome Statute.[47]

Although crimes against humanity may be committed by non-State groups, in particular terrorist organisations, case law on crimes against humanity in the UK has predominantly concerned State or State-sponsored action. This has included the Zimbabwe police's acts against political opponents of the ZANU PF party;[48] the Zimbabwe youth militia's attacks on white farmers and their workers;[49] the activities of the Basji, a volunteer paramilitary force in Iran;[50] the activities of the Afghani intelligence service[51] and the Sri Lankan police force.[52] It therefore remains to be seen whether terrorism will feature in the jurisprudence of courts and tribunals in the UK in the case of non-State organisations.

1.4 *Conclusions on Article 1F(a) Crimes*

Terrorism has not therefore featured in the UK's interpretation of war crime or crime against humanity in the context of Article 1F(a). This is somewhat surprising, given that terrorism has the potential to feature largely in the interpretation of the provision. Rather, domestic jurisprudence in the UK has focused on the definitions of Article 1F(a) crimes contained in the Statutes and jurisprudence of international criminal courts and tribunals.[53]

There are a number of reasons why terrorism may not feature in the UK's interpretation of war crimes and crimes against humanity under Article 1F(a),

47 SK *(Zimbabwe)* (n 69) [81].

48 MT *(Article 1F (a) – aiding and abetting)* (n 185).

49 SK *(Article 1F(a) exclusion) Zimbabwe* (n 210).

50 *Azimi-Rad* (n 210); *AA-R (Iran)* (n 69).

51 MH *(Syria)* (n 69).

52 AS (s.55) (n 210).

53 Kapferer notes frequent reference to relevant international instruments and decisions of international tribunals and the ICC in decisions by national courts and asylum authorities. Sibylle Kapferer, 'Revision of UNHCR's Guidelines' (n 7) 3.

which are explored further in Chapter 6. The development of Article 1F screening in the Home Office has meant that the specialised units which deal with potential Article 1F cases are primarily expert in international criminal law, and as such are likely to adhere to the interpretations of these crimes as a matter of international criminal law rather than employ the 'terrorism' label. Similarly, it has been suggested by judicial participants interviewed as part of this research that judges are more comfortable dealing with the definitions of international crimes as they appear in international instruments, rather than contending with the complex concept of terrorism.[54]

The practice of UK courts and tribunals in adhering to the definitions of Article 1F(a) crimes by reference to international criminal instruments, rather than generalised labels of categories of persons or acts, appears to accord with the ordinary meaning of the phrase 'as defined in the international instruments drawn up to make provision in respect of such crimes', in line with Article 31(1) of the Vienna rule. The ordinary meaning of this phrase, in the context of the 1951 Convention's status as an international legal instrument, indicates that crimes against peace, war crimes and crimes against humanity must be interpreted with reference to *international* instruments that define such crimes.[55] Thus, purely domestic interpretations of the crimes may not be appropriate as these words may be considered to have 'special meanings' within the terms of Article 31(4) of the Vienna rule, and as such should not be interpreted without consideration of the international legal instruments and jurisprudence that define them.

When approaching the international instruments which define the crimes listed in Article 1F(a), courts and tribunals in the UK have tended to adopt a dynamic approach, clearly considering the terms 'war crime', 'crime against humanity' and 'crime against peace' to be 'evolutive' in nature. Indeed, the concepts of 'war crime', 'crime against humanity' and 'crime against peace' are ones which have evolved and developed in international criminal law since the adoption of the 1951 Convention.[56] It has therefore been suggested that to fail to take into account more recent interpretations of these terms would be to thwart the object and purpose of the provision as well as 'gradually render the

54 See Chapters 6 and 7.

55 In accordance with Article 31 of the Vienna Convention.

56 As international law is a dynamic legal system, subsequent developments in international law may be taken into account when interpreting treaty provisions, especially where the concepts used in a treaty are open or evolving and there are subsequent developments in customary and general principles. ILC Fragmentation Report, Summary Conclusions, paras 22–23.

instrument devoid of any substance'.[57] This dynamic approach to the interpretation of Article 1F(a) crimes is reflective of the UK's approach taken to the interpretation of Article 1F, and the 1951 Convention as a whole, as considered in Chapter 2.

However, it is suggested by the present author that courts and tribunals in the UK should perhaps be more cautious when referring to contemporary definitions of Article 1F(a) crimes. Whilst Article 31(3)(c) of the Vienna rule clearly indicates that an interpreter should take into account 'relevant rules of international law' when interpreting a treaty, this provision is limited to rules 'applicable in the relations between the parties to the treaty'. Reference to more modern enumerations of the crimes listed in Article 1F(a) may therefore be inappropriate unless it is clear that the provisions truly are applicable to all parties to the 1951 Convention, having crystallised as customary international law.[58] A notable trend in UK practice is a strong reliance on the provisions of the Rome Statute. This over-reliance must be cautioned against, since the Rome Statute is in some senses narrower, and in some wider, than the customary international law definitions of the crimes listed in Article 1F(a).[59] It is therefore suggested that courts and tribunals in the UK strive to interpret Article 1F(a) in line with established rules of customary international law, in keeping with the rule of interpretation contained in Article 31 of the Vienna Convention on the Law of Treaties.[60]

57 Zimmermann and Wennholz (n 68) 609.

58 Customary international law consists of unwritten and evolving rules, created by extensive and virtually uniform State practice and *opinio juris* which are binding on all States. *North Sea Continental Shelf Cases (Federal Republic of Germany/Denmark; Federal Republic of Germany/Netherlands)* (Merits) [1969] ICJ Rep 3.

59 For example, it has been suggested that the Rome Statute is narrower than the customary international law of crimes against humanity, and the Article 1F definition should not be limited by this instrument. Gilbert, 'Current Issues' (n 188) 437. Drummond similarly suggests that the Federal Court of Appeal of Australia erred in relying on the Rome Statute without adequate justification. She argues that this could lead to unjustified inclusions or inclusions, depending on whether the Rome Statute is narrower or broader than custom. Drummond C, 'Different Sources of International Criminal Law and Exclusion: How the Federal Court of Australia in *SRYYY v Minister for Immigration and Multicultural and Indigenous Affairs* Got it Wrong and Why it Matters' (2013) 3(1) Oxford Monitor of Forced Migration 40. Hathaway and Foster also argue that exclusions ought not to be based on norms of international criminal law unless there is general consensus in contemporary international criminal instruments and jurisprudence regarding the affirmative elements of the crime and any applicable defences. Hathaway J, and Foster, M, *The Law of Refugee Status* (2nd edn, CUP, 2014) 572–586.

60 Hathaway and Foster also point out that the focus of international criminal courts and tribunals has (understandably) thus far been focused on the prosecution of the most

2 Terrorism as a Serious Non-political Crime

Article 1F(b) excludes from refugee status an individual for whom there are 'serious reasons for considering…has committed a serious non-political crime outside the country of refuge prior to his admission to that country as a refugee'.

Whilst a number of international instruments may be considered pre-runners to Article 1F(b), these provisions did not refer to terrorism, but rather to common criminals and criminals extraditable by treaty. Several resolutions of the United Nations Relief and Rehabilitation Administration (UNRRA) excluded those who had committed serious common crimes from the organisation's assistance.[61] The Constitution of the International Refugee Organisation (IRO Constitution) also excluded from its mandate ordinary criminals extraditable by treaty.[62] Similarly, Proverb 7 of the Statute of the UNHCR Statute provides the competencies of the UNHCR shall not extend to a person:

> In respect of whom there are serious reasons for considering that he has committed a crime covered by the provisions of treaties of extradition or…by the provisions of article 14, paragraph 2, of the Universal Declaration of Human Rights.

Article 14(2) of the Universal Declaration of Human Rights (UDHR) states that the right to seek and enjoy asylum may not be invoked 'in the case of prosecutions genuinely arising from non-political crimes…'[63] The UNHCR's mandate therefore does not extend to persons for whom there are 'serious reasons for

---

egregious offenders, which has resulted in a dearth of jurisprudence concerning relatively minor offenders. As such, decision-makers should be wary of mechanistic extrapolation of such jurisprudence concerning major offenders to cases involving relatively minor offenders, as is often in issue in Article 1F cases. Ibid. 570–571.

61 UNRRA Resolution 71 excluded from the organisation's assistance: 'displaced persons who may be detained in the custody of the military or civilian authorities of any of the United Nations on charges of having collaborated with the enemy or having committed other crimes against the interests or nationals of the United Nations'. United Nations Relief and Rehabilitation Administration (UNRRA) Resolution 71, para 2(a), *Functions of the Administration with Respect to Displaced Persons*, August 1945, reprinted in George Woodbridge, *UNRRA: the History of the United Nations Relief and Rehabilitation Administration* (Columbia University Press 1950) 142–143; also cited in Atle Grahl-Madsen, *The Status of Refugees in International Law*, vol. I (AW Sijthoff-Leiden 1966) 271.

62 IRO Constitution, Annex I, Part II.

63 Universal Declaration of Human Rights, UNGA Res 217 A(III) (10 December 1948).

considering' they have committed a crime covered by extradition treaties, or are fleeing legitimate prosecution for crimes which are non-political in nature.[64]

Terrorism also did not feature in the debates surrounding the drafting of Article 1F(b). Initially, those who had committed common crimes were not excluded from the scope of the Convention at all.[65] The reference to 'common criminals' in the exclusion provision was included as a result of a French proposal, and retained primarily at the insistence of the French representative.[66] However, due to the concerns of some states that the provision could be used to exclude individuals after admission to a receiving country, and for possibly trivial offences, it was agreed that only *serious* crimes committed *before* entry were at issue. During the course of the discussions, the issue of extradition was also raised, and the possible conflict between State's obligations under extradition treaties and the provisions of the Convention.[67] However,

64 See Kapferer S, 'Article 14(2) of the Universal Declaration of Human Rights and Exclusion from International Refugee Protection' (2008) 27(3) Refugee Survey Quarterly 53–75 for a detailed review of the drafting of Article 14(2) UDHR and the exclusion provisions contained in the IRO Constitution and the UNHCR Statute.

65 The draft exclusion provision prepared by the working group of the Ad Hoc Committee on Statelessness and Related Problems (the Ad Hoc Committee) was limited to those who had committed a crime against peace, war crime, or crime against humanity (as specified in Article VI of the London Charter of the International Military Tribunal), or acts contrary to the purposes and principles of the United Nations (UN). UN Ad Hoc Committee on Statelessness and Related Problems, Provisional Draft of Parts of the Definition Article of the Preliminary Draft Convention Relating to the Status of Refugees, Prepared by the Working Group on This Article' (23 January 1950) E/AC.32/L.6, Article 1B.

66 The French proposal put forth during the debates of the Ad Hoc Committee denied refugee status to any person to whom Article 14(2) UDHR applied. UN Ad Hoc Committee on Refugees and Stateless Persons 'Ad Hoc Committee on Statelessness and Related Problems, France: Proposal for a Draft Convention Preamble' (17 January 1950) E/AC.32/L.3. At the Conference of Plenipotentiaries, concerns were raised over the reference to Article 14 UDHR in the exclusion provision. UN Conference of Plenipotentiaries on the Status of Refugees and Stateless Persons 'Draft Convention Relating to the Status of Refugees. United Kingdom: Alternative Amendments to Section E of Article l' (13 July 1951) A/CONF.2/74. However, the French delegate stated it was impossible for France to agree to drop the limiting clause in the case of common-law criminals. In his opinion, 'it was important not to allow any confusion between [*bona fide* refugees] and ordinary common-law criminals'. UN Conference of Plenipotentiaries on the Status of Refugees and Stateless Persons 'Summary Record of the Twenty-fFourth Meeting' (n 198) (Mr Rochefort [France]).

67 UN Conference of Plenipotentiaries on the Status of Refugees and Stateless Persons 'Summary Record of the Twenty-Fourth Meeting' (n 198) (Mr Herment [Belgium], Mr Hoare [United Kingdom], Mr Robinson [Israel]).

ultimately the drafters declined introducing a formal connection with the law of extradition. The final text of Article 1F(b) adopted at the Conference reads as follows:

> (b) he has committed a serious non-political crime outside the country of refuge prior to his admission to that country as a refugee[68]

Terrorism did not therefore feature in the final text of Article 1F(b), nor was the issue raised during the debates surrounding the drafting of the provision, which rather focused on whether it was necessary to exclude common criminals from the scope of the Convention and possible conflicts with states obligations under treaties of extradition. Terrorism also doesn't feature in the formulations of Article 1F(b) contained in the OAU Refugee Convention, the Arab Refugee Convention or the EU Qualification Directives, in which the provision is replicated almost exactly.[69] The EU Directives specify, however, that the phrase 'outside the country of refuge prior to his or her admission as a refugee means the time of issuing a residence permit based on the granting of refugee status'.[70] The Directives also specify that 'particularly cruel actions, even if committed with an allegedly political objective, may be classified as serious non-political crimes'.[71] As will be considered below, this latter addition may be seen as giving effect to the approach taken to the interpretation of non-political crime by the UNHCR, as endorsed by the UK House of Lords decision in *T v Secretary of State for the Home Department.*[72]

Terrorism has the potential to feature largely in the interpretation of Article 1F(b) since terrorist offences are capable of constituting 'non-political' crimes

68 The final text of Article 1F was adopted by the Conference by 19 votes to none, with 2 abstentations. UN Conference of Plenipotentiaries on the Status of Refugees and Stateless Persons, 'Conference of Plenipotentiaries on the Status of Refugees and Stateless Persons: Summary Record of the Thirty-Fourth Meeting' (30 November 1951) A/CONF.2/SR.34.

69 Although under the Arab Refugee Convention exclusion is also limited to those who have 'not been acquitted under a final peremptory verdict'. Article 2(2).

70 This interpretation appears to be contrary to the clear and unambiguous language of Article 1F(b). UNHCR Background Note (n 164) 16, para 45. However, this interpretation of the temporal and geographical limitation has been included in the UK's Qualification Regulations and set out in the Home Office's APG. Qualification regulation, 7(2)(b); Home Office Exclusion APG (n 16) s 5.4. The issue has yet to come before a court or tribunal however.

71 Qualification Directives, Article 12(2)(b).

72 *T* (n 166).

where they are considered to be disproportionate to their alleged political objective, and many terrorist crimes will also be considered 'serious' within the meaning of the provision. Indeed, terrorism has featured to a large extent in the UK's interpretation of Article 1F(b). Courts and tribunals have, on a number of occasions, excluded individuals under this provision for committing crimes characterised as terrorist in nature. The Home Office's APG similarly notes that terrorist-related offences are likely to fall under this provision. However, while under the UK's approach to interpreting Article 1F(b), terrorist acts may clearly constitute 'non-political' crimes for the purpose of the provision, close examination of the jurisprudence of courts in the UK reveals that not every act so defined will automatically be considered disproportionate to its political motivation. Similarly, the Court of Appeal has recently made clear that simply labelling an act 'terrorist' is not sufficient to raise it to the level of gravity required to constitute a 'serious' crime for the purpose of Article 1F(b). Rather, regard must be had to the individual facts of each case in order to determine that a particular terrorist offence constitutes a 'serious' crime, the definition of which must be based on a 'common starting point'. The UK's interpretation of terrorism as both a 'non-political' crime and a 'serious' crime under Article 1F(b) is considered in turn below.

2.1 *Terrorism as a Non-political Crime*

The UK's practice on interpreting the term 'non-political' crime in Article 1F(b) has traditionally been to rely on the rules and principles of extradition law, particularly the scope of the political offence exception to extradition, to inform the interpretation of the phrase.[73] In the seminal case *T v Secretary of State for the Home Department*, the House of Lords drew on principles from a number of extradition cases in order to give meaning to the phrase 'non-political crime' in Article 1F(b). Although Lord Mustill noted 'There are significant differences between the two doctrines [of asylum and extradition law]', he stated:

> the reference to the "serious non-political crime" in the [1951 Convention] must surely be an echo of the political exception which had been a feature of extradition treaties for nearly a century, and one may hope that

73 There is some debate over the role that the law of extradition should play in the interpretation of 'serious non-political crime'. As noted above, both the Constitution of the IRO and the UNHCR Statute refer to extraditable crimes in the context of exclusion from refugee protection. However, the law of extradition is not explicitly referred to in the text of Article 1F(b), although the issue of Contracting States' obligations under treaties of extradition was raised during the drafting.

decisions on the political exception would provide a comprehensive framework for the few and scattered decisions on asylum.[74]

In this case, their Lordships held that for a crime to be political in nature there had to be shown a direct relationship between the ideas of the perpetrator and those of the victim, such as a crime aimed at a government or military target. In such a case, the crime would be considered political and therefore not fall within the scope of Article 1F(b). Their Lordships believed that a crime could be considered non-political in nature, despite being committed with political objectives, when no clear link exists between the crime and its alleged political objective, or when the act in question is disproportionate to the alleged objective. This was particularly the case where the crime was aimed at a civilian target or was likely to involve the indiscriminate killing or injuring of members of the public.[75] In this case, their Lordships were of the opinion that a terrorist offence which involved the indiscriminate killing of innocent civilians (in this case a bomb attack on an airport) was far removed from any political objective, and therefore could only be described as a non-political crime for the purpose of Article 1F(b).

In coming to this conclusion, the House of Lords drew on the UNHCR Handbook. This position has now been set out in the Home Office's APG,[76] and maintained by the UNHCR and other States Parties to the 1951 Convention.[77] According to the UNHCR Guidelines, '[a] serious crime should be considered non-political when other motives (such as personal reasons or gain) are the predominant feature of the specific crime committed'. Non-political motives should be considered predominant where no clear link exists between the crime and its alleged political objective, or when the act in question is disproportionate to the alleged objective.[78] In particular, the UNHCR advises that '[e]gregious acts of violence, such as those commonly considered to be of a 'terrorist' nature, will almost certainly [be considered] wholly disproportionate to any political objective'.[79] This doctrine has also now been set out in the UK's Qualification Regulations of 2006, which provides that in the construction and application of Article 1F(b), 'the reference to serious non-political crime

74 *T* (n 166) [746B]–[746C].

75 Ibid. [786H]–[787B]. See also similar comments made by the Court of Appeal in this case. *T v Secretary of State for the Home Department* (Court of Appeal) [1995] 1 WLR 545 [558G]–[559A].

76 Home Office Exclusion APG (n 16) s 5.3. Also approved by tribunal in *Gurung* (*Exclusion, Risk, Maoists*) (n 85) 151.

77 Rikhof, *The Criminal Refugee* (n 72) 310–350.

78 UNHCR Guidelines (n 65) 5, para 15. See also UNHCR Handbook (n 65) para 152.

79 UNHCR Background Note (n 164) 15.

includes a particularly cruel action, even if it is committed with an allegedly political objective',[80] replicating the language of Article 12(2)(b) of the EU Qualification Directive. The Home Office's APG explains 'Article 1F(b) may therefore include terrorist crimes' as 'terrorist acts which are wholly disproportionate to any political motive will often be "non-political."'[81]

Indeed, their Lordships in *T* stressed that terrorist offences amounted to 'serious non-political crimes' for the purpose of Article 1F(b). Lord Mustill, in his leading judgment, noted that 'terrorism is an evil in its own right, distinct from endemic violence, and calling for special measures of containment'.[82] Delineating acts of terrorism as political crimes was also the correct approach because the law of asylum 'must be applied at speed'. In contrast to the subjective criteria such as remoteness, causation, atrociousness and proportionality generally employed in extradition cases, the term 'terrorism' was considered capable of 'capable of definition and objective application'.[83] He drew on the definition of terrorism contained in the 1937 League of Nations Convention, which defined 'terrorism' as:

> criminal acts directed against a state and intended or calculated to create a state of terror in the minds of particular persons, or a group of persons or the general public.[84]

Whilst this Convention never came into force, the House of Lords was happy that it was 'serviceable'.

Following the House of Lords judgment in *T*, it appears that terrorist offences should be considered non-political in nature for the purpose of Article 1F(b). However, closer examination of the judgment reveals that their Lordships appeared to employ a specific understanding of terrorism, as indiscriminate violence directed at innocent members of the public:

> The terrorist does not strike at his opponents; those whom he kills are not the tyrants whom he opposes, but people to whom he is indifferent. They

80 Qualification Regulations, regulation 7(2).
81 Home Office Exclusion APG (n 16) s 2.5 and 5.3.
82 *T* (n 166) [772H].
83 Ibid. [772H]–[773A-C].
84 Article 1.2 of the 1937 League of Nations Convention. Considered in *T* (n 166) [772H]–[773A–C]. For a detailed consideration of the drafting of this Convention, and its influence on subsequent efforts to define terrorism, see Saul B, 'The legal response of the League of Nations to terrorism' (2006) 4(1) Journal of International Criminal Justice 78–102.

> are the raw materials of a strategy, not the objectives of it. The terrorist is not even concerned to inspire terror in the victims, for to him they are cyphers...the depersonalised and abstract violence which kills 20, or three, or none, it matters not how many or whom, so long as the broad effect is achieved.[85]

Indeed, Lord Mustill continued: 'once it is made clear that terrorism is not simply a label for violent conduct of which the speaker deeply disapproves, the term is capable of definition and objective application'.[86]

The House of Lord's determination that terrorist acts amount to serious non-political crimes therefore appears to be limited to their interpretation of 'terrorism' as indiscriminate acts of violence directed at innocent civilians, as opposed to politically motivated violent conduct *per se*. As explained in the Home Office's APG:

> Consistent with the reasoning in T v SSHD, the commission of crimes such as murder, rape and serious assault, or other violent acts which *result in indiscriminate harm or death to the public,* will usually fail to establish a sufficient link to the achievement to a political objective and should be considered to be "non-political" crimes for the purposes of Article 1F(b).[87]

The CJEU, in the *B & D* case, also appeared to interpret non-political crime under Article 1F(b) in this manner. The Court in this case referred to 'terrorist acts, which are characterised by their violence towards civilian populations'.[88]

However, the scope of terrorist-related offences, as defined in the UK, is in many cases much broader than this definition. For example, a terrorist act of violence may be directed not against the public, but against a specific political target. A violent attack against a government representative will clearly fall within the scope of the UK's domestic definition of terrorism,[89] however it is not clear that this will necessarily constitute a non-political crime for the purpose of Article 1F(b). As noted in the Home Office's APG:

---

85 *T* (n 166) [772E]–[772H].

86 Ibid. [772H]–[773A–C] (Lord Mustil).

87 Home Office Exclusion APG (n 16) s 5.3 (emphasis added).

88 *Bundesrepublik Deutschland (C-57/09) v B (C-101/09) and D* [2010] ECR 1-000 [81]: First, it is clear that terrorist acts, which are characterised by their violence towards civilian populations, even if committed with a purportedly political objective, fall to be regarded as serious non-political crimes within the meaning of point (b).

89 See the UK's domestic definition of terrorism, contained in the Terrorism Act 2000, discussed in Chapter 4.

> A link may however be established to a political crime if such methods [violent acts] are used against specific targets that are political in nature (e.g. government representatives etc) and are committed for political motives.[90]

Furthermore, a number of terrorist-related offences do not involve the commission of an act of violence at all. For example, in the UK it is a criminal offence simply to be a member of a proscribed terrorist organisation.[91] This is clearly a terrorist-related offence, and yet does not involve violence of any type. This was recognised in a case which came before the Special Immigration Appeals Commission (SIAC), in which an Algerian national had been sentenced to life imprisonment in his absence for belonging to a terrorist organisation. This was considered by the adjudicator to constitute an 'inherently political offence' in the absence of any linked and more specifically criminal behaviour.[92]

Under the UK's approach, terrorist offences are therefore capable of constituting 'non-political crimes' for the purpose of Article 1F(b), despite being committed with political motivation, where they involve attacks on civilians or violence which is disproportionate to the alleged political objective. However, not every terrorist-related offence will amount to a non-political crime under this test, as has been recognised in both the jurisprudence of courts and tribunals in the UK and in the Home Office's guidance documents.[93]

2.2 *Terrorism as a Serious Crime*

In order to fall within the scope of Article 1F(b) the crime must not only be non-political in nature but also be sufficiently 'serious'. Indeed, during the drafting of Article 1F(b) the UK representative was concerned that the provision should not be used to exclude those who had committed minor offences from the protection of the Convention.

The term 'serious crime' is not defined in the 1951 Convention itself. The UNHCR suggests that the term 'serious' is limited to 'a capital crime or a very

90 Home Office Exclusion APG, s 5.3.

91 Terrorism Act 2000, s 11.

92 *Y v Secretary of State for the Home Department* [2006] UKSIAC 36/2004 [133].

93 Indeed, Hathaway and Foster argue that one simply cannot reconcile the invocation of acts "commonly considered" to be terrorist as presumptive grounds for considering an act to be a non-political crime for the purpose of Article 1F(b). Hathaway J, and Foster, M, *The Law of Refugee Status* (n 254) 561.

grave punishable act'.[94] However, this has been described by the UK tribunal as 'an unwarranted gloss' on the term 'serious'.[95] It has further been suggested that examples of serious crimes include murder, rape, arson and armed robbery, but do not extend to minor crimes such as petty theft,[96] and that certain offences may be deemed serious if accompanied by the use of deadly weapons, involve serious injury to persons or there is evidence of serious habitual criminal conduct and other similar factors.[97] These examples of serious crime are all covered by the Border Agency's APG on exclusion, which further provide that 'crimes, though not accompanied by violence, such as large-scale fraud, may also be regarded as "serious" for the purposes of Article 1F(b)'.[98]

In determining what amounts to a 'serious crime' for the purpose of Article 1F(b) in the UK, recourse has also been made by the Home Office to s.72 of the UK Nationality, Immigration and Asylum Act 2002 (the 2002 Act), which provides a statutory definition of 'particularly serious crime' for the purpose of the exception to *refoulement* under Article 33(2) of the 1951 Convention. This provision provides that a 'particularly serious crime' is one which either attracted a custodial sentence of two years or more or, where the offence is committed outside of the UK, could have attracted a custodial sentence of two years or more had the offence been committed in the UK. Thus in *AH* (*Algeria*) the Secretary of State argued that the 1951 Convention left the issue of what constituted a 'serious crime' to be determined by the domestic courts of signatory states. The Secretary of State therefore submitted that they were entitled to rely upon the presumption in s.72: that a person convicted of an offence and sentenced to at least two years imprisonment had committed a 'particularly serious crime', which therefore fell within the scope of Article 1F(b) as a 'serious crime'. This position is also maintained in the Home Office's APG which further provides that:

> given that the Article 1F(b) requirement states exclusion will be merited following a "serious" crime, as opposed to "particularly serious," it may be appropriate to regard a crime for which a custodial sentence of 12 months

94 UNHCR Handbook (n 65) para 155. UNHCR Background Note (n 164) 14.

95 *AA* (*Exclusion clause*) *Palestine* (n 167) [66].

96 UNHCR Guidelines (n 65) para 14; UNHCR Background Note (n 164) 14, para 40.

97 UNHCR Background Note (n 164) 14, para 40. Goodwin-Gill and McAdam suggest such crimes might include burglary, theft and simple robbery, receiving stolen property, embezzlement and assault, provided aggravating factors were present. Goodwin-Gill and McAdam (n 68) 179.

98 Home Office Exclusion APG, s 5.2.

> or more upon conviction might be expected (if that crime had been tried in the United Kingdom) as a "serious crime."[99]

Under this approach, a crime will be considered sufficiently 'serious' for the purpose of Article 1F(b) if it would attract a custodial sentence of one year were it committed in the UK.

However, in *AH* (*Algeria*) the Court of Appeal gave short shrift to the Home Office's approach to the determination of 'serious' for the purpose of Article 1F(b). Sullivan LJ, in his leading judgment, stated that he did not accept that each signatory state was free to adopt its own definition of what constitutes a 'serious crime' for the purpose of the provision.[100] In his opinion, whilst the Convention left to domestic courts the decision of whether a non-political crime was 'serious' in any particular case, 'that determination must be founded upon a *common starting point* as to the level of seriousness that must be demonstrated if a person is to be excluded from the protection of the Convention'.[101] Ward LJ agreed:

> Being an international convention, it must be given an autonomous meaning. They are ordinary words and should be given their ordinary universal meaning.[102]

The Lord Justices stressed that it was not helpful to determine the level of seriousness of an offence by the precise sentence of imprisonment imposed upon an asylum applicant. Although sentence was a material factor, 'it is not the benchmark'.[103] Rather, Ward LJ stated that the term 'serious' had to be given its ordinary meaning. In the context of Article 1F(b), this meaning was given the 'appropriate colour' in that the crime committed must be serious enough to justify the withholding of protection an asylum applicant would otherwise enjoy as a person fleeing persecution.[104] In sum, Ward LJ stated:

> In deciding whether the crime is serious enough to justify his loss of protection, the Tribunal must take all facts and matters into account,

---

99 Ibid. s 5.2: 'as a guide as to what level of offending constitutes "serious," the UK Border Agency uses the definition of "particularly serious" in Section 72 Nationality, Immigration and Asylum Act 2002'.

100 *AH* (*Algeria*) (n 69) [30], [32].

101 Ibid. [31] (emphasis added).

102 Ibid. [50].

103 Ibid. [54].

104 Ibid. [52].

> with regard to the nature of the crime, the part played by the accused in its commission, any mitigating or aggravating features and the eventual penalty imposed.[105]

Whilst Sullivan LJ could accept that an offence which carried a maximum sentence of 10 years imprisonment was capable of constituting a serious non-political crime within the scope of Article 1F(b), in this case the fact that the asylum applicant had been sentenced to two years imprisonment 'placed it at the lower end of seriousness of this kind of offence'. The Court of Appeal in this case therefore stressed the need to examine cases individually in order to determine if the crime(s) in question are sufficiently serious for the purpose of Article 1F(b), regard being had to all the surrounding circumstances. When the case was remitted to the immigration tribunal, the tribunal agreed that 'serious' in the context of Article 1F(b) has an autonomous international meaning and is not to be defined purely by national law or the length of sentence imposed or likely to be imposed.[106] In the tribunal's opinion, the crimes and acts enumerated in Articles 1F(a) and (c) serve to illustrate the level of seriousness required to engage Article 1F(b).[107]

Approaches of presumptive exclusion based on generalised classifications of Article 1F crimes or length of sentence have indeed been heavily criticised.[108] Rather, it would appear that the restrictive approach that it is advised be adopted in the interpretation of Article 1F points to the need to consider the act committed by the asylum applicant individually.[109] Similarly, the principle that the provisions of the 1951 Convention be interpreted so as to have an autonomous meaning points to the need to base Article 1F(b)'s concept of serious crime on international, rather than domestic standards.[110] As such, the Court of Appeal appears to have been correct in rejecting the Secretary of

---

105 Ibid. [54].

106 *AH (Article 1F(b) – 'serious') Algeria* [2013] UKUT 382 [83].

107 Ibid. [86].

108 Zimmermann and Wennholz (n 68) 601; Gilbert, 'Current Issues' (n 188) 450; Goodwin-Gill and McAdam (n 68) 181–182.

109 The UNHCR advises that factors relevant to determining the seriousness of a crime include the nature of the act; the actual harm inflicted; the form of procedure used to prosecute the crime; the nature of the penalty for such a crime; and whether most jurisdictions would consider the act in question to be a serious crime. UNHCR Guidelines (n 65) para 14; UNHCR Background Note (n 164) 14, para 39.

110 UNHCR Guidelines (n 65) 5 para 14; UNHCR Background Note (n 164) 14, para 38. Although Goodwin-Gill and McAdam argue that standards in the potential country of asylum are relevant. Goodwin-Gill and McAdam (n 68) 178.

State's reliance on the 2002 Act, and rather stressing the need to examine cases individually in light of all the circumstances surrounding the crime for which there are serious reasons for considering the asylum applicant has committed.

Attention was also given in the *AH* (*Algeria*) case to whether terrorist offences amounted to 'serious crimes' for the purpose of Article 1F(b). Indeed, it is likely that many terrorist offences will be considered to be 'serious crimes', particularly where they involve acts such as murder, bombing and hostage taking. Thus in one case the UK tribunal noted:

> It would be difficult for the Claimant to argue that his activities in training to be an Islamic Jihad armed militant, smuggling guns, undertaking missions and preparing for a suicide mission did not constitute serious crimes under the formal, if ineffective, legal system or systems in Gaza.[111]

The tribunal drew attention to the fact that the asylum applicant 'was a would-be suicide bomber; even if his target had been a checkpoint, which is a place where many civilians gather and queue'.[112] In this case the asylum applicant's terrorist activity meant he fell within the scope of Article 1F(b). The House of Lords in *T* were also clearly of the opinion that terrorist offences amounted to 'serious non-political crimes' for the purpose of Article 1F(b). However, as there are a range of offences that may be considered terrorist in character, it is apparent that not every act considered to be terrorist or terrorist-related in nature will meet Article 1F(b)'s requirement of 'serious crime', as was the case in *AH* (*Algeria*), considered below.

In *AH* (*Algeria*), the Court of Appeal had to determine whether the asylum applicant's conviction in France amounted to a 'serious crime' for the purpose of Article 1F(b). He had been convicted in France for the terrorist-related offence of being a member of an association formed with a view to the preparation of acts of terrorism, and making fraudulent representations, in the form of a passport and identity card, with the intention of seriously disrupting public order by intimidation or terror. The Court of Appeal in this case held that it was not possible, on the basis of the very limited findings of the French Court, to conclude that this offence crossed the threshold of seriousness for the purpose of Article 1F(b). It was not clear what 'material acts' were relied upon by the French Appeal Court in the case, further than the offence of falsifying a French passport and national identity card, which it was considered the

111 *AA* (*Exclusion clause*) *Palestine* (n 167) [46].

112 Ibid. [49].

asylum applicant would use in relation to the terrorist activities of the group.[113] In particular, Sullivan LJ noted:

> While terrorism is a grave international threat, merely labelling an offence a terrorist offence is not sufficient, of itself, to establish that the offence is a serious offence for the purpose of Article 1F(b).

Whilst his Lordship noted that 'as an instrument of state policy, "nipping terrorism in the bud" is eminently sensible', he pointed out that:

> if the criminal law framed in aid of the policy foils the aspiring terrorist's intentions well before he has undertaken any, or any significant, preparatory acts, then the consequence for the purpose of Article 1F may well be that the offence of which he is convicted, at the outer boundary of criminality, will not be an offence which is so serious as to exclude him from protection under the Convention.[114]

Sullivan LJ thus emphasised the need for an act of sufficient seriousness to have been committed by an asylum applicant in order to bring him or her within the terms of Article 1F. Merely labelling an offence 'terrorist' was considered not adequate to establish that the offence is 'serious' for the purpose of Article 1F(b).

In contrast with the approach adopted by the House of Lords in *T*, the Court of Appeal in this case did not attempt to define terrorism for the purpose of Article 1F(b), nor stress that terrorist acts should fall to be excluded under the provision. Rather, the Court of Appeal directed its legal analysis away from the 'terrorism' label, and toward answering the question of whether there were serious reasons for considering the individual had committed a serious crime. The Court in this case seems to have recognised the broad sweep of some domestic anti-terrorist legislation (in this case French), and therefore cautioned against relying on the delineation of a crime as 'terrorist' when determining it is 'serious' for the purpose of Article 1F(b).

When remitted for reconsideration, the immigration tribunal in *AH* (*Algeria*) held that personal participation in a conspiracy to promote terrorist violence could amount to a particularly serious crime for the purpose of Article 1F(b). However, in common with the approach of the Court of Appeal, the tribunal stressed that this was, 'providing again that the focus is on the substance of the

---

113 *AH* (*Algeria*) [2012] (n 69) [18]–[20].

114 Ibid. [21].

conduct and undue emphasis is not given merely to the labels applied by domestic law'.[115]

Whilst account should be taken of the fact that the UN Security Council has called upon Member States to qualify terrorist acts as 'serious criminal offences',[116] the principle that the provisions of the 1951 Convention be interpreted so as to have an autonomous meaning points to the need to base Article 1F(b)'s concept of serious crime on international, rather than domestic standards. Therefore, domestic definitions of terrorism or terrorist offences may not be appropriate standards of which to base an Article 1F decision. Rather, it appears consideration should rather be given to whether the offence would be considered a serious crime by the majority of states parties to the 1951 Convention.[117] Examples of terrorist offences which would appear to meet this standard include those prohibited by international anti-terrorism convention, such as hostage taking, hijacking, and the use of explosives.[118] However, it would appear that in all cases the surrounding circumstances of the crime should be considered, to allow any relevant mitigating or aggravating circumstances be taken into account when determining whether the crime is sufficiently serious for the purpose of Article 1F(b).[119]

---

115 *AH (Article 1F(b))* (n 301) [89]. The tribunal requested the entire judgment of the French court be translated into English, noting that only a partial translation had been provided to the Court of Appeal. Upon receiving the full transcript the tribunal concluded that there was sufficient evidence to conclude that AH was senior participant in the conspiracy and that he was therefore excluded from refugee status under Article 1F(b).

116 UNSC Res 1373, para 5.

117 Indeed, Hathaway and Foster argue that the determination of whether any particular crime is 'serious' for the purpose of Article 1F(b) requires that the act was a serious crime common crime in both the state it was committed and in the state assessing refugee status, and furthermore be an extraditable crime as defined by reference to international minimum standards. Hathaway J, and Foster, M, The Law of Refugee Status (n 254) 550.

118 For example, Convention for the Suppression of Unlawful Seizure of Aircraft; International Convention against the Taking of Hostages; International Convention for the Suppression of Terrorist Bombings. It has been suggested that those crimes that are within United Nations multilateral anti-terrorist conventions can safely be assumed to be serious. Gilbert, 'Current Issues in the Application of the Exclusion Clauses' (n 188) 449. Hathaway and Foster also favour an approach by which the standards against which exclusion on grounds of terrorism is to be measures is predicated on norms set by international agreements, rather than measures specifically targeting refugees. Ibid. 561–562.

119 UNHCR Handbook (n 65) para 157.

2.3 *Conclusions on Article 1F(b) Crimes*

The UK's interpretation of the term 'non-political' crime in Article 1F(b) has traditionally been based on the rules and principles of extradition law, particularly the scope of the political offence exception to extradition. However, in *T v Secretary of State for the Home Department* the House of Lords stressed that the evil of terrorism calls for special measures of containment, and therefore held that terrorist crimes fall within the scope of Article 1F(b) as serious non-political crimes. Their Lordships drew on the definition of terrorism contained in the 1937 League of Nations Convention. However, closer examination of the judgment reveals that the House of Lords appeared to employ a specific understanding of terrorism in this case: indiscriminate violence directed at innocent members of the public. Not every terrorist-related offence will amount to a serious non-political crime under this test, as has been recognised in both the jurisprudence of courts and tribunals in the UK and in the Home Office's guidance documents.

In contrast with the approach adopted by the House of Lords in *T*, the Court of Appeal in *AH (Algeria)* did not attempt to define terrorism for the purpose of Article 1F(b), nor stress that terrorist acts should fall to be excluded under the provision. Rather, the Court of Appeal directed its legal analysis away from the 'terrorism' label, and toward answering the question of whether there were serious reasons for considering the individual had committed a serious non-political crime. Merely labelling an offence 'terrorist' was not considered adequate to establish that the offence is 'serious' for the purpose of Article 1F(b). The Court in this case seems to have recognised the broad sweep of some domestic anti-terrorist legislation, and therefore preferred an approach which focused on individual examination of each case in order to determine if the crime in question is sufficiently serious to bring it within the scope of Article 1F(b), regard being had to all the surrounding circumstances.

3 Conclusions

Although explicit reference to the Vienna rule has not been frequently made, courts and tribunals in the UK have tended to adopt a restrictive approach to the interpretation of the crimes enumerated in Articles 1F(a) and (b), an approach which tends away from expansive interpretations of these crimes and stresses the need for individual consideration of the facts of each case. To this end, generalised classifications and purely domestic interpretations of the crimes enumerated in these provisions have been rejected, resort rather being had to international instruments in order to arrive at the 'autonomous' meaning of the crimes as a matter of international law.

Terrorism has not featured to any significant extent in the UK's interpretations of the crimes that fall within the scope of Article 1F(a), resort rather being had to the statues and jurisprudence of international criminal courts and tribunals. In the context of Article 1F(b), whilst terrorism was a clear feature of the House of Lords decision in *T*, the Court of Appeal has recently emphasised that merely labelling an offence 'terrorist' is not adequate to establish that the offence is 'serious' for the purpose of Article 1F(b). The Court of Appeal rather stressed that the individual facts of each case must be considered in order to determine if the crime in question is sufficiently serious to warrant exclusion from refugee status under this provision. Indeed, a closer reading of the House of Lords judgment in *T* reveals that their Lordships had in mind a specific form of terrorism in this case – acts of indiscriminate violence directed towards innocent civilians – rather than any form of terrorism *per se*. That not every terrorist-related offence will amount to a serious non-political crime under this test appears to have been recognised in both the jurisprudence of courts and tribunals in the UK and in the Home Office's guidance documents, and is indeed the approach that appears to have been adopted to the notion of terrorism in the context of Article 1F(b) by the CJEU.

CHAPTER 4

Terrorism as Acts Contrary to the Purposes and Principles of the United Nations

Article 1F(c) of the 1951 Convention excludes from refugee status an individual for whom there are 'serious reasons for considering...has been guilty of acts contrary to the purposes and principles of the United Nations'. Several resolutions of the United Nations Relief and Rehabilitation Administration (UNRRA) might be considered forerunners of Article 1F(c). For example, UNRRA Resolution 71 excluded from the organisation's assistance:

> displaced persons who may be detained in the custody of the military or civilian authorities of any of the United Nations on charges of having collaborated with the enemy or having committed other crimes against the interests or nationals of the United Nations.[1]

The Constitution of the International Refugee Organisation (IRO Constitution) also excluded from its mandate those who had assisted enemy forces in the persecution of civilian populations or operations against the United Nations, and those who had, since the end of hostilities, participated in any organisation hostile to the government of a member of the United Nations, or had participated in any *terrorist organisation*.[2]

Despite reference to terrorist organisations in the IRO Constitution, terrorism did not feature in early formulations of Article 1F(c), nor the debates surrounding the drafting of the provision. The drafting debates rather focused on the imprecise nature of the phrase 'acts contrary to the purposes and principles of the United Nations', and the type of acts that might fall within the scope of the provision.[3] The debates surrounding the drafting of the provision

---

1 UNRRA, Resolution 71, para 2(a).

2 IRO Constitution, Annex I Part II.

3 The Canadian delegate proposed deleting these words, stating the formulation was so vague as to be open to abuse by governments wishing to exclude refugees from the protection of the Convention. ECOSOC Social Committee '160th Meeting' (1950) UN Doc E/AC.7/SR.160, 16. The UK delegate stated that he had 'doubts as to the exact meaning of the words "acts contrary to the purposes and principles of the United Nations," and felt that the adoption of such a text might make it possible for governments to exclude refugees who should not be so treated'. UN Conference of Plenipotentiaries on the Status of Refugees and Stateless Persons 'Conference

 | DOI 10.1163/9789004292062_006

suggest that Article 1F(c) was understood as applying to violations of human rights that fell short of crimes against humanity, war crimes, genocide and the subversion or overthrow of democratic regimes, committed by persons occupying government posts, such as heads of State, ministers and high officials.[4]

Terrorism is also not mentioned in the exclusion provisions of the OAU Refugee Convention, which replicate the wording of Article 1F(c) and includes an additional reference to a person who has been 'guilty of acts contrary to the purposes and principles of the Organization of African Unity'.[5] Terrorism is, however, explicitly cited in the EU Qualification Directives. The Directives exclude those 'guilty of acts contrary to the purposes and principles of the United Nations *as set out in the Preamble and Articles 1 and 2 of the Charter of the United Nations*'.[6] Furthermore, the Preambles to the Directives provide:

> Acts contrary to the purposes and principles of the United Nations are set out in the Preamble and Articles 1 and 2 of the Charter of the United Nations and are, amongst others, embodied in the United Nations Resolutions relating to measures combating terrorism, which declare that 'acts, methods and practices of terrorism are contrary to the purposes and principles of the United Nations' and that 'knowingly financing, planning and inciting terrorist acts are also contrary to the purposes and principles of the United Nations.[7]

The EU Directives thus refer directly to the Charter of the United Nations and UN resolutions relating to measures combating terrorism when interpreting the phrase 'acts contrary to the purposes and principles of the United Nations'.

The purposes and principles of the UN, as set out in the Preamble and Articles 1 and 2 of the Charter of the United Nations (UN Charter), include such purposes as maintaining international peace and security, developing friendly relations among nations and promoting and encouraging respect for human rights, and principles such as the sovereign equality of all states, fulfilling

---

of Plenipotentiaries on the Status of Refugees and Stateless Persons: Summary Record of the Twenty-ninth Meeting' (28 November 1951) A/CONF.2/SR.29 (Mr. Hoare [United Kingdom]).

4 ECOSOC Social Committee '166th Meeting' (1950) UN Doc E/AC.7/SR.166, 6–7; UN Conference of Plenipotentiaries on the Status of Refugees and Stateless Persons 'Summary Record of the Twenty-fourth Meeting' (n 198) (Mr. Hoare [United Kingdom]).

5 This should be read today as a reference to the purposes and principles of the African Union. OAU Refugee Convention, art 1(5). Zimmermann and Wennholz (n 68) 592. No provision equivalent to Article 1F(c) is included in the Arab Refugee Convention.

6 Qualification Directive, art 12(2)(c) (emphasis added).

7 2004 Qualification Directive, recital 22; 2011 Qualification Directive, recital 31.

obligations under the Charter in good faith and settling disputes by peaceful means. These are broad general statements[8] and as such it has been suggested that in certain areas the practical content of the declared purposes and principles must be determined in light of more general developments in international law,[9] including, for example, multilateral conventions adopted under the auspices of the UN General Assembly and UN Security Council resolutions.[10] This dynamic approach to the interpretation of the purposes and principles of the UN is mandated by the EU Qualification Directives, which refer to UN resolutions which declare that 'acts, methods and practices of terrorism are contrary to the purposes and principles of the United Nations' outlined in Chapter 1.[11] This has indeed been the approach adopted by courts and tribunals in the UK when considering the scope of the provision.

Terrorism has featured largely in the UK's interpretation of Article 1F(c). Drawing on the UN resolutions highlighted above, the courts and tribunals in the UK have recognised that acts of terrorism are capable of falling within the scope of Article 1F(c). The Home Office's APG similarly provides:

> Acts of terrorism are widely considered contrary to the purposes and principles of the United Nations, as set out in the United Nations Security Council Resolutions relating to measures combating terrorism (United

8 Indeed Hathaway and Foster note that 'To describe these purposes and principles as broad-ranging is surely an understatement'. Hathaway J, and Foster, M, *The Law of Refugee Status* (n 254) 590.

9 Goodwin-Gill and McAdam (n 68) 185. Roscini also notes that the UN Charter is a treaty and as such can be modified by subsequent custom. He points out that informal modification of the UN Charter was endorsed by the ICJ in the 1971 Advisory Opinion on Namibia (n 89) with regard to Article 27(3). Roscini M, 'The United Nations Security Council and the Enforcement of International Humanitarian Law' (2010) 43 Israel Law Review 339. Although Nyinah suggests that the meaning of 'purposes and principles of the United Nations' in Article 1F(c) is limited to those set forth in the UN Charter. Nyinah (n 191) 309.

10 UNHCR Background Note (n 164) 17, para 47. For example, respect for human rights has been developed through the UDHR, the 1966 International Human Rights Covenants, regional treaty arrangements such as the European Convention on Human Rights and customary international law. Roscini also suggests that promoting and encouraging respect for international humanitarian law can now be considered one of the UN purposes. Roscini M, 'The United Nations Security Council and the Enforcement of International Humanitarian Law' (n 323) 333–335. However, in light of the residual nature of Article 1F(c), breaches of international humanitarian law may more appropriately be considered under Article 1F(a).

11 UNGA Dec 1994, para 2; UNGA Dec 1996, para 2; UNSC Res 1373, para 5; UNSC Res 1377, preamble role 5; UNSC Res 1624 preamble role 8.

> Nations Security Council Resolutions 1373 and 1377 which declare that the "acts, methods and practices of terrorism are contrary to the purposes and principles of the United Nations" and that "knowingly financing, planning and inciting terrorist acts are also contrary to the purposes and principles of the United Nations."[12]

This has now been set out in statute in the UK's Immigration, Asylum and Nationality Act 2006, which provides that the construction of Article 1F(c) includes acts of committing, preparing or instigating terrorism.[13]

However, it seems that courts and tribunals in the UK have been more cautious with regard to adopting a definition of terrorism for the purpose of Article 1F(c). Although the UK's Immigration, Asylum and Nationality Act directs one to the UK's domestic definition of terrorism for this purpose, the practice of courts and tribunals in the UK has not been to adhere rigidly to this definition, but rather to draw on the definitions of terrorism contained in international sources to give content to the meaning of terrorism in the context of the provision. Indeed, the Supreme Court recently rejected the UK's domestic definition of terrorism completely, rather preferring to rely on the UNHCR's guidance when interpreting the phrase 'acts contrary to the purposes and principles of the United Nations'. While jurisprudence on Article 1F(c) in the UK has long been dominated by the definition and scope of 'terrorism' as acts contrary to the purposes and principles of the United Nations, a recent approach to the interpretation of the phrase considers whether it also covers military action which does not amount to terrorism but can nevertheless be considered to constitute 'acts contrary to the purposes and principles of the United Nations' for the purpose of Article 1F(c).

Part 1 of this chapter examines the practice of the immigration tribunal and the SIAC in the early cases involving Article 1F(c), before the adoption of domestic legislation in the UK concerning the interpretation of the provision. Part 2 considers the UK's domestic definition of terrorism, the coming into force of the EU Qualification Directive and how the intersection of these different legal regimes was approached in a number of cases before the Court of Appeal, while Part 3 considers a recent decision of the Supreme Court in which it provides long-awaited guidance on the definition of 'terrorism' for the purpose of Article 1F(c). The chapter concludes in Part 4 with a critical examination of the Supreme Court's approach to addressing the important question of whether military action against armed forces acting under UN mandate is

12 Home Office Exclusion APG s 6.2.

13 Immigration, Asylum and Nationality Act, s 54.

contrary to the purposes and principles of the United Nations for the purpose of Article 1F(c).[14]

1 The Early Cases

For over a decade the immigration tribunal and the SIAC have recognised that acts of terrorism are capable of falling within the scope of Article 1F(c).[15] In the early cases, before the adoption of the UK's 2006 Immigration, Asylum and Nationality Act which sets out in statute that acts of terrorism fall within the scope of the provision, the immigration tribunal and the SIAC drew on a number of the UN resolutions outlined above in support of this proposition.[16] These bodies therefore took a dynamic approach to the interpretation of the phrase 'acts contrary to the purposes and principles of the United Nations', an approach based in part on 1951 Convention's status as a 'living instrument'.

The meaning of the phrase 'acts contrary to the purposes and principles of the United Nations' was considered in detail by the immigration tribunal in the *KK* case in 2004. The tribunal here noted that, although Articles 1 and 2 of the UN Charter are the 'starting point' for determining the meaning of the phrase, it did not consider itself limited to the wording of these Charter provisions but also considered UN General Assembly and Security Council resolutions to be highly relevant to the interpretation of the provision. The tribunal drew attention to the rule of treaty interpretation contained in the Vienna Convention on the Law of Treaties, and considered Security Council resolutions to be evidence of subsequent practice of states parties within the meaning of Article 31(3)(b) of the Vienna rule,[17] and General Assembly resolutions, while not having the legislative force of Security Council resolutions, as evidence of subsequent agreement of states parties within the meaning of Article 31(3)(a) of the Vienna rule.[18] The tribunal noted:

---

14 This chapter is drawn in part from Singer S, 'Exclusion from Refugee Status: asylum seekers and terrorism in the UK' (2012) 1 Centre for Criminal Justice and Human Rights Working Papers Series 2–16.

15 *Mukhtiar Singh v Secretary of State for the Home Department* [2000] (unreported, SC 4/99) [68]; *Gurung (Exclusion, Risk, Maoists)* (n 85) 100.

16 *C v Secretary of State for the Home Department* [2003] UKSIAC 7/2002 [31]; *AA (Exclusion clause) Palestine* (n 167) [54]; *KK* (n 147) [21]–[29].

17 The tribunal made reference to the powers of the Security Council in Articles 24 and 48 of the UN Charter.

18 *KK* (n 147) [21]–[29].

> To fail to give full effect to these Acts is not merely to ignore the Vienna Convention: it is to prevent the Charter of the United Nations being regarded as a living instrument, capable of being adapted by interpretation and use, by agreement and endorsement, to the circumstances of changing ages.[19]

This approach was followed in a number of decisions of the tribunal and the SIAC.[20] These UN Security Council and General Assembly resolutions were therefore relied upon heavily in the UK's interpretation of Article 1F(c), to support the view that acts of terrorism fall within the scope of the provision. In support of this approach, attention was also drawn to the seminal decision of the Supreme Court of Canada in *Pushpanathan*.[21] In this case, the Canadian Court held that acts could be considered contrary to the purposes and principles of the United Nations for the purpose of Article 1F(c) in cases where:

(a) 'there was a consensus in international law that particular acts constitute sufficiently serious and sustained violations of fundamental human rights as to amount to persecution' and
(b) the acts 'are explicitly recognised as contrary to the purposes and principles of the United Nations.'[22]

The tribunal reasoned that as acts of terrorism had been explicitly recognised as contrary to the purposes and principles of the United Nations in these Security Council and General Assembly resolutions, terrorism was certainly capable of falling within the scope of Article 1F(c) under section (b) of the *Pushpanathan* approach.[23]

---

19 Ibid. [69]. Similarly, the tribunal has noted that: 'The UN, through its Resolutions, may express its principles, and affect the scope or application of the exclusion clauses. Those clauses are intended to prevent the claim of refugee status being made successfully by those whose conduct is condemned by the international community, a condemnation which can be expressed through UN Resolutions. If the Refugee Convention is properly seen as a "living document" its adaptability to the needs of the times can be reflected in the development or elaboration of UN principles affecting exclusion, as well as in the development of protection needs'. *AA (Exclusion clause) Palestine* (n 167) [53].

20 *AA (Exclusion clause) Palestine* (n 167); *Y* (n 287); *Abu Qatada v Secretary of State for the Home Department* [2007] UKSIAC 15/2005; *DD & Anor v Secretary of State for the Home Department* [2007] UKSIAC 42/2005.

21 *Pushpanathan v Canada* [1998] 1 SCR 982.

22 Ibid. [65]–[66], cited in *KK* (n 147) [76].

23 *KK* (n 147) [76].

However, in these early cases both the tribunal and the SIAC repeatedly stressed that merely characterising certain acts as 'terrorist' is 'neither necessary nor sufficient' for the act to constitute acts contrary to the purposes and principles of the UN for the purpose of Article 1F(c).[24] Rather, it was necessary to examine the meaning of the phrase 'acts contrary to the purposes and principles of the United Nations', and determine whether the acts in question were capable of falling within the scope of the provision:

> evidently the phrase [acts contrary to the purposes and principles of the United Nations] is capable of bearing a meaning not limited to acts of terrorism. For the same reason, acts which some might call terrorist might not fall within the United Nations' understanding of the word, but might nevertheless, for some other reason, fall within the class of acts that are contrary to the purposes and principles of the United Nations. But what we wish to make clear is that the entire process of analysis is properly independent of any use of the word "*terrorism*" in other contexts.[25]

The tribunal in *KK* maintained that it was 'searching for an international autonomous meaning of the relevant provisions of the Refugee Convention', and therefore purely domestic interpretations of terrorism, such as those contained in English statutes, were inappropriate.[26] Similarly, the tribunal considered its task was to determine what the UN means by 'terrorism' in their resolutions, rather than any meaning that terrorism might have by international agreement.[27]

The tribunal and the SIAC, however, declined from making any firm findings as to what the UN meant by terrorism in its resolutions, or formulating a working definition of terrorism for the purpose of Article 1F(c). Rather, the provision was repeatedly held to apply to 'acts which are the subject of intense disapproval by the governing body of the entire international community'.[28] The tribunal in KK explained:

---

24 *Y* (n 287) [148]; *Abu Qatada* (n 334) [105]; DD *& Anor* (n 334) [121].

25 *KK* (n 147) [75] (emphasis in original).

26 Ibid. [61]: 'it is not open to us to provide a purely national or local interpretation. For this reason, English statutes relating to the definition of terrorism, treatment of terrorists, or even to the interpretation of the Refugee Convention are of very limited assistance'.

27 Ibid. [74]; *AA (Exclusion clause) Palestine* (n 167) [60]; *Y* (n 287) [148].

28 *KK* (n 147) [85]. Approved in *Y* (n 287) [148]; *Abu Qatada* (n 334) [105]; *DD & Anor* (n 334) [121].

> An individual who has committed such an act cannot claim that his categorisation as criminal depends upon the attitudes of the very regime from whom he has sought to escape, because the international condemnation shows that his acts would have been treated in the same way wherever and under whatever circumstances they had been committed.[29]

In these early cases, Article 1F(c) was held to apply to a Turkish activist who had been convicted of arson and conspiracy to commit arson in relation to his part in petrol bomb attacks on a Turkish bank and travel agency in London. The fact that a DKHP flag had been placed at the scene of both incidents was considered to show the purpose of the attacks 'was to provoke a state of terror amongst those engaged in lawful Turkish businesses in the United Kingdom and thus to indicate that the fight against the Turkish Government was being pursued by violent means even here'.[30] The tribunal noted that these factors 'bring into these offences of arson both an international and a terrorist element', and therefore fell within the scope of Article 1F(c).[31] The provision was also applied to an active supporter of Egyptian Islamic Jihad (EIJ), a proscribed terrorist organisation in the UK, for his role in trying to recruit serving Egyptian Army officers for the EIJ and in planning operations on behalf of the EIJ, both in Egypt and abroad.[32] Again, the key factors here appeared to be the international dimension to the individual's activities and the political motivation underlying them.

In deciding these early cases, courts and tribunals in the UK also firmly established that Article 1F(c) is not limited to those deploying state powers, but can also extend to private individuals. As the purposes and principles of the UN to which Article 1F(c) refers are intended to govern the conduct of Member States in relation to one other, Article 1F(c) was traditionally interpreted as capable of applying only to an 'individual in a position of power in a member State and instrumental to his State's infringing these principles'.[33] Thus, during the drafting of the provision, the delegate for France explained '[t]he provision was not aimed at the man-on-the-street, but at persons occupying government

---

29 *KK* (n 147) [85].

30 Ibid. [94]. The DHKP, the Revolutionary People's Liberation Party–Front, (Turkish: Devrimci Halk Kurtuluş Partisi-Cephesi or DHKP/C) is a Marxist-Leninist party in Turkey.

31 Ibid. [95].

32 *C v Secretary of State for the Home Department* [2003] UKSIAC 7/2002.

33 UNHCR Handbook (n 65) para 163. However, see Goodwin-Gill and McAdam (n 68) 186–188, for examples of Article 1F(c)'s application to private individuals in its early years.

posts, such as heads of State, ministers and high officials'.[34] It has indeed been suggested that State officials are most likely to be capable of violating the purposes and principles of the United Nations by interfering with other States in violation of international law or depriving third persons of their human rights as protected under international law.[35] However, it cannot be disregarded that private groups or single private persons are today also subject to obligations arising under public international law.[36] Indeed, in the seminal *Pushpanathan* case the Supreme Court of Canada held that Article 1F(c) could, in some instances, extend to private actors. The Court noted that '[a]lthough it may be more difficult for a non-state actor to perpetrate human rights violations on a scale amounting to persecution without the state thereby implicitly adopting those acts, the possibility should not be excluded *a priori*'.[37] The UK tribunal has followed this approach, holding that private individuals are indeed capable of falling with the scope of Article 1F(c),[38] an approach which has been confirmed in later cases by the Court of Appeal and Supreme Court[39] and is reflected in the Home Office's APG.[40]

The Security Council and General Assembly have declared that 'acts methods and practices of terrorism' are contrary to the purposes and principles of the United Nations without limiting this determination to acts committed by State officials. This may be seen as implying that private individuals are also capable of acting against these purposes and principles.[41] Indeed, the Security Council has gone as far as to state its 'unequivocal condemnation of all acts,

34 ECOSOC Social Committee '166th Meeting' (n 318) 6–7. The representative for Chile found it difficult to see how an individual could commit such acts, since membership of the UN was confined to sovereign states. ECOSOC Social Committee '160th Meeting' (n 317) 15.

35 Zimmermann and Wennholz (n 68) 602.

36 Not least in terms of sanctions imposed by the Security Council under Chapter VII of the UN Charter. Zimmermann and Wennholz (n 68) 602.

37 *Pushpanathan* (n 335) [68].

38 *KK* (n 147) [20]: 'We are perfectly content to hold that a private individual may be guilty of an act contrary to the purposes and principles of the United Nations, and we see no difficulty in reading the words in this way. Indeed, in the light of other materials before us, we think we should have had some difficulty in confining article 1F(c) to individuals who control States'.

39 *Al-Sirri* [2009] (n 69) [39]; *DD* (*Afghanistan*) (n 69) [55], [63]–[69]; *Al-Sirri* [2012] (n 69).

40 Home Office Exclusion APG s 6.4, which provides: 'Article 1F(c) applies to anyone who commits an act which is contrary to the purposes and principles of the United Nations. That person does not have to be acting on behalf of a State or as part of an organisation. Individuals acting in a non-State capacity should be excluded under 1F(c) where their actions merit it'.

41 Zimmermann and Wennholz (n 68) 603.

methods and practice of terrorism, wherever and *by whomever committed*'.[42] It has, however, been suggested that if Article 1F(c) is applied to non-state actors, it should be restricted to 'persons in high office in government or a rebel movement that controls territory within the State or in a group perpetrating international terrorism that threatens international peace and security'.[43] It is submitted by the present author that, as the purposes and principles of the United Nations are inherently international in nature, the provision be limited to senior State officials or high ranking members of an organisation that are capable of implementing policies and large scale actions that threaten international peace and security. In particular, Article 1F(c) should not be applied to low ranking members or foot soldiers in a State-controlled or rebel organisation, particularly as exclusion of these individuals from refugee status could more appropriately be considered under Articles 1F(a) or (b) or, if committed in the host State, under the domestic criminal legal system of that country.[44]

Another issue that the tribunal and the SIAC had to grapple with in the early cases was the question of whether there are any geographical or temporal limitations to the scope of Article 1F(c). Unlike Article 1F(b), which provides the excludable act must have been committed *outside* the country of refuge *prior* to his admission to that country as a refugee', Article 1F(c) does not explicitly provide for any temporal or geographical limitations to the range of acts that may fall within the scope of the provision. Nevertheless, in a number of UK cases it was argued that Article 1F(c) similarly applies only to acts committed outside the country of refuge prior to the asylum applicant's admission to that country as a refugee. However, this argument was firmly rejected by the tribunal:

> Article 1F(c) does not contain the words "outside the country of refuge prior to his admission to that country as a refugee," which are found in

42 UNSC Res 1377, preamble para 4 (emphasis added).

43 Gilbert 'Current Issues' (n 188) 457.

44 However, Hathaway and Foster argue that transitions in the nature of global power, particularly the ability of some individuals not in a position of formal authority to threaten fundamental tenets of peaceful co-existence among states support a 'cautious evolution' towards seeing a broader range of persons as potentially subject to exclusion under Article 1F(c). Hathaway J, and Foster, M, *The Law of Refugee Status* (n 254) 589. Similarly, Sivakumaran notes that it is unclear why some commentators have argued that Article 1F(c) should be limited to high-level figures, as potentially all actors may have deleterious effects on the purposes and principles of the UN. As such, the organisational affiliation and institutional rank of the individual are but two factors to be included in determining the gravity of the act in question. Sivakumaran S, 'Exclusion from Refugee Status: The Purposes and Principles of the United Nations and Article 1F(c) of the Refugee Convention' (2014) 26(3) *International Journal of Refugee Law* 380.

> Article 1F(b). There is no reason at all to suppose that that difference is accidental. Acts which merit the condemnation of the whole international community must lead to exclusion from the benefits of the Refugee Convention whenever they occur.[45]

This view was later approved in a number of cases which appeared before the SIAC, and ultimately by the Court of Appeal and the House of Lords.[46] The Home Secretary accordingly relied on Article 1F(c) in a number of cases to revoke refugee status from those previously granted protection in the UK.[47]

This appears to be the correct interpretation of the provision. The ordinary meaning of the text of Article 1F(c) does not indicate any temporal or geographical limitations to the acts that may fall within its scope. Although Article 1F(b) includes such limitations, these are not included in the text of either Articles 1F(a) or (c), which should also be interpreted to apply to acts committed without such requirements. However, given the vague nature of Article 1F(c), and the relatively limited jurisprudence concerning its application, it has been argued by commentators that its application 'needs to take place with restraint and should be limited to residual cases in which Art. 1F(a) and (b) fail to apply'.[48] The lack of temporal or geographical limitations to the range of acts that may fall within the scope of Article 1F(c) do not mean that the provision should simply be used to cover any crime which would fall within the scope of Article 1F(b) but for the geographical and temporal limitations inherent in the provision, as not every serious non-political crime will meet the

45 *KK* (n 147) [86]–[88].

46 *Y* (n 287) [136–146]; *Abu Qatada* (n 334) [93–103]; *DD & Anor* (n 334) [109]–[122]; *MT (Algeria)* (n 147) [77]–[90]; *RB (Algeria) v Secretary of State for the Home Department* [2009] UKHL 10 [127–129], [206].

47 As considered further in Chapters 6 and 7.

48 Zimmermann and Wennholz (n 68) 610. It has been suggested that this approach makes for analytical clarity, and avoids the possibility of an overly liberal interpretation of 'acts contrary to the purposes and principles of the United Nations'. Nyinah (n 191) 310. Indeed, in its *Handbook*, the UNHCR notes that the purpose of Article 1F(c) is to 'cover in a general way such acts against the purposes and principles of the United Nations that might not fully be covered by the two preceding exclusion clauses'. UNHCR Handbook (n 65) 162. Kapferer suggests that Article 1F(b) should be applied to deal with offences involving the indiscriminate use of violence, commonly known as 'terrorist' offences. Kapferer S, 'Exclusion Clauses in Europe' (n 72) 205. Indeed, Hathaway and Foster argue that the failure to assess exclusion in relation to the most directly applicable component of Article 1F can have serious ramifications, and the amorphous nature of Article 1F(c) as too frequently applied facilitates evasion of the 'subtlety and precision' mandated by Articles 1F(a) and (b). Hathaway J, and Foster, M, *The Law of Refugee Status* (n 254) 593.

gravity required to constitute 'acts contrary to the purposes and principles of the United Nations' for the purpose of Article 1F(c). Such crimes could be better addressed by Article 33(2) of the 1951 Convention, which in any case appears a more specific provision for this set of circumstances, or the domestic criminal legal system of the host State.[49]

In these early cases, the immigration tribunal and the SIAC therefore began to define the scope and reach of Article 1F(c). These bodies adopted a dynamic approach to the interpretation of the provision, and relied on UN resolutions which declare that 'acts methods and practices of terrorism are contrary to the purposes and principles of the United Nations' in determining that acts of terrorism were capable of falling within the scope of the provision. Whilst it may initially have been doubted whether these resolutions truly represented the consensus of the international community sufficient to establish subsequent practice or agreement regarding the interpretation of the 1951 Convention,[50] it seems that the number and strength of resolutions adopted establish uncontrovertibly that terrorism may constitute acts contrary to the purposes and principles of the United Nations for the purpose of Article 1F(c).[51]

---

49 Gilbert G, 'Exclusion under Article 1F since 2001' (n 6); Hathaway J, and Foster, M, *The Law of Refugee Status* (n 254) 593–594; Zimmermann and Wennholz (n 68) 607. Indeed, Zimmerman suggests that that Article 1F(c) be considered barred in application when acts can already be subsumed under criminal law provisions of the host State. For a detailed overview of the scope of Article 33(2) see Lauterpacht E, and Bethlehem D, 'The scope and content of the principle of *non-refoulement*: Opinion' in Feller E, Türk V, and Nicholson F, (eds) *Refugee Protection in International Law: UNHCR's Global Consultations on International Protection* (CUP, 2003) 89–177. See also Zimmermann A, and Wennholz P, 'Article 33, para 2' in Andreas Zimmerman (ed) *The 1951 Convention Relating to the Status of Refugees and its 1967 Protocol: A Commentary* (OUP 2011) 1397–1423.

50 During the drafting on of UNGA Dec 1996, Liechtenstein, Switzerland, New Zealand, Mexico, Costa Rica and the Netherlands all made statements to the effect that they did not consider the declaration extended the grounds of exclusion from refugee status under the 1951 Convention. UNGA 'Summary Record of the 11th Meeting' (4 October 1996) UN Doc A/C.6/51/SR.11, 7–8. Gilbert also noted that 'it is questionable whether the General Assembly through an annexed declaration can re-state the purposes and principles of the United Nations' Gilbert, 'Current Issues' (n 188) 441. Hathaway and Harvey also note that it is problematic to view legally non-binding GA declarations as capable of redefining the scope of Article 1F(c). Hathaway and Harvey (n 61) 272. However, see Aust (n 99) 240, where he considers the 1994 UNGA Declaration of Measures to Eliminate International Terrorism to constitute subsequent agreement on the interpretation of the term 'contrary to the purposes and principles of the United Nations'.

51 Gilbert, 'Current Issues' (n 188) 456: 'What is clear after 11 September 2001 and the subsequent Security Council resolutions, particularly Resolution 1377, is that acts of

The tribunal and the SIAC in these cases, however, stressed that the purpose of such an examination was not to rely on interpretations of terrorism which exist in international instruments, nor domestic statutes defining the term, but rather to determine what the UN meant by terrorism in these resolutions. However, both these bodies declined making any firm findings as to what the UN meant by terrorism in its resolutions, or formulating a working definition of terrorism for the purpose of Article 1F(c). Rather, the provision was held to apply to 'acts which are the subject of intense disapproval by the governing body of the entire international community'. The approach of the tribunal and the SIAC in these early cases therefore seems to have been to rely on a decision-maker to recognise acts of terrorism which attract the condemnation of the international community, rather than refer definitions of terrorism which exist in international or domestic instruments. As considered below, this is in direct contrast with the approaches later taken to the interpretation of the provision.

2 The UK's Domestic Definition of Terrorism, the EU Qualification Directive and the Court of Appeal

Following the 7/7 terrorist attacks on London in 2005, the UK included two provisions concerning Article 1F in the 2006 Immigration, Asylum and Nationality Act. One of these, section 54, provides that:

---

international terrorism constituting a threat to international peace and security are contrary to the purposes and principles of the United Nations'. Ian A. MacDonald and Ronan Toal (eds) *Immigration Law and Practice in the United Kingdom*, Vol I (8th edn, Lexis Nexis 2010) 908: 'Acts of terrorism are contrary to the purposes and principles of the UN and accordingly come within the ambit of Article 1F(c) wherever and whenever committed, considering not only Articles 1 and 2 of the 1945 Charter of the United Nations (which set out the purposes and principles of the UN), but also, in the light of Article 31 of the Vienna Convention on the Law of Treaties (which sets out general rules of interpretation of treaties), subsequent Security Council and General Assembly resolutions that unequivocally condemn terrorism and terrorist acts'. Gilbert further notes that while the question of whether the UN General Assembly and Security Council can extend the limitation of Article 1F(c) through resolutions in this way, there is little to be gained from exploring this issue since any expansion by either organ can be explained in terms of providing a gloss to the purposes and principles as set out in the Charter. Courtesy of Article 25 of the UN Charter, all member states are bound to apply Chapter VII resolutions (e.g. UNSC Res 1377). Gilbert G, 'Exclusion under Article 1F since 2001' (n 6).

> [i]n the construction and application of Article 1(F)(c) of the Refugee Convention the reference to acts contrary to the purposes and principles of the United Nations shall be taken as including… (a) acts of committing, preparing or instigating terrorism…and (b) acts of encouraging or inducing others to commit, prepare or instigate terrorism.[52]

That acts of terrorism fall within the scope of Article 1F(c) was therefore formally set out in statute in the UK. In a similar manner to the tribunal, the government relied heavily on the UN Security Council resolutions which declared that 'acts methods and practices of terrorism are contrary to the purposes and principles of the UN' to justify including this provision in the Act.[53] However, in contrast to the approach which had been previously adopted by the tribunal and the SIAC, which focused on the meaning of terrorism in the UN resolutions under examination, this provision provides that'terrorism' for the purpose of the construction of Article 1F(c) has the meaning given by the UK's domestic definition of terrorism.[54]

The UK's domestic definition of terrorism, contained in the Terrorism Act 2000, is extremely wide. Section 1 of the 2000 Act encompasses certain acts and threats done in order to advance a political, religious or ideological cause, if done in order to influence the government or an international governmental organisation, or to intimidate the public or section of the public.[55] The acts or threats that may fall within this definition include not only serious violence against a person and endangering another person's life, but also acts that involve serious damage to property, whether or not this involves a risk of harm to anyone.[56] Therefore, political protest that involves demolishing a State official's car, or throwing a brick through the window of a State building, even where it was clear that neither car nor building were occupied, may fall within

52 Whether or not these acts amount to amount to an actual or inchoate offence. The other, section 55, will be considered in Chapters 6 and 7.

53 During the drafting debates surrounding the UK's Immigration Asylum and Nationality Act 2006, the Immigration Minister noted that the provision relating to Article 1F(c) was entirely consistent with UNSC Res 1373 and 1377. Hansard, HC Deb 22 October 2005, vol 438, col 284; HC Deb 16 November 2005, vol 439, col 1055 (Mr McNulty).

54 Immigration Asylum and Nationality Act 2006, s 54(2) provides that'terrorism' for the purpose of the construction of Article 1F(c) has the meaning given by s 1 of the UK Terrorism Act 2000.

55 Although if what is done involves the use or threatened use of firearms or explosives, and in order to advance a political, religious or ideological case, it is within the definition without anything further. Terrorism Act 2000, s 1(3).

56 Ibid., s 1(2).

this definition of terrorism.[57] Furthermore, the act or threat need not to be designed to influence a government or an international organisation or to intimidate the public when it involves the use of firearms or explosives. This means that any threat or use of firearms or explosives motivated by a political or ideological cause is an act of terrorism, as long as it involves serious danger to persons or serious damage to property and regardless of its purpose. For these purposes 'the government' and 'the public' are not limited to the UK, but extend to action against any government, anywhere in the world.[58] The broad scope of this legislation was made clear in two criminal cases concerning the definition of terrorism contained in the 2000 Act which recently came before the Court of Appeal and Supreme Court.

In the first of these cases, it was argued by the appellant that actions targeted at removing an unelected and unrepresentative government, in this case the Gaddafi regime in Libya, did not fall within the terms of the 2000 Act, as an unrepresentative government could not be considered a 'government' within the meaning of the Act.[59] The Court of Appeal, however, rejected this argument, noting that, given the broad terms of the 2000 Act, all governments were within its scope; there was no exemption from criminal liability for terrorist activities which were motivated or said to be morally justified by the alleged nobility of the terrorist cause.[60] As noted by the Court:

> What is striking about the language of s1, read as a whole, is its breadth. It does not specify that the ambit of its protection is limited to countries abroad with governments of any particular type or possessed of what we, with our fortunate traditions, would regard as the desirable characteristics of representative government. … Terrorism is terrorism, whatever the motives of the perpetrators.[61]

The Supreme Court also recently rejected the argument that the UK's definition of terrorism did not extend to military action by non-State groups in a

57 Steve Symonds, 'The special immigration status' (2008) 22(4) *Journal of Immigration Asylum and Nationality Law* 341–342.

58 Terrorism Act 2000, s 1(4).

59 This argument drew on provisions of international human rights instruments which recognised the right of participation in government through freely chosen representatives. Article 21 of the Universal Declaration of Human Rights and Article 52 of the International Covenant on Civil and Political Rights recognised the right of participation in government through freely chosen representatives.

60 *R v F* [2007] EWCA Crim 243.

61 Ibid. [27].

non-international armed conflict, despite the fact that such action was directed at the State's armed forces rather than civilians.[62] The Court noted that although the UK's domestic definition of terrorism is 'concerningly wide' there is no basis on which the natural, very wide, meaning of section 1 of the 2000 Act could be read restrictively.[63] The Court noted that:

> the current law allows members of any nationalist or separatist group to be turned into terrorists by virtue of their participation in a lawful armed conflict, however great the provocation and however odious the regime which they have attacked.[64]

The UK's domestic definition of terrorism is therefore extremely broad in scope. It appears to cover all politically motivated action against a government or international organisation, permitting no exceptions for those engaged in military action during armed conflicts, nor the activities of those seeking to overthrow repressive regimes, whether during an armed conflict or during peacetime.

In the asylum context, however, the interpretation given to terrorism for the purpose of Article 1F(c) by courts and tribunals in the UK has not been as comprehensive in its scope. Notably, military activity directed against a State's armed forces has been excluded from the definition of terrorism for the purpose of Article 1F(c), and courts have developed the requirement that terrorist activity must have an international dimension to constitute 'acts contrary to the purposes and principles of the United Nations' for the purpose of the provision. In attempting to define 'terrorism' for the purpose of Article 1F(c), the Court of Appeal has relied on the UK's domestic definition contained in the 2000 Act and a number of other international sources. The intersection of a number of different areas of law here has resulted in a rather confusing stream of decisions from the Court of Appeal. Much of this disparity has stemmed from the coming into force of the EU Qualification Directive.

In 2006, the same year as the UK's Immigration, Asylum and Nationality Act, the EU Qualification Directive came into force, which is incorporated into UK law by the 2006 Qualification Regulations. As noted above, the Qualification Directive defines the phrase 'acts contrary to the purposes and principles of the United Nations' by reference to the preamble and Articles 1 and 2 of the UN

62 *Gul, R. v* [2013] UKSC 64.

63 Ibid. [38].

64 Ibid. [61]. A point made by the Independent Reviewer of Terrorism Legislation in the United Kingdom, Mr David Anderson QC.

Charter and UN resolutions which declare that 'acts, methods and practices of terrorism are contrary to the purposes and principles of the United Nations'. The Court of Appeal in a number of cases has held that the Qualification Directive conditions and qualifies the application of the Terrorism Act 2000 to Article 1F proceedings, as, even at its most generous, the formulation of 'acts contrary to the purposes and principles of the UN' contained in the Directive is not as wide as section 1 of the Terrorism Act 2000.[65] As such, 'the meaning of terrorism contained in the 2000 Act has where necessary to be read down in an art. 1F case so as to keep its meaning within the scope of art 12(2)(c) of the Directive'.[66] Adopting this approach, the Court of Appeal in *Al-Sirri* noted that, 'terrorism here means the use for political ends of fear induced by violence'.[67] The Court did not consider this materially different from the second limb of Security Council Resolution 1566 of 2004:

> acts...committed with the purpose to provoke a state of terror in the general public or in a group of persons or particular persons, intimidate a population or compel a government or an international organisation to do or abstain from doing any act[68]

The Court of Appeal in this case therefore referred to a definition of terrorism contained in a UN resolution to inform the interpretation of terrorism for the purpose of Article 1F(c).

The Court of Appeal in *KJ* (*Sri Lanka*), however, didn't appear to rely on any sources, domestic or international, when it noted that military action directed against government forces did not constitute acts contrary to the purposes and principles of the United Nations.[69] The Court of Appeal in this case considered it common ground that the deliberate killing or injuring of civilians in pursuit

---

65 *Al-Sirri* [2009] (n 69) [28]–[29].

66 Ibid. [28]–[29]. Approved in *MH* (*Syria*) (n 69) [29]. Approved by the Supreme Court in *Al- Sirri* [2012]] (n 69) [36].

67 *Al-Sirri* [2009] (n 69) [30]. Although noting that there was not a present need for an elaborate definition.

68 UNSC Res 1566, para 3, cited in *Al-Sirri* [2009] (n 69) [31].

69 This case involved a member of the LTTE who had been engaged in military action against the Sri Lankan government. The facts found by the Tribunal in this case showed no more than that the asylum applicant had participated in military actions against the Sri Lankan government, and as such did not constitute serious reasons for considering that he had been guilty of acts contrary to the purposes and principles of the United Nations. *KJ* (*Sri Lanka*) (n 69) [34]–[40].

of political objects were acts of terrorism within the meaning of Article 1F(c).[70] However, participation in military action directed against government forces, which did not involve the murder or attempted murder of civilians, did not fall within the scope of the provision. Although it was noted by the SIAC in one case that this aspect of the *KJ* (*Sri Lanka*) judgment was made *per incuriam*,[71] the distinction between military action directed against government forces and attacks on civilians has been maintained in later Court of Appeal decisions.[72] Thus it has been held that *KJ* (*Sri Lanka*) is authority for the view that military action directed against the armed forces of a government, even if conducted by a proscribed terrorist organisation, does not as such constitute terrorism or acts contrary to the purposes and principles of the United Nations.[73] The Court of Appeal in *DD* (*Afghanistan*) noted that 'it is difficult to hold that every act of violence in a civil war, the aim of which will usually be to overthrow a legitimate government, is an act of terrorism within the 2000 Act'.[74] The Court in this case therefore appears to have seen its task as interpreting the UK's domestic definition of terrorism contained in the Terrorism Act of 2000. In contrast with the later Court of Appeal decision in the criminal context, noted above, the court in this case did not consider the UK's domestic definition of terrorism to be as wide-reaching in its scope as to encompass all military action against government forces.

However, the Court of Appeal has also stressed that the *KJ* (*Sri Lanka*) exception does not extend to violence of any kind against governments, such as violence against government officials. In *SS* (*Libya*), a military attack which left 165 Libyan officials dead and 159 injured was considered to be action very difficult to categorise as anything other than terrorism, and as such fell within the scope of Article 1F(c).[75] The Court of Appeal here approved the definition of terrorism in the European Council's Common Position of 2001 as authoritative guidance for the meaning of terrorism within the context of Article 12(2)(c) of the Qualification Directive.[76] The essence of this definition was:

---

70 Ibid. [34]–[36].

71 As noted by the Special Immigration Appeals Commission in SS *v Secretary of State for the Home Department* [2010] UKSIAC 56/2009.

72 In *SS* (*Libya*) (n 69), the Court of Appeal said the Special Immigration Appeals Commission was not right to have held this was made per incuriam.

73 *DD* (*Afghanistan*) (n 69) [55]–[56]. Although military action directed against UN-mandated forces did constitute acts contrary to the purposes and principles of the UN.

74 Ibid. (n 69) [55].

75 *SS* (*Libya*) (n 69) [44].

76 Council Common Position 2001/931/CFSP on the application of specific measures to combat terrorism. [2001] OJ L304/12, 93.

> the use or threat of action designed to influence a government or to intimidate a population by serious acts of violence and some acts of economic disruption.[77]

These Court of Appeal decisions therefore reveal a confusing strain of reasoning. While the Court in *Al-Sirri* appeared to consider the EU Directive referred it to a definition of terrorism contained in Security Council Resolution 1566, the Court in SS (*Libya*) instead referred to the definition contained in an EU instrument as guidance on the interpretation of terrorism within the meaning of the Directive. The Court of Appeal in *KJ* (*Sri Lanka*) and *DD* (*Afghanistan*), in contrast, appeared to be seeking to interpret the UK's domestic definition contained in the Terrorism Act 2000, although applying a more restrictive reading of this definition than has been apparent in the criminal context by excluding military activity directed against a State's armed forces.

Another issue to which some attention has been given throughout this jurisprudence is whether an international dimension is needed in order to bring a terrorist act within the scope of Article 1F(c). In *Al-Sirri*, the Court of Appeal stated it saw force in the argument that terrorism had to have an international dimension in order to fall within the scope of the EU Qualification Directive. However, in the instant case this international dimension was supplied as it 'involved the use of a safe haven in one state to destabilise the government of another by the use of violence'.[78] In a later decision, however, the Court saw nothing for a requirement of an 'international dimension' to the terrorist act, as the court in *Al-Sirri* had not had to express a definitive view for the purpose of that case.[79] The *Al-Sirri* requirement of an international dimension was, however, followed by the tribunal in a case involving a former police officer in Zimbabwe,[80] and was indeed affirmed by the Supreme Court when *Al-Sirri* was heard on appeal.

The Court of Appeal in these cases drew on a number of different instruments to inform the meaning of terrorism for the purpose of Article 1F(c). While the underlying bases of these different definitions of terrorism appear similar – acts intended to provoke a state of terror in the population or coerce

---

77 SS (*Libya*) (n 69) [25]; also relied on in SS *v Secretary of State for the Home Department* (n 385) [15]. Indeed, the SIAC in this case considered the common ground between the European Council's Common Position and the UK's definition of terrorism in the Terrorism Act 2000 to be far greater than the differences.

78 *Al-Sirri* [2009] (n 69) [32], [51].

79 SS (*Libya*) (n 69) [27].

80 MT (*Article 1F (a) – aiding and abetting*) (n 185) [99].

a state or international organisation to take (or abstain from) some sort of action – the range of acts that may fall within these definitions differ to a large extent. Thus, as noted above, the UK's domestic definition of terrorism encompasses not only serious violence against a person and endangering another person's life, but also acts that involve serious damage to property, whether or not this involves a risk of harm to anyone. In contrast, UN Security Council Resolution 1566 of 2004 suggests that terrorism should be limited to acts that are (i) prohibited under international counter-terrorism conventions and (ii) involve taking hostages, or are committed with the intent of causing death or serious bodily injury.[81] The definition of terrorism contained in the European Council's Common Position of 2001 includes kidnapping or hostage taking, attacks upon a person's life or physical integrity or causing extensive destruction to a public place or private property which is likely to endanger human life or result in major economic loss.[82] The range of acts that may fall within the scope of these definitions therefore vary, with the UK's definition of terrorism certainly representing the broadest of these three. The meaning of terrorism in the context of Article 1F(c) appears to have been confused even further in the Supreme Court's decision in *Al-Sirri*, in which it referred to the definition of terrorism contained in the UN's draft Comprehensive Convention on International Terrorism, as will be considered below.

3 The Supreme Court's Judgment in *Al-Sirri*

The interpretation of Article 1F(c) was recently considered by the UK Supreme Court in the conjoined cases *Al-Sirri* and DD (*Afghanistan*).[83] In its decision in the *Al-Sirri* case, the Court had to determine whether all activities defined as terrorism by UK domestic law were, for that reason alone, acts contrary to the purposes and principles of the United Nations, or whether such activities must also constitute a threat to international peace and security or friendly relations between nations.

81 UNSC Res 1566, para 3. There are at present a host of international counter-terrorism conventions prohibiting acts such as hostage taking, hijacking, terrorist bombings, and nuclear terrorism.

82 Council Common Position 2001/931/CFSP, replicated in Council Framework Decision 2002/475/JHA on combating terrorism. [2002] OJ L164/3, art 1.

83 *Al-Sirri v Secretary of State for the Home Department; DD (Afghanistan) v Secretary of State for the Home Department* [2012] UKSC 54.

Before the Supreme Court, it was argued by the Secretary of State that, because the United Nations had condemned terrorism but not defined the term, Member States were free to adopt their own definitions, and therefore, acts falling within the UK's domestic definition of terrorism would be acts contrary to the purposes and principles of the United Nations whether or not they had an international dimension or repercussions for international peace and security.[84] In support of this argument, a number of UN General Assembly and Security Council resolutions on the subject of terrorism were cited, sometimes including and sometimes lacking the adjective 'international'. The Supreme Court, however, rejected this argument, noting:

> it is clear that the phrase "acts contrary to the purposes and principles of the United Nations" must have an autonomous meaning. It cannot be the case that individual Member States are free to adopt their own definitions.[85]

Rather, the Supreme Court agreed with the appellants who, supported by the UNHCR, argued that Article 1F must be 'interpreted narrowly and applied restrictively' because of the serious consequences of excluding a person who has a well-founded fear of persecution from the protection of the 1951 Convention.[86]

In relation to the nature of acts that could be considered to fall within the scope of Article 1F(c), the Supreme Court agreed with the UNHCR that:

> There should be a high threshold "defined in terms of the gravity of the act in question, the manner in which the act is organised, its international impact and long-term objectives, and the implications for international peace and security."[87]

The Court drew attention to the fact that the principal purposes of the United Nations are to maintain *international* peace and security, and also noted that

84 *Al-Sirri* [2012] (n 148) [26].

85 Ibid. [36].

86 Ibid. [12]. At para 16 the Supreme Court noted that 'the article should be interpreted restrictively and applied with caution'. It was 'common ground' in *JS* (*Sri Lanka*), and must apply *a fortiori* in the context of article 1F(c).

87 UNHCR Background Note (n 164) 17–18; UNHCR, Guidelines, p. 5, cited in *Al-Sirri* (n 148) [16]. Furthermore, the Court held that 'there should be serious reasons for considering that the person concerned bore individual responsibility for acts of that character'.

the Court of Justice of the European Union (CJEU), in its decision in the *B & D* case, consistently referred to 'international' terrorism.[88] For these reasons, the appropriately cautious and restrictive approach was that advocated by the UNHCR in its Guidelines on International Protection:

> Article 1F(c) is only triggered in extreme circumstances by activity which attacks the very basis of the international community's coexistence. Such activity must have an international dimension. Crimes capable of affecting international peace, security and peaceful relations between states, as well as serious and sustained violations of human rights would fall under this category.[89]

The Supreme Court therefore held that acts of terrorism could only be considered contrary to the purposes and principles of the United Nations for the purpose of Article 1F(c) if they impacted in some significant way on international peace and security.

At para 39 of his judgment, Lord Phillips set down what he considered to be the 'essence of terrorism' for the purpose of Article 1F(c):

> the commission, organisation, incitement or threat of serious acts of violence against persons or property for the purpose of intimidating a population or compelling a government or international organisation to act or not to act in a particular way.[90]

Lord Phillips drew here on the definition of terrorism in Article 2 of the UN's draft Comprehensive Convention on International Terrorism, and also referred to the Court of Appeal's statement in *Al-Sirri*, noted above: 'the use for political ends of fear induced by violence'. In his Lordship's opinion, it seemed very likely that 'inducing terror in a civilian population or putting such extreme pressures upon a government will also have the international repercussions referred to by the UNHCR'.[91]

As to the question of whether actions taken in one state to destabilise the government of another would supply this 'international character', the Court concluded that this would depend on the facts of the individual case. However, the Court considered that it 'clearly would be enough if the government

88 *Al-Sirri* [2012] (n 148) [37].
89 UNHCR Guidelines (n 65) para 17. Cited in *Al-Sirri* [2012] (n 148) [38].
90 *Al-Sirri* [2012] (n 148) [39].
91 Ibid. [39].

(or those in control) of one state offered a safe haven to terrorists to plot and carry out their terrorist operations against another state', as this would have clear implications for inter-state relations. Although the Court did note that the same would not be true of simply being in one place and doing things which have a result in another. The test is 'whether the resulting actions have the requisite serious effect upon international peace, security and peaceful relations between states'.[92]

The Court of Appeal in its decisions restricted the scope of the UK's domestic interpretation of terrorism for the purpose of Article 1F(c) either by reading down the scope of the UK's definition or adopting more restrictive approaches allegedly based on the UK definition itself. However, the Supreme Court in *Al-Sirri* rejected the UK's domestic definition of terrorism for the purpose of Article 1F(c), and referred exclusively to international legal instruments and guidance to inform the interpretation of the provision. In particular, the Supreme Court drew attention to the definition of terrorism contained in the UN's draft Comprehensive Convention on International Terrorism. Negotiations on this counter-terrorism treaty have fallen into deadlock, primarily because of the problem of finding an all-encompassing definition of terrorism and the related issue of whether such a definition should apply to national liberation movements.[93] Nevertheless, the negotiations on this convention resulted in a draft definition of terrorism in 2005, which covers acts such as death or serious bodily injury to any person, serious damage to public or private property and damage to property resulting or likely to result in major economic loss when the purpose is to intimidate a population or to compel a government or international organisation to do or abstain from doing any act.[94] It is this definition of terrorism that Lord Phillips referred to in his judgment, albeit for the purpose of Article 1F(c) this appears to be qualified by the requirement that the activity attacks 'the very basis of the international community's coexistence' and impacts in some significant way on international peace and security.

The Supreme Court's determination that a terrorist act must have an international dimension in order to fall within the terms of Article 1F(c) appears to accord with the ordinary meaning of the terms of the UN Charter. As noted by Lord Phillips: 'the principal purposes of the United Nations are to maintain international peace and security, to remove threats to *that* peace, and to

92 Ibid. [40].

93 See for example preamble role 9, United Nations General Assembly, draft Comprehensive Convention on International Terrorism, UN Doc A/59/894.

94 Ibid. art 2(1).

develop friendly relations among nations'.[95] The CJEU in the *B & D* case also appear to have interpreted the UN resolutions on terrorism to refer to 'international terrorists'.[96] Similarly, the court's endorsement of the UNHCR's position that Article 1F(c) is triggered only in extreme circumstances, by activity which attacks the very basis of the international community's coexistence, appears to be in line with international guidance on the interpretation of the provision. For example, in *Pushpanathan* the Supreme Court of Canada made clear that a very high threshold must be reached before an act could be considered to fall within Article 1F(c), and that not every act condemned by the UN could, for that reason alone, be considered contrary to its purposes and principles.[97] Thus, in *Pushpanathan* itself, the Canadian Court held that the crime of drug trafficking did not come within the scope of Article 1F(c), despite co-ordinated efforts of the UN to suppress the activity, through treaties, declarations and institutions.[98] Indeed, given the breadth of subjects covered by multilateral UN instruments, the UNHCR similarly advises that:

> Equating any action contrary to such instruments as falling within Article 1F(c) would…be inconsistent with the object and purpose of the provision. Rather, it appears that Article 1F(c) only applies to acts that offend the principles and purposes of the United Nations in a fundamental manner.[99]

95 *Al- Sirri* [2012] (n 148) [37] (emphasis in original).

96 *Bundesrepublik Deutschland v B and D* (n 283) [83]: 'Those include Resolutions 1373 (2001) and 1377 (2001) of the UN Security Council, from which it is clear that the Security Council takes as its starting point the principle that international terrorist acts are, generally speaking and irrespective of any State participation, contrary to the purposes and principles of the United Nations'.

97 For example, in this case drug-trafficking was not considered an act contrary to the purposes and principles of the UN, despite co-ordinated efforts of the UN to suppress the activity, through treaties, declarations and institutions.

98 UNHCR similarly advises that attempts to apply Article 1F(c) to people trafficking or smuggling is misguided. UNHCR Background Note (n 65) 18, para 48.

99 Ibid. 17, para 47. It has also been suggested that '[i]n interpreting the ambit of these decisions, some care is needed, first, because of the very divergent definitions of terrorism; and, secondly, because the exclusive focus of the UN Security Council Resolutions after 11 September 2001 has been on Al Qaeda and a long list of named organisations and individuals allegedly associated with it, rather than on Turkish Kurds fighting for self-determination or Muslims in Gujerat, India, fighting against extremist communalism, but who have nevertheless been labelled as terrorists by the EU or under Indian anti-terrorist legislation'. MacDonald and Toal (n 365) 908. Gilbert similarly notes that not every General Assembly or even Security Council resolution reflects a purpose or principle of the UN

The Supreme Court's endorsement of the UNHCR's guidance in this respect would therefore appear to accord with the ordinary meaning of the provision and is in line with the restrictive approach that is advised be adopted in its interpretation.[100] Indeed, simply labelling certain acts 'terrorist' can hardly be considered to elevate those acts to be of interest to the United Nations or those concerned with its purposes and principles. Rather, it should be shown that the acts in question are of sufficient gravity to be of concern to the international community and impact in some fundamental way on international peace and security.[101]

Importantly, the Supreme Court appears to have approved the distinction made in earlier Court of Appeal decisions between military action directed against government forces and acts of violence directed at civilians, the former being excluded from the definition of terrorism for the purpose of Article 1F(c). As a primary problem that states encounter when attempting to agree upon a

---

such that acts automatically fall within the scope of Article 1F(c). Gilbert G, 'Exclusion under Article 1F since 2001' (n 6).

100 Indeed, in light of the vague nature of the phrase 'acts contrary to the purposes and principles of the United Nations', a number of commentators have suggested that article 1F(c) may be open to abuse by governments seeking to exclude refugees illegitimately. From its inception, some states considered it too vague and imprecise to be included in the terms of the 1951 Convention. Grahl-Madsen, in his commentary on the 1951 Convention, noted that during the drafting of Article 1F 'those who pressed for the inclusion of the clause had only vague ideas as to the meaning of the phrase'. Atle Grahl-Madsen, *The Status of Refugees,* (n 256) 283. The principle that Article 1F be interpreted restrictively would therefore seem to apply particularly in the context of Article 1F(c). UNHCR Background Note (n 164) 17, para 46. The UNHCR notes the 1951 Convention's *travaux* also provide limited guidance as to the types of acts that would deprive a person from the benefits of refugee status, although there is some indication the provision was meant to cover violations of human rights which, although falling short of crimes against humanity, were nevertheless of an exceptional nature. See also Gilbert, 'Current Issues' (n 188) 455–456, in which he suggests '[t]here is a danger that the phrase is so imprecise as to allow States to exclude applicants without adequate justification'. Goodwin-Gill and McAdam also note that 'Article 1F(c) is potentially very wide'. Goodwin-Gill and McAdam, (n 68) 190. Hathaway and Foster note that 'an exclusion clause once thought to be applicable only in the limited circumstances of grave abuse of government authority has today become something of a ravenous omnivore'. Hathaway J, and Foster, M, *The Law of Refugee Status* (n 254) 594.

101 Hathaway and Foster note that this approach holds promise as a means of giving substantive content to Article 1F(c) in a manner which both constrains overly aggressive interpretations of the provision and can ground future interpretation and application of the clause. Hathaway J, and Foster, M, *The Law of Refugee Status* (n 254) 595–596.

definition of terrorism concerns the question of whether an exception should be made for the activities of national liberation movements, the exclusion of this form of military activity from the interpretation of terrorism for the purpose of Article 1F(c) might go some way in dispelling concerns regarding the lack of international consensus on this issue. However, it must be noted that whilst the Supreme Court considered that activity directed against armed government forces did not fall within the definition of terrorism for the purpose of Article 1F(c), action against UN-mandated combatant forces *did* constitute acts contrary to the purposes and principles of the UN for the purpose of the provision, albeit not within the 'terrorism' rubric.[102]

In this case, the Supreme Court drew on the definition of terrorism contained in the UN's draft Comprehensive Convention on International Terrorism. This is in contrast to the approach adopted in the Court of Appeal decisions, in which reference was made to the definitions contained in UN Security Council Resolution 1566, the European Council's Common Position on Terrorism and the UK's domestic definition of terrorism contained in the Terrorism Act 2000. That different sources have been relied on in these decisions is reflective not only of the multiple definitions of terrorism that exist in international and domestic legal instruments, but also the intersection here of three different legal systems: that of the United Nations, the European Union and the UK's domestic legal regime. Courts in the UK have therefore taken different approaches to determining the appropriate legal instruments that should be referred to in the interpretation of terrorism for the purpose of Article 1F(c).

It is not entirely clear which definition of terrorism (if any) should be relied on when interpreting the meaning of the terrorism for the purpose of Article 1F(c), although it appears that recourse to definitions of terrorism in international instruments adopted under the auspices of the UN might be preferable to those adopted in a regional or domestic context. As famously noted by Lord Steyn in *ex parte Adan*: 'In principle there can only be one true interpretation of a treaty'.[103] Employing the UK's domestic definition of terrorism in the interpretation of Article 1F(c) would likely fragment the interpretation of the provision across states parties to the 1951 Convention. Similarly, reliance on regional standards such as the EU's Common Position, which is applicable only to EU Member States, has the potential to splinter of the meaning of Article 1F(c) across different regions of the world.

Indeed, in relation to the regional European system, the Qualification Directive itself states that the 1951 Convention constitutes the 'cornerstone of

102 As considered in Section 4.

103 *Ex parte Adan* (n 145) [515]–[517] (Lord Steyn).

the international legal regime for the protection of refugees' and that the provisions of the Directive were adopted to guide Member States 'in the application of the [1951] Convention'.[104] In the *B & D* case, the CJEU concluded these provisions meant the Directive must 'be interpreted...in a manner consistent with the 1951 Geneva Convention'.[105] It might therefore be better to approach the definition of terrorism for the purpose of Article 12(2)(c) of the Qualification Directive in a manner which accords to the interpretation of Article 1F(c) of the 1951 Convention.[106] Under this approach, reference to definitions of terrorism which are universal in their scope, rather than those that appear in EU regional instruments, may be more appropriate. Indeed, the preamble to the Directive itself does not refer to acts contrary to the purposes and principles of the United Nations by reference to regional or domestic interpretations of terrorism, but rather by reference to the UN Charter and UN resolutions relating to measures combating terrorism.

Being international in scope, the Supreme Court's reference to the draft UN Comprehensive Convention might be considered an appropriate basis for determining the meaning of terrorism for the purpose of Article 1F(c). However, as noted above, negotiations on this convention have fallen into deadlock because the international community has as yet been unable to agree on a definition of terrorism for the purpose of the instrument. Attempts have also been made to include terrorism as one of the core international crimes within the jurisdiction of the International Criminal Court (ICC). Reference to the

---

104 Recitals 3, 16 and 17.

105 *Bundesrepublik Deutschland v B and D*, (n 283), [78].

106 Hugo Storey argues that the Directive leaves the Refugee Convention intact as the governing international treaty on asylum law and the Directive furnishes interpretive guidance on the application of key elements of the refugee definition contained in the 1951 Refugee Convention. Hugo Storey, 'EU Qualification Directive: a brave new world?' (2008) 20 International Journal of Refugee Law 7. Symes and Lambert suggest that where the 1951 Convention and its case law appear more generous than the QD, the Convention should be regarded as authority. Symes bases his argument on preamble 3 to the Directive, which acknowledges the 1951 Convention provides the cornerstone of refugee protection, whilst Lambert bases her argument on Article 307 EC which provides for the primacy of agreements entered into before conflicting European ones. Helene Lambert, 'The EU Asylum Qualification Directive, its Impact on the Jurisprudence of the United Kingdom and International Law (2006) 55 International and Comparative Law Quarterly 161. Mark Symes, 'The Refugee Qualification Directive' (2006) Electronic Immigration Network. Boccardi also notes the potential of Article 63 EC for challenging EU action on the grounds it is incompatible with the 1951 Convention. Boccardi I, *Europe and Refugees: Towards an EU Asylum Policy* (n 7) 139.

crime of terrorism as defined in an international criminal instrument might be considered an proper basis for the meaning of the term for the purpose of Article 1F(c), particularly given Article 1F's close relationship with international criminal law.[107] Furthermore, reference to a crime *of* terrorism, rather than an instrument in which terrorism is defined only to criminalise ancillary conduct,[108] or where no criminal offences are created at all,[109] might be considered more fitting when seeking to determine whether an individual might be 'guilty' of acts contrary to the purposes and principles of the UN. However, these attempts to date have failed, as states have been unable to agree on a definition of the crime.[110]

Alternately, the customary crime of terrorism recently declared by the Special Tribunal for Lebanon might be considered particularly appropriate source for the meaning of the term in the context of Article 1F(c). In addition to the benefits of defining a *crime* of terrorism, the customary status of the Tribunal's definition would appear to make it applicable to all states parties to the 1951 Convention, thereby avoiding the fragmentation of interpretation that might occur were national or regional definitions of terrorism employed, or indeed, newly formulated definitions contained in instruments such as the Statute of the ICC, which might not be applicable to all states parties to the 1951 Convention. The Tribunal's assessment of customary law in this decision is, however, highly controversial, and the validity of recognising a crime of terrorism under customary international law severely criticised. It therefore remains to be seen whether the Tribunal's approach will be followed by courts and tribunals around the world, particularly as since the decision is not binding on courts other than the Tribunal itself.[111]

In the absence of a universally accepted definition of terrorism it may therefore be preferable to focus on what the immigration tribunal in the early cases

---

107 As is most evident in Article 1F(a)'s reference to 'crime against peace, war crime, or crime against humanity', the crimes that fell within the jurisdiction of the International Military Tribunal at Nuremberg. More recently, the Rome Statute of the ICC has been held to be the 'starting point' for the interpretation of the crimes that fall within the scope of Article 1F(a). *JS (Sri Lanka), R* UKSC (n 69) [8]–[9].

108 Such as the UK's domestic definition of terrorism.

109 Such as UNSC Res 1566 and the EU Common Position of 2001.

110 UNGA 'Final Act of Conference of Plenipotentiaries on the Establishment of an International Criminal Court' (17 July 1998) UN Doc A/CONF.183/10, Resolution E. A definition of terrorism was also not included following the Review Conference in Kampala in 2010.

111 Indeed the Supreme Court itself in *Al-Sirri* stated that 'there is as yet no internationally agreed definition of terrorism', *Al- Sirri* [2012] (n 148) [37].

termed 'acts which are the subject of intense disapproval by the governing body of the entire international community'. These would appear to include acts prohibited by international anti-terrorism conventions such as those relating to hostage taking, hijacking, terrorist bombings and nuclear terrorism, which are politically motivated and committed with the intent of causing death or serious bodily injury, as referred to in Security Council Resolution 1566. Indeed, in the early cases the tribunal saw its task as determining what the UN meant by 'terrorism' in its resolutions rather than any meaning that terrorism might have by international agreement or domestic legislation.[112]

In practice, however, the Supreme Court's endorsement of the UNHCR's position regarding the threshold to be employed in Article 1F(c) cases may have gone some way to dispelling many of the differences that exist between these different definitions of terrorism. An act of politically motivated violence that is considered to 'attack the very basis of the international community's coexistence', being assessed with regard to its gravity and impact on international peace and security, would likely fall under all the formulations of terrorism set out in the above legal instruments. The Supreme Court's endorsement of the UNHCR's high threshold here is important, because it is in line with the restrictive approach that is advised be adopted in the interpretation of Article 1F and also enables account to be taken of the unique and exceptional nature of the provision. As such, there may be a limit to the utility of employing external standards to determine the meaning of terrorism for the purpose of Article 1F(c). While these legal sources may prove useful in adding meaning to the term, what ultimately should be shown in each case is that the activity in question 'attacks the very basis of the international community's coexistence'. This approach enables account to be taken of the unique and exceptional nature of Article 1F(c) and its context in an international treaty of a humanitarian character, rather than as a means of criminal prosecution and punishment.

While the Supreme Court appeared to adopt a narrow interpretation of the meaning of terrorism for the purpose of Article 1F(c) in its decision in *Al-Sirri*, the same cannot be said for the second case considered by the Court, that of *DD (Afghanistan)*. This case did not concern the meaning of terrorism for the purpose of the provision, but rather other acts that may be considered to constitute acts contrary to the purposes and principles of the United Nations, in particular, military action against forces acting under UN mandate, as will be considered below.

---

112 *KK* (n 147) [74]; *AA (Exclusion clause) Palestine* (n 167) [60]; *Y* (n 287) [148].

4 Action against UN Mandated Forces as Acts Contrary to the Purposes and Principles of the United Nations

In *DD* (*Afghanistan*), the second case which came before the Supreme Court, the Court had to determine whether armed insurrection directed not only against government forces, but also against a UN-mandated force supporting that government, constituted acts contrary to the purposes and principles of the United Nations for the purpose of Article 1F(c).

The case concerned an asylum applicant, DD, who had been engaged in offensive and defensive military operations in Afghanistan against both Afghan government forces and the UN-mandated International Security Assistance Force (ISAF), established by the UN Security Council to assist the new Afghan authority and provide security for UN troops in Afghanistan.[113] Before the Court of Appeal, the Secretary of State had argued that the asylum applicant's actions constituted acts of terrorism and as such were acts contrary to the purposes and principles of the United Nations. As noted above, the Court of Appeal, however, held that military actions against the Afghan military forces were not necessarily terrorist in nature, and as such not contrary to the purposes and principles of the United Nations for the purpose of Article 1F(c).[114] In particular, the Court of Appeal drew attention to the fact that there was no evidence that DD had been involved in the commission of gross human rights violations against the civilian population. There was a distinction between armed attacks against civilians, on the one hand, and armed forces on the other, and as such DD's simple participation in armed conflict against the Afghan forces did not amount to terrorism for the purpose of Article 1F(c).

However, notwithstanding the fact that DD's actions did not amount to terrorism for the purpose of Article 1F(c), the Court of Appeal considered DD's direct military action against UN-mandated forces to be a 'clear example' of action contrary to the purposes and principles of the United Nations.[115] The Court reasoned that, since the UN Security Council implements the UN purpose of maintaining international peace and security, attacks against Security Council-mandated forces carrying out that mandate was action contrary to the purpose and principles of the United Nations, and as such fell within the scope

113 This force was initially mandated by Security Council Resolution 1386 of 20 December 2001 for a period of six months, its mandate being extended both temporally and geographically by a number of later resolutions. United Nations Security Council, Resolution 1386 UN Doc S/RES/1386.

114 *DD* (*Afghanistan*) (n 69) [56].

115 Ibid. [64]–[65].

of Article 1F(c). The Supreme Court therefore had to determine whether the Court of Appeal had been correct in deciding that military action against UN-mandated ISAF forces fell within the scope of Article 1F(c) of the 1951 Convention as acts contrary to the purposes and principles of the United Nations.

Before the Supreme Court, it was argued on behalf of the DD that participation in an armed attack against forces operating under and carrying out a UN mandate does not, without more, engage Article 1F(c). It was argued that armed insurrection is not, in itself, contrary to the purposes and principles of the United Nations for a number of reasons:

Firstly, it was argued that the appropriate legal framework for determining the lawfulness of actions against UN-mandated forces is international humanitarian law, which governs situations of internal and international armed conflict. Under international humanitarian law, UN-mandated non-combatant peacekeeping forces enjoy special protection against attack.[116] However, it was pointed out that combatant forces such as ISAF acting under UN-mandate do not enjoy such protection. Therefore, there was a fundamental distinction between military action directed at UN-mandated peacekeeping forces and UN-mandated combatant forces. Since UN-mandated combatant forces enjoy no special protection under international humanitarian law, simply engaging in military action against these forces was not illegitimate under the laws of war, and as such, it was argued, did not constitute acts contrary to the purposes and principles of the United Nations.

Furthermore, attention was drawn to the guidance provided by the Canadian Supreme Court in the *Pushpanathan* case.[117] It will be recalled that the Canadian Court held that acts could be considered contrary to the purposes and principles of the United Nations for the purpose of Article 1F(c) where: (i) 'a widely accepted international agreement or United Nations resolution explicitly declares that the commission of certain acts is contrary to the purposes and principles of the United Nations…[and] such declarations or resolutions represent a reasonable consensus of the international community', or (ii) 'there is consensus in international law that particular acts constitute sufficiently serious and sustained violations of fundamental human rights as to amount to persecution'.[118] DD's actions did not amount to serious and sustained violations of fundamental human rights, nor had the Security Council

116 *Al- Sirri* [2012] (n 69) [59]–[60]. For example, the 1994 Convention and 2005 Protocol on the Safety of United Nations and Associate Personnel.

117 *Pushpanathan* (n 335).

118 Ibid. [65]–[66].

ever sought to categorise opposition, even armed opposition, to UN-mandated forces as contrary to the purposes and principles of the United Nations. Consensus did not exist that attacks on UN-mandated forces are contrary to the purposes and principles of the United Nations.

It was therefore argued that military action against UN-mandated forces should only provide a basis for exclusion under Article 1F(c) where (i) the act or acts in question constitute a crime in international law; or (ii) the act or acts, which must be of sufficient gravity to have a negative impact on international peace and security, have been specifically identified as contrary to the purposes and principles of the UN, either by a clear decision of the Security Council acting within its competence, or by way of agreement or consensus among states at large.[119] DD's actions against UN-mandated combatant forces did not amount to a crime in international law, nor had they been specifically identified as contrary to the purposes and principles of the UN by the Security Council or consensus of States at large. Therefore, it was argued that these actions did not fall within the scope of Article 1F(c) as acts contrary to the purposes and principles of the UN.

In its judgment, the Supreme Court accepted the points made concerning the distinction between ISAF combatant forces and UN-mandated peacekeeping forces, but did not consider these differences material to the issue of whether DD was excluded from refugee status by virtue of Article 1F(c). In the Courts opinion:

> The question which rules of law apply to attacks on ISAF and [UN peacekeeping forces] is categorically different from (and irrelevant to) the question whether an attack against either body is contrary to the purposes and principles of the United Nations.

The Court stated that this question 'must be determined in an examination of all the relevant facts', which included the terms of the Security Council Resolutions by which ISAF was mandated.[120]

The Supreme Court drew attention to the purpose of the ISAF forces: to maintain peace and security in Afghanistan and thereby assist in the maintenance of international peace and security. The Court considered the maintenance of international peace and security to be one of the most important purposes set out in Article 1 of the UN Charter. Although the UN Security Council had never sought to categorise opposition to UN-mandated forces as

119 *Al-Sirri* [2012] (n 69) [62].
120 Ibid. [65].

contrary to the purposes and principles of the United Nations, the Court noted that it was not suggested, either by the UNHCR or the Supreme Court of Canada in *Pushpanathan*, that this was the only criterion for determining whether actions could be considered contrary to the purposes and principles of the United Nations.[121] The Court noted that, in *Pushpanathan*, the Supreme Court of Canada did not have to consider whether an attack on a UN body or UN-mandated force fell within the scope of Article 1F(c), and there was therefore no basis for restricting the approach to 1F(c) to that laid out in that case.[122]

In the Court's view, the correct test was that put forward by the UNHCR:

> Article 1F(c) is only triggered in extreme circumstances by activity which attacks the very basis of the international community's coexistence. Such activity must have an international dimension. Crimes capable of affecting international peace, security and peaceful relations between states, as well as serious and sustained violations of human rights would fall under this category.[123]

On this test, the Court considered an attack on ISAF forces was in principle capable of being an act contrary to the purposes and principles of the United Nations. The Court noted that the fundamental aims and objectives of ISAF accorded with the first purpose stated in Article 1 on the UN Charter: the maintenance of international peace and security. By attacking ISAF, the asylum applicant was seeking to frustrate this purpose. The Court concluded: 'To hold that his acts are in principle capable of being acts contrary to the purposes and principles of the United Nations accords with common sense and is correct in law'.[124]

The Supreme Court in this case therefore took a much broader view of action that was capable of falling within the scope of Article 1F(c). Although again endorsing the UNHCR's guidance concerning the gravity of the act in question and its impact on international peace and security, the court held that DD's activities could constitute acts contrary to the purposes and principles of the UN despite a lack of international consensus to this effect. In contrast to acts of terrorism, which have repeatedly been held to constitute acts contrary to the purposes and principles of the UN in a number of resolutions of the Security Council and General Assembly, the UN had never sought to categorise action against UN-mandated forces as contrary to its purposes and

121 Ibid. [66].

122 Ibid. [67].

123 UNHCR Guidelines (n 65) para 17. *Al-Sirri* [2012] (n 69) [66].

124 *Al-Sirri* [2012] (n 69) [68].

principles. Despite this, the Supreme Court held that DD's actions were capable of falling within the scope of Article 1F(c).

While it may be true that interpreting action against UN-mandated forces as 'acts contrary to the purposes and principles of the United Nations' seems to accord with 'common sense', it may however be unfortunate that the Supreme Court in this case chose to depart from the guidance provided by the Canadian Supreme Court in *Pushpanathan* regarding the need for international consensus.[125] Article 1F's status as a provision of an international convention indicates that it should be interpreted in accordance with the rule of treaty interpretation contained in the Vienna Convention on the Law of Treaties, that is, the provision must be interpreted in good faith, in light of its context and object and purpose. It has already been noted above that these considerations mandate a restrictive approach to the interpretation of Article 1F(c), as advocated by the Supreme Court in this case. The debates surrounding the drafting of Article 1F(c) suggest that it was originally understood as applying to acts such as gross violations of human rights, war crimes and genocide. However, under the Vienna rule an interpretation of Article 1F(c) must also take into account subsequent practice and agreement of states parties to the treaty.[126] Subsequent agreement and state practice may take a variety of forms, but what is crucial is that the agreement or practice establishes 'the agreement of the parties' to the treaty.

Applying these rules of treaty interpretation to the terms of Article 1F(c), it would appear that the meaning of the phrase 'acts contrary to the purposes and principles of the United Nations' may be expanded, taking into account this subsequent practice and agreement where this represents 'the agreement

125 Although Sivakumaran points out that acts are rarely explicitly characterised as contrary to the purposes and principles of the UN, as international bodies do not generally have international refugee law in mind when considering such acts. Similarly, characterisation as such should not be determinative of an acts status for the purpose of Article 1F(c). As such, the Pushpanathan approach is both over- and under- inclusive. Sivakumaran S, 'Exclusion from Refugee Status' (n 358) 371.

126 Vienna Convention, art 31(3). Thus in *KK*, the Immigration and Asylum Tribunal considered the UN resolutions declaring 'acts methods and practices of terrorism are contrary to the purposes and principles of the United Nations' to constitute subsequent state practice and agreement, and therefore clearly relevant to the interpretation of the phrase 'purposes and principles of the United Nations' for the purpose of Article 1F(c). *KK* (n 147) [25]–[29]. See also Aust (n 99) 240, where he considers the 1994 UNGA Declaration of Measures to Eliminate International Terrorism to constitute subsequent agreement on the interpretation of the term 'contrary to the purposes and principles of the United Nations'.

of the parties' to the Convention. This requirement appears much like the Canadian Court's guidance in *Pushpanathan,* that a certain level of international 'consensus' that certain acts constitute acts contrary to the purposes and principles of the UN is required before they can be considered to fall within the scope of Article 1F(c). However, as was pointed out in the case, such consensus does not exist in relation to action directed against UN-mandated forces. Indeed, as a matter of policy, UN Security Council resolutions do not characterise armed opposition to UN-mandated forces as contrary to the purposes and principles of the UN. Any such characterisation would foreclose the possibilities for negotiated settlement, and would also go against the principle that the law of armed conflict should apply equally to both parties.[127] Similarly, there do not appear to be any 'relevant rules of international law' prohibiting military action against UN-mandated combatant forces that can be drawn on to expand the meaning of Article 1F(c) in this way.

Thus, whilst there is clearly a dynamic aspect to both the UN Charter and the 1951 Convention, the interpretation of the phrase 'acts contrary to the purposes and principles' should not be expanded in the absence of clear international practice or agreement in this respect. Indeed, the UNHCR has stressed that the exclusion clauses in the 1951 Convention are exhaustive, and '[w]hile these grounds are subject to interpretation, they cannot be supplemented by additional criteria in the absence of an international convention to that effect'.[128] The Supreme Court may therefore have been misplaced in departing from the clear guidelines provided by the Canadian Court in *Pushpanathan*. Indeed, even under the UNHCR's approach, which the Supreme Court considered to be the 'correct test' in Article 1F(c) cases, the court appears to have been misguided in determining that attacks on UN-mandated forces constitute acts contrary to the purposes and principles of the United Nations for the purpose of Article 1F(c). The UNHCR's guidance clearly refers to '*Crimes* capable of affecting international peace, security and peaceful relations between states'.[129] As considered above, DD's actions did not amount to a crime under international criminal law, nor were they in violation of the rules of international

127 Guy Goodwin-Gill, 'Article 1F(c) of the 1951 Convention: Denying refugee status because of acts contrary to the purposes and principles of the United Nations' (lecture given as part of the International Refugee Law Seminar Series, Refugee Law Initiative, London) (11 October 2011). Indeed, Sivakumaran points out that this is close to bringing back the notion of 'just war', by which different rules apply to the righteous and wrongful sides. Sivakumaran S, 'Exclusion from Refugee Status' (n 358) 368.

128 UNHCR Guidelines (n 65) 2; UNHCR Background Note (n 164) 4.

129 Emphasis added.

humanitarian law.[130] It therefore seems the Supreme Court's decision was flawed in this point and should be revisited.

The Supreme Court's decision in this aspect of the case clearly has wide-reaching effects. It has been noted that, as a result, any individual that attacks a UN body or a UN-mandated body would be acting in a manner contrary to the purposes and principles of the UN for the purpose of Article 1F(c), irrespective of whether or not the victims in question are civilians or combatants and whether or not there has been compliance with the applicable international law.[131] This sits uneasily with the principle of combatant immunity, universally recognised as a norm of international humanitarian law that provides an individual cannot be prosecuted for lawful acts of war, and the principle of equality of obligation of belligerents.[132] It is submitted that the better approach would have been to follow the guidance provided by the Canadian Court in *Pushpanathan*, and limit the application of Article 1F(c) to acts which either constitute gross violations of fundamental human rights, or are explicitly recognised as contrary to the purposes and principles of the UN by a widely accepted international agreement or UN resolution which represents a reasonable consensus of the international community.

5 Conclusions

It is well established in the UK's interpretation of Article 1F(c) that acts of terrorism are capable of falling within the scope of the provision. In the early cases, the tribunal and the SIAC stressed that the purpose of their examination was not to rely on interpretations of terrorism which exist in international instruments or domestic statutes, but rather to determine what the UN meant by terrorism in its resolutions. The provision was therefore held to apply to 'acts which are the subject of intense disapproval by the governing body of the entire international community'. In contrast, the Court of Appeal, in a number of decisions following the coming into force of the EU Qualification Directive and the UK's domestic legislation on the meaning of terrorism for the purpose of Article 1F(c), relied on a variety of instruments when interpreting the meaning of terrorism for the purpose of the provision. The Court furthermore

130 It has been suggested that compliance with the applicable law should be an important part of the decision on exclusion. Sivakumaran S, 'Exclusion from Refugee Status' (n 358) 368–369, 372–377.

131 Sivakumaran S, 'Exclusion from Refugee Status' (n 358) 368.

132 Ibid. 568–570.

developed an exception for military action directed against a government's armed forces, and in a number of cases held the terrorist activity must have an international dimension in order to fall within the scope of Article 1F(c).

In its decision in the conjoined cases *Al-Sirri* and *DD* (*Afghanistan*), the Supreme Court rejected the UK's domestic definition of terrorism entirely for the purpose of Article 1F(c). The Court instead followed the UNHCR's guidance in holding that, in order to fall within the scope of the provision, the act in question must 'attack the very basis of the international community's coexistence', being assessed with regard to its gravity and impact on international peace and security. The Supreme Court drew on the definition of terrorism contained in the UN's draft Comprehensive Convention in formulating the 'essence' of terrorism for the purpose of Article 1F(c):

> the commission, organisation, incitement or threat of serious acts of violence against persons or property for the purpose of intimidating a population or compelling a government or international organisation to act or not to act in a particular way

Whilst this UN convention may be a more appropriate point of reference than definitions of terrorism contained in regional or domestic instruments, negotiations on this convention have fallen into deadlock and the present author therefore suggests that it should be approached with caution. However, the Supreme Court's endorsement of the UNHCR's position may, for the purpose of Article 1F(c), have gone some way to dispelling many of the differences that exist between the various definitions of terrorism that exist in international law. Importantly, the Supreme Court also appears to have approved the distinction made in earlier Court of Appeal decisions between military action directed against government forces and acts of violence directed at civilians, and has stressed that, in order to fall within the scope of Article 1F(c), the acts in question must have an international dimension. The Supreme Court's endorsement of the UNHCR's guidance in general appears to accord with the ordinary meaning of the provision and is in line with the restrictive approach that is recommended to be adopted in its interpretation. The Home Office's APG, however, still refers to terrorism for the purpose of Article 1F(c) as defined in section 1 of the Terrorism Act 2000, and needs to be updated in this respect.[133]

In contrast to its narrow interpretation of terrorism for the purpose of Article 1F(c), the Supreme Court appeared to adopt an expansive approach to the interpretation of the provision when determining that military action

133 Home Office Exclusion APG, s 6.2.

directed against combatant forces acting under UN-mandate is action contrary to the purposes and principles of the UN. It appears that the Supreme Court may have been misguided in this aspect of the case. The principles of international law which govern the interpretation of the 1951 Convention, and leading international guidance on the interpretation of Article 1F(c) in particular, indicate that international consensus is required to expand the meaning of the phrase 'acts contrary to the purposes and principles of the United Nations' in this way. In the case of action directed against UN-mandated combatant forces, this consensus is clearly lacking. It therefore seems the Supreme Court's decision was flawed in this point and should be revisited.

CHAPTER 5

Responsibility and Membership of a Terrorist Organisation

Perhaps the most important aspect of Article 1F is the level of complicity in the commission of Article 1F acts that must be established for an asylum applicant to be excluded from refugee status. Whilst Article 1F clearly applies to those who personally perpetrate excludable acts, responsibility may also arise where the asylum applicant has contributed to or been complicit in the commission of such crimes. Terrorism has featured to a large extent in the UK's interpretation of responsibility for the purpose of Article 1F. This has arisen primarily in relation to the extent to which an asylum applicant can be held responsible for the commission of the activities of a terrorist group or organisation of which they are a member. Since terrorism has featured largely in the interpretation of individual responsibility as a result of membership of an organisation in the context of Article 1F, this mode of incurring responsibility for Article 1F acts will be the primary focus of this chapter.

Article 1F excludes from the benefits of the 1951 Convention those for whom there are serious reasons for considering have 'committed' or 'been guilty of' the acts specified therein. The IRO Constitution went a little further than this. In addition to 'war criminals, quislings and traitors' and ordinary criminals extraditable by treaty, the IRO Constitution excluded from the organisation's mandate those who had 'participated' in any organisation with the purpose of overthrowing the government of a UN Member State, 'participated' in any terrorist organisation or 'become leaders' of movements hostile to the government of a UN Member State.[1] However, these forms of responsibility were not included in the terms of Article 1F, nor were they raised during the drafting of the provision. During the drafting of Article 1F, reference was repeatedly made

1 IRO Constitution, Annex I Part II, Article 6: '(a) participated in any organization having as one of its purposes the overthrow by armed force of the Government of their country of origin, being a Member of the United Nations; or the overthrow by armed force of the Government of any other Member of the United Nations, or have participated in any terrorist organization; (b) become leaders of movements hostile to the Government of their country of origin being a Member of the United Nations or sponsors of movements encouraging refugees not to return to their country of origin'.

 | DOI 10.1163/9789004292062_007

to those who had 'committed' one of the enumerated acts, rather than being a member of or participated in a particular organisation or movement.[2]

The OAU Refugee Convention similarly makes reference to those who have 'committed' or 'been guilty' of the crimes and acts listed in its exclusion provision. The Arab Refugee Convention rather refers to individuals that have 'been convicted' of a war crime, crime against humanity, terrorist crime or serious non-political crime. However, Article 1F's 'serious reasons for considering' clearly mandates that a lower standard of proof is required than a criminal conviction.[3] Indeed, the EU Qualification Directives do not include the requirement that an individual must be convicted of a crime in order to be excluded from refugee status, but rather replicate Article 1F's references to those who have 'committed' or 'been guilty' of excludable acts. The Directives furthermore specify that the exclusion provisions apply 'to persons who incite or otherwise participate in the commission of the crimes or acts mentioned therein'.[4]

The EU Qualification Directives' reference to those who 'incite or otherwise participate' in the commission of an Article 1F act may be seen as reflecting the well established principle of international criminal law, by which, although criminal liability clearly attaches to the physical perpetration of a crime,

2 Although the formulation of Article 1F referred to those who had '*committed* a crime specified in Article VI of the London Charter of the International Military Tribunal' or '*falls under*' the provisions of article 14(2), UDHR, the reference to an individual falling under the terms of the UDHR appears to have been understood by delegates to mean an individual having 'committed' the acts specified therein. Thus, in criticising reference to the UDHR in paragraph (b), the UK delegate noted that the clause would seem to include refugees who had 'committed' a crime, no matter how trivial, provided it was a non-political crime. The UK delegate was further concerned that persons who 'committed' minor crimes in their country of refuge should not be excluded from the benefits of the Convention. UN Conference of Plenipotentiaries on the Status of Refugees and Stateless Persons 'Twenty-ninth Meeting' (n 348) (Mr. Hoare [United Kingdom]). The final text of Article 1F(b) ultimately adopted at the Conference refers to an individual who has 'committed' a serious non-political crime…'. The text of Article 1F(c) was similarly revised during the drafting debates to refer to an individual who has 'committed' acts contrary to the purposes and principles of the United Nations. However, this was finally amended to refer to a person who has been 'guilty of' acts contrary to the purposes and principles of the United Nations. UN Conference of Plenipotentiaries on the Status of Refugees and Stateless Persons 'Twenty-ninth Meeting'.

3 See Chapter 7 for interpretation of 'serious reasons for considering' and standard of proof required in Article 1F cases. The wording 'has been guilty of' contained in Article 1F(c), as opposed to the 'has committed' contained in the previous two paragraphs of Article 1F, cannot be interpreted as inserting a different threshold for individual responsibility in the context of Article 1F(c). Zimmermann and Wennholz (n 68) 603.

4 Qualification Directives, Art. 12(2)(3).

liability also attached to various forms of participation in the commission or attempted commission of the act. The rationale for this approach to responsibility for participation in an international crime was outline by the Appeals Chamber of the ICTY as follows:

> Most of these crimes do not result from the criminal propensity of single individuals but constitute manifestations of collective criminality: the crimes are often carried out by groups of individuals acting in pursuance of a common criminal design. Although some members of the group may physically perpetrate the criminal act (murder…), the participation and contribution of the other members of the group is often vital in facilitating the commission of the offence in question. It follows that the moral gravity of such participation is often no less – or indeed no different – from that of those actually carrying out the acts in question.[5]

Thus an individual may be held responsible for the commission of an international crime through various modes of participation. For example, Article VI of the London Charter provides that individual responsibility for crimes against peace, war crimes and crimes against humanity attaches to 'Leaders, organizers, instigators and accomplices participating in the formulation or execution of a common plan or conspiracy to commit any of the foregoing crimes' who are responsible for 'all acts performed by any persons in execution of such plan'. Article 7(1) of the ICTY Statute similarly provides:

> A person who planned, instigated, ordered, committed or otherwise aided and abetted in the planning, preparation or execution of a crime referred to in articles 2 to 5 of the present Statute, shall be individually responsible for the crime.[6]

The Rome Statute of the ICC for the first time explicitly systematises the requirements of individual criminal responsibility, and in Article 25(3) distinguishes modes of criminal participation to which individual responsibility attaches.[7] Furthermore, the *ad hoc* tribunals of Rwanda and former Yugoslavia

5 *Prosecutor v Tadic* (Appeal Judgment) ICTY-94-1-A (15 July 1999) [191].

6 Articles 2–5 define war crimes, the crime of genocide and crimes against humanity.

7 These are: (a) the commission a crime, whether as an individual, jointly with another, or through another person; (b) ordering, soliciting or inducing the commission of a crime; (c) aiding, abetting or otherwise assisting in the commission of the crime, or; (d) in any other way contributing to the commission or attempted commission of the crime by a group of

have developed in their jurisprudence the concept of 'joint criminal enterprise', whereby an individual may be held criminally responsible for participating in crimes committed by a group where they share a 'common plan or purpose'.[8]

The UN resolutions on terrorism similarly declare not only that 'acts, methods, and practices of terrorism are contrary to the purposes and principles of the United Nations', but also that 'knowingly financing, planning and inciting terrorist acts are also contrary to the purposes and principles of the United Nations'.[9] Indeed, in Resolution 1377 the Security Council stressed that 'the financing, planning and preparation of as well as *any other form of support* for acts of international terrorism are similarly contrary to the purposes and principles of the Charter of the United Nations'[10]

In the UK, Regulation 7(3) of the Qualification Regulations provides that Articles 1F(a) and (b) of the 1951 Convention apply 'to a person who instigates or otherwise participates in the commission of the crimes or acts specified in those provisions', echoing Article 12(3) of the EU Qualification Directives.[11] Section 54 of the UK Immigration, Asylum and Nationality Act 2006 goes further for the purpose of Article 1F(c), providing that the reference to acts contrary to the purposes and principles of the United Nations shall be taken as including... (a) acts of committing, preparing or instigating terrorism...and (b) acts of encouraging or inducing others to commit, prepare or instigate terrorism. Responsibility for Article 1F crimes in the UK is therefore not limited to those who physically perpetrate them, but extends to those who instigate or participate in the commission of such crimes. Although these provisions provide different modes of liability for Article 1F(c), as opposed to Articles 1F(a) and (b), in practice courts and tribunals in the UK have relied on the same approaches to responsibility under all three limbs, as will be considered throughout the course of this chapter.

Terrorism has featured largely in the UK's interpretation of Article 1F responsibility in the jurisprudence of courts and tribunals in the UK, particularly where an individual has not personally committed one of the crimes or acts

---

persons acting with a common purpose. Articles 25(3)(e) and (f) also criminalise certain preparatory actions.

8 *Prosecutor v Tadic* (n 460).

9 UNGA Dec 1994, para 2; UNGA Dec 1996, para 2; UNSC Res 1373, para 5; UNSC Res 1377, preamble para 5; UNSC Res 1624, preamble para 8.

10 UNSC Res 1377, preamble para 5 (emphasis added).

11 Qualification Directives, Art. 12(2): 'Paragraph 2 applies to persons who instigate or otherwise participate in the commission of the crimes or acts mentioned therein'.

listed in Article 1F, but is a member of, or associated with, a terrorist organisation that has committed such a crime. The UK Supreme Court has, however, recently disapproved the previous guidance on responsibility which focused on the terrorist nature of the organisation of which the individual was associated, and applied an interpretation which is more akin to that employed in international criminal law, although there still appear to be significant divergences between the approaches adopted in the refugee and criminal legal contexts. Parts 1 and 2 of this chapter examine the *Gurung* approach to Article 1F responsibility, and the difficulties encountered when trying to apply this approach in practice. In Part 3 the recent decisions of the Supreme Court and Court of Appeal are examined, while in Parts 4 and 5 there is a wider discussion of these different approaches to Article 1F responsibility and their interplay with the standards of liability employed in international criminal law.

1 The *Gurung* Doctrine

The leading case on Article 1F exclusion in the UK for a number of years was *Gurung v Secretary of State for the Home Department*, a starred decision of the immigration tribunal which pre-dated the UK Qualification Regulations and the EU Qualification Directive.[12] In the *Gurung* decision, the tribunal sought to provide guidance on the interpretation of Article 1F following the recent 9/11 terrorist attacks on the United States. The tribunal in this case advocated a dynamic approach to interpreting the provision, and noted that '[i]n deciding such issues as complicity we will need to look more and more to international criminal law definitions'.[13]

One of the key issues the tribunal had to determine in this case was whether simple membership of an organisation that had committed acts or crimes proscribed by Article 1F was enough to bring an individual within the scope of the provision. Whilst the tribunal acknowledged that mere membership of an organisation that committed such acts was not generally enough to bring an individual within the scope of Article 1F,[14] it went on to state:

> it would be wrong to say that an appellant only came within the Exclusion Clauses if the evidence established that he has personally participated in acts contrary to the provisions of Art. 1F. *If the organisation is one or has*

12 *Gurung (Exclusion, Risk, Maoists)* (n 85).

13 Ibid. [34].

14 Ibid. [104].

> *become one whose aims, methods and activities are predominantly terrorist in character, very little more will be necessary.*[15]

The tribunal held that there was a presumption an asylum applicant was excluded from refugee status under Article 1F where they were a voluntary member of an organisation that was 'predominantly terrorist in character', even if there was no evidence the individual had personally participated in the terrorist activities of the group. The tribunal considered this form of complicity necessary in order to adequately reflect the realities of modern-day terrorism, as the 'terrorist acts of key operatives are often possible only by virtue of the infrastructure of support provided by other members who themselves undertake no violent actions'.[16] The tribunal did, however, stress that:

> whilst complicity may arise indirectly, it remains essential in all cases to establish that the appellant has been a voluntary member of such an organisation who fully understands its aims, methods and activities, including any plans it has made to carry out acts contrary to Art. 1F.[17]

Although the tribunal observed that international criminal law and international humanitarian law should be the principal sources of reference when dealing with issues such as complicity in international crimes, and referred to the Rome Statute and the ICTY's Statute and jurisprudence,[18] the tribunal did not go on to analyse these sources. Rather, individual responsibility under the *Gurung* approach may be incurred where an individual is a voluntary member of an organisation that is 'predominantly terrorist in character'.

In reaching this conclusion, the tribunal in *Gurung* drew on a long standing line of jurisprudence on the interpretation of Article 1F responsibility, established by the Canadian Federal Court of Appeal in the seminal *Ramirez* decision.[19] Since this decision pre-dated the statutes of the *ad hoc* tribunals and the Rome Statute, the Canadian Court based its analysis of individual responsibility in large part on domestic US and Canadian decisions, commentaries of academic writers, and the London Charter of the International Military Tribunal (IMT). Drawing particularly on the London Charter's reference to '[l]eaders,

---

15 Ibid. [105] (emphasis added).

16 *Gurung* (*Exclusion, Risk, Maoists*) (n 85) [106].

17 Ibid. [108].

18 Ibid. [109].

19 *Ramirez v Canada* (*Minister of Employment and Immigration*) [1992] 2 FC 306 (Federal Court of Appeal), [23].

organizers, instigators and accomplices' in its Article VI, the Court held that Article 1F exclusion attaches not only to those that had physically perpetrated an Article 1F crime, but also accomplices and abettors. The question then remained 'What degree of complicity is required to be an accomplice or abettor?' In its judgment, the Canadian Court based its analysis of Article 1F responsibility on the concept of 'personal and knowing participation in persecutorial acts'.[20] In the case of crimes committed by a group, the court was of the opinion that 'complicity rests...on the existence of a shared common purpose and the knowledge that all of the parties in question may have of it'.[21] The requirement of 'personal and knowing participation' meant that 'mere membership in an organization which from time to time commits international offences is not normally sufficient for exclusion from refugee status'.[22] However, the court went on to state that 'where an organization is principally directed to a *limited, brutal purpose*...mere membership may by necessity involve personal and knowing participation in persecutorial acts'.[23] On this reasoning, responsibility so as to give rise to exclusion may be incurred as a result of simple membership of an organisation, where the organisation is considered particularly violent in nature. The Canadian approach to Article 1F individual responsibility found widespread support within jurisdictions such as New Zealand, the UK and the United States, and was also approved by the UNHCR.[24]

Although the UNHCR advises that 'membership per se of an organisation that commits or incites others to carry out violent crimes is not necessarily decisive or sufficient to exclude a person from refugee status',[25] it further notes that 'the purposes, activities and methods of some groups are of a particularly violent nature, with the result that voluntary membership thereof may also raise the presumption of individual responsibility'.[26] This presumption of individual responsibility reverses the burden of proof, so it rests on the asylum

20 Ibid. [23].

21 Ibid. [19].

22 Ibid. [16]. This conclusion was supported by the jurisprudence of the IMT, which excluded from criminal responsibility persons who had no knowledge of the criminal purposes or acts of the organisation of which they were a member.

23 Ibid., [17] (emphasis added).

24 Rikhof J, 'War Criminals Not Welcome; How Common Law Countries Approach the Phenomenon of International Crimes in the Immigration and Refugee Context' (2009) 21(3) International Journal of Refugee Law 453–507. Rikhof includes a detailed analysis of the approaches to Article 1F responsibility adopted in the United States, Canada, Australia and New Zealand.

25 UNHCR Background Note (n 164) para 59.

26 UNHCR Guidelines (n 65) para 19.

applicant to demonstrate that they have not been involved in the criminal activities of the organisation. In the context of membership of a terrorist organisation, in its 2001 document, 'Addressing Security Concerns', published shortly following the 9/11 terrorist attacks, the UNHCR stated:

> Where, however, there is sufficient proof that an asylum-seeker belongs to an extremist international terrorist group, such as those involved in the 11 September attacks, voluntary membership could be presumed to amount to personal and knowing participation, or at least acquiescence amounting to complicity in the crimes in question.[27]

This approach therefore presumes individual responsibility where an asylum applicant is a voluntary member of an 'extremist terrorist organisation'. This paragraph of the UNHCR's 2001 document was cited by the AIT in the *Gurung* decision in support of its conclusion that an individual could be excluded under Article 1F for mere membership of an organisation that is 'predominantly terrorist in character'. There are a number of difficulties with applying this approach to Article 1F responsibility in practice, however, as will be considered in the following section.

2 The Problems in Identifying an 'Extreme Terrorist Organisation'

The *Gurung* approach to Article 1F responsibility based on simple membership of an organisation grounds individual responsibility in the *nature* of the organisation, i.e. whether the organisation is 'predominantly terrorist in character'. One of the main difficulties with this approach surrounds the issue of determining whether an organisation is 'predominantly terrorist in character' so as to fall within the *Gurung* doctrine.[28]

Many States and international organisations have adopted their own lists of proscribed terrorist organisations.[29] However, automatic exclusion based on membership of an organisation included in one of these proscribed lists has been cautioned against. In its recent Advisory Opinion, the CJEU stated that:

27 UNHCR 'Addressing Security Concerns without Undermining Refugee Protection – UNHCR's Perspective' (29 November 2001) para 18.

28 Saul notes that it is questionable whether front-line decision-makers can easily make such complex judgments. Saul B, 'Protecting Refugees in the Global "War on Terror"' (n 5).

29 For example, see UK Terrorism Act 2000, Schedule II; Council Common Position 2001/931/CFSP, 93.

> the fact that a person has been a member of an organisation which, because of its involvement in terrorist acts, is on the [proscribed list of terrorist organisations adopted by the European Union]…does not automatically constitute a serious reason for considering that that person has committed 'a serious non-political crime' or 'acts contrary to the purposes and principles of the United Nations'.[30]

Rather, the CJEU was of the opinion that regard must be had to the specific facts of each case individually. Although membership of an organisation included on such a list is a factor to be taken into account during the exclusion decision, 'the mere fact that the person concerned was a member of such an organisation cannot automatically mean that that person must be excluded from refugee status'.[31] Indeed, the UNHCR itself has cautioned against exclusion based on membership of a proscribed organisation, noting that 'lists established by the international community of terrorist suspects and organisations…would be drawn up in a political, rather than a judicial process and so the evidentiary threshold for inclusion is likely to be much lower [than ICTY/ICTR indictments]'.[32] Similarly, the UNHCR notes that '[n]ational lists of terrorist suspects or organisations will tend to have a lower evidentiary threshold than their international counterparts, due to the lack of international consensus'.[33] This is amply demonstrated in the UK context, as considered below.

The UK's list of proscribed terrorist organisations is contained in Schedule 2 of the Terrorism Act 2000. Organisations are included in this list at the discretion of the Secretary of State, where he or she believes that the organisation is 'concerned in terrorism'.[34] The subjective nature of this test, coupled with the broad definition of terrorism contained in Section 1 of the Terrorism Act 2000, means the decision to include an organisation within this list is at the discretion of the Secretary of State. It is not therefore clear that organisations included in this list will necessarily meet the threshold necessary to be considered 'predominantly terrorist in character' under the *Gurung* doctrine.

---

30 *Bundesrepublik Deutschland v. B and D*, (n 283) [99].

31 Ibid. [88].

32 UNHCR Background Note (n 164) para 106.

33 Ibid. para 109.

34 UK Terrorism Act 2000, s 3(4), see also s 3(5). At present there are 59 proscribed terrorist organisations contained in this schedule. The Home Office Exclusion APG advise that: 'Case owners should consider exclusion particularly carefully where there is evidence that an individual has been convicted of an offence under Section 11 of the Terrorism Act 2000 (belonging, or professing to belong, to a proscribed organisation)'. Home Office Exclusion APG, s 2.4.3.

Thus the Court of Appeal has held that, although the Kurdistan Workers' Party (Partiya Karkeren Kurdistan: PKK) was included in the UK's list of proscribed terrorist organisations, there was 'no suggestion that it fell at the extreme end of the continuum'[35] so as to give rise to the *Gurung* presumption of exclusion.[36] Similarly, the Court of Appeal has held that the Tamil Tigers (LTTE), again included on the UK's list of proscribed terrorist organisations, could not be considered 'predominantly terrorist in character' under the *Gurung* doctrine.[37]

The UNHCR advises that a presumption of exclusion should arise only where the list has a credible basis and if the criteria for placing a particular organisation on the list are such that all members can reasonably be considered to be individually involved in violent crimes.[38] In the absence of an international list of proscribed terrorist organisations with a clear and credible legal basis, it therefore falls to the national courts to determine whether an organisation is 'predominantly terrorist in character' so as to give rise to the *Gurung* presumption of Article 1F exclusion. The tribunal in *Gurung* suggested considering organisations along a 'continuum' for this purpose with, at one end:

> an organisation that has very significant support amongst the population and has developed political aims and objectives covering political, social, economic and cultural issues. Its long term aims embrace a parliamentary, democratic mode of government and safeguarding of basic human rights. But it has in a limited way or for a limited period created an armed struggle wing in response to atrocities committed by a dictatorial government.[39]

The tribunal considered that in such a case an adjudicator should be extremely slow to conclude an applicant's mere membership of the organisation raises any real issue under Article 1F. However, at the other end of the continuum, the tribunal hypothesised an organisation which:

---

35 See below for the Gurung 'contimuum approach' to determining the nature of an organisation.

36 *MH (Syria)* (n 69) [36].

37 Since the organisation 'pursued its political ends in part by acts of terrorism and in part by military action directed against the armed forces of the government of Sri Lanka'. *KJ (Sri Lanka)* (n 69) [38].

38 UNHCR Background Note (n 164) 62.

39 *Gurung (Exclusion, Risk, Maoists)* (n 85) [112].

> has little or no political agenda or which, if it did originally have genuine political aims and objectives, has increasingly come to focus on terrorism as a modus operandi. Its recruitment policy, its structure and strategy has become almost entirely devoted to the execution of terrorist acts which are seen as a way of winning the war against the enemy, even if the chosen targets are primarily civilian. Let us further suppose that the type of government such an organisation promotes is authoritarian in character and abhors the identification by international human rights law of certain fundamental human rights.[40]

In the case of this latter type of organisation, the tribunal was of the opinion that 'any individual who has knowingly joined such an organisation will have difficulty in establishing he or she is not complicit in the acts of such an organisation'.[41] Thus, following the Canadian *Ramirez* decision, the tribunal considered the key factor in establishing Article 1F responsibility rested on the nature of the organisation: 'The more an organisation makes terrorist acts its *modus operandi*, the more difficult it will be for a claimant to show his voluntary membership of it does not amount to complicity'.[42]

However, a more recent trend in state practice has been to move away from focus on the nature of an organisation when determining whether an asylum applicant is responsible for the commission of Article 1F acts. As noted above, in its recent Advisory Opinion, the CJEU stated that the fact that an asylum applicant had been a member of a proscribed terrorist organisation does not automatically constitute serious reasons for considering they are individually responsible for the crimes committed by that group.[43] Rather, the Court stressed that there must be an individual assessment of the facts of each case, so as to make it possible to determine whether there are serious reasons for considering the individual committed, instigated or participated in an Article 1F crime or act within the meaning of the Qualification Directive.[44] Indeed, a number of problems with the *Gurung* approach to Article 1F responsibility

40 Ibid. [113].

41 Ibid. [113].

42 Ibid. [151].

43 *Bundesrepublik Deutschland v B and D* (n 283) [99].

44 Ibid. [94]. The CJEU similarly advised that, rather than focus on the terrorist nature of an organisation, Article 1F exclusion: 'is conditional on an assessment on a case-by-case basis of the specific facts, with a view to determining whether the acts committed by the organisation concerned meet the conditions laid down in those provisions and whether individual responsibility for carrying out those acts can be attributed to the person concerned' *Bundesrepublik* [99].

were highlighted by the Court of Appeal and Supreme Court in the seminal *JS* (*Sri Lanka*) case, which concerned exclusion under Article 1F(a).[45]

In the *JS* (*Sri Lanka*) case, both the Court of Appeal and the Supreme Court considered the level of responsibility required to bring an individual within the scope of Article 1F. The Court of Appeal stated it did not find it helpful to try and place organisations along a 'continuum' as suggested by the tribunal in *Gurung*.[46] In his leading judgment, Toulson LJ noted that 'it provides a subjective and unsatisfactory basis for determining whether as a matter of law an individual is guilty of an international crime'.[47] Firstly, he considered that the tribunal:

> rolled up a number of factors which might cause somebody wedded to the ideals of western liberal democracy to take a more or less hostile view of the organisation and to use an assessment of where the organisation stands in relation to those values in deciding whether its armed acts were "proportionate."[48]

In Toulson LJ's opinion, factors such as whether the organisation's long term aims embraced a democratic mode of government did not seem relevant to the question of individual responsibility for the purpose of Article 1F.[49] Indeed, his Lordship considered the fundamental problem with the continuum approach adopted by the tribunal in *Gurung* was that it:

> takes the decision maker's eye off the really critical questions whether the evidence provides serious reasons for considering the applicant to have committed the actus reus of an international crime with the requisite mens rea and invites a less clearly focused judgment.[50]

The Supreme Court in the *JS* (*Sri Lanka*) case also criticised the 'continuum' approach, stating that '[t]he reality is that there are too many variable factors involved in each case, some militating one way, some the other, to make it helpful to try to place any given case at some point along a continuum'.[51] Lord Brown, in his leading judgment, found it 'more troubling still' that:

---

45 *JS* (*Sri Lanka*), *R* EWCA (n 69) [95]; *JS* (*Sri Lanka*), *R* UKSC (n 69).

46 *JS* (*Sri Lanka*), *R* EWCA (n 69) [95] [111].

47 Ibid. [112].

48 Ibid. [112].

49 Ibid. [113].

50 Ibid. [114]. Approved by the Supreme Court *JS* (*Sri Lanka*), *R* UKSC (n 69) [45].

51 *JS* (*Sri Lanka*), *R* UKSC (n 69) [32].

> the tribunal in these paragraphs introduces considerations which properly have no place at all in determining how article 1F applies. Whether the organisation in question is promoting government which would be "authoritarian in character" or is intent on establishing "a parliamentary, democratic mode of government" is quite simply nothing to the point in deciding whether or not somebody is guilty of war crimes. War crimes are war crimes however benevolent and estimable may be the long-term aims of those concerned. And actions which would not otherwise constitute war crimes do not become so merely because they are taken pursuant to policies abhorrent to western liberal democracies.[52]

The Supreme Court and Court of Appeal in these cases therefore disapproved the *Gurung* approach to exclusion. Rather than focus on the nature of the organisation in question when determining Article 1F responsibility, both the Court of Appeal and the Supreme Court preferred to approach the issue from the basis of international criminal law, as considered below.

3 Towards Convergence with International Criminal Law

In the *JS* (*Sri Lanka*) cases, both the Court of Appeal and Supreme Court preferred to approach the issue of Article 1F responsibility by employing the standards of international criminal law, rather than focus on the nature of an organisation of which an asylum applicant was a member.

In his leading judgment in the Court of Appeal, Toulson LJ based the standard of individual responsibility in Article 1F cases on the ICTY's doctrine of joint criminal enterprise,[53] formulating the requirements for joint criminal enterprise liability as follows:

> in order for there to be joint enterprise liability, there first has to be a common design which amounts to or involves the commission of a crime provided for in the statute. The actus reus requirement for criminal liability is that the defendant must have participated in the furtherance of the joint criminal purpose in a way that made a significant contribution to the crime's commission. And that participation must have been with the

52 Ibid. [32].

53 After referring to the Rome Statute of the ICC, the ICTY Statute, and considering in some detail the *Tadic* decision of the ICTY and subsequent ICTY jurisprudence.

> intention of furthering the perpetration of one of the crimes provided for in the [Rome] statute.[54]

His Lordship thus aligned Article 1F responsibility closely with international criminal jurisprudence on individual responsibility, departing from the 'personal and knowing participation' standard traditionally employed by States Parties to the 1951 Convention. Toulson LJ's approach rather focuses on the level of participation of the asylum applicant in the commission of the international crime, employing the standards of *mens rea* and *actus reus* established by the ICTY. In particular, the individual must have made a 'substantial contribution' to the commission of the crime, with the mens rea intent of furthering the perpetration of one of the crimes enumerated in the Rome Statute.

As regards membership of an extremist organisation, Toulson LJ noted that:

> [a] person who becomes an *active* member of an organisation devoted exclusively to the perpetration of criminal acts may be regarded as a person who has conspired with others to commit such acts and will be criminally responsible for any acts performed in pursuance of the conspiracy.[55]

However, Toulson LJ cautioned that he used the words 'active member' deliberately, since issues of responsibility were unlikely to present a problem in the case of an active member of an organisation dedicated entirely to terrorist activities.[56] However, he considered that 'it is another matter if an organisation pursues its political ends in part by acts of terrorism and in part by other means. Joining such an organisation may not involve conspiring to commit criminal acts or in practice doing anything that contributes significantly to the commission of criminal acts'.[57] Toulson LJ's approach therefore departs from the *Gurung* decision of the tribunal in two important respects. Firstly, his Lordship bases Article 1F responsibility predominantly on the standards of individual responsibility established by the ICTY's doctrine of joint criminal enterprise, rather than the 'personal and knowing participation' standard traditionally employed by States Parties in the refugee context. Secondly, membership of an organisation will only give rise to Article 1F responsibility where the individual was an 'active member' of an organisation 'devoted exclusively

54 As this case concerned exclusion under Art. 1F(a), the court referred to the definition of war crimes contained in the Rome Statute *JS (Sri Lanka), R* EWCA (n 69) [95] [104], [119].

55 *JS (Sri Lanka), R* EWCA (n 69) [95] [107] (emphasis added).

56 Ibid. [107].

57 Ibid. [107].

to the perpetration of criminal acts', rather than a voluntary member of an organisation that is 'predominantly terrorist in character'. The Court of Appeal in *JS* (*Sri Lanka*) thus set a much higher standard of complicity required to give rise to exclusion under Article 1F, particularly in relation to membership of a 'terrorist organisation'.

The UK Supreme Court in *JS* (*Sri Lanka*) similarly based its analysis of Article 1F responsibility largely on international criminal sources.[58] In disapproving the *Gurung* approach to individual responsibility, Lord Brown in his leading judgment stated that the correct approach to Article 1F responsibility is that 'article 1F disqualifies those who make "a substantial contribution to" the crime, knowing that their acts or omissions will facilitate it'.[59] However, Lord Brown considered Toulson LJ's formulation of Article 1F responsibility in the Court of Appeal too narrowly drawn, as it 'is all too easily read as being directed to specific identifiable crimes'. Rather, Lord Brown considered that liability should attach to wider concepts of common design, 'such as the accomplishment of an organisation's purpose by whatever means are necessary'.[60] Lord Brown therefore stated:

> Put simply, I would hold an accused disqualified under article 1F if there are serious reasons for considering him voluntarily to have contributed in a significant way to the organisation's ability to pursue its purpose of committing war crimes, aware that his assistance will in fact further that purpose.[61]

Thus under Lord Brown's formulation of Article 1F responsibility, it must be established that the individual made a 'substantial contribution' to the criminal purpose of the organisation, although this does not need to be directed toward the commission of a specific crime. It will suffice if the individual intended to further the organisation's general criminal purpose.

Lord Brown furthermore outlined a number of factors which should be taken into account by a decision maker when determining Article 1F responsibility, which 'ultimately must prove to be the determining factors in any case'. These include: (i) the nature and the size of the organisation (ii) whether and, if so, by whom the organisation was proscribed, (iii) how the asylum-seeker came to be recruited, (iv) the length of time he remained in the organisation

58 Including the Rome Statute of the ICC, the ICTY Statute, and the ICTY's decision in *Tadic*.
59 *JS* (*Sri Lanka*), *R* UKSC (n 69) [35].
60 Ibid. [38].
61 Ibid. [38].

and what, if any, opportunities he had to leave it, (v) his position, rank, standing and influence in the organisation, (vi) his knowledge of the organisation's war crimes activities, and (vii) his own personal involvement and role in the organisation.[62]

The Supreme Court's decision in *JS* (*Sri Lanka*) has been followed by a number of decisions of the Court of Appeal and tribunal in Article 1F(a) cases.[63] It has also been approved by the Supreme Court and Court of Appeal in relation to Article 1F(c), where it has been held that 'the *JS* (Sri Lanka) criteria 'inevitably apply when it is article 1F(c) which is under consideration'.[64] The Home Office's APG has similarly been amended to include the Supreme Court's jurisprudence:

> membership of, or employment in, an organisation which uses violence, or the threat of violence, as a means to achieve its political or criminal objectives is not enough on its own to make a person guilty of an international crime, and is not sufficient to justify exclusion from refugee status…the exclusion clauses will apply if there are serious reasons for considering that the individual has voluntarily contributed in a significant way to the organisation's ability to pursue its purpose of committing war crimes, aware that the assistance will in fact further that purpose. If the person was aware that in the ordinary course of events a particular consequence would follow from his actions, he would be taken to have acted with both knowledge and intent.[65]

The guidance also include Lord Brown's 'factors' which must be taken in to account in every case, and acknowledges that although the 'judgment related to Article 1F(a) cases, the test articulated on this issue by the Supreme Court extends to Article 1F generally (i.e. crimes and acts other than war crimes)'.[66]

---

62 Ibid. [30].

63 CM (*Article 1F(a) – superior orders*) *Zimbabwe* [2012] UKUT 236 (IAC); *MT* (*Article 1F (a) – aiding and abetting*) (n 185); *Azimi-Rad* (n 210); *AA-R* (*Iran*) (n 69); *AS* (*S.55*) (n 210).

64 AH (*Algeria*) (n 69) [13]; DD (*Afghanistan*) (n 69) [47]; see also *Al-Sirri* [2012] (n 148).

65 Home Office Exclusion APG, s 3.3. The Home Office guidance previously provided that: 'On the Gurung test, however, where the organisation concerned is one whose aims, methods and activities are predominantly terrorist in character, it may be sufficient for little more than simple membership of and support for such organisations to be taken as acquiescence amounting to complicity in their terrorist acts'. UK Border Agency, Asylum Policy Instructions: Exclusion: Articles 1F and 33(2) of the Refugee Convention (2008), s 2.4.3.

66 Ibid. s 3.3.

The approach to Article 1F responsibility laid down by the Supreme Court in *JS Sri Lanka* has also been followed by the New Zealand Supreme Court and most recently the Supreme Court of Canada, in which the *JS* approach to responsibility was elaborated on to a large extent.[67] There therefore appears to be an emerging trend among some states parties to the 1951 Convention to determine Article 1F responsibility by focusing on the level of participation of the individual in the commission of an Article 1F crime, rather than simply looking to the nature of the organisation of which they are a member. This move appears to have been influenced to some degree by the jurisprudence of courts in the UK. The following sections will discuss these approaches to Article 1F responsibility, and their relationship with the standards of criminal liability employed in international criminal law.

4 International Criminal Law and the *Gurung* Doctrine

In the *JS* (*Sri Lanka*) cases, both the Supreme Court and Court of Appeal chose to depart from the 'personal and knowing participation' approach of the tribunal in *Gurung*, and rather draw on the standards of responsibility employed in international criminal law. This may be seen as a positive development in the jurisprudence surrounding Article 1F, as it would appear that international criminal instruments are a more appropriate source for determining the standards of responsibility in the context of the provision. In *Gurung* itself the tribunal noted that '[i]n deciding such issues as complicity we will need to look more and more to international criminal law definitions'.[68] Indeed, at least in the context of Article 1F(a) it would appear that resort to international criminal law sources is warranted.

The ordinary meaning of the phrase 'has committed' in Article 1F indicates that, in order to be excluded from refugee status, an asylum applicant must have been *individually* involved in the commission (or attempted commission) of the act, i.e. that some form of individual responsibility be established. The context of this term in Article 1F(a)'s reference to international crimes 'as defined in the international instruments drawn up to make provision in respect of such crimes' suggests that the standard of individual responsibility that

67 The New Zealand Supreme Court in *Attorney General v Tamil X* [2010] (n 172) [68], noted with approval the UK Supreme Court decision in *JS* (*Sri Lanka*), as did the Canadian Supreme Court *in Ezokola v. Canada* (n 172) 40.

68 *Gurung* (*Exclusion, Risk, Maoists*) (n 85) [35].

must be established for the purpose of Article 1F(a) should similarly be drawn from the international instruments employed to define such crimes.[69] This conclusion is reinforced when the term is viewed in its context: since the object and purpose of Article 1F(a) is to deny suspected international criminals the protection of the 1951 Convention, excluding those who would not be considered criminally responsible for the acts in question would run counter to the rationale of the provision, and indeed the protective purpose of the 1951 Convention as a whole.

Similarly, Article 1F(c) makes reference to acts which are necessarily international in nature. As such, it would appear that the standard of individual responsibility for Article 1F(c) should be interpreted by reference to the international criminal sources employed in the interpretation of responsibility for the purpose of Article 1F(a). Whilst the acts referred to in Article 1F(c) may not necessarily be defined as international crimes, acts 'contrary to the purposes and principles of the United Nations' must meet a threshold of international condemnation approaching that of international crime.[70] Responsibility for these acts may therefore be considered to fall to be governed by the rules and principles of responsibility for that exist as a matter of international law.[71] Furthermore, applying well established rules of individual responsibility to Article 1F(c) maintains the protective objective of the 1951 Convention by ensuring a level of certainty in the application of what is an inherently vague ground of exclusion. Although Article 1F(c) employs the terminology 'been guilty of' rather than 'committed', it does not appear that this wording should be read as introducing a higher threshold of responsibility, such as actual conviction for the act in question, as Article 1F's reference to 'serious reasons for

69 Indeed, as the 1951 Convention is silent on the meaning of the term 'committed', international legal instruments may be relevant to the interpretation of the term since '[t]he parties are taken to refer to customary international law and general principles of law for all questions which the treaty does not itself resolve in express terms', and furthermore may be presumed not to intend to act inconsistently with generally recognised principles of international law. ILC Fragmentation Report, Summary Conclusions, para 19. Since the concept of individual responsibility is a well established principle of international criminal law, recourse to international criminal law instruments to determine the meaning of 'committed' gives effect to the principle of harmonisation, by which norms of international law should be interpreted to as to give rise to a single set of compatible obligations.

70 *Al-Sirri* [2012] (n 148).

71 In the absence of a definition of 'been guilty of' in the 1951 Convention, states parties may be presumed to refer to the standards of individual responsibility that exist as a matter of international criminal law.

considering' clearly mandates that a lower standard of proof is required than a criminal conviction.[72]

In contrast to sub-paragraphs (a) and (c) of Article 1F, Article 1F(b) does not necessarily concern the exclusion of the perpetrators of crimes of an international nature, but rather those that have committed 'serious non-political crimes'. It may therefore be thought inappropriate to apply standards of individual responsibility that concern international crimes to a provision that generally covers those of a lesser character. However, it has been suggested that the international sources concerning individual responsibility for international crimes should also be considered the appropriate standard in respect of Article 1F(b).[73] The absence of clear international standards defining individual responsibility for serious non-political crimes means that any other approach would result in the fragmented application of individual responsibility in Article 1F(b) cases, depending on the criminal law of the domestic regime in which the asylum application fell to be considered. The principle that the 1951 Convention be interpreted so as to have one true autonomous meaning mandates an interpretive approach that applies internationally agreed rules and principles of individual responsibility to the application of the provision.

It may therefore be concluded that resort to international criminal law standards of responsibility is warranted for Article 1F(a) crimes, and, in the absence of clear international standards defining individual responsibility for serious non-political crimes and acts contrary to the purposes and principles of the United Nations, may also be appropriate sources for determining responsibility in the context of Articles 1F(a) and (c).[74]

---

72 See Chapter 7 for interpretation of 'serious reasons for considering' and standard of proof required in Article 1F cases. The wording 'has been guilty of' contained in Article 1F(c), as opposed to the 'has committed' contained in the previous two paragraphs of Article 1F, cannot be interpreted as inserting a different threshold for individual responsibility in the context of Article 1F(c). Zimmermann and Wennholz (n 68) 603.

73 ECRE, 'Position on Exclusion' (n 84) para 37.

74 However, some caution must be exercised when incorporating criminal law standards into the refugee status determination procedure. See for example Jennifer Bond's critique of the UNHCR's reliance on international criminal standards when applying Article 1F in relation to situations of mass influx. In particular, the UNHCR's practice of not taking into account mitigating circumstances while simultaneously relying on criminal law standards that presume such factors form part of the analysis. Bond J, 'Excluding Justice: The Dangerous Intersection between Refugee Claims, Criminal Law, and 'Guilty' Asylum Seekers' (2012) 24(1) International Journal of Refugee Law 37–59. The Michigan Guidelines similarly point out that, in contrast with criminal trials, decisions on refugee exclusion are binary – an individual either is or is not excluded from refugee status and as such this

If international criminal law standards are seen as the appropriate sources for determining Article 1F responsibility, then the problems with the *Gurung* approach to Article 1F exclusion appear even more pronounced. It will be recalled that under the *Gurung* doctrine, responsibility for the commission of Article 1F crimes could be incurred where an individual was a voluntary member of an organisation that is 'predominantly terrorist in character'. This approach to Article 1F responsibility based on simple membership of an organisation grounds individual responsibility in the *nature* of the organisation. However, this appears inconsistent with the standards of responsibility in international criminal law.

Whilst the various forms of participation which give rise to individual responsibility in international criminal law have different requirements regarding the *actus reus* and *mens rea*, they all share a common characteristic: under international criminal law, an individual cannot be held responsible for the criminal acts of an organisation as a result of their simple membership of that group. Although the London Charter contained provisions which effectively attributed individual responsibility on the basis of membership of a criminal organisation,[75] criminal responsibility on the basis of group membership has been consistently rejected by the ICTY.[76] As noted by the ICTY Trial Chamber in *Kvocka*:

> mere membership in a criminal organisation would not amount to co-perpetrating or aiding and abetting in the criminal endeavour implemented by that organization, despite knowledge of its criminal purpose. For liability to attach, it must be shown that either (1) the accused participated in some significant way, or (2) the accused held such a position of responsibility – for example commander of a sub-unit – that participation could be presumed.[77]

---

determination is not tempered by the sentencing process. Michigan Guidelines on the Exclusion of International Criminals, Sixth Colloquium on Challenges in Refugee Law, University of Michigan, 22–24 March 2013, para 3.

75 London Charter, arts 9 and 10. The IMT applied these provisions in criminalising several organisations including the Leadership Corps of the Nazi Party, the Gestapo, the SD, and the SS. Noted in Rikhof J, 'Complicity in International Criminal Law and Canadian Refugee Law' (2006) 4 Journal of International Criminal Justice 720.

76 *Prosecutor v Kvocka et al.* (Trial Judgment) ICTY-98-30/1-T (2 November 2001) [281]; *Prosecutor v Milutinovic et al.* (Appeal Judgment) ICTY-99-37-AR72, (21 May 2003) [24]-[26], [31]; *Prosecutor v. Milomir Stakic* (Trial Judgment) ICTY-97-24-T, (31 July 2003) [433]; *Prosecutor v. Blagoje Simic et al.* (Trial Judgment) ICTY-95-9-T, (17 October 2003) [153].

77 *Prosecutor v Kvocka et al.* (n 531) [281].

International criminal law does not focus on the nature of the group or organisation of which the individual is part when determining criminal responsibility, but rather whether the individual knowingly made a 'substantial' or 'significant' contribution to the commission of a crime, be this through committing the crime; participating in a 'joint criminal enterprise'; planning, instigating, ordering or aiding and abetting the planning, preparation or execution of the crime.[78]

Furthermore, it is not clear that the reversal of the burden of proof implied in the *Gurung* presumption of exclusion where the applicant is a voluntary member of an 'extremist terrorist organisation' is warranted in the context of Article 1F. Indeed, reversing the burden of proof appears to contravene one of the fundamental principles of international criminal law: the presumption of innocence.[79] Whilst the refugee status determination is an administrative decision, and therefore not subject to the right to fair trial contained in many human rights instruments,[80] it is generally recognised that the process is

---

78 For joint criminal enterprise (JCE) I: *Prosecutor v. Radoslav Brdjanin* (Appeal Judgment) ICTY-99-36-A, (3 April 2007) [430]; For JCE II: *Prosecutor v Kvocka et al.* (n 531) [97]; *Prosecutor v Tadic* (Appeal Judgment) (n 460). JCE III requires a lower standard of contribution, but the status of JCE II and III as a matter of customary international law are not clear. A person who 'solicits', 'induces' or 'orders' the commission of a crime must have been 'substantially contributing' to the conduct of the perpetrator. *Prosecutor v Kordic and Cerkez* (Appeal Judgment) ICTY-95-14/2-A, (17 December 2004) [27], [42]; *Sylvestre Gacumbitsi v. The Prosecutor* (Appeal Judgment) ICTR-2001-64-A, (7 July 2006) [129]. Aiding, abetting or otherwise assisting the principal to a crime can also suffice as a basis for criminal responsibility. Although the assistance need not be essential, it must have had a 'substantial effect' on the commission of the crime. *Prosecutor v Aleksovski* (Appeal Judgment) ICTY-95-14/1-A (24 March 2000) [162]; *Prosecutor v Blaskic* (Appeal Judgment) ICTY-95-14-A (29 July 2004) [46]; *Prosecutor v Vasiljevic* (Appeal Judgment) ICTY-98-32-A (25 February 2004) [102]; *Prosecutor v Tadic* (Appeal Judgment) (n 460). [229]. Subjectively, the individual must have been aware that they were supporting the commission of the crime and wished to provoke the commission of the crime, or be aware that there was a 'substantial likelihood' the commission of the crime would result from their actions.

79 The principle of the presumption of innocence, recognised in Art. 66 of the Rome Statute, provides: 'Everyone shall be presumed innocent until proved guilty before the Court in accordance with the applicable law'. To this end, '[t]he onus is on the Prosecutor to prove the guilt of the accused'.

80 For example, Council of Europe (CoE) European Convention for the Protection of Human Rights and Fundamental Freedoms (4 November 1950) ETS 5, Art. 6; UNGA International Covenant on Civil and Political Rights (16 December 1966) 999 UNTS 171, Art. 14. See Maaouia v France [2000] ECHR, application 39652/98.

subject to basic requirements for a fair procedure.[81] Indeed, it is well established in UK jurisprudence that in Article 1F decisions the burden of proof lies upon the Secretary of State to establish that Article 1F applies.[82] Bearing in mind the serious consequences of exclusion from refugee status, an approach that reverses the burden of proof has the potential to seriously compromise the protective object and purpose of the 1951 Convention.[83] Perhaps for these reasons, the UNHCR warns that caution must be exercised where such a presumption of responsibility arises, 'to consider issues including the actual activities of the group, its organisational structure, the individual's position in it, and his or her ability to influence significantly its activities, as well as the possible fragmentation of the group'.[84] However, these factors advocated by the UNHCR still focus primarily on determining the nature of the organisation, an aspect of the refugee status determination procedure that has presented considerable problems in practice and does not appear to be in line with the standards of individual responsibility employed in international criminal law.[85]

---

81 MacDonald Toal (n 365) 820; Gilbert, 'Current Issues' (n 188) 439, 461. The UNHCR Executive Committee formulated basic requirements for a fair procedure in 28th session in 1977. The ECRE recommend that safeguards of procedural fairness such as the presumption of innocence are entailed in Article 1F cases. ECRE, 'Position on Exclusion' (n 84) para 9.

82 As was recognised in the *Gurung* decision itself. *Gurung* (*Exclusion, Risk, Maoists*) (n 85) [93]-[94]. MT (*Article 1F (a) – aiding and abetting*) (n 185) [74]; *Azimi-Rad* (n 210) [15].

83 The Lawyers Committee for Human Rights also argues that it is contrary to the principle of procedural fairness to require an asylum applicant to demonstrate they are not implicated in excludable crimes. Lawyers Committee for Human Rights, 'Safeguarding the Rights of Refugees under the Exclusion Clauses: Summary Findings of the Project and a Lawyers Committee for Human Rights Perspective' (2000) 12 (Special Supplement) International Journal of Refugee Law 325. Saul also argues there is a real danger that the application of the presumption will lead to automatic and peremptory exclusion without affording a fair procedure. Saul B, 'Protecting Refugees in the Global "War on Terror" (n 5).

84 UNHCR Guidelines (n 65) para 19. Also noted by the tribunal in *Gurung* (*Exclusion, Risk, Maoists*) (n 85) [110].

85 Indeed it appears the UNHCR is revising this position. In her update on the UNHCR Guidelines on Exclusion, Kapferer notes that '[t]he notion of a "presumption" should not be understood to suggest that it could be justified to apply exclusion in the absence of sufficient factual basis supporting a finding of individual responsibility'. She further provides that 'denial of international refugee protection flowing from membership alone or otherwise based on criteria that are not in line with the requirements for establishing individual responsibility under international law would not be in keeping with the 1951 Convention'. Sibylle Kapferer, 'Revision of UNHCR's Guidelines' (n 7) 6.

The departure of the Supreme Court and the Court of Appeal from the *Gurung* approach to Article 1F responsibility in the *JS* (*Sri Lanka*) case may therefore be seen as a positive development in the jurisprudence on Article 1F responsibility. As was noted above, the *Gurung* approach to responsibility where an asylum applicant is a member of an organisation that is 'predominantly terrorist in character' is not in line with the standards of individual responsibility employed in international criminal law, which rather mandates an approach that focuses on the contribution to the commission of the crime made by an individual, rather than their membership of a particular organisation or group. However, the Supreme Court's decision in *JS* (*Sri Lanka*) is not without its difficulties, as will be considered below.

5 International Criminal Law and Lord Brown's Formulation of Article 1F Responsibility

In formulating the test of Article 1F responsibility in *JS* (*Sri Lanka*), Lord Brown based his approach on the ICTY's doctrine of joint criminal enterprise.[86] The doctrine of joint criminal enterprise can be traced back to the seminal case of *Tadic*, in which the ICTY Appeals Chamber held this mode of participation was grounded in post-World War II jurisprudence that had become part of customary international law, and was implicitly contained in Article 7(1) of the ICTY Statute.[87] This concept has subsequently also been adopted by the ICTR and hybrid criminal courts.[88]

Under the doctrine of joint criminal enterprise, a participator in a criminal act will be deemed individually responsible as a perpetrator of the act where there exists a 'common plan, design or purpose' among a plurality of persons

86 *JS* (*Sri Lanka*), *R* UKSC (n 69) [15]-[20].

87 *Prosecutor v Tadic* (Appeal Judgment) (n 460) [188] and subsequent. Participation in a joint criminal enterprise is a form of 'commission' under ICTY Statute Article 7(1). *Prosecutor v Krnojelac* (Appeal Judgment) ICTY-97-25-A (17 September 2003) [73].

88 *Prosecutor v Simba* (Trial Judgment) ICTR-01-76-T (13 December 2005) [385] et seq; *Prosecutor v Brima* (Appeal Judgment) SCSL-2004-16-A (20 June 2007) (Special Court for Sierra Leone) [61] et seq; *Prosecutor v Perriera*, Special Panels for Serious Crimes East Timor (27 April 2005) [19] et seq. According to the jurisprudence of the ICTY, the notion of joint criminal enterprise encompasses three different categories: the 'basic form', the 'systematic form' and the 'extended form', and each of these categories create different requirements regarding the respective *actus reus* and *mens rea*. However Lord Brown limited himself to the basic form of JCE, finding the other categories unhelpful. *JS* (*Sri Lanka*), *R* UKSC (n 69) [19].

which amounts to or involves the commission of a crime against international law, and the accused participates in this common design.[89] Whilst the individual need not have physically perpetrated the crime, they must have contributed to the common plan. The ICTY's joint criminal enterprise therefore has at its core: (i) a common plan, (ii) a significant contribution to that plan, and (iii) knowledge and criminal intent. However, in formulating the test for Article 1F responsibility Lord Brown curiously only mentions in passing the very aspect which makes joint criminal enterprise a unique form of liability in international criminal law: a common plan or design. Although Lord Brown's formula is couched in joint criminal enterprise language, it has been pointed out that the lack of reference to a common design makes it resemble another form of criminal liability, namely, aiding and abetting.[90]

Aiding or abetting can suffice as a basis for criminal responsibility in international law, as provided in Article 25(3)(c) Rome Statute and recognised under customary international law.[91] Although the assistance need not be essential, it must have had a 'substantial effect' on the commission of the crime.[92] The assistance can include encouraging the perpetrator, providing the means for the crimes commission or granting other moral support.[93] The person granting the assistance must be aware that his or her contribution is supporting the commission of the crime, however, it is not necessary that the aider and abettor knows the precise crime that was intended and that was committed, but he must be aware of the essential elements of the crime.[94] Crucially, in order for an individual to be found liable under this secondary mode of participation there is no requirement that they be part of or contribute to a 'common plan or design'.

Lord Brown's lack of reference to the crucial 'common plan' element of joint criminal enterprise means that either he has provided an incomplete definition of joint criminal enterprise, or he has collapsed all aspects of complicity into one type of criminal liability: aiding and abetting.[95] It has been suggested that in reality the judgment only seems to represent one type of extended liability, and that in practice this may lead the immigration tribunal to try and fit

---

89 *Prosecutor v Tadic* (Appeal Judgment) (n 460) [188].

90 As noted by Rikhof in *The Criminal Refugee* (n 72) 254–255.

91 *Prosecutor v Furundzija* (Trial Judgment) ICTY-95-17/1-T (10 December 1998) [192] et seq.

92 *Prosecutor v Aleksovski* (n 533) [46]; *Prosecutor v Vasiljevic* (n 533) [102]; *Prosecutor v Tadic* (Appeal Judgment) (n 460) [229].

93 *Prosecutor v Furundzija* (n 546) [231] et seq.; *Prosecutor v Tihomir Blaskic* (n 533) [48].

94 *Prosecutor v Aleksovski* (n 533) [162]; *Prosecutor v Vasiljevic* (n 533) [102].

95 Rikhof, *The Criminal Refugee* (n 72) 254–255.

all forms of participation into the 'straightjacket' of joint criminal enterprise, rather than other easier and often more appropriate forms of extended liability.[96] Perhaps for this reason more recent decisions of the immigration tribunal have preferred to focus on the aiding and abetting form of liability in the context of Article 1F.[97]

Furthermore, attention must be drawn to the list of 'factors' outlined by Lord Brown in the Supreme Court, which he advised should be taken into account by a decision maker when determining Article 1F responsibility, and which 'ultimately must prove to be the determining factors in any case'.[98] It will be recalled that these factors included (i) the nature and the size of the organisation (ii) whether and, if so, by whom the organisation was proscribed, (iii) how the asylum-seeker came to be recruited, (iv) the length of time he remained in the organisation and what, if any, opportunities he had to leave it, (v) his position, rank, standing and influence in the organisation, (vi) his knowledge of the organisation's war crimes activities, and (vii) his own personal involvement and role in the organisation.[99]

Although an individual's standing an rank in an organisation may be relevant to an assessment of whether an individual is responsible for the commission of crimes under international criminal law,[100] factors such as the nature and size of the organisation and whether or not it is proscribed appear to tend

96 Ibid. 254–255. Gilbert similarly notes that domestic courts are increasingly referring to decisions of the international courts and tribunals when determining Article 1F responsibility, although the simpler inchoate crimes of aiding and abetting would usually suffice. Gilbert G, 'Exclusion under Article 1F since 2001: two steps backwards, one step forward' (n 6).

97 *MT (Article 1F (a) – aiding and abetting)* (n 185) [131]; *AS (S.55)* (n 210) [99].

98 *JS (Sri Lanka), R* UKSC (n 69) [30].

99 Ibid., [30].

100 Anyone that orders the commission of a crime under international law is criminally liable. An order assumes the existence of a hierarchal relationship, typically military in nature. The perpetrator uses his or her authority to cause another person to commit a crime. *Prosecutor v Kordic and Cerkez* (n 533) [28]; *The Prosecutor v Nahimana, Barayagwiza, Ngeze* (Appeal Judgment) ICTR-99-52-A (28 November 2007) [481]. Article 28 Rome Statute furthermore provides that commanders and superiors are responsible for crimes committed by forces under their effective command and control, because of their failure to exercise proper control over such forces. The Statutes of the ICTY and ICTR provides that the fact that a crime was committed by a subordinate: 'does not relieve his or her superior of criminal responsibility if he or she knew or had reason to know that the subordinate was about to commit such acts or had done so and the superior failed to take the necessary and reasonable measures to prevent such acts or to punish the perpetrators thereof'. ICTY Statute Article 7(3); ICTR Statute Article 6(3).

back towards the *Gurung* and *Ramirez* focus on the nature of an organisation when determining Article 1F responsibility. This may make it possible for tribunals to engage in an assessment of whether the organisation is 'predominantly terrorist in character'.[101] As noted above, criminal liability in international criminal law focuses on the contribution of the individual to the commission of an international crime, rather than details of an individual's membership of a particular organisation. Indeed, in his separate opinion in the *JS (Sri Lanka)* case, Lord Kerr cautioned:

> While the six factors that counsel identified will frequently be relevant to that evaluation, it seems to me that they are not necessarily exhaustive of the matters to be taken into account, nor will each of the factors be inevitably significant in every case. One needs, I believe, to concentrate on the actual role played by the particular person, taking all material aspects of that role into account so as to decide whether the required degree of participation is established.[102]

It appears that Lord Brown's reliance on these factors is a move back towards the *Gurung* and *Ramirez* approach to responsibility and away from than that of the international criminal tribunals. While examination of these factors might prove practically useful to decision makers unfamiliar with the standards of individual responsibility employed in international criminal law, this approach may import factors into an assessment of Article 1F responsibility that are not strictly relevant.[103]

6 Conclusions

Terrorism has featured to a large extent in the UK's interpretation of responsibility for the purpose of Article 1F. This has arisen primarily in relation to the extent to which an asylum applicant can be held responsible for the commission of the activities of a terrorist group or organisation of which they are a

---

101 Rikhof, *The Criminal Refugee* (n 72) 254.

102 *JS (Sri Lanka), R* UKSC (n 69) [55].

103 Indeed, this factor approach was developed in Canadian jurisprudence and therefore Lord Brown's endorsement of this approach might be seen as a step back towards the *Ramirez* approach to exclusion. Simeon J C, 'Complicity and Culpability' (n 72) 130. See also Rikhof J, 'War criminals not welcome' (n 479) 465 for development of the 'factor approach' in Canada.

member. The leading case on Article 1F responsibility in the UK for a number of years was the *Gurung* decision of the immigration tribunal, in which responsibility for the commission of an Article 1F act could be presumed where the individual was a voluntary member of an organisation that is 'predominantly terrorist in character'. However, a number of practical difficulties emerge when trying to characterise an organisation in this way. An approach which is based on the inclusion of an organisation in a proscribed terrorist list has been cautioned against, and in many cases such groups may be fractured and pursue their political objectives in part through acts of terrorism, but also engage in legitimate acts of political persuasion. Indeed, the Supreme Court and Court of Appeal recently disapproved the *Gurung* approach to exclusion, preferring to approach the question of Article 1F responsibility through recourse to standards of criminal liability employed in international criminal law rather than focus on the 'terrorist' nature of an organisation.

The Supreme Court's approach to determining Article 1F responsibility appears to be a positive development in the jurisprudence surrounding Article 1F, as it would appear that international criminal standards are a more appropriate source for determining the standards of responsibility in the context of the provision. However, the Supreme Court's formulation of Article 1F responsibility is not without its difficulties. Lord Brown's formulation of Article 1F responsibility seems to collapse all aspects of criminal complicity into one type of criminal liability, an approach that may in practice prove difficult for immigration tribunals to apply in practice and lead them away from applying other easier and often more appropriate forms of extended liability. Furthermore, Lord Brown's reliance on a number of 'factors' when determining whether an individual may be considered responsible for the commission of an Article 1F act may import considerations that are not strictly relevant to such an assessment, and indeed seems to tend back towards the *Gurung* focus on the 'terrorist' nature of an organisation of which an individual is a member.

CHAPTER 6

The Application of Article 1F

The UK does not at present publish comprehensive data on exclusion from refugee status under Article 1F. This means that it is extremely difficult to establish what is happening in practice in relation to the application of the provision on the ground As explained by a member[1] of the Home Office's Special Cases Unit (SCU):

> SCU 1: "But of course at the root of all this, which is for you, and for me and for the judiciary, is the lack of reliable data. It isn't recorded by them it isn't recorded by us, particularly at appeal."

A number of sources are therefore drawn on in this chapter in an attempt to provide an overview of the application of Article 1F in the UK. These sources include data provided by the Home Office in response to a number of Freedom of Information (FOI) requests made by the present researcher, questionnaires and interviews conducted with immigration judges sitting in tribunals throughout the UK, interviews conducted with legal practitioners and a member of the Home Office's SCU team and analyses of published cases concerning Article 1F.[2] These sources will be employed in answering a number of questions relating to exclusion under Article 1F in the UK:

- When is Article 1F raised?
- Which limb of Article 1F is relied upon in exclusion decisions?
- How often is Article 1F raised, and has this changed over time?
- Who is being excluded under Article 1F?

Throughout this examination particular attention will be given to the application of Article 1F to suspected terrorists.

---

1 The interviewee has ten years experience of working for both the War Crimes Unit and Special Cases Unit within the Home Office. They have personally handled and overseen scores of Article 1F cases and was the lead Home Office official on the *JS* (*Sri Lanka*) case.

2 See Methodology section in Chapter 1.

 | DOI 10.1163/9789004292062_008

1 When Article 1F is Raised

Article 1F can be raised at a number of stages during the asylum process in the UK: at the initial decision of the Home Office, on appeal or to revoke or cancel refugee status previously granted. The majority of asylum applications which raise Article 1F issues are handled by the Home Office's Special Cases Unit (SCU).[3] A small number of Article 1F cases are also dealt with by the Criminal Casework Directorate.[4] When an asylum applicant is deemed to fall under Article 1F in the initial decision of the Home Office, their asylum application is refused and the reasons for this decision are communicated to them in a 'Reasons for Refusal' letter. The Secretary of State will also issue a certificate (known as a section 55 certificate) to the effect that Article 1F has been applied.[5] Article 1F may additionally be raised in the Reasons for Refusal letter as a supplementary ground of refusal, i.e. the application for asylum is refused on the grounds that the applicant does not have a well-founded fear of persecution, but even if they did have such a fear they would nevertheless be excluded from refugee status by virtue of Article 1F.

When an individual has not been excluded from refugee status under Article 1F at initial decision, exclusion may nevertheless be raised at the appeal stage, either by the Home Office or the appeal tribunal. This normally occurs when an asylum application has been refused by the Secretary of State on the grounds that the asylum applicant does not in fact have a well-founded fear of persecution and the applicant appeals this decision. Article 1F issues may arise before the tribunal when Article 1F was raised as a supplementary ground of

---

3 The SCU team deals not only with asylum cases, but also manages residence permits, visas and citizenship applications where these cases raise issues of the applicant's criminal conduct. In addition, the SCD screens applicants who have applied for resettlement through the UNHCR, to ensure that individuals who fall to be excluded under Article 1F are not resettled in the UK via this route. A Watch List is also maintained by several bodies working with state security in order to identify individuals who attempt to enter the UK at visa posts, airports and other checkpoints. Individuals for whom there are serious reasons for considering fall within the scope of Article 1F are refused entry to the UK. Maria Bergram Aas, 'Exclusion from Refugee Status: Rules and practices in Norway, Canada, Great Britain, The Netherlands and Denmark' (2013) Norwegian Directorate of Immigration, 109–110.

4 The Criminal Casework Directorate manages cases of foreign criminals facing deportation.

5 Immigration, Nationality and Asylum Act 2006, s 55 (this was previously s 33 of the UK Anti-terrorism Crime and Security Act 2001, which has now been repealed and replaced by s 55 of the 2006 Act).

refusal in the Reasons for Refusal letter or as a result of additional evidence given by the asylum applicant during cross-examination. Immigration Judges have a legal duty to consider exclusion in cases that raise Article 1F criminality issues even when this has not been raised by the Home Office.[6]

Article 1F may also be raised by the Secretary of State to cancel or revoke a grant of refugee status from a person previously recognised as a refugee.[7] Cancellation of refugee status may occur where information subsequently comes to light which provides serious reasons for considering the individual should have been excluded by virtue of Article 1F. In this case, a person's refugee status may be cancelled on the basis that Article 1F applies. Additionally, an individual's refugee status may be revoked where, subsequent to the grant of asylum, a person engages in activity falls within the scope of Article 1F(a) or (c).[8]

From the sources analysed, it seems that in the overwhelming majority of cases Article 1F is raised by the Home Office at initial decision. Figure 1 shows the responses given when judicial participants were asked when, in their experience, Article 1F is most often raised. Over 85% of judicial participants indicated Article 1F is most often raised in the initial decision of the UKBA.[9]

> Judge B: "I think mostly in my experience exclusion cases mostly present when the decision maker has made a section 55 certification. Before it gets to the first tier tribunal it's already an exclusion case really. I certainly, in my very limited experience, haven't seen anything in the last couple of years where the Secretary of State has tried to raise it in the course of proceedings."

This finding is supported by the cases analysed as part of this research. Table 1 shows when Article 1F was raised in these cases, and reveals that in 52% of cases the individual was excluded under Article 1F at initial decision, and in a

6 *Gurung (Exclusion, Risk, Maoists)* (n 85) [151].

7 Home Office Exclusion APG, Part 7.

8 Article 1F(b) is geographically and temporally limited to acts committed outside the country of refuge prior to being committed to that country as a refugee. Articles 1F(a) and (c) are not limited in this manner.

9 In a pattern common to a number of figures in this chapter, the percentages cited in this figure total more than 100%. This is because a number of judicial participants indicated more than one option in their response. Percentages are therefore given as 'percentage of respondents providing a positive answer' to the particular instance when Article 1F is raised, rather than as a 'percentage of respondents'.

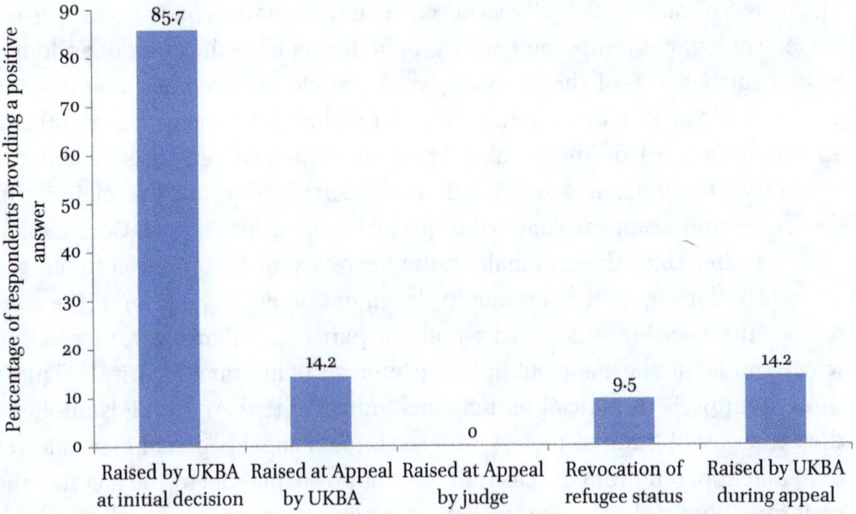

FIGURE 1 *When immigration judges consider Article 1F is most often raised (n = 21).*[10]

TABLE 1 *When Article 1F is raised, case analysis (n = 25).*[11]

	Secretary of state: initial decision	Secretary of state: supplementary reasons	Secretary of state: on appeal	Secretary of state: revocation	Immigration judge
Frequency	13	2	3	4	4
% of total cases[12]	52%	8%	12%	16%	16%

10 For 11 participants the question was not applicable as they stated Article 1F had never been raised before them. 2 participants stated that too few cases had come before them to be able to answer the question. Data was missing for 2 participants.

11 Appeals heard together concerning 1F were counted as separate cases. This analysis excludes duplicate cases as they proceeded through the high courts. In one case analysed the immigration judge also raised limb (b) of Article 1F, where (a) and (c) were the grounds of the initial decision of the Secretary of State, so in total there were 25 cases but 26 instances of Article 1F being raised.

12 Percentages rounded to nearest whole number.

further 8% of cases Article 1F was raised by the Secretary of State in the reasons for refusal letter as a supplementary ground for refusing the grant of asylum.

In a further 16% of the cases analysed, Article 1F was relied upon by the Secretary of State to revoke refugee status that had previously been granted to an individual. All of these cases involved suspected terrorists whom the Secretary of State sought to exclude under Article 1F(c). In the majority of these cases initial appeal went to the Special Immigration Appeals Commission (SIAC) rather than the tribunal, as the Secretary of State had certified the appeals under s.97 of the Nationality, Immigration and Asylum Act (the 2002 Act) as the decision was based wholly or partly in reliance on information which should not be made public in the interests of national security.[13] Figure 1 shows that 9.5% of judicial participants indicated that Article 1F is raised by the Secretary of State to revoke refugee status. That this percentage is lower than that apparent from the case analysis may be explained by the fact that the majority of judicial participants that responded to questionnaires had experience sitting at the tribunal rather than the SIAC, and it is therefore likely they would not have come across cases in which revocation of refugee status was intertwined with national security issues.

Article 1F is also frequently raised during appeal, either by a tribunal judge or Home Office Presenting Officer (HOPO), when it hasn't previously been considered by the Home Office at initial decision. Table 1 shows that in 12% of the cases analysed as part of this research Article 1F was raised by the Home Office during the appeal. Similarly, Figure 1 shows that 14.2% of judicial participants indicated that Article 1F is raised by the Border Agency during the appeal.

> Judge 3: "In the cases that have come before me the vast majority have arisen during oral evidence at which it becomes apparent that there are issues which the UKBA have not previously taken on board and they decide during the course of the hearing that they wish to consider Article 1F."
>
> Judge D: "It was raised by a HOPO at the hearing which to me was an example of someone who has thought it should have been raised earlier."
>
> Judge 10: "Once arose as a result of answers given in [cross examination of the asylum applicant]."

However, no judicial participants indicated Article 1F is often raised by an immigration judge during the appeal. In only 16% of the cases analysed as part

13 See Chapter 7 for the appeals procedure.

of this research was Article 1F raised by the immigration judge hearing the case at appeal, rather than by the Home Office. However, it is clear that there is a legal duty on tribunal judges to consider Article 1F if the issue arises, even if this hasn't been raised by the Secretary of State.[14]

> Barrister E: "I'm certainly conscious of cases where exclusion wasn't raised by the decision maker, where it then fell to be raised by the tribunal *ex officio*, sometimes without the assistance of the decision maker having considered exclusion at all."
> SCU 1: "Another issue which stretches back to the *Gurung* determination, which is still good law to some extent, is the notion that if we don't raise the exclusion clause it's still incumbent on the judge to consider it."

Article 1F was raised by tribunal judges, rather than the Home Office, in the earliest reported Article 1F cases analysed as part of this research: the seminal cases *T v Secretary of State for the Home Department* and *Gurung v Secretary of State for the Home Department*.[15] Since the *Gurung* determination in 2002, however, Article 1F has only been raised by the judiciary in two of the cases analysed, and in one of these cases Article 1F(b) was simply considered in addition to the 1F(a) and (c) grounds relied upon by the Secretary of State. Thus while the early cases show a predominance of Article 1F being raised by the judiciary, this trend does not seem to have continued in more recent cases.

It may be concluded that in the overwhelming majority of Article 1F cases exclusion is raised by the Home Office at initial decision, although it is also relied upon by the Home Office to revoke refugee status and is sometimes raised during the course of an appeal by the Home Office or occasionally by an immigration judge.

A similar pattern appears when Article 1F is raised in relation to suspected terrorists. Table 2 shows when Article 1F was raised in the cases involving suspected terrorists analysed as part of this research. In 40% of the cases analysed Article 1F was raised by the Secretary of State at initial decision or as a supplementary ground for refusal (as compared to 60% in the overall case analysis). The proportion of cases in which Article 1F is raised by the Secretary of State on appeal remains similar, with 13% for cases relating to suspected terrorists and 12% in the overall case analysis. However, in the cases involving suspected terrorists there is a marked increase in the number of cases in which Article 1F is relied upon to revoke refugee status (27% in cases involving suspected

14 See n 564 and accompanying text.

15 *T* (n 166); *Gurung (Exclusion, Risk, Maoists)* (n 85).

TABLE 2 *When Article 1F is raised in relation to suspected terrorists, case analysis (n = 15).*[16]

	Secretary of state: initial decision	Secretary of state: supplementary reasons	Secretary of state: on appeal	Secretary of state: revocation	Immigration judge
Frequency	4	2	2	4	3
% of total[17] cases	27%	13%	13%	27%	20%

terrorists as opposed to 16% in the overall case analysis). There is also a slight increase in the proportion of cases in which exclusion is raised by the immigration judge (20% in cases involving suspected terrorists as opposed to 16% in the overall case analysis), although this result appear to be influenced to a large degree by the early *T* and *Gurung* cases considered above.

It therefore seems to be more common for Article 1F to be relied upon by the Secretary of State to revoke refugee status in cases involving suspected terrorists. Indeed, there were no cases analysed in which Article 1F was relied upon to revoke refugee status other than in relation to suspected terrorists.

This difference may be due to the nature of the criminal acts at issue. Individuals excluded on the basis they have committed a war crime or crime against humanity (under Article 1F(a)) are likely to have committed this act outside the UK, since these are crimes committed in the context of an armed conflict or a widespread and systematic attack upon a population. Similarly, Article 1F(b) requires serious non-political crimes to have been committed *outside* the country of refuge *prior* to his admission to the country as a refugee. In cases involving crimes that are allegedly committed outside the UK it is more likely that exclusion under Article 1F will be considered during the initial asylum application process rather than at a later date, as it is unlikely that information which implicates the individual in the commission of an excludable crime will be brought to the attention of the Home Office by a foreign state after an individual has been granted refugee status (unless it is a particularly high profile case). Conversely, under Article 1F(c) individuals may be excluded for committing terrorist acts in the UK, after being granted refugee status, since

16 Appeals heard together concerning 1F were counted as separate cases. This analysis excludes duplicate cases as they proceeded through the high courts.

17 Percentages rounded to nearest whole number.

there are no similar temporal and geographical limitations as are found in Article 1F(b).[18] An individual suspected of committing a serious crime in the UK or abroad after being granted refugee status will therefore likely fall to be excluded under Article 1F(c), and such a case will concern revocation of previously granted refugee status. Since terrorism has explicitly been held to fall under Article 1F(c), it is likely that a number of the individuals excluded from refugee status under this provision will be described as terrorists. Article 1F is therefore more likely to be relied upon to revoke refugee status where the individual is alleged to be a terrorist and falls under Article 1F(c), as considered in Section 2.3 below.

Overall, it seems that in the majority of cases Article 1F is raised in the initial decision of the Home Office, although in cases which involve suspected terrorists the provision is often relied upon to revoke refugee status.

2 The Limb of Article 1F That is Relied upon

From the above discussion it is clear that the question of when Article 1F is raised is intimately linked to the limb of Article 1F that is relied upon to exclude an individual from refugee status, which is the topic of this section.

2.1 *The Limb of Article 1F Relied upon by the Secretary of State*

The vast majority of cases that are referred to the Home Office's SCU and ultimately excluded under Article 1F by the Home Office at initial decision fall under 1F(a) (war crime or crime against humanity). Figure 2 displays the mean number of initial decisions, per annum, that the different limbs of Article 1F were relied upon by the UK Border Agency between 2008 and 2013. Article 1F(a) was relied upon in nearly 80% of exclusion decisions, with Article 1F(b) (serious non-political crime) and Article 1F(c) (acts contrary to the purposes and principles of the United Nations) relied upon approximately equally.

The reliability of the information displayed in Figure 2 may be limited however, in that the data outlines the refusals based on limbs (a), (b) and (c) of Article 1F separately, and does not therefore indicate instances where the limbs were relied upon in conjunction, or indeed, where no particular limb of Article 1F was specified in the refusal decision. However, the responses provided by judicial participants to the questionnaires appear to support the reliability of the trends indicated by the Home Office data, as considered below.

---

18 See Chapter 4. Indeed, in the majority of revocation cases the key issue concerned the temporal and geographical limitations of Article 1F(c).

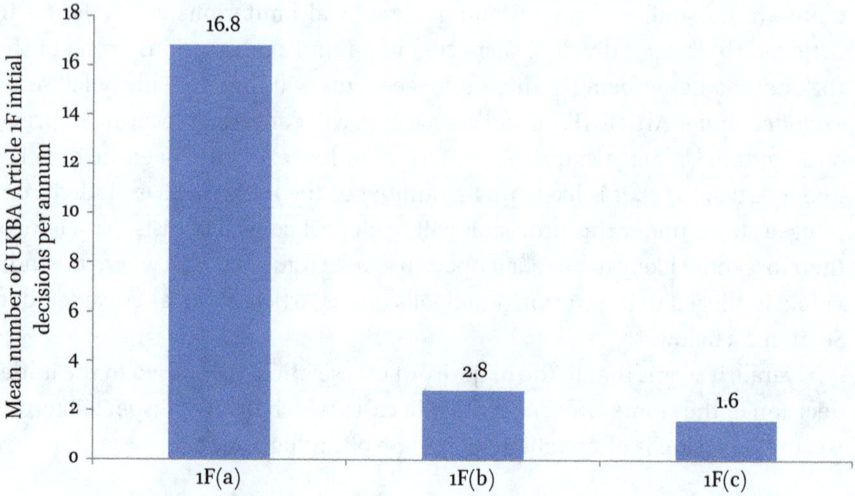

FIGURE 2 *The mean number of UKBA Article 1F initial decisions per annum, 2008–2013.*[19]

Figure 3 shows the data provided by judicial participants when asked which limb(s) of Article 1F they consider to be most often relied upon by the Home Office in Article 1F decisions. Figure 3 reveals a similar pattern of results to the Home Office data, in that judicial participants consider Article 1F(a) to be by far the most frequently relied upon limb of Article 1F, whilst Article 1F(c) is the least frequently relied upon. It also appears that judicial participants do not consider it very common for the different limbs of Article 1F to be relied upon in combination (only 15% of participants indicated this option), and no participants raised the issue of no particular limb(s) of Article 1F being specified in the refusal decision.[20] This serves to increase the reliability of the Home Office data, as it appears to be a minority of cases in which the limbs of Article 1F are relied upon in conjunction and no instances of non-specification of the limb relied upon has been raised.

> Judge 2: "1F(b) used to be virtually only limb. 1F(a) now more common."
> Judge D: "I think it's usually one that's relied on and it's usually war crimes [1F(a)]."

19 Figures for 2012 and 2013 are provisional.

20 Again, percentages cited in this figure total more than 100%, as a number of judicial participants selected more than one limb of Article 1F in their response. Percentages are therefore given of respondents providing a positive answer to the limb of Article 1F in question.

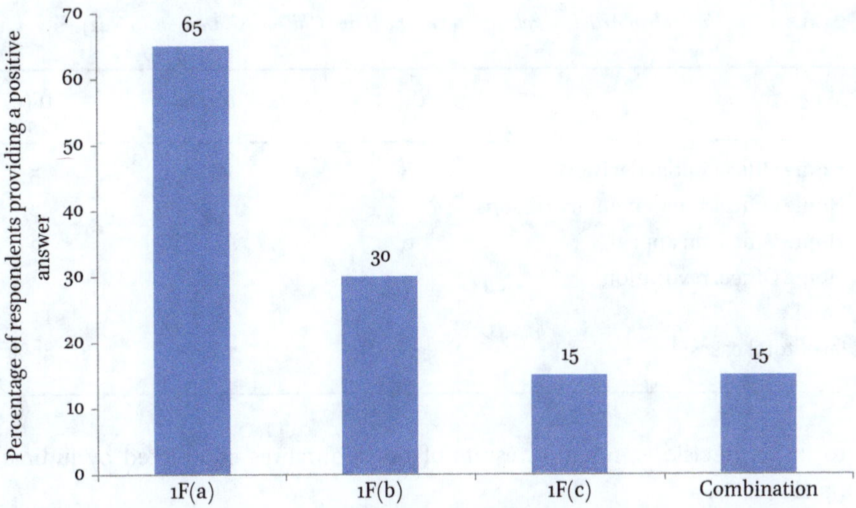

FIGURE 3 *The limb of Article 1F judicial participants consider is most often relied upon by the Home Office (n = 20).*[21]

Judge 14: "b and c."
Judge 23: "The allegation in my one case was involvement in a crime against humanity [1F(a)]."
Judge 33: "Generally all three."
Judge B:" I suppose to the extent that I get feedback...there seem to be more 1F(a)'s."

The results of the Home Office data and responses of judicial participants analysed above reveal that Article 1F(a) is overwhelmingly the limb of Article 1F that is relied upon by the Home Office in exclusion decisions. However, the results of the case analysis conducted as part of this research reveal somewhat more nuanced results. Table 3 shows the number of cases in which the different limbs of Article 1F were relied upon by the Home Office, and reveals that although Article 1F(a) is relied upon by the Home Office in a large number of cases, it is 1F(c) that is relied upon most frequently. Indeed, Article 1F(c) was relied upon by the Home Office in 59% of cases.

That Article 1F(c) is relied upon in such a large proportion of these cases is curious, as it doesn't accord with the data provided by the Home Office relating

21 For 11 participants the question was not applicable as they stated Article 1F had never been raised before them. 3 participants stated that too few cases had come before them to be able to answer the question. Data was missing for 2 participants.

TABLE 3 *The limb of Article 1F relied upon by the Home Office, case analysis (n = 22).*[22]

When raised	1F(a)	1F(b)	1F(c)
Home Office: initial decision	8	2	5
Home Office: supplementary reasons	0	0	2
Home Office: on appeal	0	2	2
Home Office: revocation	0	0	4
Total	8	4	13
% of total cases[23]	36%	18%	59%

to initial decisions, nor the results of questionnaires completed by judicial participants.

The reason for the large number of 1F(c) cases that appear in the case analysis may be due to the nature of the provision itself. As considered in Chapter 4, jurisprudence on the meaning of the phrase 'acts contrary to the purposes and principles of the United Nations' that appears in Article 1F(c) is still very much in development. It may therefore simply be the case that permission to appeal to the Upper Tribunal and higher courts is allowed in more cases involving Article 1F(c) than the other limbs of Article 1F which are more certain in their scope, as the judiciary seek to clarify this area of law. Therefore the high number of Article 1F(c) cases that appear in the case analysis may not be truly representative of the proportion of cases involving this ground of exclusion.

The low number of Article 1F(c) cases that appear in both the Home Office data and responses of judicial participants might also be due to the nature of the cases concerned. A large number of the cases in which Article 1F(c) was relied upon by the Home Office involved revocation of refugee status where the initial appeal went to the SIAC rather than the tribunal. All of these cases involved revocation of refugee status as a result of the individual's suspected terrorist activities after they were granted refugee status in the UK.[24] That these revocation cases were not picked up on in the responses of judicial

22 Appeals heard together concerning 1F were counted as separate cases. This analysis excludes duplicate cases as they proceeded through the high courts. In two cases (b) and (c) were relied upon in conjunction while in one case (a) and (c) were relied on in conjunction.

23 Percentages rounded to nearest whole number.

24 *Abu Qatada* (n 334); *bb v Secretary of State for the Home Department* [2006] UKSIAC 39/2005; *Y* (n 287); *C v Secretary of State for the Home Department* (n 330).

participants is unsurprising, as the overwhelming majority of judges that responded to the questionnaires sat in the immigration tribunals rather than the SIAC.[25] The revocation cases were also not covered by the Home Office data, which relates only to initial decisions of the Border Agency and therefore do not include instances where Article 1F is raised at a later time, i.e. upon appeal or revocation.

That Article 1F(c) was relied upon by the Secretary of State in these revocation cases may be explained by the fact that, as considered above, the acts that may fall within the scope of this limb of Article 1F are not temporally or geographically limited. As such, this provision can therefore be relied upon to exclude individuals on the basis of acts committed in the UK after being granted refugee status.

However, it may be concluded that, aside from when Article 1F is relied upon to revoke refugee status, in the overwhelming majority of Article 1F cases one limb of Article 1F is relied upon by the Home Office, and this is Article 1F(a): war crime or crime against humanity. It seems there are two primary reasons that this limb of Article 1F is relied upon over and above (b) and (c), which relate to the development of Article 1F screening by the Home Office and the nature of asylum applications in the UK, as will be considered in more detail below.

2.1.1 The Development of Article 1F Screening by the Border Agency

An important reason that 1F(a) is relied upon by the Home Office at initial decision over and above the other grounds of exclusion seems to be related to the development of Article 1F screening by the Home Office. From the mid-1990's to the early 2000's there was 'virtually no application of 1F at all'[26] by the Home Office. However, in 2003 the War Crimes Unit of the Border Agency was established. This Unit's remit was closely tied to the government policy of no safe haven for war criminals. It was at this stage that the Border Agency began proactively screening asylum applications for possible exclusion under Article 1F. Because the specialisation of the War Crimes Unit was the commission of international crimes, this category of exclusions received the most attention.

> SCU 1: "We were dealing with international crimes and that was our remit… In fact before we were assimilated into Special Cases we probably hardly ever thought of Article 1F(b) or (c)."

25 See Methodology section in Chapter 1.

26 SCU 1.

Systematic screening of immigration cases in search of individuals who should be excluded under Article 1F(a) started in 2005, whereas screening for 1F(b) and (c) cases is still in the early stages of development.[27] The War Crimes Unit was fully assimilated into the Special Cases Unit in 2009 and over the last three years has also begun to focus more on screening for 1F(b) and (c) grounds for exclusion.

> SCU 1: "1F(b) will probably be increasingly used as we at the Directorate take in more cases, but again you're probably talking two or three years down the line."

At present over 80% of cases referred to the SCU and excluded from refugee status at initial decision by the Home Office fall under Article 1F(a).[28]

2.1.2 The Nature of Asylum Claims

Another reason that Article 1F(a) is relied upon by the Home Office over the other limbs of Article 1F relates to the nature of asylum claims in the UK. Unsurprisingly, a large number of asylum applications in the UK emanate from conflict-ridden zones. As explained by the Home Office in their Immigration Statistics report:

> World events have an effect on which nationals are applying for asylum at any particular time. For example, there have been increases in the number of applicants from Syria since the outbreak of the Syrian civil war in early 2011. Since the early nineties increasing numbers of people have sought asylum from Eritrea in the circumstances of international concern over human rights within the country.[29]

Figure 4 displays the top ten nationalities that applied for asylum in the UK in 2013. This year saw Pakistan, Iran, Sri Lanka and Syria the top countries of nationality of asylum applicants in the UK. The years 2012, 2011 and 2010 also saw Pakistan, Iran and Sri Lanka as top countries of nationality of asylum applicants, while there were also a substantial number of applicants from

---

27 Aas 'Exclusion from Refugee Status' (n 561) 110.

28 Ibid. 110.

29 Home Office, Immigration Statistics October to December 2013, Section 8.3, Asylum table as 01 q. https://www.gov.uk/government/publications/immigration-statistics-october-to-december-2013/immigration-statistics-october-to-december-2013#asylum-1> accessed 2 December 2014.

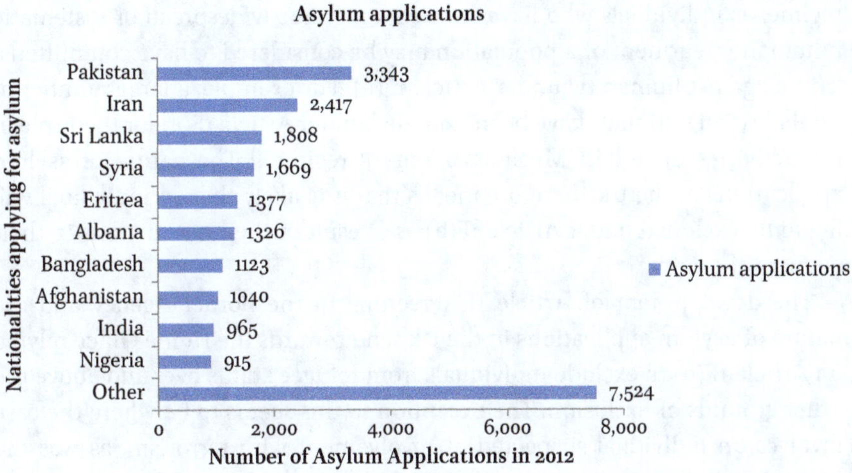

FIGURE 4 *The top ten nationalities applying for asylum in the UK in 2012 (Total number of applications = 23,507).*[30]

Afghanistan, Syria and Libya. In 2010 Zimbabwean nationals came top with 2,435 applications for asylum.

Countries like Sri Lanka, Afghanistan, Syria and Libya, which feature highly in the countries of nationality, have all experienced large scale internal or international conflicts in recent years. Asylum applicants from conflict zones that are suspected of committing serious crimes are likely to have committed this crime in the context of the armed conflict. As such, their crime is likely to fall under Article 1F(a) as a 'war crime'.

> Barrister H: "A lot of people claiming asylum will be claiming asylum in the context of having taken a side in a conflict, and when you take a side in a conflict and find your case is that you're going to be in trouble in your own country because you are deemed as being 'on the other side', it's not that surprising that issues about what you did as part of your activity in the conflict might raise an exclusion issue."

Asylum applicants who come from non-conflict zones may also fall under Article 1F(a) where they have played a role in the activities of a repressive

30 Home Office, Immigration Statistics October to December 2013, Section 8.3, Asylum table as 01 q. https://www.gov.uk/government/publications/immigration-statistics-october-to-december-2013/immigration-statistics-october-to-december-2013#asylum-1.

regime, as individuals who have assisted a regime's widespread or systematic inhumane treatment of a population may be considered to have committed a 'crime against humanity' under Article 1F(a). For example, a large number of Zimbabwean nationals have been excluded under Article 1F(a) for their role in the activities of Robert Mugabe's Zanu-PF regime.[31] The nature of asylum applications in the UK therefore means that it is likely that an individual will fall to be excluded under Article 1F(a) as a result of their past actions in their country of origin.

The development of Article 1F screening in the Border Agency and the nature of asylum applications in the UK tend towards the Home Office relying on Article 1F(a) to exclude individuals from refugee status over and above the other grounds of exclusion. The exception to this seems to be where the case involves an individual suspected of involvement with terrorism, as was the case with the revocation cases discussed above. The limb of Article 1F relied upon by the Home Office to exclude suspected terrorists from refugee status will be considered in Section 2.3 below.

2.2 *The Limb of Article 1F Raised by Immigration Judges*

In a very small number of cases analysed as part of this research Article 1F was raised by the immigration judge hearing the case at appeal, rather than by the Home Office. Table 4 shows the number of cases in which the different limbs of Article 1F were raised by an immigration judge hearing an asylum appeal. In the majority of these cases 1F(b) was raised. These include the seminal cases *T v Secretary of State for the Home Department* and *Gurung v Secretary of State for the Home Department,* which both involved the exclusion of suspected terrorists and are the earliest reported Article 1F cases analysed as part of this

TABLE 4 *The limb of Article 1F raised by immigration judges, case analysis (n = 4).*[32]

When raised	1F(a)	1F(b)	1F(c)	Total
Immigration judge	0	3	1	4

31 CM *(Article 1F(a) – superior orders) Zimbabwe* [2012] UKUT 236 (IAC); SK *(Zimbabwe)* (n 69); MT *(Article 1F (a) – aiding and abetting)* (n 185).

32 This analysis excludes duplicate cases as they proceeded through the high courts. In one case 1F(a) and (c) had been relied upon by the Home Office at initial decision and the tribunal also chose to consider 1F(b).

research. It may be tentatively concluded that Article 1F(b) is the most common limb of Article 1F raised by immigration judges, although the sample size is too small to make any firm findings on this matter.

It has been suggested that Article 1F(b) might be the preferred limb of Article 1F raised by immigration judges because the provisions relationship with the law of extradition makes it more familiar to judges than the concepts 'war crime', 'crime against humanity' or 'acts contrary to the purposes and principles of the United Nations'.

> Barrister E: "And in a sense I would have thought, considering the case law, that in most cases where (b) is raised nowadays, the courts find that easier because that refers to concepts with which they are more familiar because that is non-political crime, a concept of law which most lawyers have grown up with and most judges will have had exposure to elsewhere. Concepts under (a) are much more based in public international law, and of course the fast moving and changing area of international criminal law, which they may not be familiar with. And 1F(c) is in one sense not connected to any area of law they might be familiar with because it doesn't link into identifiable crimes or acts but is linked to a number of concepts such as the purposes and principles of the United Nations and acts contrary to those purposes and principles, neither of which are easy concepts to identify or construe."

However, it is not possible to make any firm findings here since Article 1F seems to be raised by the judiciary in only a minority of cases.

2.3 *The Limb of Article 1F Relied upon in Relation to Suspected Terrorists*

Figure 5 shows the number of cases analysed as part of this research in which the different limbs of Article 1F were raised by the Secretary of State in relation to suspected terrorists. In the overwhelming majority of cases concerning suspected terrorists Article 1F(c) was raised by the Secretary of State. Indeed, 1F(c) was relied upon in 83% of cases, while in the remaining 17% Article 1F(c) was relied upon in conjunction with 1F(b). There were no instances of the Home Office relying exclusively on 1F(b), and 1F(a) was not relied upon at all in relation to suspected terrorists.

It therefore seems that in the majority of cases involving suspected terrorists Article 1F(c) is relied upon by the Home Office as the ground of exclusion. This is unsurprising, since terrorism has explicitly been declared to fall within the scope of Article 1F(c) in resolutions of the United Nations General Assembly and Security Council, the EU's Qualification Directive and domestic

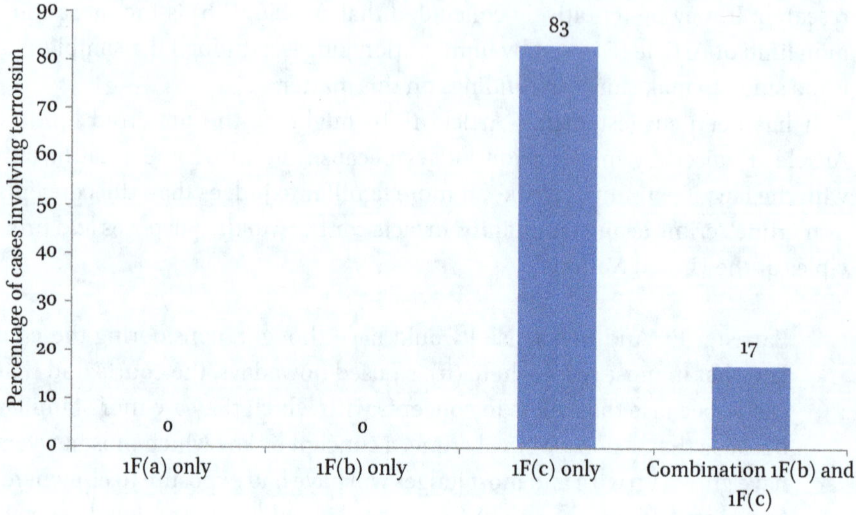

FIGURE 5 *The limb of Article 1F relied upon by the Secretary of State in cases involving terrorism, case analysis (n = 12).*[33]

legislation. As noted above, all the cases analysed as part of this research in which Article 1F was relied upon to revoke refugee status concerned the exclusion of suspected terrorists under Article 1F(c).

2.3.1 The Use of Articles 1F(b) and 1F(c) to Exclude Suspected Terrorists from Refugee Status

Historically, 1F(b) was the limb of Article 1F relied upon to exclude suspected terrorists from refugee status. This was the limb of Article 1F raised by immigration judges in the early cases *T* and *Gurung*. In both of these cases, the judiciary explicitly held that, although Article 1F(b) refers to serious *non-political* crimes, terrorists acts are capable of falling within the scope of the provision.[34]

> Judge B: "I think if you go back to the period straight after 9/11 then it was mainly 1F(b) that was being used."

However, in more recent years there seems to have been a move on the part of the Secretary of State to rely on Article 1F(c) rather than 1F(b). There seem to be a number of reasons for this change in approach.

---

33 Appeals heard together concerning Article 1F were counted as separate cases. This analysis excludes duplicate cases as they proceeded through the high courts.

34 See Chapter 3.

Firstly, as noted above, Article 1F(c) is not temporally or geographically limited in the same manner as Article 1F(b), and can therefore be relied upon in cases involving revocation of refugee status. Indeed, in the majority of revocation cases the key legal issue that had to be determined by the SIAC was whether or not Article 1F(c) is geographically or temporally limited.[35] The SIAC held it was not,[36] and therefore the Secretary of State has been free to rely on this provision to exclude individuals who have allegedly committed terrorist acts in the UK after being granted refugee status. As noted above, all the cases analysed as part of this research in which Article 1F was relied upon to revoke refugee status concerned the exclusion of suspected terrorists under Article 1F(c).[37]

A further reason that Article 1F(c) may have been relied on by the Secretary of State over 1F(a) and (b) concerns the nature of the acts the asylum applicant is alleged to have been involved in. Article 1F(b) requires that a specific crime be committed and that the crime be 'serious'. Similarly, for an act to fall within the scope of Article 1F(a) it must meet the level of gravity required to constitute an international crime. Whilst the implication of Article 1F(c) is that for an act to be considered 'contrary to the purposes and principles of the United Nations' it must be a serious crime, this requirement is not explicitly mentioned in the provision and therefore there has been greater scope for interpretation on this point. As the UN has repeatedly declared that 'acts methods and practices of terrorism are contrary to the purposes and principles of the United Nations' without referring to a legal definition of the term, the meaning of terrorism for the purpose of Article 1F(c) in recent years has not been clear.[38] In the UK this resulted in the extremely broad definition of terrorism being employed in the interpretation of the provision and the Supreme Court has only recently held that only acts that violate the purposes and principles of the United Nations in a 'fundamental manner' fall under Article 1F(c).[39] As such, the nature of acts considered to fall within Article 1F(c) in recent years may

35 See Chapter 4.

36 A point confirmed by the House of Lords in *rb* (*Algeria*) (n 360).

37 Indeed, Hathaway and Foster note that all too often the fact that Article 1F(c) is not temporally limited is relied upon as a basis for ignoring the true purpose of the provision in favour of an approach that focuses on the security of the host state, a factor more appropriately considered under Article 33(2) of the 1951 Convention. As a result, Article 1F(c) has today become something of a 'ravenous omnivore'. Hathaway J, and Foster, M, *The Law of Refugee Status* (n 254) 594.

38 For judicial definitions of terrorism for the purpose of Article 1F(c) see Chapter 4.

39 Immigration, Asylum and Nationality Act 2006, s 54; *Al-Sirri* [2012] (n 13).

have been greater in scope than those considered to fall under Articles 1F(a) or (b).[40]

In many cases the Secretary of State may have chosen to rely on Article 1F(c) over the other limbs of Article 1F, as this ground of exclusion may have been interpreted as including a broader scope of excludable acts. As terrorism has explicitly been held to fall under Article 1F(c) in UN resolutions and regional and domestic legislation, it is unsurprising that, when relying on this provision, these individuals were described as 'terrorists' by the Home Office. A large proportion of judicial participants also considered Article 1F(c) was often relied upon by the Home Office in cases involving suspected terrorists, as will be considered below. However, it may that in practice Article 1F(a) is being relied upon in the vast majority of cases involving suspected 'terrorists', and these individuals are simply not being described as such.

2.3.2 The Use of Article 1F(a) in Relation to Suspected Terrorists

Figure 6 shows the responses provided by judicial participants when asked which limb of Article 1F they consider to be most often relied upon by the Home Office in relation to individuals suspected of involvement with terrorism. The majority of participants that responded to this question considered Articles 1F(a) and (c) were most often relied upon, with Article 1F(b) relied upon much less regularly. Two participants indicated a combination of limbs was relied upon, one of which specified the combination was 1F(a) and (c).

Whilst the responses of judicial participants support the finding that in a large proportion of cases concerning suspected terrorists Article 1F(c) is relied upon by the Home Office, a curious result is that a large proportion of judicial participants also considered 1F(a) is often relied upon. In the cases analysed as part of this research there were no instances in which Article 1F(a) was raised in relation to suspected terrorists. Indeed, the word 'terrorism' was not

---

40 Indeed, There have also been a number of cases in which Article 1F(c) was relied upon by the Home Office to exclude from refugee status individuals who had been engaged in military activity against governmental forces. It appears that Article 1F(c) was relied on in these cases rather than Article 1F(a), as the acts in question did not constitute war crimes within the meaning of Article 1F(a). The Court of Appeal however in a number of cases rejected the argument that violence directed against governmental military forces constituted terrorism for the purpose of Article 1F(c), maintaining a distinction between activity directed against civilians and against government forces. This has been confirmed by the Supreme Court in *Al-Sirri* [2012] (n 13). See Chapter 4 for further consideration of this distinction.

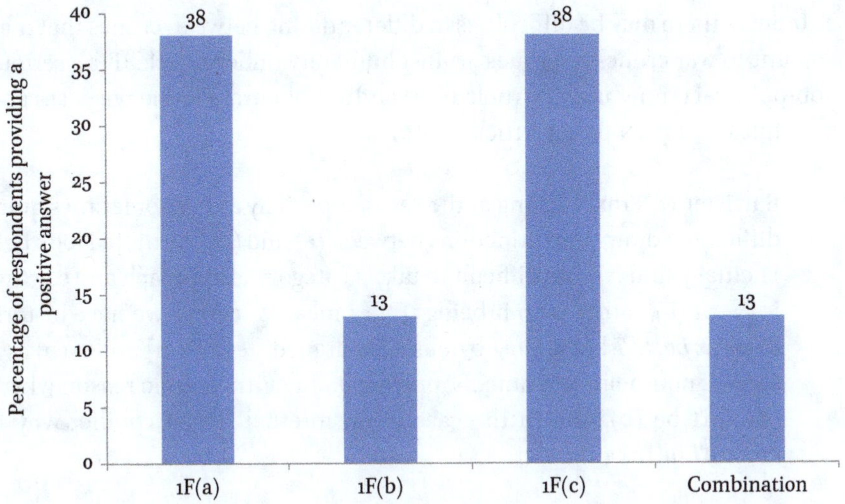

FIGURE 6 *The limb of Article 1F judicial participants consider is most often relied upon by the Home Office in relation to suspected terrorists* ($n = 12$).[41]

mentioned in any of the cases analysed in which Article 1F(a) was considered.[42]

The implication here is that, whilst 'terrorism' may not explicitly feature in the majority of cases in which the Home Office relies on Article 1F(a) to exclude individuals from refugee status, judicial participants nevertheless perceive the individuals to be terrorists. For example, a military combatant engaged in an armed conflict for whom there is evidence they committed atrocities against civilians will likely be excluded from refugee status by the Home Office not on the basis that they are a 'terrorist' as such, but, as the alleged act was committed in the context of an armed conflict, under Article 1F(a) on the basis that they have committed a 'war crime'. Nevertheless, that the individual is alleged to have committed atrocities against civilians may mean that judicial participants perceive the individual to be a terrorist, even if this terminology does not feature in the Home Office's grounds for exclusion nor the tribunal determination.

41 For 22 participants the question was not applicable as they stated Article 1F had never been raised before them in relation to an individual suspected of involvement with terrorism. 1 participant stated that too few cases had come before them to be able to answer the question. Data was missing for 1 participant.

42 Except in relation to the disapproving the *Gurung* approach to complicity in the *JS* (*Sri Lanka*) cases. There was one 1F(a) case in which reference was made to initial decision of tribunal in which terrorism mentioned, but did not constitute substance of case.

Indeed, there may be difficulties in differentiating between crimes that may amount to war crimes or crimes against humanity under Article 1F(a), serious non-political crimes under Article 1F(b) and acts contrary to the purposes and principles of the UN under Article 1F(c).

> Barrister E: "From looking at the cases, especially as it is sometimes quite difficult to draw the distinctions between (a) and (c), the more I look at it I actually find it quite difficult to take a categorical approach and say this is (a) or (c), rather than it being 1F. ... I mean of course we have historically, *ex parte T* being the obvious case, argued [terrorism] under (b) as a serious non-political crime... Applying it after *T* there is no reason why it couldn't be (b), and in the case of an internal armed conflict why it couldn't be (a) either."

The Home Office's asylum process guidance itself points out that:

> 'Acts of terrorism are widely considered contrary to the purposes and principles of the United Nations, and may potentially fall within Article 1F(c). But they may also fall within Article 1F(b) because acts of terrorism are not necessarily political crimes, or even within Article 1F(a)'.[43]

The responses of judicial participants indicate that in a number of cases in which the asylum applicant could potentially be classed as a 'terrorist', or are perceived as such by the judiciary, the Home Office relies on Article 1F(a) rather than 1F(c) to exclude the individual from refugee status. There are a number of reasons this might be the case.

Firstly, as noted above, the development of Article 1F screening in the Border Agency means that the units within the Home Office that consider Article 1F cases have been more specialised in the definitions of war crimes and crimes against humanity than 'terrorism' per se. Therefore, when the past activities of an asylum applicant could equally be characterised as a crime against humanity or an act of terrorism, it may be that the Border Agency staff are more familiar with crime against humanity and therefore classify the act as such. It is also acknowledged that Article 1F(a) offences are easier to define than 'acts contrary to the purposes and principles of the United Nations', and as such this is a more concrete ground of exclusion, as considered further below.

Furthermore, the nature of asylum applications in the UK might tend towards acts being classified as war crimes or crimes against humanity rather

43 Home Office Exclusion APG, s 2.5.

than acts of terrorism. As noted above, a large proportion of asylum applications in the UK are from nationals of conflict-ridden countries or those fleeing repressive regimes. It is therefore likely that an excludable act was committed in the context of an armed conflict or in support of such a regime, which may tend towards exclusion being considered under Article 1F(a), a provision more suited to consideration of such crimes, rather than Article 1F(c) which is more uncertain in its scope. This may also be because the interpretation of 'terrorism' by courts and tribunals in the UK does not include a number of forms of military activity committed during armed conflict.[44]

Where it is difficult to differentiate whether an excludable act should fall under Article 1F(a) or (c), overall Article 1F(a) may be the preferred ground of exclusion for the Home Office because it refers to more concrete international legal standards contained in international criminal law instruments than the imprecise phrase 'acts contrary to the purposes and principles of the United Nations' contained in Article 1F(c). Furthermore, international guidance on the interpretation of Article 1F(c) stresses that, due to the vague nature of Article 1F(c), it should only be relied upon in exceptional circumstances. Where possible, recourse should rather be made to the more certain Articles 1F(a) or (b).[45,46]

> SCU 1: "I think 1F(c) is vague and difficult to pin down. Most of the reasons to exclude someone are covered by 1F(a) and 1F(b) anyway, 1F(c) has a sort of residual character. It has also been, perhaps wrongly, used as a counter-terrorism exclusion clause."
>
> Judge B: "I think my reading of it anyway is that *Al-Sirri* essentially confirms UNHCR approach in that it [1F(c)] shouldn't be the first recourse

44 See n 600.

45 Indeed, Articles 1F(a) and (b) provide adequate means to exclude individuals who have perpetrated serious terrorist crimes from the protection of the 1951 Convention. These provisions furthermore lay out far more specific requirements than Article 1F(c) in relation to the material elements of the crime. It has therefore been suggested that Article 1F(c) should be approached as an 'exclusion of last resort'.

46 Nyinah (n 191) 310. Hathaway and Foster also point out that the amorphous nature of Article 1F(c) as too frequently applied facilitates the evasion of the rigours of pursuing exclusion under the most applicable grounds, a result of which is that 'all of the subtlety and precision mandated by Arts. 1(F)(a) and (b) is lost'. They argue that Article 1F(c) ought to be applied 'in a way that does not ride roughshod over other aspects of Art. 1(F) and the Convention more generally', and be given a meaning that allows it to perform a distinct function. Hathaway and Foster, *The Law of Refugee Status*, n 68, 593–594. See Chapter 4 for more.

just because something that looks like terrorism is involved. And so if you take 1F(c) out of the picture, then I suppose 1F(a) is the most obvious clause to use. And…it's easier for a judge to look at a case and say are there certain crimes being committed here by reference to international legal standards than saying well is this person a terrorist, and what does that mean in terms of the combination of our domestic terrorism legislation and the Refugee Convention and the Qualification Directive and so on so…its easier for us than trying to engage with the issue of terrorism *per se.*"

Barrister E: "*JS* (*Sri Lanka*) is the classic case in the Supreme Court where it is not classed as terrorism [but as a war crime]."

Barrister A: "An act of terrorism could in principle be a war crime of course. There's no reason to exclude terrorism from war crimes, it's a matter of applying international law, and determining what is a war crime. And 1F(b), serious non-political crime, again, it could fall within that. And UNHCR's view is absolutely clear, that because you've got more clearly defined provisions in 1F(a) and 1F(b), you really want to be starting there. If you're looking at a situation in the context of an armed conflict, then you need to analyse the whole case under IHL [international humanitarian law]. And if something is a war crime under IHL, then you'd be looking at a case of exclusion based on 1F(a)."

Overall, Article 1F(a) seems to be the limb of Article 1F overwhelmingly relied upon by the Home Office in exclusion decisions, although in cases where terrorism is explicitly cited as the ground of exclusion it seems to be Article 1F(c) that is relied upon over and above the other limbs of Article 1F. Whilst the predominance of Article 1F(a) cases may simply be a fortunate result of the nature of asylum claims and the history of Article 1F screening in the Border Agency, the Home Office's trend towards relying on Article 1F(a) over the other grounds of exclusion where possible ensures recourse to more objective international legal norms than the vague terms 'terrorism' and 'acts contrary to the purposes and principles of the United Nations' encapsulated in Article 1F(c), and appears to be in line with the residual character of Article 1F(c) and the restrictive approach it advised be adopted in the interpretation of the provision.

3 How Often Article 1F is Raised

At present, the Home Office's SCU receives around 150–200 potential Article 1F referrals per year. Ultimately around a quarter of potential Article 1F cases that are referred to the SCU result in an exclusion decision.[47] Table 5 shows the number of individuals excluded from refugee status under Article 1F at initial decision by the UKBA between 2008 and 2013. This data reveals that Article 1F exclusion decisions represent an extremely small number of initial UKBA decisions in the UK, on average only 0.1% of initial decisions and 0.2% of refusals.[48] It is also notable that Article 1F(a) (war crime, crime against humanity) is by far the limb of Article 1F most often relied upon by the UKBA at initial decision.

Exclusion under Article 1F therefore represents an extremely small number of initial decisions made by the Border Agency. The Home Office data is displayed in chart form in Figures 7 and 8. These figures reveal that there has been a slight increase in the use of Article 1F during this time period. The main feature of this increase has been a rise in reliance on Article 1F(a), which rose from 11 to 26 in the period 2008–2010, before falling again from 2011–2013.[49] The

TABLE 5 *The number of UKBA Article 1F exclusions at initial decision, 2008–2013.*[50]

Year	Total initial decisions	Total refusals under Article 1F	Refusals under Article 1F(a)	Refusals under Article 1F(b)	Refusals under Article 1F(c)	Refusals under Article 1F as a proportion of initial decisions
2008	19,398	14	11	0	3	0.07%
2009	24,287	20	16	3	1	0.08%
2010	20,261	26	26	0	0	0.13%
2011	17,380	31	23	5	3	0.18%
2012	16,774	21	15	5	1	0.13%
2013	17,647	16	10	4	2	0.09%

47 SCU 1. This seems to include instances where Article 1F is raised as a supplementary ground of refusal.

48 Data on the total number of refusals made by the UKBA were also included in the data provided by the Home Office but due to space constraints have not been included in Table 5.

49 Although the data for 2012 and 2013 is provisional. The reason for this dip seems to be restructuring of SCU at UKBA. SCU 1: 'Internally we'd just been restructured, the war crimes unit was essentially disbanded, it's actually not that less people were eligible for 1F(a) exclusion, it's probably just that we just weren't getting round to processing the cases as quickly because we were dealing with new workstreams as a result of the restructure ... The key point is that we were getting more work and had less staff'.

50 Data for 2012 and 2013 is provisional.

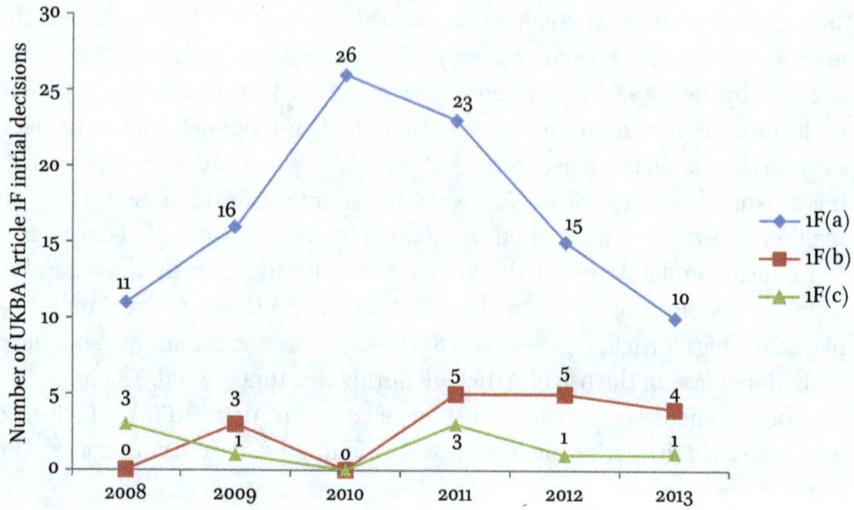

FIGURE 7 *The number of* UKBA *Article 1F initial decisions 2008–2013.*[51]

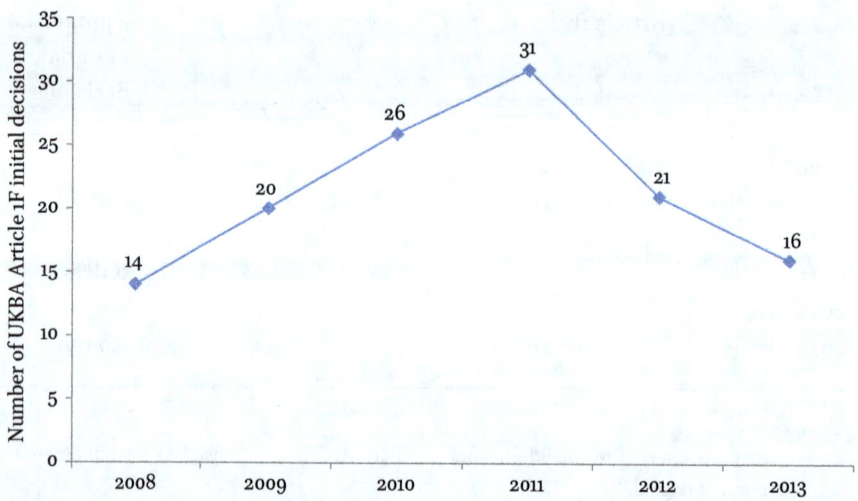

FIGURE 8 *The total number of* UKBA *Article 1F initial decisions 2008–2013.*[52]

51 Data for 2012 and 2013 is provisional.

52 Data for 2012 and 2013 is provisional.

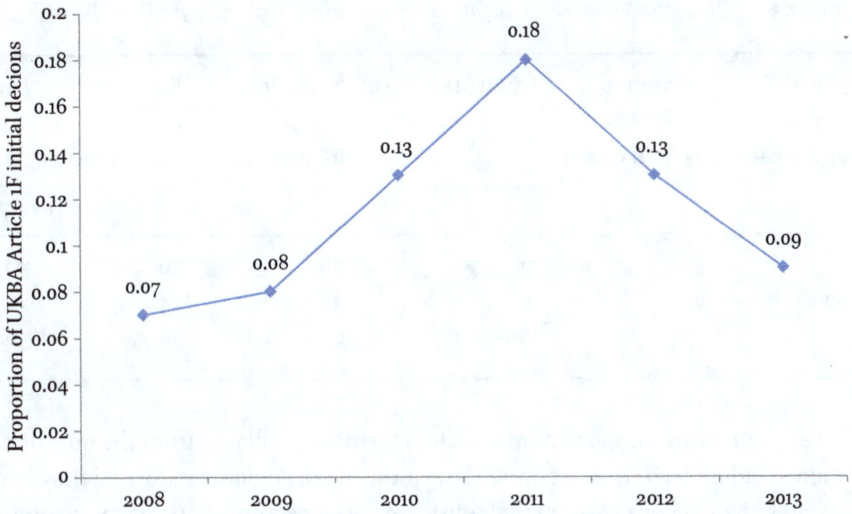

FIGURE 9 *The total number of UKBA Article 1F initial decisions 2008–2013 as proportion of total initial decisions.*[53]

use of Article 1F(c) and (b) appear to have remained relatively constant over this time period, with only a very small increase in the use of Article 1F(b) in 2011 and 2013. When the number of Article 1F initial decisions is given as a proportion of the total number of decisions made by the UKBA rather than by frequency, the same trends can be observed (see Figure 9).

Figures 7, 8 and 9 show that, while there has been a slight increase in the use of Article 1F at initial decision between 2008 and 2013, there has not been a significant increase and exclusion under Article 1F has remained exceptionally applied.

Table 6 details the responses given by judicial participants when asked how often, in their experience, Article 1F is raised by the Home Office. The results support the conclusion that Article 1F is raised very infrequently in the UK. The overwhelming majority of participants (97.3%) indicated that Article 1F is raised by the Home Office "Rarely" or "Never."[54]

53 Data for 2012 and 2013 is provisional.

54 It must also be noted that a number of judicial participants explained that although they indicated 'Rarely' as their response, they had actually only had strictly speaking less than 1% of Article 1F cases. Similarly, a number of participants indicated 'Never' although they had come across a small number of Article 1F cases, but not enough to meet the 1% threshold of 'Rarely'. These inaccuracies, however, do not detract from the conclusion that the overwhelming majority of participants considered Article 1F to be raised 'Rarely' or 'Never'.

TABLE 6 *How often judicial participants consider Article 1F is raised by the Home Office.*

Percentage of respondents providing a positive answer	**Very often (61–80% of asylum cases)**	**Often (41–60% of asylum cases)**	**Sometimes (21–40% of asylum cases)**	**Rarely (1–20% of asylum cases)**	**Never**
n	36	36	36	36	36
Frequency	0	0	1	24	11
Percent %	0%	0%	2.8%	66.7%	30.6%

These figures are supported by anecdotal evidence collated from the questionnaires and interview transcripts. Many judicial participants indicated they had dealt with only 1 or 2 cases in their entire experience, some had dealt with none.

> Judge 23: "As far as I can remember I have only ever had one case."
> Judge 7: "Only 1 time in entire career."
> Judge D: "The number of cases where Article 1F is used is very infrequent… It's only going to be a couple a year at the moment. …it's not a big issue. At the moment it's not a big issue."
> Judge 29: "Sorry to be unhelpful but in all my years of sitting [14 years] this issue has never been raised before me."
> Judge 13: "I do not recollect the last time I dealt with such an appeal."
> Judge 10: "Only done 4 in all the time I've been sitting."
> Judge 11: "My perception is that Art 1F is rarely used. The topic was covered in a Training Conference some years ago and only one [Immigration Judge] in my group had any practical experience of the exclusion clause."
> Judge 16: "I have only twice come across it."
> Judge 18: "Unlike some other jurisdictions (e.g. Canada), Article 1F is rarely used in the UK."

Judicial participants reported a very low number of Article 1F cases. Indeed, a number of participants indicated they could not complete the questionnaire as they had never come across such a case. Some indicated they had dealt with so few cases they could not reliably provide responses to many of the questions.[55] The responses of judicial participants support the exceptional nature

55 For 11 judicial participants the remainder of the questionnaire was not applicable as they stated Article 1F had never been raised before them in relation to an individual

of Article 1F decisions apparent from the Home Office data. However, there are a number of factors that must be taken into account when considering the small number of Article 1F cases that have come before judicial participants.

One reason that a number of judicial participants that responded to questionnaires may have encountered a particularly small number of Article 1F cases is that decisions to allocate cases by the Presidential team may be made on the basis of a Judges' seniority or experience. Judges who are not senior and/or do not have experience in Article 1F cases may not therefore be allocated these cases as often as other judges who have more relevant experience.

Another reason judicial participants may have encountered a particularly small number of Article 1F cases is due to the limitations on the right of appeal against a decision to exclude under Article 1F.[56] An individual excluded from refugee status under Article 1F but who can nevertheless not be removed from the UK on human rights grounds may appeal against the Secretary of State's decision to grant him limited leave to remain. However, the right to appeal the Secretary of State's refusal of the asylum claim is limited to those who have been granted leave to enter or remain in the UK for a period exceeding one year.[57] An individual excluded under Article 1F who cannot be removed from the UK on human rights grounds will be granted Restricted Leave, a form of leave is usually granted for a maximum period of six months at a time.[58] An individual excluded from refugee status will therefore have to have this form of leave renewed twice before they have leave to appeal to the tribunal against the exclusion decision.

> SCU 1: "There is also a little kind of grey area in this: have you heard of restricted leave? Some of these cases that are excluded that may appear in your figures are not necessarily going into the appeal system, and sometimes they can be on restricted leave for quite a long time."

However, all the data employed in this study supports the conclusion that Article 1F decisions represent an extremely small proportion of the total

---

suspected of involvement with terrorism. Various participants were unable to answer specific questions as too few cases had come before them, as specified in the individual results tables and figures throughout this chapter.

56 See Chapter 7 for more on this.

57 2002 Nationality, Immigration and Asylum Act, s 83.

58 Home Office, 'Interim Asylum Instruction: Restricted Leave', 28 May 2012, s.1.5 <https://www.gov.uk/government/uploads/system/uploads/attachment_data/file/257436/restricted-leave-article-1f-pdf.pdf> accessed 4 December 2014.

TABLE 7 *How often judicial participants with experience in Article 1F cases consider Article 1F is raised by the Home Office in relation to an individual suspected of involvement with terrorism (n = 23).*[59]

Percentage of respondents providing a positive answer	Very often (61–80% of Article 1F cases)	Often (41–60% of Article 1F cases)	Sometimes (21–40% of Article 1F cases)	Rarely (1–20% of Article 1F cases)	Never (0% of Article 1F cases)
n	23	23	23	23	23
Frequency	3	3	3	3	11
Percent %	13%	13%	13%	13%	48%

number of asylum decisions made in the UK: the use of this provision appears be very exceptional.

3.1 *How Often Article 1F is Raised in Relation to Suspected Terrorists*

In total, 36% of judicial participants that completed questionnaires as part of this research had had experience in a case in which Article 1F had been raised in relation to a suspected terrorist. Table 7 shows the responses of judicial participants with experience in Article 1F cases when asked how often they considered Article 1F is raised by the Home Office in relation to an asylum applicant suspected of involvement with terrorism. The majority of judicial participants stated that such a case had never been raised before them, whilst those that had heard such a case were divided over how often Article 1F is raised is this respect.

Case analysis reveals a much higher proportion of Article 1F cases involving individuals suspected of involvement with terrorism, with 67% of the cases concerning terrorism.[60]

There are a number of factors which may explain the difference between the case analysis results and the responses of judicial participants. Firstly, it may simply be that individuals excluded on the ground they are suspected of

59 For 11 participants the question was not applicable as they stated Article 1F had never been raised before them. 2 participants stated that too few cases had come before them to be able to answer the question.

60 16 of 24 cases. Appeals heard together concerning 1F were counted as separate cases. This analysis excludes duplicate cases as they proceeded through the high courts.

involvement with terrorism are more often granted leave to appeal to the higher courts and tribunals. Indeed, 73% of the Article 1F cases analysed in which terrorism was raised concerned exclusion under Article 1F(c), whilst a further 13% concerned exclusion on (b) and (c), respectively.[61] As noted previously, the phrase 'acts contrary to the purposes and principles of the United Nations' contained in Article 1F(c) is particularly vague, as is the term 'terrorism'. These cases may appear more often in the case analysis simply because leave to appeal to the higher courts and tribunals is granted more often in cases concerning Article 1F(c) as higher courts seek to clarify this area of law.

Another reason for the difference between the case analysis results and the responses of judicial participants may relate to the nature of the cases themselves. Cases involving suspected terrorists are much more likely to go to appeal before the SIAC rather than the tribunal, as the cases are more likely to be based on evidence that the Secretary of State considers should not be made public in the interest of national security. Indeed, 40% of the Article 1F cases concerning suspected terrorists that were analysed as part of this study were heard by the SIAC.[62] Since the judicial participants that responded to questionnaires as part of this study overwhelmingly have experience of the tribunal system rather than experience sitting at the SIAC, they may not have come across as many of these cases.

> Judge A: "I can't remember dealing with a pure terrorism case. They tend to be allocated to judges at Field House, which is part of SIAC, because special security clearance is needed to deal with some of this evidence."

It may therefore be that in practice a higher number of Article 1F cases involve suspected terrorists than indicated by the judicial participants that took part in this research.

4 The Increase in the Application of Article 1F

Although the Home Office data indicates that the use of Article 1F has remained fairly constant over the last five years (see Figures 7, 8 and 9), there has been an increase in the application of the provision by the Home Office in the last

61 11 of the 15 cases were solely based on 1F(c), two on 1F(b) and (c) together and two on 1F(b) alone.

62 Six of the 15 cases. All of these cases concerned Article 1F(c), rather than (b) or (a).

decade. Before the establishment of specialised units within the Border Agency it seems there was very little application of Article 1F by the Home Office.

> SCU 1: "Historically, mid-90's to early noughties where there was no War Crimes Unit, there was no aggressive use of screening, virtually no application of 1F at all…basically before my team existed, the old War Crimes Unit, you would be talking about less than 5 exclusions a year, we're talking tiny figures, so although we might have figures of 30 per year [at present], that is actually representing quite a significant sea change."
> Interviewer: "So you do think there has been quite a big increase then?"
> SCU 1: "Yes, yes, in comparison to 10 years ago. So I would say since probably about 2004, from then on there was a general pick up in exclusion under the Convention, but we are not talking scores of people each year."
> SCU 1: "A really key point from my perspective is that 10 years ago it [Article 1F] wasn't really being used at all but there has been a marked increase since about 2004. This is further evidenced by the number of cases, involving 1F(a) in particular, that have made it to the Upper Tribunal, Court of Appeal or Supreme Court in the last five years. There is little doubt in my mind that this has been as a direct result of our screening for suspects. All of the cases that have made the higher courts were originally referred to us."

The establishment of specialised units within the Border Agency seems to have contributed to an increase in the application of Article 1F by the Home Office.

Judicial participants, however, were divided over whether or not there had been an increase in the use of the provision. Figure 10 displays the responses provided by judicial participants when asked if they considered the use of Article 1F had increased, decreased or remained the same in the time they had been sitting as an immigration judge. Whilst there were clearly differences of opinion between judicial participants, the majority of participants were of the opinion that the number of Article 1F cases had remained the same in the time they had been sitting. Less than half this number thought use of the provision had increased, and a very small minority felt it had decreased.

> Judge 2: "It appears to go up and down but overall, and surprisingly, I don't see it has gone up."
> Judge 14: "[Increased] In the sense that it was raised hardly at all but a little more now."
> Judge D: "Increase. Definitely using it more."
> Judge A: "It tends to come in waves."

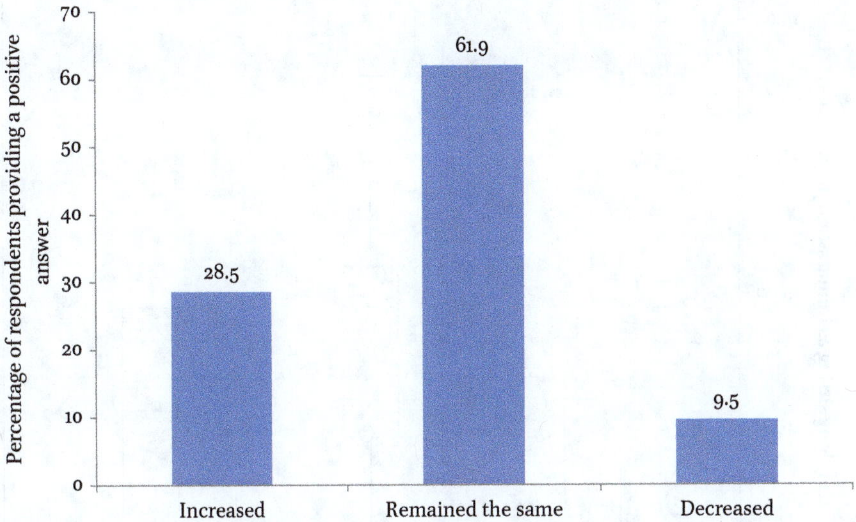

FIGURE 10 *Judicial participant's opinion on whether the use of Article 1F had increased, decreased or remained the same in the time they had been sitting (n = 21).*[63]

When these responses were analysed according to the number of years the participants had been sitting as immigration judges, no clear link emerged between the response given and how long judicial participants had been sitting.

Figure 11 shows how long judicial participants had been sitting as immigration judges, divided by the response given to the question of whether the use of Article 1F had increased, decreased or remained the same in the time they had been sitting. Those that considered the use of the provision had remained the same had a higher median number of years sitting (13 years) than those that considered the use of the provision had increased (9 years) or decreased (10.75 years). Judicial participants that considered the use of the provision had remained the same also had a wider range of years sitting (18 years) than those that considered the use of Article 1F had increased (13 years) or decreased (7.5 years), encapsulating both those with the longest and shortest experience sitting as an immigration judge. However, the differences between these groups are so small that it is not safe to draw conclusions as to whether the length of time the judicial participants had been sitting as immigration judges

63 For 11 participants the question was not applicable as they stated Article 1F had never been raised before them. 3 participants stated that too few cases had come before them to be able to answer the question. Data was missing for 1 participant.

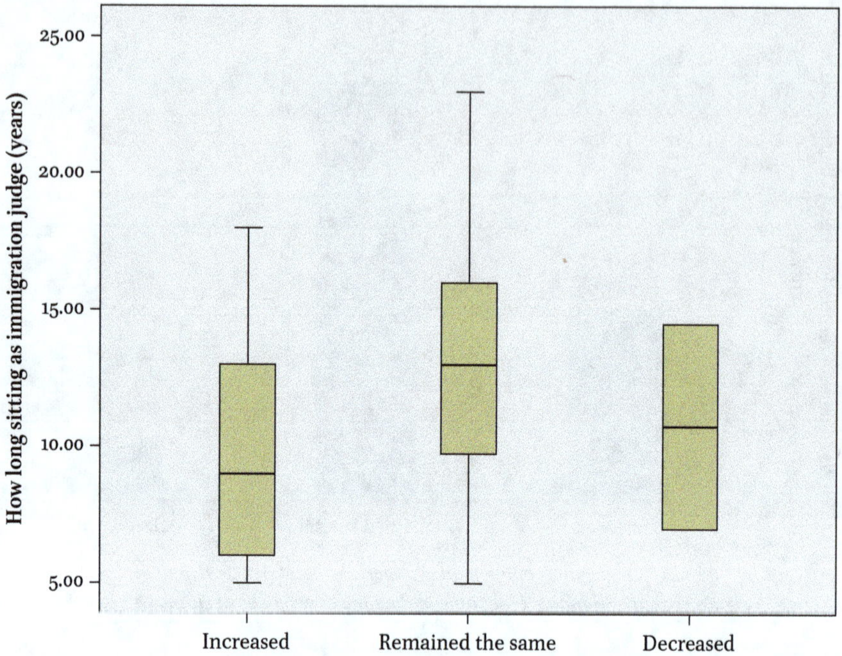

FIGURE 11 *How long judicial participants had been sitting as immigration judges, divided by the response given to the question of whether the use of Article 1F had increased, decreased or remained the same in the time they had been sitting* ($n = 21$).[64]

influenced their opinion on whether or not the frequency with which Article 1F is applied has changed over time.

Judicial participants were divided over whether or not there had been an increase in the use of Article 1F, although most participants indicated they thought the use of the provision had remained the same during the time they had been sitting as an immigration judge.

Judicial participants that had experience in Article 1F cases involving suspected terrorists were also divided as to whether there had been an increase in the number of these cases. Figure 12 shows the responses of judicial participants when asked whether the number of cases in which Article 1F is raised in relation to those suspected of involvement with terrorism had increased, decreased or remained the same in the time they had been sitting. Of the judicial participants that had experience in Article 1F cases involving terrorism, the

64 For 11 participants the question was not applicable as they stated Article 1F had never been raised before them. 3 participants stated that too few cases had come before them to be able to answer the question. Data was missing for 1 participant.

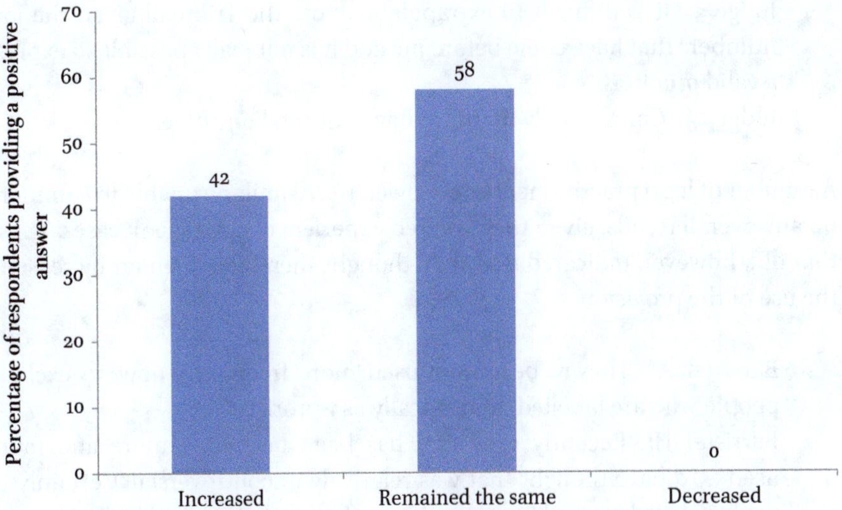

FIGURE 12 *Judicial participant's opinion on whether the use of Article 1F had increased, decreased or remained the same in relation to an individual suspected of involvement with terrorism in the time they had been sitting (n = 12).*[65]

majority felt the use of Article 1F had either increased or remained the same in relation to those suspected of involvement with terrorism. No judicial participants indicated use of the Article 1F had decreased.

Judicial participants were again divided in opinion, although, significantly, no participants considered the number of cases in which Article 1F is raised in relation to those suspected of involvement with terrorism had decreased in the time they had been sitting.

However, a number of judicial participants found it difficult to comment on overall trends in the use of Article 1F, given the limited number of Article 1F cases that had come before them.

> Judge A: "Overall there could be an increased percentage of the total number of cases that are coming through but I don't think any of us would know."
>
> Judge B: "Very difficult to say."

65 For 22 participants the question was not applicable as they stated Article 1F had never been raised before them in relation to an individual suspected of involvement with terrorism. 1 participant stated that too few cases had come before them to be able to answer the question. Data was missing for 1 participant.

> Judge 3: "It is difficult to extrapolate across the Tribunal given the low numbers that have come before me and it is not really possible to express a valid opinion."
> Judge 23: "Cannot reply to this as have only had one case."

A number of legal practitioners interviewed were similarly unable to comment on any overall trends, given their limited experience in Article 1F cases. Those that did, however, indicated that they thought there had been an increase in the use of the provision.

> Barrister A: "They're becoming used more frequently now, to exclude people who are labelled domestically as terrorists."
> Barrister H: "Recently exclusion has been becoming more and more used... I'd have thought that was relatively uncontroversial. Certainly in the last decade, possibly going a bit further back than the last decade, the last decade and a half."
> Solicitor A:"I think there has been an increase in number of exclusion cases based on Article 1F(a) and (c), and I think this is likely to continue."
> Barrister B: "I think now they're [the Home Office] much more on the ball [in relation to raising Article 1F]."

The cases analysed as part of this research show that there has been an increase in the number of Article 1F cases brought before courts and tribunals in the UK. Figure 13 shows the number of Article 1F cases heard before courts and tribunals, per year, from 1996 to 2013. Between 1996 and 2002 there was not a single Article 1F case in the sample. However, aside from a significant decrease in 2008, from 2002 onwards there seem to have been a steady stream of cases, overall showing an increase over this time period.

These case analysis results may be influenced by the fact that more tribunal decisions have been reported in the last decade than two decades ago. However, even allowing for this influence it seems that there has been an increase in the number of cases in which Article 1F is raised, particularly from the latter half of the 1990s.

Analysis of Article 1F cases involving suspected terrorists revealed similar results. Figure 14 shows the total number of Article 1F cases concerning suspected terrorists analysed as part of this research, divided by year. Between 1996 and 2002 there was not a single Article 1F case involving a suspected terrorist in the sample. However, again, aside from a significant decrease in 2008, from 2002 onwards there seem to have been a steady stream of cases, showing

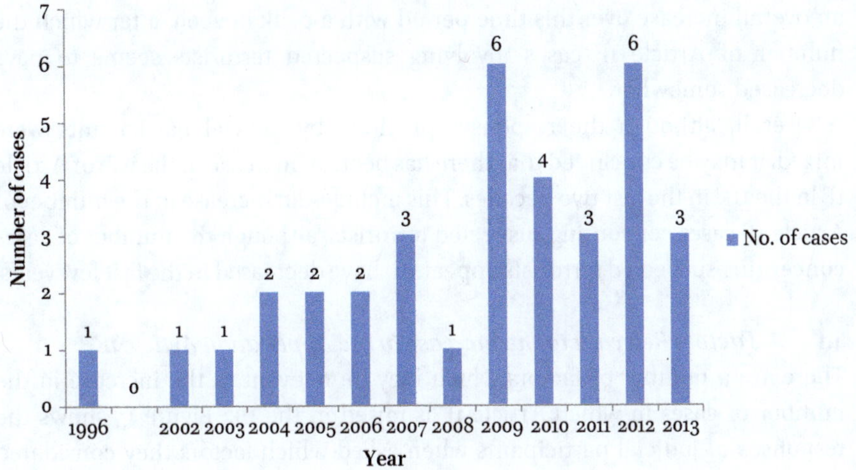

FIGURE 13 *Total number of Article 1F cases, by year, case analysis (n = 35).*[66]

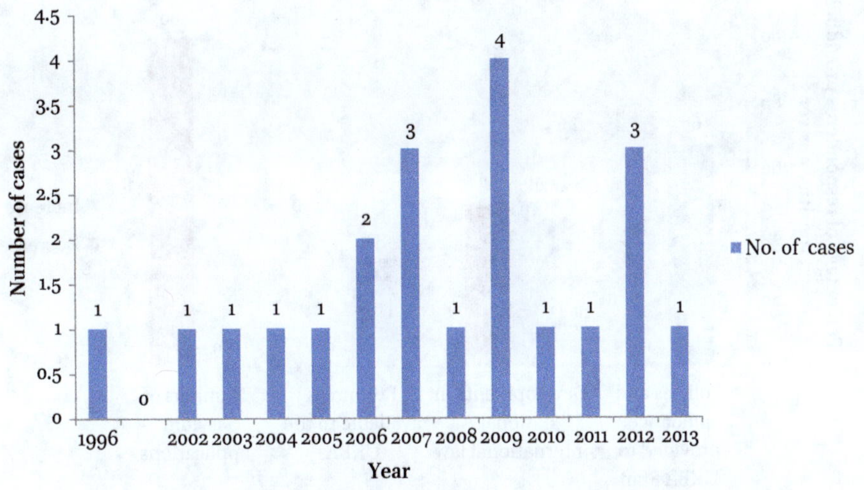

FIGURE 14 *Total number of Article 1F cases concerning suspected terrorists, by year, case analysis (n = 21).*[67]

66 Appeals heard together concerning 1F were counted as separate cases.

67 Appeals heard together concerning 1F were counted as separate cases.

an overall increase over this time period with a peak in 2009, after which the number of Article 1F cases involving suspected terrorists seems to have decreased somewhat.

Overall, although the responses provided by judicial participants were mixed, it may be concluded that there has been an increase in the use of Article 1F in the UK in the last two decades. This includes an increase in the number of Article 1F cases concerning suspected terrorists, although the number of cases concerning suspected terrorists appears to have decreased in the last few years.

4.1 *Factors Relevant to the Increase in the Application Article 1F*

There are a number of factors which may be relevant to the increase in the number of cases in which Article 1F is raised in the UK. Figure 15 shows the responses of judicial participants when asked which factors they considered relevant to any increase or decrease in the use of Article 1F. The majority of participants that thought the use of Article 1F had increased considered poli-

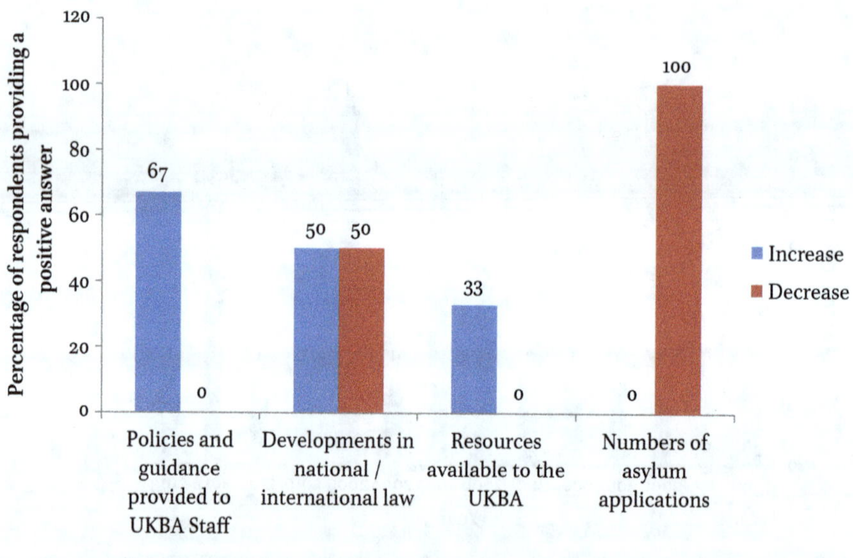

FIGURE 15 *Factors judicial participants considered relevant to change in the number of Article 1F cases (n = 8).*[68]

68 6 judicial participants considered the number of cases in which Article 1F is raised had increased, whilst 2 thought it had decreased. For 13 participants the question was not applicable as they considered the number of cases in which Article 1F is raised had remained the same. For 11 participants the question was not applicable as they stated Article 1F had never been raised before them. 3 participants stated that too few cases had come before them to be able to answer the question. Data was missing for 1 participant.

cies and guidance provided to UKBA Staff and developments in national/international law to be relevant factors in this increase, while some also considered the resources available to the UKBA to be important. Some participants who though the use of Article 1F had decreased also stated developments in national/international law was a relevant factor, although overwhelmingly the number of asylum applications was considered to be the most relevant factor by this group.[69]

As noted above, no judicial participants with experience in Article 1F cases involving suspected terrorists considered the number of these cases had decreased. Figure 16 shows the responses of judicial participants who

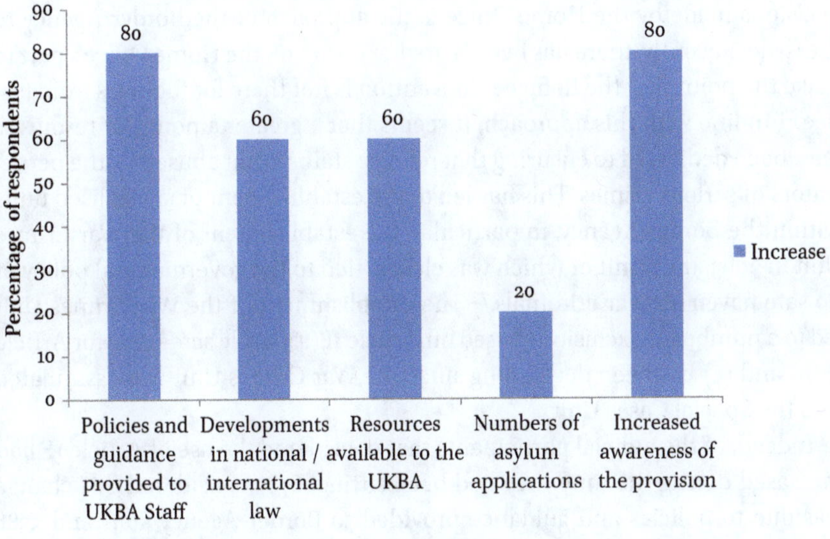

FIGURE 16 *The factors judicial participants considered relevant to increase in the use of Article 1F in relation to those suspected of involvement with terrorism ($n = 5$).*[70]

---

69 The influence of these factors on the number of Article 1F decisions in the uk, and the disparate responses of judicial participants in this respect, are explored further in Sections 4.1.1–4.1.3 below.

70 For 22 participants the question was not applicable as they stated Article 1F had never been raised before them in relation to an individual suspected of involvement with terrorism. For 7 participants the question was not applicable as they considered the use of Article 1F in relation to individuals suspected of involvement with terrorism had remained the same. 1 participant stated that too few cases had come before them to be able to answer the question. Data was missing for 1 participant. Judge 14: 'It is not obvious to me what determines HO decision making'.

considered the number of cases involving suspected terrorists had increased when asked what factors they considered relevant to this change. 80% of judicial participants considered policies and guidance provided to UKBA staff and increased awareness of the provision to be relevant factors to the increased use of Article 1F in relation to suspected terrorists, and 60% also cited legal developments and resources available to the UKBA to be relevant. Only 20% of judicial participants considered number of asylum seekers to be a relevant factor.

The potential influence of a number of these factors on the application of Article 1F in the UK will now be considered in more detail below.

4.1.1 The Policies and Resources of the Border Agency

A factor which seems to have had a great impact on the number of Article 1F decisions made by the Home Office is the approach of the Border Agency to the issue. Recently, there has been 'a greater desire on the Home Office's part to make the point that the Refugee Convention is not there for fugitives from justice'.[71] In line with this approach, it seems that a greater amount of resources have been dedicated to ensuring that refugee status is not abused by the perpetrators of serious crimes. This has led to the establishment of specialised units within the Border Agency, in particular, the establishment of the War Crimes Unit in 2003, the remit of which was closely tied to the governmental policy of no safe haven for war criminals.[72] The establishment of the War Crimes Unit led to a number of exclusions based on Article 1F(a), while screening for Article 1F(b) and (c) has been developing since the War Crimes Unit was assimilated into the Special Cases Unit.

Indeed, of the judicial participants that considered the use of Article 1F had increased during the time they had been sitting, 67% considered this change was due to policies and guidance provided to Border Agency staff and 33% considered it was due to the resources available to the Border Agency. Of those that considered the application of Article 1F to suspected terrorists had increased this percentage increased to 80% and 60% respectively.

> Judge D: "I just think it's because they've had better training, the caseworkers."
> Judge 2: "I thought about ticking all of these but given that many more cases than are recognised have 1F overtones I think the most important factor by far is resources."

---

71 Barrister H.

72 As considered in section 2.1.1.

> Judge 14: "I am unaware of any concerted effort on the part of the UKBA to identify this issue."
> Judge 3: "I would consider any such change being as a result of the resources available to the UKBA to undertake proper research and analysis of the claims made."
> Judge 35: "There is a specialist war crimes section of the UKBA."

The amount of time and resources Border Agency staff have to dedicate to investigating potential Article 1F cases clearly has a huge impact on the number of Article 1F decisions made. As noted by one barrister 'it's a very tiny number [of cases], but they soak up a huge amount of resources when they come up'.[73] Indeed, the SCU member interviewed as part of this research indicated that the drop in the number of Article 1F(a) decisions in 2011 (see Figure 11) was due to a restructuring of the SCU and consequent drop in resources.[74] The allocation of resources and policies by the Home Office has therefore clearly had a great impact on the number of Article 1F decisions made by the Border Agency.

4.1.2 Numbers of Asylum Applications

The number of asylum applications made in the UK may also influence the number of Article 1F decisions made by the Home Office. Figure 17 shows the number of asylum applications made per year in the UK for the years 2001–2013, and demonstrates that there has been a dramatic reduction in the number of asylum applications in the last decade.

The fall in the number of asylum application in the UK may affect the number of Article 1F decisions made by the Home Office in two ways. Firstly, it might be expected that, as fewer individuals are applying for asylum in the UK, fewer individuals would fall under Article 1F and be eligible for exclusion.

> Judge B: "I noticed one of the bullet points in your questionnaire was the fall in asylum numbers and I'm sure that may play a significant part in whatever answer you're going to get. Because if you've got a drastic reduction in asylum figures it's not surprising that you don't see many exclusion cases."

Figure 15 shows that 100% of judicial participants that considered the use of Article 1F had decreased indicated that numbers of asylum applications was a relevant factor in this decrease, whilst no participants that considered the use

73 Barrister D.

74 See n 610 and accompanying text.

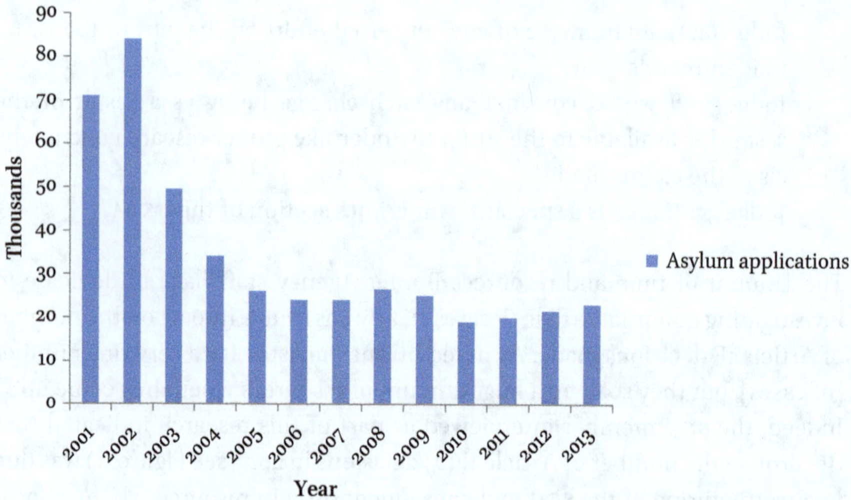

FIGURE 17 *The number of asylum applications made in the UK per calendar year, 2001–2013.*[75]

of Article 1F had increased felt this was a relevant factor. However, the fall in the number of asylum applications might also mean that the Border Agency is able to dedicate more time and resources to potential Article 1F cases.

> Judge 15: "This area has tended to develop once the Home Office were no longer completely overwhelmed by the number of asylum applications."

Figure 16 reveals that 20% of judicial participants that considered the use of Article 1F in relation to suspected terrorists had increased felt that number of asylum applications was relevant to this increase. It is not therefore possible to conclusively state the impact of the drop in the number of asylum applications on the number of Article 1F decisions made by the Home Office.

4.1.3 Judicial Awareness

Another factor which may have contributed to the increase in the number of Article 1F cases is increased judicial awareness of the provision. As noted previously, in the earliest cases analysed as part of this research, *T* and *Gurung*, Article 1F was raised by the tribunal rather than the Home Office. As suggested by two interviewees, the trend towards applying Article 1F more often in the

75 Source: Home Office, Immigration Statistics October to December 2013, Section 8.2, Asylum table as 01 https://www.gov.uk/government/publications/immigration-statistics-october-to-december-2013/immigration-statistics-october-to-december-2013#asylum-1.

UK may have originated in the judiciary's increased awareness of the provision, which was later picked up on by the Home Office.

> Barrister H: "I think that back 10 or so years ago, certainly in the 1990's there were very few exclusion decisions. And then particularly with cases like *Gurung*, the tribunal, some of the more on the ball tribunal judges, realised the Refugee Convention treated exclusion under Article 1F as mandatory, so that any approach that might have been the previous practice, along the lines of 'it's a matter for the Secretary of State in a refusal decision to decide whether or not they're excluded' changed slightly into a business of saying that where the evidence brings up a question of exclusion then exclusion must be considered by the appeal tribunal if it hasn't been considered by the Secretary of State, on the basis of the Article 1F wording. And so from then you have more and more the tribunal making a point which the Secretary of State very much picked up on, and so it tends to be more of an issue."
>
> Judge B: "After 9/11 we obviously had a lot of discussions not only within the UK but also through the International Association of Refugee Law Judges who were very exercised about what were the implications for the work of judiciaries involved in asylum work... I think that [the time of the *Gurung* decision] was a time when we all took stock about what we were doing in relation to the exclusion clauses and all these issues, start to look at inclusion first or exclusion first. I suppose *Gurung* in many ways reflects what we all thought was the right approach then."

The tribunal's *Gurung* decision in 2002 seems to have had a great impact in bringing Article 1F into the fore of judicial awareness. Indeed, the tribunal in *Gurung* held that it was incumbent on tribunal judges to consider Article 1F, even where this was not raised by the Home Office.[76] It is from the date of the *Gurung* determination onwards that Article 1F cases seem to arise more often before courts and tribunals in the case analysis.

> Judge D: "The one case (in private practise) I thought it was relevant was a Bosnian case and I think if that case was in court now it would have been raised as a war crimes issue. But back then the decision maker did not deal with it."

76 *Gurung (Exclusion, Risk, Maoists)* (n 85) [151].

However, it must be noted that the increase in the number of Article 1F cases following the *Gurung* determination may also have been due to the establishment of the War Crimes Unit within the Home Office, as the periods coincide.

4.1.4 Developments in National and International Law

50% of judicial participants who considered there had been an increase in the use of Article 1F indicated developments in national and/or international law was a factor relevant to this change. 60% of participants that considered the use of Article 1F in relation to suspected terrorists had increased also felt that this was a relevant factor. However, 50% of participants that considered there had been a decrease in the use of Article 1F also cited developments in national and/or international law as a factor relevant to this decrease.

As noted throughout the course of this book, in the past two decades there have been significant legal developments in relation to Article 1F and the 1951 Convention as a whole. At the international level, a number of resolutions of the UN General Assembly and Security Council have called on States to exclude terrorists from refugee status and have influenced the interpretation of 'acts contrary to the purposes and principles of the United Nations' under Article 1F(c). Regional regimes of refugee protection have also undergone development, including in particular the establishment of the EU's Common European Asylum System, and the UNHCR and other international bodies have issued detailed guidance on the interpretation and application of Article 1F. Other regimes of international law which are often drawn on in the interpretation of Article 1F have also undergone significant development, particularly international human rights, criminal and humanitarian law, and this has influenced the interpretation of the provision domestically. At the national level, in part in response to these international developments, legislation and guidance has been adopted concerning the interpretation and application of the provision, and there has been a substantial increase in the number of cases concerning Article 1F being heard by the appellate courts of not only the UK but many other states parties to the 1951 Convention.

These legal developments may influence the application of Article 1F in a number of ways. While these developments may have in some ways resulted in restrictive state policies and legislation concerning the application of Article 1F, there has also been a great focus on ensuring that decisions to exclude are in line with international human rights and refugee law and that Article 1F be interpreted restrictively and applied with caution. Particularly in light of the mixed responses provided by judicial participants noted above, it is not possible to draw general conclusions as to the relevance of legal developments on the frequency with which Article 1F is applied in the UK. Indeed, overall it seems that the factor that has had the greatest impact on the frequency with which Article 1F is applied is the establishment of specialised units within the Home Office.

5 Who is Being Excluded under Article 1F

The final question that will be examined in this section is who is being excluded under the Article 1F. Figure 18 shows the number of Article 1F exclusions made in the initial decision of the Border Agency between 2008 and 2013, divided by country of nationality of the asylum applicant. The data reveals that, between 2008 and 2013, of a total of 128 Article 1F exclusion decisions at initial decision the highest number related to nationals of Zimbabwe (26 Article 1F decisions), followed by nationals of Afghanistan (16 Article 1F decisions), Iraq (16 Article 1F decisions), and Sri Lanka (14 Article 1F decisions). It is notable that the majority of these decisions concerned exclusion under Article 1F(a), rather than the other limbs of Article 1F.[77]

Figure 19 shows the number of Article 1F cases analysed as part of this research divided by nationality of the asylum applicant. A large number of these cases also concern nationals of Zimbabwe, Afghanistan and Sri Lanka, although nationals of Iraq did not feature so highly, with only one reported case. Nationals of Egypt and Algeria also featured highly in the cases analysed, although these did not feature significantly in the Home Office data. Nationals of countries that were also not featured in the Home Office data include Jordan, Nepal and Syria.

By far the largest number of Article 1F cases in the Home Office data concerned nationals of Zimbabwe. Nationals of Zimbabwe also featured highly in the cases analysed as part of this research. These cases involved Zimbabweans that supported the Mugabe regime, and include a member of the Zanu PF youth militia involved in attacks on white-owned farms, a soldier in the Zimbabwean army and a former police officer. Nationals of Afghanistan and Sri Lanka also featured highly in both the Home Office data and case analysis. Nationals of Afghanistan were members of various Islamic militias, particularly Jamait-e-Islami, the Taliban and Hizb-e-Islami, and also the KhAD

77 Zimbabwe: all but one were article 1F(a) cases. Afghanistan: 11 article 1F(a) cases, three article 1F(b) and two article 1F(c). Iraq: all article 1F(a) cases. Sri Lanka: all but one were article 1F(a) cases.

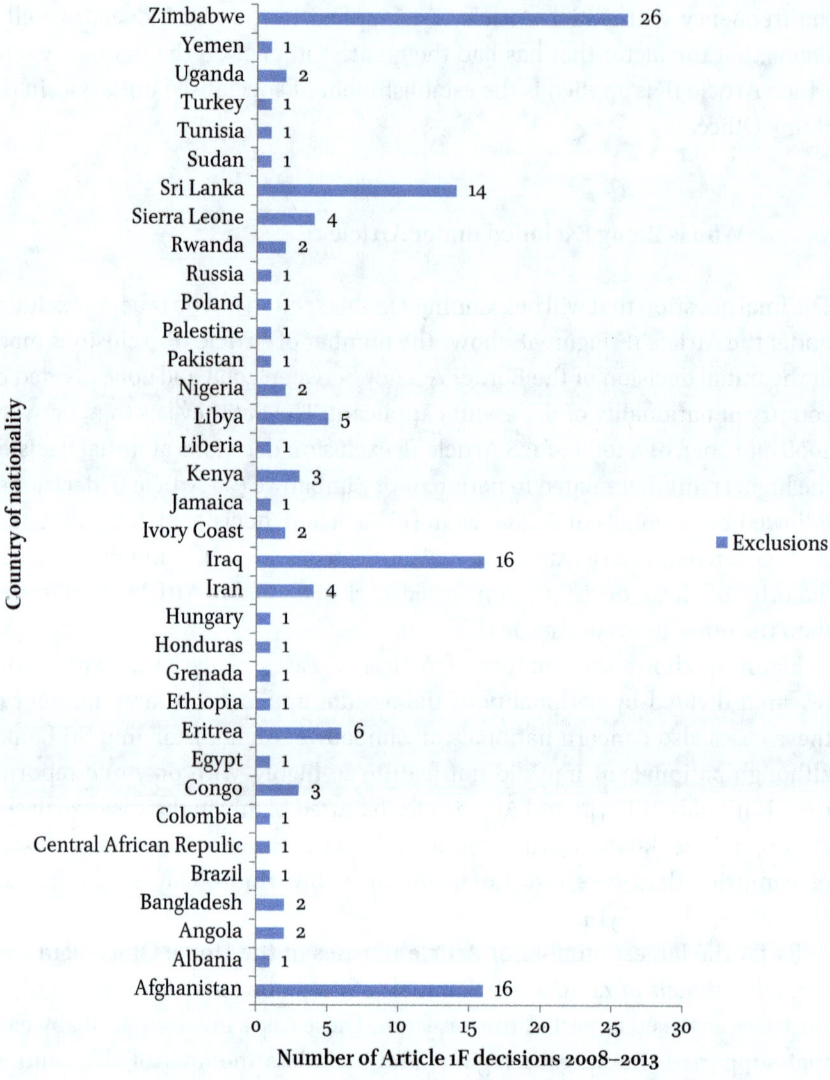

FIGURE 18 *The number of* UKBA *initial Article 1F decisions from 2008–2013, divided by country of nationality (n = 128).*

Intelligence Service. Sri Lankan nationals were primarily members of the Tamil Tigers (LTTE), although a recent case concerned a former member of the Sri Lankan police force. Libyans also feature in both the case analysis and the Home Office data, and in the case analysis relate to a member of the Libyan Islamic Fighting Group (LIFG). Nationals of two countries in the case analysis

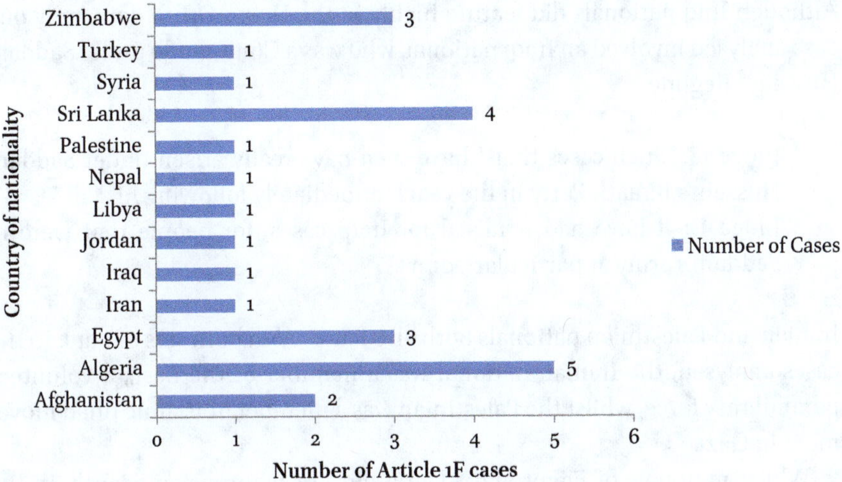

FIGURE 19 *Article 1F cases divided by country of nationality, case analysis (n = 25).*[78]

were PKK members: Syria and Turkey, although Syria did not feature in the Home Office data.[79]

> Judge 15: "The countries currently productive of Article 1F exclusions are Sri Lanka (LTTE involvement), Turkey (PKK) and Afghanistan (Various possibilities)."
> Judge A: "Mainly people from Sri Lanka and Libya."
> Judge 14: "Afghan commander of Taliban group."
> Judge D: "I think they have raised it in two Libyan cases in the last two years."
> Barrister B: "I think the commonest is probably the LTTE. I've also dealt with exclusion when national security issues have been raised. In particular in relation to imputed connection with Al-Qaida."

78 This analysis excludes duplicate cases as they proceeded through the high courts.

79 Shah suggests that Turkish nationals have increasingly relied on the Ankara agreement to gain 'establishment' status in the UK, thereby avoiding applying for asylum. This could explain the small number of Turkish nationals that appear in the Home Office data and Figure 19. Shah P, 'Activism in the European Court of Justice and changing options for Turkish citizen migrants in the United Kingdom' in: Kay Hailbronner, Bilgin Tiryakioglu, Esin Kucuk and Katja Schneider (eds.) *Vatandaşlık, Göç, Mültecive Yabancılar Hukukundaki Güncel Gelişmeler* (*Current Developments in Citizenship, Immigration, Refugee Law and Law of Foreigners*), (Union of Turkish Bar Associations, 2009) 299–326.

Although Iraq nationals did feature highly in the Home Office data, only one case analysed involved an Iraqi national, who was a Commando under Saddam Hussein's Regime.

> Judge 18: "Such cases that I have seen have really arisen under Saddam Hussein's Ba'aath Party in the years immediately following his fall."
> Judge D: "I have had it raised for Iraqi cases, for people that were in Saddam's army at particular points."

Iranian and Palestinian nationals both also featured in both sets of data. In the cases analysed, the Iranian national was a member of the Basij, a volunteer paramilitary force, whilst the Palestinian was a member of Islamic Jihad movement in Gaza.

Whilst nationals of Egypt and Algeria did not feature significantly in the Home Office data, a number of cases involving nationals of these countries emerged in the case analysis. The Egyptian nationals were suspected of involvement with Islamic terrorist organisations and Al-Qaida, whilst most of the Algerian nationals were similarly suspected of involvement with Islamic terrorist organisations, both in Algeria and Europe, although one Algerian national was rather suspected of committing serious fraud in Algeria. The early *Gurung* determination in 2002 also involved a Nepalese national who was a member of the Nepalese Communist Party. It also seems that Article 1F has been applied to Rwandan nationals in the past.

> Judge B: "We had some high profile people from Rwanda, particularly say back in 2000, up till about 2008, they're not so frequent anymore."

The most notable result of this analysis is that overwhelmingly Article 1F cases involve members or supporters of State regimes or rebel organisations, rather than individuals acting alone or in small groups. Supporters of repressive State regimes include members of the Zanu PF youth militia; a soldier in the Zimbabwean army and a police officer in Zimbabwe; a member of the KhAD Intelligence Service in Afghanistan; a Commando under Saddam Hussein's Ba'aath Regime in Iraq; a member of the Sri Lankan police force and a member of the Basij paramilitary force in Iran. Members of non-State rebel groups also featured highly in the case analysis, and include members of the LTTE in Sri Lanka, the LIFG in Libya and the PKK. A large number of individuals were members of various cross-border Islamic militias including Jamait-e-Islami, the Taliban, Hizb-e-Islami, Al-Qaida and the Jihad Islamic movement.

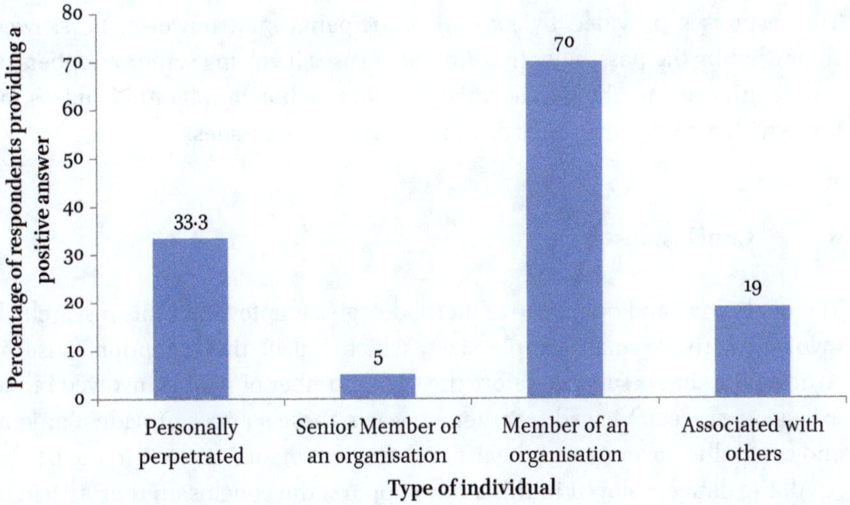

FIGURE 20 *The responses of judicial participants when asked which type of individual Article 1F cases most often involve (n = 21).*[80]

That the majority of Article 1F cases involve individuals who are members of organisations that commit Article 1F crimes rather than act alone is supported by the responses of judicial participants that took part in this research. Figure 20 shows the responses of judicial participants when asked which type of individual Article 1F cases most often concern. The overwhelming majority of judicial participants (70%) indicated that Article 1F cases most often concern individuals who are a member of an organisation that has committed a serious crime, rather than a senior member of such an organisation (5%). A third of judicial participants indicated that Article 1F cases most often involve those who have personally perpetrated a serious crime, while 19% considered that Article 1F was most often raised in relation to an individual 'associated' with others that have committed a serious crime.

> Judge 23: "It was alleged that the person was a member of an organisation that committed the crime."
> Judge 14: "Most appellants appearing in Tribunal do not claim to be the highest leaders of the movements to which they belong but rather junior commanders/footsoldiers/ordinary members."

80 For 11 participants the question was not applicable as they stated Article 1F had never been raised before them. 2 participants stated that too few cases had come before them to be able to answer the question. Data was missing for 1 participant.

The responses provided by judicial participants may, however, be skewed somewhat by the possibility that Article 1F cases involving senior members of an organisation might be allocated to more senior immigration judges, or those with greater experience dealing with exclusion issues.

6 Conclusions

The qualitative and quantitative methodologies employed in this research all involve relatively small sample sizes, which reflect the exceptional use of Article 1F in the UK, and therefore the small number of people involved in the exclusion process. Viewed together, however, these sources provide a unique and compelling overview of the use and application of Article 1F in the UK.

All the data employed in this study supports the conclusion that Article 1F decisions represent an extremely small proportion of the total number of asylum decisions made in the UK: the use of this provision appears be very exceptional. Overall, it seems that in the majority of cases when Article 1F is relied upon it is raised in the initial decision of the Home Office, either as a primary or supplementary ground for refusal. However, in cases which involve suspected terrorists the provision is also often relied upon to revoke refugee status. It seems that Article 1F is rarely raised by an immigration judge where it has not previously been considered by the Home Office. The majority of Article 1F cases involve nationals of Zimbabwe, Afghanistan, Sri Lanka, and Iraq, Libya, Egypt and Algeria. Article 1F cases predominantly involve members of a State or non-State organisation that has committed serious crimes, rather than individuals acting alone or in small groups. Such organisations include State regimes such as Saddam Hussein's Ba'aath regime in Iraq and Robert Mugabe's Zanu PF regime in Zimbabwe. Non-state 'terrorist' rebel groups include the PKK, LTTE and LIFG and also a large number of Islamist militias including the Taliban and Al-Qaida.

Article 1F(a) appears to be the limb of Article 1F overwhelmingly relied upon by the Home Office in exclusion decisions. The Home Office's predominant focus on excluding individuals for committing war crimes and crimes against humanity under Article 1F(a), rather than the other limbs of Article 1F, appears to be primarily related to the development of screening within the Border Agency and the associated allocation of resources. The remit of specialised units within the Home Office has been closely tied to the governmental policy of 'no safe haven for war criminals', with the result that these units are more specialised in the definitions of war crimes and crimes against humanity than 'serious non-political crime' and 'acts contrary to the purposes and principles of the United Nations' that appear under Articles 1F(b) and (c). The establishment of such units also appears to have led to an increase in the application of Article 1F in the UK in the past decade, although the provision still appears to be applied exceptionally in practice. An interesting consequence of this focus on Article 1F(a) is that many individuals who could very readily be depicted as 'terrorists' are not described as such in the exclusion decision. It is suggested that the Home Office's trend towards relying on Article 1F(a) over the other grounds of exclusion makes for a more principled approach to exclusion from refugee status than reference to vague terms such as 'terrorism', and is in line with the restrictive approach it is advised be adopted in the interpretation of Article 1F.

In cases where terrorism is explicitly cited as the ground of exclusion, it seems to be Article 1F(c) that is relied upon over and above the other limbs of Article 1F. That this ground of exclusion is relied upon to exclude terrorists from refugee status is unsurprising, as 'terrorism' has explicitly been held to fall within the scope of the provision in both international instruments and domestic legislation. Furthermore, this limb of Article 1F may be a preferable ground of exclusion for the Home Office as it is not temporally or geographically limited in the same manner as Article 1F(b). The Home Office has therefore relied upon Article 1F(c) in a number of cases to revoke refugee status. Another reason Article 1F(c) might be a preferable ground for excluding terrorists is that the scope of acts that fall within this ground of exclusion may until recently have been considered broader in scope than those under Articles 1F(a) and (b). Indeed, although Article 1F(b) was the limb of Article 1F traditionally relied on to exclude terrorists from refugee status, this provision appears to now be very rarely applied in the UK.

CHAPTER 7

The Exclusion Process

The 1951 Convention does not set out procedures for the determination of refugee status, nor the process by which an individual may be considered for exclusion from refugee status under Article 1F. It is therefore left to contracting states to establish appropriate procedures in this respect.[1] However, in accordance with the Vienna rules, states must apply the 1951 Convention in good faith.[2] The UNHCR and other commentators have therefore distilled a number of procedural requirements from international human rights law instruments, which it is recommended be applied to refugee status determination process to ensure fair and efficient procedures.[3] In the UK, the majority of procedural issues which would affect a fair hearing in the immigration appeal tribunals are covered in the Tribunal's procedure rules.[4] The UK is also party to the EU's Procedures Directive, which forms part of the EU's Common European Asylum System in setting down minimum standards on procedures for refugee status determination in Member States.[5] However, an examination of the entire span of refugee status determination procedures and processes in the UK is beyond the scope of this chapter, which rather focuses specifically on the procedures

1 UNHCR Handbook (n 65) para 189.

2 Terje Einarsen, 'Drafting History of the 1951 Convention and the 1967 Protocol' in Andreas Zimmerman (ed) *The 1951 Convention Relating to the Status of Refugees and Its 1967 Protocol: A Commentary* (OUP, 2011) 40.

3 UNHCR Guidelines (n 65) Part III; UNHCR 'Global Consultations on International Protection/ Third Track: Asylum Processes (Fair and Efficient Asylum Procedures)' (31 May 2001) EC/GC/01/12; UNHCR 'Improving Asylum Procedures: Comparative Analysis and Recommendations for Law and Practice – Key Findings and Recommendations' (March 2010). ECRE, 'Position on Exclusion' (n 84). Gilbert also argues that Article 6 ECHR (right to fair trial) should apply to a status determination hearing considering exclusion because of their close relationship to a criminal charge. Gilbert G, 'Exclusion and Evidentiary Evidence' (n 22) 163–167; Gilbert G, 'Exclusion under Article 1F since 2001' (n 6).

4 Tribunal rules and legislation: <www.justice.gov.uk/tribunals/rules> accessed 12 December 2013.

5 Council Directive 2005/85/EC on Minimum Standards on Procedures in Member States for Granting and Withdrawing Refugee Status. [2006] OJ L326, 13–34. Although the UK decided not to opt-in to the 2013 recast of the Directive. Directive 2013/32/EU of the European Parliament and of the Council of 26 June 2013 on common procedures for granting and withdrawing international protection (recast). [2013] OJ L180/60.

 | DOI 10.1163/9789004292062_009

and processes by which an individual is considered for exclusion from refugee status under Article 1F.

Part 1 of this chapter therefore focuses on the process by which an Article 1F decision is made within the Home Office, and the evidence relied upon to support such a decision. In Part 2, the practical and legal consequences of an Article 1F decision on an excluded individual are explored, while in Part 3 the treatment of evidence and the legal issues involved in Article 1F cases before the immigration tribunal and the Special Immigration Appeals Commission (SIAC) are examined. Again, a large part of this research is drawn from the interviews conducted and cases analysed as part of this research.

1 The Exclusion Decision

1.1 *The Referral Process*

When an individual applies for asylum in the UK, their application is considered by a Home Office caseworker, who will interview them and assess their claim for protection. Decision makers are instructed to consider both whether an applicant has a well-founded fear of persecution so as to qualify as a refugee under the 1951 Convention, and then whether the applicant falls to be excluded by virtue of Article 1F.[6] If an issue of Article 1F criminality arises, the case is referred to the Special Cases Unit (SCU). Around 80% of the cases referred to the SCU fall under Article 1F(a) (war crime; crime against humanity).[7]

The SCU's research team provides caseworkers with specialised country profiles which are aimed at assisting the identification of applicants who could potentially fall under Article 1F. About 60 country profiles have been developed and are updated every six months, and include information on organisations that operate in the relevant country, state bodies including the military, the general history of the country and other relevant factors.[8] Article 1F issues often come to light during the asylum applicant's interview.

> SCU 1: What we say to caseworkers initially is to err on the side of caution. With a 1F case basically we would expect anybody who is confessing to either being involved in obvious sorts of organisations and armed groups, Taliban whatever it might be, or they're saying they've otherwise been

6 Home Office Exclusion APG, s 2.4.

7 See Chapter 6.

8 Aas 'Exclusion from Refugee Status' (n 561) 110.

involved in a crime, they would be expected to be referred to my department.

A large number of potential Article 1F issues come to light as a result of the asylum applicant's own testimony. A caseworker's assessment of the credibility of the applicant is therefore an important factor in determining whether or not a case raises potential Article 1F issues and should be referred to the SCU for further investigation.

Particularly in the early years of Article 1F screening in the Border Agency, there seem to have been a number of cases in which Article 1F was not raised due to caseworkers' negative findings on credibility. Indeed, a number of judicial participants noted that Home Office decision-makers often refuse an asylum application on credibility grounds, denying the asylum applicant is fleeing persecution, rather than raise Article 1F, even when it is apparent that the case may raise Article 1F criminality issues.

> Judge D: "Instead of saying '1F' they said 'we don't believe you' which is another way of the Home Office dealing with the issue is to simply state that the applicant is not credible and refuse the application on credibility grounds rather than deal with a 1F scenario which might lead to positive credibility findings and insufficient evidence for exclusion."
> Judge 28: "...What is more a problem is when the UKBA do not raise [Article 1F] as they do not think the claim is credible yet if I find for the Appellant Article 1f or often Article 33(2) should be considered."
> Judge A: "It's a Home Office view that if they can 'not believe' anything, they won't believe it. Which I find, I and colleague judges, land up are more and more unhappy with. Particularly when you're looking at the 1F situations, the degree of institutional disbelief that the Home Office present doesn't actually help their case at all, because it sets anyone looking at the situation objectively against the Home Office position."
> Judge E: "In First-tier tribunal decisions now you'll often see asylum dealt with first and then they'll go on to the different lower levels of protection... But then it's very rarely Article 1F there, it's just 'I don't believe you when you say you were part of the MDC[9] and can't be sent back because you can't demonstrate loyalty to the President'."

9 Refers to the Movement for Democratic Change, the main opposition party in Zimbabwe.

Negative findings on credibility were identified by judicial participants as a major factor which contributed to Article 1F not being raised by the Home Office in asylum decisions. An individual cannot be excluded from refugee status under Article 1F if they would not otherwise qualify for protection due to a well-founded fear of persecution. However, in a system in which a large number of asylum applications that are refused on credibility grounds go on to appeal, and are ultimately considered credible by an immigration judge, considering any potential Article 1F issues at initial decision would increase the efficiency of the asylum system and lessen the possibility that undeserving applicants 'slip through the net'.[10] Indeed, the Border Agency's Asylum Process Guidance (APG) provides:

> If an applicant's account of his Article 1F-related activities is not credible, those findings cannot justify a decision to exclude. But there must also be argument on exclusion to ensure that should an Immigration Judge believe the applicant and conclude that he is a refugee, consideration is given to exclusion.[11]

These instructions make clear that even when an asylum applicant's account is not credible, potential Article 1F issues must nevertheless be considered. In this situation, Article 1F could be relied upon by the Home Office as a supplementary ground of refusal. The fact that a number of participants involved in this research identified credibility as an issue indicates that this is possibly an area which should be explored further by the Home Office.

There are a number of reasons that caseworkers may opt to refuse an asylum application on credibility grounds without thoroughly considering any potential Article 1F issues. Firstly, caseworkers are under constant pressure to make decisions on and resolve asylum applications quickly. Article 1F cases, however, are extremely time consuming. They involve specialised areas of law and investigation by the SCU may take a considerable amount of time. Caseworkers may therefore be deterred from referring a potential Article 1F case when the faster route may be simply to refuse the asylum application on credibility grounds.

10 Credibility is indeed a problem that plagues refugee status determination procedures in general. See the UNHCR's recent report on the topic: UN High Commissioner for Refugees (UNHCR), Beyond Proof, Credibility Assessment in EU Asylum Systems (May 2013). The Home Office also produces asylum process guidance on credibility, which are currently being revised in light of the UNHCR's report. UK Border Agency, Asylum Process Guidance, 'Considering Asylum Claims and Assessing Credibility' (2012).

11 Home Office Exclusion APG, s.2.4.

Secondly, it may be that caseworkers are not familiar with or confident in identifying and applying Article 1F to asylum applications that come before them.

> Judge 1: "I worked as an asylum and immigration solicitor prior to becoming a judge and found that 1(f) was rarely if ever raised even in cases where I would have expected that it would be a factor (eg former Yugoslavia). My conclusion was that BA staff were not confident in using this provision to refuse asylum applicants."

Cases that give rise to potential Article 1F issues are extremely rare. However, as shown in this chapter, it is crucial that caseworkers are trained in identifying potential Article 1F cases and refer these cases to the SCU team for further investigation.

The importance of considering Article 1F, even as a supplementary ground for refusal, is made clear from the histories of the cases analysed as part of this research. In 8% of the cases analysed Article 1F was relied upon by the Home Office as a supplementary ground of refusal in the initial decision.[12] These cases include the seminal *DD (Afghanistan)* case that made its way all the way to the Supreme Court, and the *SS (Libya)* case which was heard before the Court of Appeal, both of which resulted in the individuals concerned being excluded under Article 1F. Had Article 1F not raised by the Home Office as a supplementary ground of refusal, there is no guarantee that in these cases the issue would have been spotted by an immigration judge or Home Office Presenting Officer (HOPO) on appeal. Early identification and investigation of potential Article 1F issues within the Border Agency is likely to avoid long and protracted appeals in which Article 1F issues have to be considered afresh, and also lessens the possibility that those who should be excluded under the provision 'slip through the net'.[13]

1.2 *The Collation of Evidence*

Cases that are referred to the SCU are considered by their research team which is made up of country specialists, experts in conflict, international relations

12 This percentage is rounded to the nearest whole number.

13 As noted by Boccardi, improved decision making increases the efficiency of national asylum systems by reducing processing times and the need for lengthy appeals. Boccardi I, 'Confronting a False Dilemma: EU Asylum Policy between "Protection" and "Securitisation"' (n 24) 244.

and international criminal law.[14] The SCU receives around 150–200 potential Article 1F referrals per year. Of these, in at least 50% of cases there is insufficient evidence to take the case further. In the remaining 50% of cases further interviews are conducted and research undertaken by the SCU team. Ultimately around a quarter of potential Article 1F cases that are referred to the SCU result in an exclusion decision.[15]

1.2.1 Testimony of the Asylum Applicant

In cases where there is sufficient evidence to pursue the Article 1F issue, further interviews of the asylum applicant are conducted by an Interviewing Officer, based on background research conducted by the SCU team. In some cases the research officer will be present during the interview in order to provide relevant information.[16] Interviews are obviously a key source of evidence on which the Home Office rely in Article 1F cases.

> Judge 15: "Usually the clue has been given by confessional evidence."
> Barrister H: "In a lot of exclusion cases the evidence will be the person's own statements in evidence, in probably the majority in practice of exclusion cases that I've come across. I'd suggest that in the majority of exclusion cases, and in the majority of the reported exclusion cases, the evidence comes from the mouth as it were of the person who is at risk of being excluded."
> Judge 14: "Home office are not very good at obtaining evidence to show behaviour alleged if matter not admitted by applicant."
> Barrister E: "I think in most cases the evidence that determines exclusion is in fact the evidence of the asylum seeker himself rather than positive evidence collated by the Home Office. One exception may be the area of war crimes, where research is being done and where there is a political commitment to do everything to make sure war criminals do not use the UK as a refuge. Certainly in most terrorism-related cases I would have thought, except perhaps for some of the most high-profile of cases, a

14 Aas 'Exclusion from Refugee Status' (n 561) 110.

15 SCU 1: 'I think we're talking about 150–200 asylum cases that get referred to our department every year. Out of those, *at least* half of them there's insufficient evidence to take them any further, and then maybe there's a quarter that we end up having interviews and doing further research on. But ultimately those who actually end up being identified as a 'runner' for exclusion, if we said we had 200 referrals per year, would be no more than 50'.

16 Aas 'Exclusion from Refugee Status' (n 561) 110.

> large part of the evidence, if not all the evidence that determines exclusion comes from the applicant himself."

Recent jurisprudence of the Supreme Court has placed a great deal of emphasis on the need for an Article 1F decision to be based on the individual facts of each case.[17] The Border Agency's APG therefore provides that 'the individual circumstances of the case must be fully explored at interview when exclusion is an element to the case'.[18] A great deal of work therefore needs to go into the task of ascertaining the specifics of each situation.

> Barrister G: "If you were applying the Supreme Court judgment [in *JS* (*Sri Lanka*)] you've got to be really on top of that country situation and you need to have some specific grip on the facts, and then you probably need quite an adept interviewer, you need someone who, it's not just an issue of the basic questions 'tell me your story', you actually need someone who is able to look and see and draw from the interview the requisite information. I think that what the judgment [in *JS* (*Sri Lanka*)] does is it places a lot more emphasis on that fact finding investigation, you've got to delve quite deeply into the facts in order to develop a case that's going to be able to withstand scrutiny in the courts. …The UK Border Agency has to work a bit harder to justify these cases."

However, some concerns have been raised over how effectively these interviews are conducted. Interviewing Officers may not be specialised in the specificity and type of information needed to substantiate an Article 1F refusal. In some cases this may leave room for the asylum applicant to later change or modify their account on appeal.

> SCU 1: "There is a probable need to do more at interview stage. We find that applicants are likely to be more truthful early on in the process. Once a case gets to appeal the applicant's story could have changed markedly and that is why we could do with tightening things up at interview, to reduce their 'wriggle room'. This is something we will be looking at in 2014."

Ineffective interviewing may also result in unnecessary delays and the need for repeated interviews. Solicitor A reported that his client was interviewed over

17 *JS* (*Sri Lanka*), *R* UKSC (n 69), see also *AH* (*Algeria*) (n 69).

18 Home Office Exclusion APG, s 2.6.

five times on the instruction of the War Crimes Unit. In his opinion, it would have been better if the War Crimes Unit had conducted the interview directly as this would have saved the need for repeated interviews and improved the quality of the refusal letter.[19] It might therefore be recommended that the SCU has a more direct role in the interviewing process in future.

Concerns have also been raised as to whether asylum applicants are generally informed of the purpose of these further interviews. The Border Agency's Asylum Process Guidance clearly states that during interviews '[t]he applicant must be given an opportunity to explain their level of involvement in the crime or act and the motivation or reasoning behind their actions', and that the question of whether he has a valid defence must also be explored.[20] However, some legal practitioners cited cases in which their clients had not been informed why further interviews were being conducted. Solicitor A, for example, stated that neither he nor his client were informed that the purpose of the further interviews was to collect evidence to exclude the asylum applicant under Article 1F, even though the interviews had been ongoing for over 1½ years.[21]

> Barrister B: "In context of their initial decisions, it's very unsatisfactory if you interview someone, you refuse their asylum claim and you then purport to exclude them, and you haven't actually put the suspicions on the allegation to them in the course of the interview, to ask for their comment."

Indeed, this issue was even noted by the tribunal in one of the cases analysed as part of this research:

> We bear in mind that the record of her asylum interview does not show that she was given as full an opportunity as is envisaged in Asylum Policy Instructions to answer questions relating to her possible involvement in crimes against humanity.[22]

It therefore seems that there are a number of ways in which the interview process within the Home Office could be improved. Closer involvement of the SCU team with Interviewing Officers has begun, and a need to provide Article 1F

---

19 Solicitor A.

20 Home Office Exclusion APG, s 2.6.

21 Solicitor A.

22 *MT (Article 1F (a) – aiding and abetting)* (n 185) [74].

interviewers with further training has been identified. This will likely greatly improve the quality and efficiency of the interview process and help to reduce the need for repeated interviews. Interviewing Officers should also be fully aware that the purpose of the interview must be communicated to the asylum applicant, so they have a chance to explain and answer any allegations put to them. This would not only add a greater degree of fairness to the process, but also hopefully lessen the prospect of lengthy appeals in which the asylum applicant has to make further representations in order to address the allegations made.

1.2.2 Other Evidence Relied Upon

Although the testimony of the asylum applicant is an extremely important source of evidence that the SCU team draws on in Article 1F cases, exclusion decisions are very rarely based solely on an asylum applicant's own testimony.

> SCU 1: "Evidence. Yes it could be the person's testimony but it would never solely be the person's testimony. The context in which they operate is often key to the decision and this is also something that some immigration judges overlook or don't understand."

Indeed, an asylum applicant may completely deny the criminal allegations made.

> Barrister H: "There are however a number of cases I've dealt with where evidence doesn't come from what the person's said, the person virulently denies the evidence which relates to 'serious reasons for considering'. And then you get more interesting issue."

Particularly in relation to Article 1F(a) and (c) cases, the SCU team 'rely on absolutely tonnes of open sourced reporting' to corroborate or refute an asylum applicant's testimony: 'UN, Human Rights Watch, Amnesty, academics, books, periodicals, journals, regional news reporting'.[23]

> SCU 1: "Any sort of 1F(c) type stuff, 1F(a), is always contextualised. Our Iraqi Ba'athist regime evidence runs to about 4 boxes of A4. Tamil Tigers, that's another one with a significant caseload… If it's a 1F(a) case there's definitely plenty for judges to look at."

---

23 SCU 1.

For example, in the *MT* case, which concerned a former police officer in Zimbabwe, the Upper Tribunal was presented with an extensive array of background material. In total 61 documents were considered, these included oral and written evidence from two expert witnesses, reports from the Zimbabwe Human Rights NGO Forum, Human Rights Watch, Amnesty International, the US State Department, Physicians for Human Rights, Freedom House Report, the Redress Trust and the African Commission on Human and Peoples Rights.[24]

> SCU 1: "Sometimes we can place the person at a particular spot, 'I was working in this prison, this was my role, I wasn't involved in any abuses', but we'll say 'well circumstantially you were there for five years, we've got these three Human Rights Watch reports that say torture was systematic all the time, everybody in the town knew about it', and we would say circumstantially there are serious reasons to consider that you at least were part of a joint criminal enterprise of that, i.e. you would have known about the abuses and your role would have made a significant contribution to them. This doesn't strike us as a particularly outlandish premise."

A number of legal practitioners interviewed as part of this research seemed overwhelmed by the amount of material relied on by the Home Office in Article 1F cases.

> Solicitor A: "I was extremely surprised by the length and depth of the UKBA war crimes unit report and the size of the Home Office bundle and the tremendous amount of work which had to be done. ...The report provided by the UKBA was 105 pages long, and full of footnotes. The report included 125 factual points."
>
> Barrister B: "I think in some cases, in one case in particular, we were swimming in evidence, between the two sides I think there was around 5000 pages of evidence. ...I remember getting incredibly long letters explaining why they were excluding, with millions of individual allegations."

The only exception to the SCU's extensive reliance on open sourced documents seems to be certain types of Article 1F(b) cases which involve the alleged individual commission of specific crimes, committed by the asylum applicant as a private actor rather than as part of a State regime or rebel organisation.

24 *MT* (*Article 1F (a) – aiding and abetting*) (n 185), Annex.

> SCU 1: "The only time we might rely just on a person's confession, and this is increasing a little bit, is around 1F(b) stuff. Because 1F(b), sometimes it's quite hard to corroborate that. [*Gives example of a case of revenge killings*] now it's going to be very hard for us to corroborate that happened, but in the context of the country, in the context of the fact that this guy has given a broadly credible account."

The SCU team also rely on a large amount of legal information: 'a 50 page summary document, all up to date case law, international criminal law and domestic law'.[25] One judicial participant in particular found the legal information provided by the Border Agency very useful.

> Judge 9: "In one case, UK BA provided a very useful report from a specialised body within UK BA, which included references to case law from other jurisdictions."

However, a number of judicial participants and legal practitioners were concerned that the evidence relied upon by the Home Office, and allegations made, are often too generalised, and based predominantly on circumstantial evidence.

> Barrister B: "They're often not very accurate in what they mean. They'll try to link conduct associated with a war crime or whatever, yet they don't really mean that, it's a more a generalised allegation, that you are a member of a movement... I think basically what happens is that the Home Office will make these allegations, looking in very generous terms, and they don't actually really test the basis of the allegations. ...they do quite often make particular allegations, quite often based on a very bland, rather speculative reading of the facts, which they don't then properly test."

Solicitor A stated that although the Border Agency report was over 105 pages long, it was very circumstantial and overly general. The basic gist was that if an individual was in a certain place at a certain time they were implicated, and there was no real consideration of the individual circumstances of the applicant.[26] For example, the detention centre at which the asylum applicant Solicitor A represented had worked at was not mentioned in the report relied

---

25 SCU 1.

26 Solicitor A.

upon by the Home Office, but the report mentioned other detention centres where torture took place. Therefore the Home Office concluded that torture took place in the detention centre at which the asylum applicant worked, even though this centre was not specifically cited in the report.[27] A number of judicial participants also raised concerns regarding the nature of evidence relied upon by the Home Office.

> Judge A: "When the Home Office are dealing with senior members of the organisation, what they tend to do is cut and paste into the refusal letter news broadcasts saying that senior members of x were involved in a particular day with this activity, and because that happened and you were in the area, you're one of those. And what the appellant can often establish is either they weren't there, or the news item that's being used against them is inaccurate."
> Judge 19: "The Home Office is generally loathe to try and prove anything."
> Judge D: "It's very generalised, that's the trouble, and that's why I think they're not successful because the evidence is just not specific enough in the cases I've had."

The concerns raised by judicial participants regarding the generality of the evidence relied upon by the Home Office in Article 1F cases were put to the SCU team member interviewed as part of this research. He pointed out that one of the major problems encountered by his team is that immigration judges often do not have an understanding of the regime or organisation the asylum applicant is alleged to be a member of, or the context of the Article 1F allegation.

> SCU 1: "Often an immigration judge has limited conception of the organisation that person is a member of, the country they were operating in, the security apparatus they were operating in – they've got the objective evidence which sometimes can be quite voluminous and due to the vagaries of the appeal system there is often limited opportunity for judges to read around the topic. My team has, for example, looked at over a thousand Iraqi cases where there are indicators the applicant has been involved in abuses; we understand about this regime inside and out, whereas an immigration judge, with respect, doesn't, so they find it very hard to contextualise who that person is and what they may have done."

27 Solicitor A.

For this reason, the SCU team member thought his team often had greater success with Zimbabwean cases, as immigration judges might be more familiar with the context of what has been happening in the country.

> SCU 1: "I think Judges think 'well it's bad, I know it's bad, they say bad things about Britain, they invaded farms'. I'm being simplistic but you know what I mean, they can understand that more easily, they can contextualise it."

The fact that immigration judges may not have more than a rudimentary understanding of the country situation in issue before an Article 1F case comes before them means that the Home Office often has a difficult task making out the Article 1F allegation. Another factor pointed out by the SCU team member is that often immigration judges are unfamiliar with the nature of evidence required in Article 1F cases.

> SCU 1: "They possibly have a problem with circumstantial evidence, which of course can convict you in a criminal court. The fact is just because you've only got evidence that the Iranian security force wholesale committed these types of crimes, and this guy says 'this was my job, I would get people and drag them out of cars', just because we've not been able to say 'it happened in this town on this day and here's a photo of him doing it', we would and do still argue there are serious reasons for considering that he was involved."

The SCU team member, and indeed a number of judicial participants themselves, stated that immigration judges often want more specific evidence of a particular crime being committed at a particular time, rather than circumstantial evidence that the asylum applicant was involved in the activities of a particular regime or organisation.[28] Similarly, the SCU team member pointed out that immigration judges often want to see an individual who is personally responsible for committing the crime, rather than those who assisted in the commission of a crime.

> SCU 1: "One of the things I think judges struggle with is this issue of wanting the 'smoking gun', wanting the kind of 'we want to see the rapist not the guy who caught the woman that detained her in a cell for three days'. For a lot of immigration judges that doesn't seem to compute. Of course

28 See comments above.

> from our perspective we are driven entirely by international legal information and UK precedents."

Whilst the Supreme Court has stressed that an asylum applicant cannot fall to be excluded under Article 1F simply for being a member of a brutal organisation, they also made clear that, in order to fall under Article 1F, the asylum applicant does not have to personally commit an excludable act. Rather, it is sufficient if the individual made a significant contribution to the organisation's criminal purpose.[29] However, criminal responsibility is an extremely complex area of law, and one with which many immigration judges will not be immediately familiar. As will be considered in Section 3.1, it is therefore unsurprising that some confusion arises as to the nature of evidence, involvement or crime required to bring an asylum applicant within the scope of Article 1F.

Although there have been concerns raised regarding the non-specifity of evidence relied upon by the Home Office in Article 1F cases, much of this concern may arise from unfamiliarity with what is required to bring an individual within the scope of Article 1F. Indeed, the SCU team member pointed out that the small number of asylum applicants excluded under Article 1F by the Home Office indicates that there is not an 'exclusion culture' within the department.

> SCU 1: "But the point is that although we try and be creative with the exclusion clauses we don't try and just exclude people for the sake of it. Certainly in the last seven, eight years there's quite a bit of rigour attached to what we do. There is no exclusion culture, which I think your stats bear out really."

It therefore appears that aside from the testimony of an asylum applicant a large amount of evidence is relied upon by the SCU team to support an Article 1F decision. This includes international and domestic legal information, and, particularly in cases falling under Article 1F(a) and (c), a large amount of open

29 Lord Brown considered Toulson LJ's formulation of Article 1F responsibility in the Court of Appeal too narrowly drawn, as it 'is all too easily read as being directed to specific identifiable crimes'. Rather, Lord Brown considered that liability should attach to wider concepts of common design, 'such as the accomplishment of an organisation's purpose by whatever means are necessary'. *JS (Sri Lanka), R* UKSC (n 69) [38]. See also *DD (Aghanistan) EWCA* (n 69), where the Court of Appeal held that it was not a prerequisite for a finding in relation to the Article 1F(c) that a specific identifiable crime or act of terrorism had to be proved.

sourced material.[30] Although the SCU team clearly draws on a large amount of evidence in formulating Article 1F decisions, and indeed a number of legal representatives appeared overwhelmed by the volume of evidence produced in Article 1F cases, concerns have been raised regarding the non-specificity of the evidence relied upon, in particular that the information is often too generalised and based predominantly on circumstantial evidence. However, it seems that much of this concern may arise from unfamiliarity with what is required to bring an individual within the scope of Article 1F, a point which will be considered further in Section 3.1 below.

2 The Consequences of Exclusion

2.1 *The Relevance of Article 1F for Removal*

An individual who is excluded from refugee status by virtue of Article 1F is denied the rights and benefits that attach to a grant of asylum under the 1951 Convention.[31] Thus individuals excluded from refugee status under Article 1F do not benefit from the 1951 Convention's right of non-return to persecution (non-*refoulement*).[32] Where possible, the Secretary of State will seek to remove an excluded individual from the UK.[33] However, exclusion from the protection of the 1951 Convention (or the EU Qualification Directive) does not mean that the individual will cease to benefit from the protections offered by other international instruments, particularly human rights instruments. Importantly, an individual excluded from refugee status under Article 1F will still benefit from the protection offered by the European Convention on Human Rights (ECHR). For example, the individual may allege that their life will be at risk (Article 2), they will suffer inhuman or degrading treatment

30 There are, however, a minority of cases in which an Article 1F decision is made in the Home Office on a case that has not gone through the SCU team. For example, the *MH (Syria)* (n 69), case that was heard before the Court of Appeal did not begin as an SCU case. It is not possible to draw conclusions on the evidence relied upon in those cases that were not dealt with by the SCU team.

31 Immigration Rule 334. In the UK, asylum is granted if a person is recognised as a refugee. Those excluded under Article 1F will also be excluded from subsidiary/humanitarian protection.

32 Refugee Convention, Article 33. See also Qualification Directives, Article 21.

33 Home Office, 'Interim Asylum Instruction: Restricted Leave' (n 618), s.1.3, see also s.10. 'Those individuals refused asylum and Humanitarian Protection because Article 1F applies and there are no barriers to their removal must be prioritised for enforcement action and removal'.

(Article 3), unlawful detention (Article 5) or an unfair trial (Article 6) on return. The rights embodied in these provisions apply to all individuals within the jurisdiction of the UK whether or not they have engaged in criminal conduct.[34] Although excluded individuals do not benefit from the protection against *refoulement* contained in the 1951 Convention, they will nevertheless continue to benefit from the protections of human rights instruments and cannot be removed from the UK where to do so would breach the UK's human rights obligations.[35]

Since asylum applicants may be excluded from refugee status under Article 1F *despite* a well-founded fear of persecution in their country of origin, in many cases individuals excluded from refugee status can nevertheless not be removed, as to do so would be in breach of the UK's human rights obligations as the individual will be at risk. The practical impact of exclusion from refugee status under Article 1F is therefore said to have lost much of its significance.

> Judge 19: "Since a person cannot be excluded from human rights protection exclusion under 1F is not as important as it might at first seem."
> Barrister C: "The long stop that is now in place of non-extradition or non-deportation to a country where your human rights will be violated has really removed the question of 'are you a refugee or not' from the centrality of what is at hand. Now that you've got your article 3, article 6, article 8 protections, in any event from deportation or extradition to a country that will torture you, abuse you, expose you to a trial on methods obtained by torture or a grossly or flagrantly unfair trial, the Refugee Convention is no longer the only protection you have."

34 See for example the decisions of the European Court of Human Rights in *Soering v United Kingdom* [1989] 11 EHRR 439; *Chahal v United Kingdom* (1997) 23 EHRR 413; *Saadi v Italy* (Application No. 37201/06). Boccardi notes that as a result of the ECtHR's landmark judgment in *Chahal*, Article 3 ECHR is broader than the prohibition against *refoulement* contained in the 1951 Convention, since no derogations to Article 3 ECHR are allowed. Boccardi I, 'Confronting a False Dilemma: EU Asylum Policy between "Protection" and "Securitisation"' (n 24) 209. For a concise analysis of the prohibition against removal to torture in international law see Duffy A, 'Expulsion to Face Torture? Non-refoulement in International Law' (2008) 20(3) International Journal of Refugee Law 373–390.

35 It must also be noted that practical barriers to removal often exist. Travel documents may have been lost or destroyed, transport to countries of origin/previous habitual residence may not be forthcoming and the governments of such countries may not be fully cooperative with regard to securing the return of such 'undesirables'.

> Judge E: "Well one of the problems is that most regional organisations like the European Union have now adopted far-reaching protection measures and so old fashioned asylum is now less important than it used to be. And also the deal that was done between the States when they negotiated the Refugee Convention and the Protocol was that you could put yourself outside protection by particularly bad behaviour of one type or another, but the [European] Convention won't have that, however badly you behave you can't put yourself outside certain categories of protection. ...I think Article 1F basically is now a bit of a backwater."
> Barrister H: "In effect exclusion is meaningful only for a person who is otherwise going to be protected. If you're excluded from the inner sanctum of the refugee protection but you're not entitled to protection in the first place then it doesn't really make all that much difference anyway does it?"

Since many individuals excluded from refugee status under Article 1F cannot (at least immediately) be removed from the UK, it is not overly clear what the benefits of excluding individuals under Article 1F are for the Home Office.

Indeed, a number of participants that took part in this research suggested that the Home Office raising an Article 1F issue based on an asylum applicant's own evidence may in some cases support the applicant's credibility and thus claim to protection. Furthermore, it was pointed out that if the Home Office argues that the asylum applicant has committed a serious crime or been a member of a prominent organisation in their country of origin this will often bolster their claim to protection. A number of participants therefore questioned why in practice the Home Office would wish to raise an Article 1F point at all.

> Judge 20: "As I see it (and from the occasional 1F cases that I have done), it rarely makes sense for the Home Office to raise Article 1F. When they do so, the Home Office are arguing on the one hand that the appellant has (for example) committed some atrocity/crime against humanity in his/her home country. But arguing on the other hand that there is no real risk of someone doing serious harm to the appellant if he/she returns to his/her home country."
> Judge D: "An allegation of Article 1F by the Home office can also be seen as an admission by the Home Office that the Appellant is at least partially credible rather than a complete dismissal of his claim and the focus is then not primarily on credibility."

> Barrister B: "One case [I was involved in] didn't in fact go ahead in the end. [The Home Office] withdrew ahead of a four day hearing, because I think they recognised they weren't going to win on risk on return. And in a sense pushing the exclusion didn't make a great deal of sense to them really, as they knew they were going to lose on risk. They were perfectly entitled to maintain the exclusion, not have it maintained in court, and grant limited transit of leave, which is what they did. So in some cases it's almost counter-intuitive to push it at times."

However, the SCU team member interviewed as part of this research pointed out that there is in fact no disincentive for the Home Office to apply Article 1F to those that fall within its scope, as applying the provision has minimal bearing on whether or not the individual can be removed from the country.

> SCU 1: "Article 1F is a key part of the Refugee Convention, it is also extremely important to government policy and wider European policy. The individual's returnability is immaterial to its application. If we didn't apply it then we could effectively be waving perpetrators of extremely serious crimes through to British Citizenship, which is both politically and morally unacceptable."

Once an individual is referred to the SCU team, the practice seems to be that, whether or not an asylum applicant can be removed from the UK, any potential Article 1F issues are pursued and applied.

> SCU 1: "Has there been any pressure around whether we should just refuse this person on credibility grounds? We know they're a war criminal but we'll just refuse them and say 'you can go back'. No that doesn't happen and, to be frank, in the majority of cases would not make someone more 'returnable'."

It therefore seems that the Home Office will pursue exclusion under Article 1F whether or not the asylum applicant can be removed from the UK. In the case of an applicant whose asylum claim is refused as they are not considered to have a well-founded fear of persecution, and can therefore be removed, Article 1F is often relied upon by the Home Office as a supplementary ground of refusal. This practice ensures full consideration of any potential Article 1F issues at initial decision and thus avoids the possibility of long and protracted appeals in which Article 1F issues have to be considered afresh if, on appeal, an immigration judge determines the applicant would in fact face risk on return.

The practice also avoids the possibility that those who should be excluded under the provision 'slip through the net' at the appeal stage. Furthermore, although the application of Article 1F to those who would face risk on return no longer means they can be removed from the UK, exclusion under Article 1F does indeed have serious practical consequences for those who remain in the UK, as will be considered below.

2.2 *Excluded Individuals in the UK*

Even if a failed asylum applicant cannot be removed from the UK, exclusion under Article 1F has serious practical consequences for individuals that remain. They are denied many of the social and economic rights that attach to a grant of asylum. Excluded individuals are also denied the identity papers and travel documents refugees are entitled to on recognition of their status. As of September 2011, individuals who are excluded from refugee status by virtue of Article 1F, but cannot be removed from the country due to the UK's human rights obligations, are subject to a Restricted Leave policy.[36] In contrast to the five years leave granted to those recognised as refugees, under the Restricted Leave policy individuals are generally granted leave to remain in the UK for a maximum of six months at a time. A number of restrictions may be attached to this form of leave, including restrictions on employment; residence; education and a requirement that the individual report to an immigration officer at regular intervals.[37] The grant of leave is reviewed prior to the six month

36 Home Office, 'Interim Asylum Instruction: Restricted Leave' (n 618). This policy of Restricted Leave replaced the previous policy of granting six months Discretionary Leave, which did not include the restrictions and conditions which now attach to Restricted Leave. This policy of restricted leave resembles the 'special immigration status' set out in Sections 130–137 of the Criminal Justice and Immigration Act 2008, which was the government's response to defeat in the High Court and Court of Appeal over the longstanding failure and ultimate refusal of the Home Office to grant discretionary leave to a group of Afghan national who hijacked an aircraft to travel to the UK. However, this section of the 2008 Act has not come into force. See Symonds S, 'The special immigration status' (n 371) for details of this incident and the special immigration status.

37 The conditions that may be imposed under the Restricted Leave policy are essentially at the discretion of the Secretary of State. However the policy does include some guidelines on their application. In relation to employment, the presumption is that permission to work will normally be restricted rather than completely denied, and that written consent from the Home Office will be required to take up new employment, change employment or take on a new role at the current employers. There's also a presumption that excluded individuals will be prohibited from working in certain professions, such as those involving vulnerable persons, public sector roles or those relating to the legal profession. In relation to residence, a person is normally required to notify the Home Office of a change of

expiration date, and if the person can still not be deported, leave is renewed. As explained in the Casework Instruction:

> The policy imposes a short period of leave and appropriate conditions while removal options continue to be pursued. Persons excluded from refugee protection (and from Humanitarian Protection) continue to be a priority for removal even where removal cannot currently be enforced. Such cases will remain under close review by UK Border Agency and will be removed at the earliest opportunity. These reviews will be conducted at six monthly intervals as a minimum, prior to the expiry of the Restricted Leave.[38]

Exclusion under Article 1F does therefore have serious practical consequences for individuals that cannot be deported from the UK in terms of family reunification, employment and the ability to travel, and may include a number of the restrictions cited above. Furthermore, this form of leave is extremely precarious, and is frequently reviewed with an eye to removing the individual from the UK at the earliest possibility.

> SCU 1: "We can prevent people from settling here, we can prevent them from having their families come over...we also have to bear in mind the system as a whole: if we don't exclude someone at the earliest juncture the likelihood is that they will still stay here. The whole picture is that if we don't exclude there's a very good chance that person could end up being a British citizen."

---

address, and in some cases seek consent before they change address. Persons may also be required to live in a certain areas. There's also a presumption that a person is prohibited from spending three consecutive nights away from their home address, or more than 10 nights away altogether during a six month period. In relation to reporting the presumption is that all cases must report regularly to an immigration officer. The presumption here is monthly reporting, although again this can be more frequent if deemed necessary. Caseworkers are instructed that these cases are amongst the highest priority cases for compliance action and that missed reporting events without satisfactory explanation should be referred to the local prosecution team for consideration. Finally, there is a presumption that any form of study at an educational institution, be it on campus or distance learning, is prohibited. The conditions imposed on a grant of Restricted Leave can of course be more stringent if considered necessary by the Home Office. Failure to abide by any of these conditions is a criminal offence and may lead to prosecution and imprisonment. Home Office, 'Interim Asylum Instruction: Restricted Leave' (n 618).

38 Home Office, 'Interim Asylum Instruction: Restricted Leave' (n 618), s 1.9.

> Barrister B: "If you're left without leave or a period of short leave, then this has all sorts of implications in terms of your ability to be reunited with your family, to get employment, because no employer's going to look at you if you only have six months leave."
>
> Barrister H: "In terms of the leave people get, of course it's an enormous issue. If you succeed in showing that you are at risk of sufficiently bad harm if you're removed from the country then the difference between being excluded and not being excluded is enormous, because if you're not excluded then you'll either get refugee status or humanitarian protection, and that's a relatively safe status to have, you normally get 5 years leave and then an application for indefinite leave. If you're excluded from the Refugee Convention for 1F reasons you'll automatically be excluded from humanitarian protection as well…and you'll get this six months excluded leave status which is a very unhappy status for people. You have all sorts of restrictions put on you and you can't leave the country. So yes it has enormous consequences. And then there's all these types of new restrictions where they restrict your right to work, and the rest of it, which is potentially very damaging… It's been made very clear, and increasingly clear over the years, you're a very unwelcome guest in this country, tolerated but not wanted, tolerated for the time being. Plus of course it means your status *vis a vis* protection is extremely vulnerable, it is reviewed, you need to reapply every six months and it gets reviewed, with a hostile eye."

Although Article 1F may be said to have lost much of its *raison d'etre*, exclusion from refugee status clearly does still have a large amount of practical significance for individuals that remain in the UK. There are of course a number of other reasons the Home Office would wish to exclude individuals from refugee status under Article 1F, even if exclusion means they cannot be immediately removed from the country.

Firstly, the purpose of Article 1F must be borne in mind. As explained in the Border Agency's APG: 'Article 1F is…intended to protect the integrity of the asylum process from abuse'.[39] As a matter of international policy, excluding suspected criminals from refugee status under Article 1F promotes the integrity of the international refugee protection regime by ensuring undeserving individuals do not claim the protection of the 1951 Convention. Furthermore, application of the provision ensures that such persons do not misuse the institution of asylum to evade legitimate prosecution.

---

39 Home Office Exclusion APG, s.2.1.

> SCU 1: "And also of course there are links to helping other jurisdictions, international tribunals etc. If a country like the UK wasn't active in the Article 1F field it would be a dereliction of duty… The exclusion clause is mandatory. We are required to apply them, that's what international and our own law says."

Ultimately, however, it seems that the greatest benefit to the Home Office in excluding individuals from refugee status under Article 1F is that it leaves the door open to future removal, and prevents the excluded individual from establishing firmer ties to the UK that may result in their permanent settlement.[40] In the year 2012, following the introduction of the new policy, 35 individuals were granted Restricted Leave in the UK.[41] In 2013, the number of individuals granted Restricted Leave was 16.[42] This figure corresponds exactly with the number of individuals excluded from refugee status in that year, so it seems that individuals excluded under Article 1F are currently being granted Restricted Leave in the UK as a matter of routine, i.e. it doesn't appear to be the case that these individuals are being removed from the UK. This is likely due to the human rights obstacles to removal highlighted above.

2.3 *The Right to Appeal*

Exclusion from refugee status under Article 1F also has repercussions in terms of an individual's right to appeal against such a decision. An asylum applicant excluded from refugee status under Article 1F who cannot be removed from the UK on human rights grounds may appeal against the Secretary of State's decision. However, the right to appeal the Secretary of State's refusal of an asylum claim is limited to those who have been granted leave to enter or remain in the UK for a period exceeding one year.[43] An individual excluded under Article 1F and granted Restricted Leave for a period of six months will therefore have to have this form of leave renewed twice before they have leave to appeal to the tribunal. This process takes a considerable period of time and meanwhile leaves the individual in a precarious legal position. For this reason a number of challenges to Article 1F decisions are brought under judicial review.

---

40 Although it must be noted that imposing restricted leave on individuals is not the only means by which British citizenship can be prevented, as there are good character and criminal offence bars to citizenship.

41 FOI Response 28840. Kept on file with author.

42 FOI Response 31164. Kept on file with author.

43 Nationality, Immigration and Asylum Act 2002, s 83.

> Barrister B: "Under Home Office policy, if you're granted refugee status, you get 5 years. If you get excluded, they will only give you 6 months at a time. And if they give you 6 months at the outset, then you can't appeal that. Once you get to 12 months, you can appeal, and at that point you can test the allegations. Otherwise you have to go on judicial review. And in something like exclusion allegations judicial review is pretty hopeless really, because you need a full review merits hearing, live evidence, all the things you need under judicial review."

The type of leave granted to those excluded under Article 1F therefore seriously impacts the possibility of appealing such a decision. Furthermore, the often voiced concerns[44] regarding the difficulty of asylum seekers to access adequate legal representation is even more acute in Article 1F cases, since the legal and factual issues raised are extremely complex and unfamiliar to many legal practitioners.

> Barrister A: "And it's a real concern, especially where a lot of people don't get proper representation, or any representation. How on earth are you expected to navigate your way through the finer points of Article 1F(c) without the help of a legal team? It would be impossible doing it by yourself, it would be pretty bad if you only had a high street solicitor with no expertise in refugee law. And it also wouldn't be great if you had a mediocre barrister, or simply not enough hours. The cases will show you how complex this area of law is."

Exclusion from refugee status under Article 1F therefore impacts the right to appeal against a refused asylum application, a problem that may be exacerbated by the complex legal and factual issues that surround Article 1F decisions which may not be familiar to many legal representatives.

Overall, exclusion from refugee status under Article 1F does therefore have serious legal and practical consequences for individuals. An exclusion decision limits the type of leave an individual may be granted to a six months renewable form of leave, which may include restrictions on employment; residence;

---

44 Earlier in 2013 Asylum Aid published three reports into the state of legal aid funding and legal representation in asylum cases. The three reports, 'Justice at Risk', 'Rethinking Asylum Legal Representation' and 'Right First Time' are all available at the Asylum Aid website www.asylumaid.org.uk. <http://www.asylumineurope.org/> accessed 12 December 2013.

education and a requirement that the individual report to an immigration officer at regular intervals. Excluded individuals will furthermore not benefit from many of the social and economic rights that attach to a grant of asylum, and will have their grant of leave regularly reviewed with an eye towards removal. Excluding an individual from refugee status under Article 1F ultimately leaves the door open to future removal and prevents the excluded individual from establishing firmer ties to the UK that may result in their permanent settlement. It is therefore essential that these decisions are reviewed robustly at the appeal stage, which is the topic of the next section.

3 The Appeal

As noted in Chapter 6, Article 1F issues may be raised at an appeal against the Secretary of State's refusal of an asylum claim where the Secretary of State relies on Article 1F as either the primary or as a supplementary ground for refusing the asylum application in the initial decision, or where Article 1F is raised by an immigration judge or Home Office Presenting Officer during the course of the hearing. Appeals lie in the first instance to the First-tier tribunal, which involves a full re-hearing of the case during which the asylum applicant is likely to make further representations and be cross examined. Appeals to the Upper Tribunal are on the ground of error of law only.

If the Home Office's initial decision was wholly or partly taken in reliance on information which should not be made public in the interests of national security, the relationship between the UK and another country, or otherwise in the public interest, the Secretary of State may certify the appeal under s.97 of the Nationality, Immigration and Asylum Act of 2002. In these cases appeal lies to the Special Immigration Appeals Commission (SIAC) rather than the tribunal. In this section appeals before the tribunal and before the SIAC will be considered in turn.

3.1 *Appeal to the Tribunal*

The procedures of Article 1F hearings before the tribunal do not differ substantially from other asylum appeals. The main exception is where the Secretary of State has certified the case under s.55 of the Immigration, Asylum and Nationality Act 2006 that Article 1F or 33(2) of the 1951 Convention apply to the asylum applicant. In these cases, an immigration judge must begin by considering whether the certificate it made out and, if so, dismiss the rest of the asylum claim, although any human rights considerations raised in the appeal will still have to be taken into account.

This practice of considering exclusion before inclusion does not appear to be contrary to the 1951 Convention as a matter of law. However, the UNHCR Guidelines advise that, 'given the possible serious consequences of exclusion, it is important to apply [the exclusion clauses] with great caution and only after a full assessment of the individual circumstances of the case'.[45] States do not appear to be under a legal duty to consider the claim for protection before consideration of exclusion.[46] However, in order to ensure fair procedure in the application of Article 1F it is likely that the context in which the crime is alleged to have occurred, the surrounding circumstances, and the treatment an individual is likely to face on return will need to be examined.[47] The UNHCR therefore advises that a 'holistic approach facilitates full assessment of the factual and legal issues of the case and is necessary in exclusion cases, which are often complex'.[48] It seems that, in practice, immigration judges prefer to consider the case as a whole, an approach which appears to be in line with the guidance provided by the UNHCR.

> Judge B: "By statute you've got to look at whether the certificate is made out or not, so you're essentially required to look at the exclusion issue first although I think in practice we, for want of another word we look at it holistically, because I think it's broadly accepted that you can't decide an exclusion issue in isolation from the account, from the narrative of the asylum seeker, but you know that's actually what our jurisdiction demands that we make a decision on the certificate."

---

45 UNHCR Guidelines (n 65) 2, para 2. See also UNHCR 'Summary Conclusions on the Concept of "Effective Protection" in the Context of Secondary Movements of Refugees and Asylum-Seekers (Lisbon Expert Roundtable, 9–10 December 2002) (February 2003).

46 Hathaway and Harvey, 'Framing Refugee Protection' (n 61) 264; Goodwin-Gill and McAdam (n 68) 178; Hathaway J, and Foster, M, *The Law of Refugee Status* (n 254) 531.

47 This is at least as concerns Article 1F(b). Goodwin-Gill and McAdam (n 68) 178. See also Amarasinha S D and Isenbecker M, 'Terrorism and the Right to Asylum under the 1951 Convention and the 1967 Protocol Relating to the Status of Refugees – A Contradiction in Terms or Do Opposites Attract?' (1996) 65(2) Nordic Journal of International Law 226, and Nyinah (n 191) 299. However, Hathaway and Foster argue that 'there may be little value in assessing the other elements of the refugee definition before turning to the question of exclusion', although there may be practical logic in considering the whole of the protection claim in a single hearing. Hathaway J, and Foster, M, *The Law of Refugee Status* (n 254) 531.

48 UNHCR Background Note (n 164) 36, para 99. The Lawyers Committee for Human Rights also advise that using exclusion as a test for admissibility is inconsistent with the exceptional nature of the exclusion clauses, and precludes the capacity to carry out a full examination of all the circumstances of a case. Lawyers Committee for Human Rights, 'Safeguarding the Rights of Refugees (n 538) 325. See also ECRE, 'Position on Exclusion' (n 84) para 8.

The need to adopt an holistic approach to Article 1F cases was indeed stressed by the tribunal in the seminal *Gurung* decision:

> The place of the Exclusion Clauses in the overall schema of the Convention also demonstrates that exclusion issues should never be examined in complete isolation from the examination of the appellant`s overall claim. The approach must always be holistic.[49]

The immigration tribunal recently held that 's.55 does not require a decision on exclusion from asylum to be made at the outset of a hearing and prior to consideration of any other matters'.[50] The tribunal pointed out that:

> it would be artificial to make a finding on [the exclusion case and the substantive asylum claim] entirely separately from the other. An assessment of whether an appellant is excluded from refugee protection, even if the standard for that assessment is different, must take account of his evidence as a whole, not just a part of it.[51]

As such, the tribunal considered that s.55 requires the tribunal in its *written determination* to decide exclusion from refugee status first, before proceeding to address any other head of claim, rather than prohibiting consideration of the substantive asylum claim per se.[52]

Another way in which Article 1F appeals differs from other asylum appeals is that the burden of proof rests on the Secretary of State to make out the exclusion decision, as is noted by the Home Office's APG.[53]

> Judge B: "In the context of the remaking of the decision there may be issues about the Secretary of State being expected to go first because of the evidential burden."

49 *Gurung (Exclusion, Risk, Maoists)* (n 85) [39].

50 *AS (S.55)* (n 210) [29].

51 Ibid. [27].

52 Ibid. [30].

53 Home Office Exclusion APG, s 3.2: 'The evidential burden of proof rests with the Secretary of State to show that Article 1F applies, not for the applicant to show that it does not. See also UNHCR Background Note (n 65) 7, para 18; *Gurung (Exclusion, Risk, Maoists)* (n 85) [93]–[94]. *MT v Secretary of State for the Home Department* (n 240) [74]; *AA (Art. 1F(a): Complicity: Arts. 7 and 25 ICC Statute: Iran)* [2011] UKUT 339 [15].

Furthermore, s.34 of the Anti-Terrorism, Crime and Security Act 2001 explicitly precludes an immigration judge from balancing or considering the proportionality of the extent of persecution feared by an asylum applicant against the gravity of the Article 1F crime or act alleged to have been committed.[54] Indeed, the notion that any balancing exercise should be adopted in deciding Article 1F cases has been robustly and repeatedly refuted by courts and tribunals in the UK.[55] Again, although there is no legal duty on states to balance the persecution feared by an asylum applicant against the crime or act they have allegedly committed, the UNHCR advises this practice 'is an important safeguard in the application of Article 1F', derived from 'the nature and rationale of the exclusion clauses and the overriding humanitarian object and purpose of the 1951 Convention'.[56] It might therefore be advised that a proportionate or balancing approach be adopted when determining Article 1F cases, although the apparent tendency of immigration judges to consider cases 'holistically' might, in practice, mitigate the preclusion of such considerations set out in UK legislation. It must also be remembered that any risk an asylum applicant would face on return will be considered in the context of whether the applicant's removal from the UK would breach the UK's human rights obligations.[57]

The main ways the procedures of Article 1F hearings before the tribunal differ from other asylum appeals is that the burden of proof rests on the Secretary of State to make out the exclusion decision, and UK legislation directs a decision maker to consider exclusion before inclusion and precludes a balancing test be adopted in relation to the extent of persecution feared by an asylum applicant on return. However, in practice it appears that immigration judges tend to consider Article 1F cases holistically, an approach which accords with UNHCR guidance on the topic. Another manner in which Article 1F hearings differ from other asylum appeals relates to the standard of proof employed in such cases, which will be considered further in Section 3.1.3.

---

54 See also Home Office Exclusion APG, s 3.10.

55 *Gurung (Exclusion, Risk, Maoists)* (n 85) [96]; *T* (n 166) [555B]; *Abu Qatada* (n 334) [106]; *DD & Anor* (n 338) [123]. Hathaway and Foster similarly argue that it is appropriate to dispense with the view that there is a duty to balance criminality and risk in Article 1F cases. Hathaway J, and Foster, M, *The Law of Refugee Status* (n 254) 565.

56 UNHCR Background Note (n 164) 28, para 77. See also Zimmermann and Wennholz (n 68) 608–609.

57 See also Home Office Exclusion APG, s 3.10.

3.1.1 The Legal Issues

At the appeal hearing, the Home Office is represented by a Home Office Presenting Officer (HOPO), or for some significant cases the Home Office instructs a barrister from the Treasury Solicitor's Department to conduct the case. Some concerns were raised by participants in this research regarding the familiarity of HOPOs with Article 1F issues. In light of the complex legal and factual issues that Article 1F cases frequently raise, the amount of time HOPOs have to prepare cases was also highlighted as an issue of concern.

> Judge 6: "HOPOs seem to have limited knowledge of the issue. When I have occasionally raised the issue at review hearings I am always told they will need to take advice."
> SCU 1: "Unfortunately due to the appeals system in general, it is often the case that a PO will have virtually no time to prepare for a 1F hearing."

Article 1F cases are extremely specialised and involve complex areas of law, and the provision is raised in an extremely small number of cases. It is therefore unsurprising that HOPOs may not be overly familiar or confident in dealing with the provision. Indeed, a number of immigration judges themselves expressed frustration over the lack of experience they had in the complex legal issues involved in Article 1F cases.

> Judge B: "Our problem is that we don't do enough cases to become expert in it [Article 1F] in any distinct way. So when we get one we have to sort of do our best, which is a bit frustrating because you make the effort to get to grips with the case law and you may not deal with it for another 3, 6 months."
> Judge 9: "I found the issued raised in these appeals very complex. Especially as there was no evidence of any direct involvement with the offences."

These concerns were echoed by other participants interviewed as part of this research.

> Barrister E: "I think one of the difficulties judges find with 1F(a) which is shown clearly by the way the Court of Appeal dealt with *JS*, is that concepts like joint criminal enterprise in international criminal law is something judges find difficult, our Court of Appeal found difficult, I think our Supreme Court found difficult. ...[This] can lead to a

> greater divergence of practice it seems to me and understanding, and therefore a greater need for clear guidance by the higher courts, and consequently cases lasting longer and even the higher courts being inconsistent
> SCU 1: I think immigration judges struggle with international criminal law, circumstantial evidence and criminal responsibility… Why would a family lawyer in Scotland, sitting as a part time immigration judge, understand issues such as customary international law?"

However, it was stressed by the SCU team member interviewed that this was not a criticism of the judges involved, but simply a consequence of the complex areas of law at issue and the fact that Article 1F cases are allotted a similar timescale to other immigration appeals which do not raise such complex areas of law. He suggested that more time and consideration should be given by immigration judges to these cases at the appeals stage.

> SCU 1: "But that isn't a significant criticism of the judges, that's more about CMRs [Case Management Reviews], directions hearings, shouldn't they be asking for reading time, shouldn't judges have an opportunity to read over the reports, come up with questions they might want to ask, direct the Secretary of State or the other side to come back on x, y and z and potentially run the cases in a more effective way?"

The SCU team member stated that the unfamiliarity of many immigration judges with the legal concepts involved meant that it was sometimes difficult for his team to succeed in Article 1F cases.

> SCU 1: "I think there's quite a complexity of issues involved in the question of 'can we convince that judge'. It's quite difficult to convince someone of something if they're starting from a position of ignorance of the law and the contextual issues."

However, it does seem that recent clarification of the law by the Supreme Court has helped provide immigration judges with guidance on how to approach Article 1F decisions. This guidance seems to have had an impact on how the judiciary approach the provision in the tribunal.

> SCU 1: "Article 1F for judges can be difficult, but one thing I would say is that since about 2010 you can almost, if we say *JS* (*Sri Lanka*) is a

> watershed, I think since then the law has been getting clearer... I think since *JS* the law has just settled down a little bit and judges understand it more."
>
> Judge B: "I think now we probably consider that the law is settled, particularly after *Al-Sirri* clarifying 1F(c)."

Indeed, the clarity provided by higher courts appears to have impacted the number of cases that are successful before the tribunal. The SCU team member interviewed as part of this research indicated that until a few years ago it may have been the case that Article 1F cases tended to fail more often than not before the tribunal.

> SCU 1: "Anecdotally, I would say that up until probably 08 09, we've been going since about 2004, we saw more allowed appeals, however this has changed since around 2010."

However, since the Supreme Court decided the *JS* (*Sri Lanka*) case in 2010, his opinion was that 'since then the law has been getting clearer...the law has just settled down a little bit and judges understand it a bit more'. In consequence, 'the number of allowed appeals we've seen at the First-tier in the last couple of years has really reduced, so that suggests that we aren't losing that many...since about 2010 we've had less allowed appeals so we seem to be doing better'. Overall, he states that his team 'don't see that many allowed appeals at the moment'.[58]

The responses of judicial participants regarding the success of Article 1F cases before the tribunal were mixed:

> Judge A: "I certainly have never accepted one myself, and I'm not aware other colleges have ever actually conceded to (a) (b) or (c)."
>
> Judge 18: "If raised, it invariably succeeds, perhaps because it is raised so infrequently in this country."
>
> Judge D: "To my knowledge none of the cases that I've seen or I've heard or been involved in have [the Home Office] been successful."
>
> Judge 28: "Very small size therefore statistical basis is not reliable but I would say Home Office only raise it where it is at least arguable and therefore in public interest it is raised."

---

58 SCU 1.

A major factor highlighted by a number of participants that took part in this research is that problems often emerge at the appeal stage due to the unfamiliarity of both HOPOs and immigration judges with the legal issues raised by Article 1F cases. Again, it must be stressed that this is not a criticism of those involved in the appeal process, but rather a natural consequence of the infrequency of Article 1F cases and the complex legal issues involved. However, it does seem that recent clarification of the law by the appellate courts has helped provide further guidance on how to approach Article 1F decisions, and as a result there has been a greater success rate for the Home Office before the tribunal.

3.1.2 The Evidential Issues

The unfamiliarity of immigration judges with Article 1F cases also seems to have influenced their treatment of the evidence upon which Home Office exclusion decisions are based. In Section 1.2 a number of these issues were considered. In particular, the SCU team member interviewed as part of this research noted that some of the main problems his team encountered when cases went to appeal were:

- Often immigration judges have a limited conception of the country situation and the regime the asylum applicant is alleged to be part of, and so they find it difficult to contextualise the case.
- Many judges do not seem to understand the legal relevance of circumstantial evidence, and rather prefer to be presented with evidence of a specific act occurring at a particular place and time
- Often judges want a 'smoking gun', an individual that physically perpetrated a crime rather than someone who assisted or furthered the commission of a criminal purpose.

Again it must be stressed that this is not a criticism of the judges involved, but simply a consequence of the complex areas of law and evidence at issue, and the fact that Article 1F cases are allotted a similar timescale to other immigration appeals which do not raise such complex issues.

Another manner in which the SCU team member considered Article 1F cases sometimes struggled at appeal relates to the testimony of the asylum applicant. As noted above, in Article 1F cases an asylum applicant's testimony is often relied upon as evidence of their involvement with the commission of an excludable act. However, the interview process within the Border Agency often results in the applicant having a degree of flexibility to change their story on appeal. The SCU team member conceded that this was often related to the way in which interviews are conducted within the Home Office.

> SCU 1: "Basically interviewing a suspected criminal, even when applying a relatively low standard of proof, requires different skills from those needed to establish if they have a well-founded fear of persecution."

Often on appeal asylum seekers revise or change their account of involvement in Article 1F acts. There are a number of reasons that asylum applicant's might present different accounts of their involvement with certain regimes and organisations on appeal than during initial interviews by the Home Office. During the initial asylum claim applicants might think that stating they were a senior member of a particular organisation or military force that was, for example, engaged in military activity against a government, might bolster their claim to protection as it would more likely establish that they would be at risk on return. However, by the appeal stage the asylum applicant might realise the potential Article 1F repercussions of claiming such involvement, and change their story accordingly.

> SCU 1: "Do people think that giving information about being involved in heinous crimes, in torture or whatever it might be, do they think that will help them with their claim? I think some people do."

The SCU team member interviewed as part of this research highlighted that many immigration judges are often very credulous of asylum applicants when they change their testimony on appeal.

> SCU 1: "Applicants change their stories often, and I would argue that judges are often a little bit too credulous, a little bit too quick to accept an evidential *volte face*."

In addition to the treatment of open-sourced evidence examined in Section 1.2.2, a key issue raised by participants that took part in this research regarding evidential issues on appeal concerned the testimony of the asylum applicant. As highlighted in Section 1.2.1, one way in which this process could be improved is training for SCU interviewing officers specialised in handling potential Article 1F cases. This would help improve the quality of initial decisions and furthermore lessen the possibility of asylum applicants continuously changing their stories on appeal. In common with immigration judges' unfamiliarity with the legal issues involved in Article 1F cases appears to be their unfamiliarity with how to treat the evidence relied upon by the Home Office in Article 1F decisions. Again it is suggested that greater time could be allotted to cases that raise Article 1F issues, to enable those involved to fully consider the complex legal and evidential issues involved. A related legal issue which impacts on the treatment of Article 1F cases on appeal is the standard of proof to be employed in such cases, as considered below.

3.1.3 The Standard of Proof

An issue related to the treatment of evidence before the tribunal is the standard of proof employed in Article 1F cases. Article 1F of the 1951 Convention requires that there be 'serious reasons for considering' an individual has committed or been guilty of the acts referred to in the provision.[59] The meaning of the phrase 'serious reasons for considering' has attracted some measure of uncertainty, as it does not easily accord with the traditional standards of proof employed by courts and tribunals in the UK.

The standard of proof imposed on Article 1F cases by the phrase 'serious reasons for considering' is unique and unknown in other areas of law. There seems to be widespread agreement that this standard of proof does not require an individual to have been criminally prosecuted for the offence in question, nor that the standard of proof equate to that required to justify a finding of guilt at a criminal trial: in the UK, 'proof beyond reasonable doubt'.[60] However below the standard of criminal guilt it is not clear what the standard of proof required by the phrase 'serious reasons for considering' entails. The UNHCR has suggested that the Article 1F standard of proof should be high enough to ensure that *bona fide* refugees are not excluded erroneously, and hence 'balance of probabilities is too low a threshold.[61] The Lisbon Expert Roundtable

59 This standard is generally understood as a means of accommodating the practical constraints of access to less evidence than is normally available in a criminal trial. Michigan Guidelines on the Exclusion (n 529).

60 UNHCR Handbook (n 65) para 149; UNHCR Guidelines (n 65) 9, para 35; Gilbert, 'Current Issues' (n 188) 470.

61 UNHCR Background Note (n 164) 38, para 107. See also Zimmermann and Wennholz (n 68) 593; Gilbert, 'Current Issues' (n 188) 470. The Lawyers Committee for Human Rights suggest the phrase should be interpreted as 'clear and convincing reasons' requiring the existence of 'clear and convincing evidence' which is detailed, specific and credible and reliable in nature. Lawyers Committee for Human Rights, 'Safeguarding the Rights of Refugees' (n 538) 329.

suggested that, as a minimum, 'serious reasons' should be interpreted to mean 'clear evidence sufficient to indict'.[62]

Canadian jurisprudence has long held that that 'serious reasons' requires more than mere suspicion of guilt, but less than the balance of probabilities.[63] That this standard of proof is lower than the balance of probabilities test has been followed in other Commonwealth jurisdictions, including Australia and New Zealand.[64] However, jurisprudence in the UK has stressed that, rather than attempting to equate the standard of proof with that employed in criminal or civil cases, the better approach is to focus on the ordinary meaning of the words. Thus the Court of Appeal in *Al-Sirri* stressed that the phrase serious reasons for considering 'sets a standard above mere suspicion. Beyond this, it is a mistake to try to paraphrase the straightforward language of the Convention: it has to be treated as meaning what it says'.[65] This approach was approved by the UK Supreme Court in *JS* (*Sri Lanka*), and followed by the New Zealand Supreme Court in *Tamil X*.[66]

More recently, the UK Supreme Court considered the meaning of the phrase 'serious reasons for considering' in the *Al-Sirri* case, and appeared to follow the approach of the Court of Appeal in focusing on the ordinary meaning of the words as the Court noted that 'it is unnecessary to import our domestic

62 UNHCR 'Summary Conclusions on the Concept of "Effective Protection" (n 690).

63 *Ezokola v Canada (Citizenship and Immigration)* (n 172) 40, Introduction; *Mugesera v Canada (Minister of Citizenship and Immigration)* [2005] 2 S.C.R. 100, 2005 SCC 40 (Supreme Court of Canada); *Lai v Canada (Minister of Citizenship and Immigration)* [2000] FCA 125 [25].

64 *Jasarevski v Minister of Citizenship and Immigration* [2012] FC 1145. At [16] the court stated "it is important to bear in mind the tests is 'serious reasons for considering', a threshold which is lower than that of the balance of probabilities." *Garate (Gabriel Sequeiros) v Refugee Status Appeals Authority* [1998] NZAR 241 (High Court of New Zealand), in which the court held the test of "serious reasons for considering" that an individual has been guilty of crimes against humanity is a lower standard of proof than the balance of probabilities. *FTZK and the Min for Immigration and Citizenship* 23 May 2012 [2012] AATA 312 [66] citing *Arquita* [2000] FCA 1889, also *Kuruparan* et al [2012] FC 745 [17], [83] citing *Sivakumar* [1994] 1 FC 433.

65 *Al-Sirri* [2009] (n 69) [33].

66 *JS* (*Sri Lanka*), *R* UKSC (n 69) [39]. More recently the New Zealand courts have followed the UK Court of Appeal in *Al-Sirri* in taking the view that "the Refugee Convention simply means what it says" and that "adding glosses by analogy with civil litigation or criminal prosecution simply confuses matters": see Hammond J in *Tamil X v Refugee Status Appeals Authority; Attorney-General (Minister of Immigration) v Y* [2009] NZCA 488, [2009] 2 NZLR 73 [77], [79]; upheld by the Supreme Court in *Attorney General (Minister of Immigration) v Tamil X* [2010] NZSC 107, [2011] 1 NZLR 721 [39].

standards of proof into the question' and 'the task of the decision-maker is to apply the words of the Convention'. However, the Supreme Court went on to suggest that:

> The reality is that there are unlikely to be sufficiently serious reasons for considering the applicant to be guilty unless the decision-maker can be satisfied in the balance of probabilities that he is.[67]

The Supreme Court in this case therefore appears advocate the balance of probabilities test in Article 1F cases. This is despite also stressing that the task of a decision maker is to 'apply the words of the Convention'. Although the Court's statements on the standard of proof in the *Al-Sirri* case were *obiter*, they seems to have been followed by the tribunal and the Court of Appeal. The Court of Appeal recently interpreted the Supreme Court's guidance to mean that '[i]t is for the Secretary of State to prove on the balance of probabilities that an individual should be excluded'.[68] The tribunal similarly noted that the standard of proof required by 'serious reasons for considering' equated to the civil standard of proof: more probable than not.[69] It is therefore likely that the balance of probabilities test will be the standard of proof adopted in future Article 1F cases. Indeed, at least one immigration judge interviewed as part of this research appears to have been employing the balance of probabilities as the standard of proof in Article 1F cases, even before the Supreme Court's decision in *Al-Sirri*.

> Judge A: "I use the balance of probabilities test: 'is it more likely than not that what I've been told by the appellant is correct, when I weigh that against the Home Office assertion?' You can skew the result by doing it the other way round. You can start off with view that the Home Office operates a credible set of assertions, and it's for the appellant to knock these down. I don't do it that way because I think the burden of proof is on the Home Office."

---

67 *Al- Sirri* [2012] (n 69) [75]. The Supreme Court arrived at this statement after drawing the following conclusions: (1)"Serious reasons" is stronger than "reasonable grounds"; (2)The evidence from which those reasons are derived must be "clear and credible" or "strong"; (3)"Considering" is stronger than "suspecting" or "believing." It requires the considered judgment of the decision-maker; (4) The decision-maker need not be satisfied beyond reasonable doubt or the standard required in criminal law; (5)It is unnecessary to import our domestic standards of proof into the question.

68 *AA-R (Iran)* (n 69) [7].

69 *AH (Article 1F(b))* (n 301) [82].

The Supreme Court's statements on the standard of proof in the *Al-Sirri* case weren't well received by the SCU team member interviewed as part of this research. He argued that the Supreme Court's judgment isn't in line with accepted Commonwealth jurisprudence on the interpretation of the phrase, and furthermore is not suitable in the Article 1F context, since exclusion from refugee status is different in nature and consequences from a criminal trial.

> SCU 1: "For a start, and *Al-Sirri* hasn't really helped this very much, they basically said they would expect serious reasons for considering to mean balance of probabilities in reality, which is quite unhelpful because linguistically the two phrases clearly mean something very different. I prefer to follow *JS* and apply the natural meaning of the phrase. 'Serious reasons for considering' is no more the civil standard than the civil is the criminal. Simply the three standards mean entirely different things."

Despite these reservations, it seems that the balance of probabilities is the standard of proof that is likely to be employed by the tribunal in future Article 1F cases.

3.2 *Appeal to the SIAC*

Exclusion decisions wholly or partly taken in reliance on information which should not be made public in the interests of national security are certified by the Secretary of State under s.97 of the Nationality, Immigration and Asylum Act 2002. In these cases appeal lies to the Special Immigration Appeals Commission (SIAC) rather than the tribunal. The sources relied upon in this research indicate that only a small number of cases that come before the SIAC involve Article 1F issues. This is because the majority of cases that come before the SIAC concern appeals against decisions to deport or exclude individuals from the UK or revoke UK citizenship. Article 1F is not relevant in decisions to exclude from the UK or revoke citizenship, and is only of minor relevance to decisions to deport. Since appellants can resist deportation on human rights grounds, even when excluded from refugee status under Article 1F, 'consequently, little, if any, attention was paid to Article 1F in the great majority of cases'.[70]

> Judge E: "Asylum as such is very rarely a determinative question in SIAC because it is dealing with mainly deportation cases where issues under the European Convention are usually more relevant, and exclusion from

70 Judge E.

> citizenship, deprivation of citizenship, where the issue doesn't arise, and exclusion [from the United Kingdom] where it also doesn't arise...it rarely has to consider it at all. In only two cases [in SIAC] was Article 1F of decisive importance."

Examination of appeal to the SIAC is therefore a relatively small section of this research.

The majority (57%) of Article 1F cases analysed as part of this research in which appeal went to the SIAC rather than the tribunal involved revocation of refugee status due to suspected terrorist activities of the individuals concerned, in which the Secretary of State relied on Article 1F(c).[71] In these cases, exclusion under Article 1F was a supplementary issue considered by the Commission in the course of the judgments, which primarily concerned whether or not there was risk on return for the individuals concerned. The two cases in which Article 1F was a decisive issue before the SIAC concerned an individual excluded under Article 1F(b) for allegations of fraud in Algeria, and a member of the Libyan Islamic Fighting Group (LIFG) that the Secretary of State sought to exclude from refugee status under Article 1F(c).

3.2.1 Legal and Evidential Issues

The SIAC may decide to hold closed hearings in which it considers evidence which should not be made public, during which the interests of the appellant are represented by a Special Advocate who is appointed by the Attorney-General (or in Scotland, by the Lord Advocate) for that purpose. The Special Advocate is not at liberty to discuss those proceedings with the appellant.[72]

The closed nature of SIAC proceedings means it is not possible to fully consider the nature of evidence relied upon by the Secretary of State in these cases. Indeed, the use of closed hearings in SIAC cases has elicited a large degree of concern.

> Barrister F: "It's totally unfair, there's no doubt about that. There's nothing worse than being involved in a one-sided trial. There's nothing worse than having a client who is not given the evidence against them. You're given very broad assertions of 'this person is believed to be involved with

71 This is compared to 16% revocation cases overall, and 27% for cases involving suspected terrorists. 57% therefore represents quite a large proportion of these cases.

72 See Clayton G, *Textbook on Immigration and Asylum Law* (4th edn, OUP, 2010) 259–261, for an account of the history and development of the SIAC.

> x, y and z' and nothing to back it up. And that is just fundamentally unfair, and I don't think you can really deny that. ... They're extraordinary, you do your part of the case and the doors close and it goes on behind closed doors. ... You should go and see one it's very interesting. They go on in the basements of Field House. You'll get a sense of what it's like to be shut out of a case which effectively will determine your client's life. It's extraordinary."

However, in most of the cases analysed as part of this research the only Article 1F issue that the Commission had to consider related to whether there are any geographical or temporal limitations to the scope of Article 1F(c), i.e. could the appellant be excluded under Article 1F(c) as a result of acts committed in the UK after being granted refugee status. In the majority of these cases there seemed little doubt that the individual concerned had committed the acts in question.

It seems that the type of evidence relied upon by the Secretary of State in SIAC cases differs from that relied upon when Article 1F is raised in relation to individuals suspected of committing war crimes or crimes against humanity, as outlined in Section 1.2 above. This is not surprising, since evidence that gives rise to national security issues, particularly those of a terrorist nature, will often be supplied by the intelligence services of the UK or other countries, rather than the open-sourced material that is often relied upon in Article 1F(a) war crimes cases.

> Judge E: "Again it's pretty unlikely that the Home Office would rely on Article 1F because that requires the collection of a good deal of information which they won't necessarily have, as I think is demonstrated by the only two SIAC cases in which it has arisen."
>
> Barrister F: "You basically get what's called a Security Services Assessment, which is a summary. So it will say something like 'whatever the name of your client is, is assessed to be an associate of x, y and z'. If you're lucky it might say something like 'in July 2002 it is assessed that your client went on holiday with Mr X and then Mr Y was there'. That's if you're very lucky, normally it will just say 'He is assessed to be involved in furthering the activities of some organisation', and then it will tend to have loads of information about other individuals who your client is assessed to be associated with and about all this stuff, and very little actually about your own client, that's my experience. There's never actually any evidence, they don't really give you any actual documents. That's largely because their assessment is put together on the basis of intelligence, sources from

> wire taps, from tip-offs, you don't get any of that, they put it all together. They paint the picture, and you just get the painted picture but you don't get any of the underlying evidence which is extremely frustrating, it's extremely frustrating."

Unfortunately, as a proportion of the evidence on which the Secretary of State relies to exclude individuals from refugee status before the SIAC cannot be made public, further information on the evidence relied upon in these cases was not available.[73]

4 Conclusions

In this chapter, the process by which an individual is excluded from refugee status under Article 1F, and the consequences of such exclusion in the UK, has been examined. This examination reveals that, although the application of Article 1F to those who would face risk on return no longer means they can be removed from the UK, exclusion under Article 1F does indeed have serious practical consequences for those who remain in the UK. Furthermore, excluding an individual from refugee status under Article 1F leaves the door open to future removal and prevents the excluded individual from establishing firmer ties to the UK that may result in their permanent settlement.

As to the process by which an exclusion decision is made, early identification and investigation of potential Article 1F issues within the Home Office is essential, as this is likely to avoid long and protracted appeals in which Article 1F issues have to be considered afresh, and also lessens the possibility that those who should be excluded under the provision 'slip through the net'. Within the Home Office, closer involvement of the SCU team with Interviewing Officers has begun and a need to provide Article 1F interviewers with further training has been identified. This will likely greatly improve the quality and efficiency of the interview process and help to reduce the need for repeated interviews.

73 As a result of his analysis of the practice of the US, Australia, the UK and Canada in excluding suspected terrorists from refugee status, Kidane suggests that the UK has the best administrative review process. This is primarily because the SIAC's members have diverse but complementary expertise, the decisions of which clearly reflect the maturity of the panel. However, he notes that none of these states provides a system that would endure appropriate levels of procedural due process. Kidane W, 'The Terrorism Bar to Asylum' (n 3) 368–370.

The main ways the procedures of Article 1F hearings before the tribunal differ from other asylum appeals is that the burden of proof rests on the Secretary of State to make out the exclusion decision, and UK legislation directs a decision maker to consider exclusion before inclusion and precludes a balancing test be adopted in relation to the extent of persecution feared by an asylum applicant on return. However, in practice it appears that immigration judges tend to consider Article 1F cases holistically, an approach which may mitigate the effect of this legislation.

It appears that, aside from the testimony of an asylum applicant, a large amount of evidence is relied upon by the SCU team to support an Article 1F decision. This includes international and domestic legal information and a large amount of open sourced material. However, concerns have been raised regarding the non-specificity of the evidence relied upon, in particular that the information is often too generalised and based predominantly on circumstantial evidence. It seems that some of this concern may arise from unfamiliarity with what is required to bring an individual within the scope of Article 1F. Indeed, a recurring theme raised by participants that took part in this research relates to the unfamiliarity of immigration judges and HOPOs with the issues raised by Article 1F cases. It is therefore suggested that, at a minimum, greater time could be allotted to cases that raise Article 1F issues, to enable those involved to fully consider the complex legal and evidential matters involved. A further option which could be pursued is the establishment of a specialised tribunal with the expertise and resources to fully consider the complex issues raised by Article 1F cases. This was a suggestion put forward by the SCU team member interviewed as part of this research. A specialised tribunal could manage Article 1F cases centrally in London, employing skilled and highly trained adjudicators with expertise in international criminal and humanitarian law.[74] It is expected that the establishment of such a tribunal would greatly improve the quality of decision making and add a greater degree of fairness and efficiency to Article 1F proceedings. However, it is unlikely that a specialised tribunal will be established for this purpose when such a small number of cases are involved.

74 The ECRE advises that only skilled and highly trained adjudicators should be called on to undertake the consideration of the exclusion clauses. ECRE, 'Position on Exclusion' (n 84) paras 10 and 52.

Conclusions

This research began with the expectation that the past decade would have seen a dramatic increase in the number of instances in which an individual was excluded from refugee status for their suspected role in terrorist activities or organisations in the UK. This expectation was based on a number of factors, including the prominent role played by the UK in the adoption of UN resolutions calling on Member States to exclude terrorists from refugee status; the introduction of primary legislation in the UK incorporating a broad definition of terrorism in the interpretation of Article 1F(c), and; the concerns of a number of commentators that the absence of a universally accepted definition of terrorism could result in the abuse of Article 1F to exclude genuine refugees from the protection of the 1951 Convention. This research therefore began with the belief that the last decade would have seen a dramatic increase in the number of individuals being excluded from refugee status on grounds of 'terrorism', particularly under Article 1F(c) of the 1951 Convention.

However, all the data employed in this study supports the conclusion that Article 1F decisions represent an extremely small proportion of the total number of asylum decisions made in the UK: the use of this provision appears be very exceptional. Although there has been an increase in the use of Article 1F in the UK in the last two decades, including an increase in the number of Article 1F cases concerning suspected terrorists, the number of cases in which the Home Office has excluded individuals from refugee status for committing terrorist acts remains infrequent and seems to have decreased in the last four years. The increase in the application of Article 1F in the UK has predominantly been in relation to those suspected of committing war crimes or crimes against humanity under Article 1F(a) rather than involvement in terrorist activities. Exclusion from refugee status under Articles 1F(b) and (c), in which terrorism has featured, has remained truly exceptional.

Indeed, courts and tribunals in the UK have repeatedly stressed that Article 1F is not to be equated with a simple anti-terrorist measure. Instead, the practice of courts and tribunals has been to examine whether a particular act meets the definition of one or more of the crimes or acts enumerated in Article 1F, rather than rely on the characterisation of the act or individual as 'terrorist' in nature. To this end, domestic definitions of the crimes and acts listed in Article 1F have been rejected and courts and tribunals have rather looked to international legal sources to determine the 'autonomous meaning' of the provision as a matter of international law.

 | DOI 10.1163/9789004292062_010

The limb of Article 1F that has been relied on in the UK in the overwhelming majority of cases is Article 1F(a) – serious reasons for considering an individual has committed a war crime or a crime against humanity. The practice of both courts and tribunals in the UK and the Home Office has been to look to sources of international criminal law to determine whether the act in question amounts to a war crime or crimes against humanity within the meaning of the provision. A result of this approach is that individuals who could very readily be depicted as 'terrorists' or members of a terrorist organisation are not described as such. Rather, reference is made to the statutes and jurisprudence of international criminal courts and tribunals to determine whether an individual is responsible for the commission of an international crime. This approach appears to accord with the ordinary meaning of the provision and is in line with the restrictive approach it is advised be adopted in the interpretation of Article 1F. However, it is suggested that courts and tribunals in the UK should perhaps be more cautious when referring to contemporary definitions of Article 1F(a) crimes. A notable trend in UK practice is a strong reliance on the provisions of the Rome Statute, which must be cautioned against since the Rome Statute is in some senses narrower, and in some wider, than the customary international law definitions of the crimes listed in Article 1F(a).

The predominant focus on Article 1F(a) and international criminal sources within the Home Office appears to be largely a result of the close relationship of the Special Cases Unit (and its predecessor the War Crime Unit) with the governmental policy of 'no safe haven for war criminals', with the result that these units are more specialised in the definitions of war crimes and crimes against humanity than 'serious non-political crime' and 'acts contrary to the purposes and principles of the United Nations' under Articles 1F(b) and (c). Furthermore, increased reliance on Article 1F(a) rather than the other limbs of Article 1F may be a consequence of the nature of asylum claims in the UK. A large number of asylum applicants in the UK emanate from conflict zones or are fleeing repressive regimes. Crimes committed by these individuals are therefore likely to have been committed in the context of an armed conflict or in support of such a regime, and therefore fall within the scope of Article 1F(a).

In common with the approach adopted in the interpretation of the crimes enumerated in Article 1F(a), courts and tribunals in the UK have recently begun to look towards international criminal sources in order to determine the standard of responsibility necessary for an individual to be excluded under Article 1F. In advocating an approach more closely aligned with international criminal law, the Supreme Court and Court of Appeal disapproved the previous guidance on Article 1F responsibility which focused on the 'terrorist' nature of an organisation of which an individual is a member. The Court of Appeal and Supreme Court preferred to rely on the doctrine of joint criminal enterprise formulated by the ICTY. While this approach is clearly a positive development in the jurisprudence surrounding Article 1F, the Supreme Court's formulation of this mode of liability appears to have confused and conflated it with other modes of responsibility in international criminal law. Furthermore, the Supreme Court's reliance on a number of 'factors' when determining Article 1F responsibility appears to have brought such an examination back to the issue of the nature of an organisation. As such, the formulation of Article 1F responsibility may need to be revisited.

The limb of Article 1F that has traditionally been relied on in the UK to exclude suspected terrorists from refugee status is Article 1F(b) – serious reasons for considering an individual has committed a serious non-political crime. In the early cases concerning the interpretation of this provision, the House of Lords established that those who commit terrorist crimes are capable of being excluded from refugee status for committing a serious non-political crime, despite such acts being committed with allegedly political motivation. However, the Court of Appeal recently stressed that merely labelling an offence 'terrorist' is not adequate to establish that the offence is 'serious' for the purpose of Article 1F(b). Rather, the Court was of the opinion that the individual facts of each case must be considered in order to determine if the crime in question is sufficiently serious to warrant exclusion from refugee status under the provision. The application of Article 1F(b) in the UK has indeed remained truly exceptional; the provision is raised in relation to only a handful of individuals each year. This may be a result of the Home Office's predominant focus on international crimes, as outlined above. Other factors which may have contributed to the low frequency with which this provision is raised in the UK relate to the limitations inherent in the provision. Unlike Articles 1F(a) and (c), Article 1F(b) is geographically and temporally limited to crimes committed outside the host state before an individual's entry as a refugee. Article 1F(b) may not be most readiliy available ground of exclusion in many cases.

The limb of Article 1F under which terrorism has featured most strongly in the UK's interpretation and application is Article 1F(c) – serious reasons for considering an individual is guilty of acts contrary to the purposes and principles of the United Nations. That terrorism has featured largely in the UK's interpretation of this provision is unsurprising, as UN resolutions, UK legislation and the EU Qualification Directives explicitly provide that acts of terrorism fall within its scope. The reference in UK legislation to the UK's broad domestic definition of terrorism in this respect led to the present researcher's expectation that a large number of individuals might potentially fall to be excluded under this provision. However, much like Article 1F(b), the application of Article 1F(c) in the UK appears to have remained exceptional.

When interpreting 'terrorism' for the purpose of Article 1F(c), courts and tribunals in the UK have looked to international definitions of the term rather than rely on the UK's domestic legislation. These bodies have furthermore developed in their jurisprudence a distinction between military activity directed against governmental armed forces and violence directed against civilians (the former held to not fall within the meaning of terrorism for the purpose of the provision) and a requirement that such activity have an international dimension in order to constitute 'acts contrary to the purposes and principles of the United Nations'. Indeed, the Supreme Court recently rejected the UK's domestic definition of terrorism for the purpose of Article 1F(c) entirely, and relied on guidance provided by the UNHCR in stressing that, in order to fall within the scope of the provision, the terrorist activity in question must 'attack the very basis of the international community's coexistence', being assessed with regard to its gravity and impact on international peace and security. In the context of Article 1F(c), this approach may have gone some way to dispelling many of the differences that exist between the different definitions of terrorism that exist in international and domestic law, such acts being likely to fall under all these definitions.

Furthermore, as a primary problem that states encounter when attempting to agree upon an international definition of terrorism concerns the question of whether an exception should be made for the activities of national liberation movements, the exclusion of military activity directed against government forces from the meaning of terrorism for the purpose of Article 1F(c) might go some way in dispelling concerns regarding the lack of international consensus on this issue. In the absence of a clear universally accepted definition of terrorism, however, it may be preferable to focus on what the immigration tribunal in the early cases termed 'acts which are the subject of intense disapproval by the governing body of the entire international community'. These would appear to include acts prohibited by international anti-terrorism conventions such as those relating to hostage taking, hijacking, terrorist bombings and nuclear terrorism, which are politically motivated and committed with the intent of causing death or serious bodily injury, as referred to in Security Council Resolution 1566.

In practice, Article 1F(c) appears to have been applied to two main types of cases. The provision has been relied on by the Secretary of State to revoke refugee status from a number of individuals who were suspected of committing terrorist acts within the UK. As these terrorist acts were committed in the UK after the individuals had been granted refugee status, Article 1F(b) could not be relied on. In the majority of these cases, appeal against the Secretary of State's decision went to the SIAC rather than the tribunal, as the decision was in part based on security sensitive information. The main issue the SIAC had to resolve in these cases concerned the issue of whether there are any temporal or geographical limitations to the scope of Article 1F(c), rather than an examination of the meaning of terrorism for the purpose of the provision. There have also been a number of cases in which Article 1F(c) was relied upon by the Home Office to exclude individuals who had been engaged in military activity against governmental forces. It appears that Article 1F(c) was relied on in these cases rather than Article 1F(a), as the acts in question did not constitute war crimes within the meaning of Article 1F(a). The Court of Appeal in a number of cases rejected the argument that violence directed against governmental military forces constituted terrorism for the purpose of Article 1F(c), maintaining the above noted distinction between activity directed against civilians and against government forces.

Although courts and tribunals in the UK appear to have been increasingly restrictive in their interpretations of 'terrorism' in the context of Article 1F(c), a recent development has seen the provision expanded to apply to attacks directed at UN-mandated combatant forces. It appears that the Supreme Court and Court of Appeal may have been misguided in this respect. The principles of international law which govern the interpretation of the 1951 Convention, and leading international guidance on the interpretation of Article 1F(c) in particular, indicate that international consensus is required to expand the meaning of the phrase 'acts contrary to the purposes and principles of the United Nations' in this way. In the case of action directed against UN-mandated combatant forces, this consensus is clearly lacking. It is therefore suggested that the Supreme Court's decision was flawed in this point and should be revisited.

The process by which an individual is excluded from refugee status under Article 1F was also examined as part of this research. The exclusion process within the Home Office appears to be subject to a fair amount of rigour, no doubt due to the establishment of exclusion units with expertise in Article 1F issues. However, some areas have been identified for further improvement. Closer involvement of the SCU team with Interviewing Officers has begun and a need to provide Article 1F interviewers with further training has been identified. This will likely greatly improve the quality and efficiency of the interview process and help to reduce the need for repeated interviews. The SCU team rely on a large amount of evidence to support an Article 1F decision, including the testimony of the asylum applicant, international and domestic legal information and a large amount of open sourced material. However, concerns have been raised regarding the non-specificity of the evidence relied upon, in particular that the information is often too generalised and based predominantly on circumstantial evidence. It seems that some of this concern may arise from unfamiliarity with what is required to bring an individual within the scope of Article 1F.

Indeed, a recurring theme raised by participants that took part in this research relates to the unfamiliarity of many immigration judges and HOPOs with the issues raised by Article 1F cases. It is therefore suggested that, at a minimum, greater time could be allotted to Article 1F cases. A further option which could be pursued is the establishment of a specialised tribunal with the expertise and resources to fully consider the complex issues raised by Article 1F cases. A specialised tribunal could manage Article 1F cases centrally in London, employing skilled and highly trained adjudicators. Although Article 1F may be said to have lost much of its *raison d'etre*, exclusion from refugee status still has serious practical and legal consequences for the individuals involved. It is therefore essential that Article 1F decisions are made with a high degree of factual and legal expertise and specialised knowledge, in order to give due consideration to the complexities involved in such cases and the serious consequences of exclusion from refugee status under Article 1F of the 1951 Convention.

Bibliography

Books and Monographs

Aust A, *Modern Treaty Law and Practice* (2nd ed, CUP, 2007).

Aust A, *Handbook of International Law* (2nd ed, CUP, 2010).

Boccardi I, *Europe and Refugees: Towards an EU Asylum Policy* (Kluwer Law International, 2002).

Brouwer E, Catz P, and Guild E (eds), *Immigration, Asylum and Terrorism: A Changing Dynamic in European Law* (Recht & Samenleving, 2003).

Brownlie I, *Principles of Public International Law* (7th ed, OUP, 2008).

Clayton G, *Textbook on Immigration and Asylum Law* (4th ed, OUP, 2010).

Conte A, *Human Rights in the Prevention and Punishment of Terrorism* (Springer, 2010).

Feller E, Türk V, and Nicholson F (eds), *Refugee Protection in International Law: UNHCR's Global Consultations on International Protection* (CUP, 2003).

Gardiner R, *Treaty Interpretation* (OUP, 2008).

Goodwin-Gill G, and McAdam J, *The Refugee in International Law* (3rd ed, OUP, 2007).

Grahl-Madsen A, *The Status of Refugees in International Law*, vol. I (AW Sijthoff-Leiden, 1966).

Hailbronner K, Tiryakioglu B, Kucuk E, and Schneider K (eds), *Vatandaşlık, Göç, Mültecive Yabancılar Hukukundaki Güncel Gelişmeler (Current Developments in Citizenship, Immigration, Refugee Law and Law of Foreigners)* (Union of Turkish Bar Associations, 2009).

Hathaway J, *The Law of Refugee Status* (CUP, 1991).

Hathaway J, *The Rights of Refugees under International Law* (CUP, 2005).

Hathaway J, and Foster, M, *The Law of Refugee Status* (2nd ed, CUP, 2014).

Letsas G, *A Theory of Interpretation of the European Convention on Human Rights* (OUP, 2007).

MacDonald IA, and Toal R (eds), *Immigration Law and Practice in the United Kingdom*, vol. I (8th ed, Lexis Nexis, 2010).

McAdam J (ed), *Forced Migration, Human Rights and Security* (Hart Publishing, 2008).

Noll G, Proof, *Evidentiary Assessment and Credibility in Asylum Procedures* (Martinus Nijhoff, 2005).

Rikhof J, *The Criminal Refugee: The Treatment of Asylum Seekers with a Criminal Background in International and Domestic Law* (Dordrecht, 2012).

Saul B, *Defining Terrorism in International Law* (OUP, 2006).

Saul B, *Defining Terrorism in International Law* (OUP, 2008).

Schabas WA, McDermott Y, and Hayes N (eds), *The Ashgate Research Companion to International Criminal Law: Critical Perspectives* (Ashgate Publishing Company, 2013).

Shelton D (ed), *The Oxford Handbook of International Human Rights Law* (OUP, 2013).

Turksen U, *Protection Seekers, States and the New Security Agenda – A Comparative Analysis of the Impact of Anti-terrorism Legislation on the Law Relating to Asylum Seekers in the United Kingdom, the United States of America and Australia* (2008) PhD, West of England, 58–9185.

Woodbridge G, *UNRRA: The History of the United Nations Relief and Rehabilitation Administration* (Columbia University Press, 1950).

Zanchettin M, *Asylum and Refugee Protection after September 11: Towards Increasing Restrictionism?* (Refugee Study Centre, 2003).

Zimmerman A (ed), *The 1951 Convention Relating to the Status of Refugees and Its 1967 Protocol: A Commentary* (OUP, 2011).

Chapters and Articles

Aas MB, 'Exclusion from Refugee Status: Rules and Practices in Norway, Canada, Great Britain, The Netherlands and Denmark' (2013) *Norwegian Directorate of Immigration*.

Amarasinha SD, and Isenbecker M, 'Terrorism and the Right to Asylum under the 1951 Convention and the 1967 Protocol Relating to the Status of Refugees – A Contradiction in Terms or Do Opposites Attract?' (1996) 65 *Nordic Journal of International Law* 223–240.

Arato J, 'Subsequent Practice and Evolutive Interpretation Techniques of Treaty Interpretation over Time and Their Diverse Consequences' (2010) 9 *The Law and Practice of International Courts and Tribunals* 443–494.

Bernhardt R, 'Evolutive Interpretation, Especially of the European Convention on Human Rights' (1999) 42 *German Yearbook of International Law* 11–25.

Blake N, 'Exclusion from Refugee Protection: Serious Non-political Crimes after 9/11' (2003) 4 *European Journal of Migration and Law* 425–447.

Boccardi I, 'Confronting a False Dilemma: EU Asylum Policy between "Protection" and "Securitisation"' (2007) 60 *Current Legal Problems* 204–257.

Bond J, 'Excluding Justice: The Dangerous Intersection between Refugee Claims, Criminal Law, and "Guilty" Asylum Seekers' (2012) 24(1) *International Journal of Refugee Law* 37–59.

Brouwer E, 'Immigration, Asylum and Terrorism: A Changing Dynamic, Legal and Practical Developments in the EU in Response to the Terrorist Attacks of 11.09' (2003) 4 *European Journal of Migration and Law* 399–424.

Cassese A, 'The Multifaceted Criminal Notion of Terrorism in International Law' (2006) 4 *Journal of International Criminal Justice* 933–958.

Clark T, 'Rights Based Refuge, the Potential of the 1951 Convention and the Need for Authoritative Interpretation' (2004) 16 *International Journal of Refugee Law* 584–608.

Drummond C, 'Different Sources of International Criminal Law and Exclusion: How the Federal Court of Australia in *SRYYY v Minister for Immigration and Multicultural and Indigenous Affairs* Got It Wrong and Why It Matters' (2013) 3(1) *Oxford Monitor of Forced Migration* 35–42.

Duffy A, 'Expulsion to Face torture? Non-refoulement in International Law' (2008) 20(3) *International Journal of Refugee Law* 373–390.

Einarsen T, 'Drafting History of the 1951 Convention and the 1967 Protocol', in Andreas Zimmerman (ed) *The 1951 Convention Relating to the Status of Refugees and Its 1967 Protocol: A Commentary* (OUP, 2011) 37–74.

European Council on Refugees and Exiles (ECRE), 'Position on Exclusion From Refugee Status' (2004) 16(2) *International Journal of Refugee Law* 257–285.

European Council on Refugees and Exiles (ECRE), *The Impact of the EU Qualification Directive on International Protection*, October 2008.

Fitzmaurice G, 'The Law and Procedure of the International Court of Justice 1951–4: Treaty Interpretation and other Treaty Points' (1957) 33 *British Yearbook of International Law* 210–212.

Fitzmaurice M, 'The Practical Working of the Law of Treaties', in Malcolm Evans (ed) *International Law* (2nd ed, OUP, 2006) 157–215.

Fitzmaurice M, 'Dynamic (Evolutive) Interpretation of Treaties: Part I' (2008) 21 *Hague Yearbook of International Law* 101–153.

Fitzmaurice M, 'Interpretation of Human Rights Treaties', in Dinah Shelton (ed) *The Oxford Handbook of International Human Rights Law* (OUP, 2013) 739–771.

French D, 'Treaty Interpretation and the Incorporation of Extraneous Legal Rules' (2006) 55(2) *International and Comparative Law Quarterly* 281–314.

Gibney M, 'Security and the Ethics of Asylum after 11 September' (2002) 13 *Forced Migration Review* 40–42.

Gilbert G, 'Current Issues in the Application of the Exclusion Clauses', in Erika Feller, Volker Türk, and Frances Nicholson (eds) *Refugee Protection in International Law: UNHCR's Global Consultations on International Protection* (CUP, 2003) 425–478.

Gilbert G, 'Exclusion and Evidentiary Evidence', in Gregor Noll, Proof (ed) *Evidentiary Assessment and Credibility in Asylum Procedures* (Martinus Nijhoff, 2005) 161–178.

Gilbert G, 'Exclusion under Article 1F since 2001: Two Steps Backwards, One Step Forward' (2012) University of Essex, School of Law, Working Papers Series.

Goodwin-Gill G, 'Forced Migration: Refugees, Rights and Security', in Jane McAdam (ed) *Forced Migration Human Rights and Security* (Portland, 2008) 1–17.

Goodwin-Gill G, 'Article 1F(c) of the 1951 Convention: Denying Refugee Status because of Acts Contrary to the Purposes and Principles of the United Nations', Lecture Given as Part of the International Refugee Law Seminar Series, Refugee Law Initiative, London, 11 October 2011.

Guild E, and Garlick M, 'Refugee Protection, Counter-Terrorism, and Exclusion in the European Union' (2010) 29(4) *Refugee Survey Quarterly* 63–82.

Hathaway J, and Harvey C, 'Framing Refugee Protection in the New World Disorder' (2001) 34 *Cornell International Law Journal* 257–320.

Juss S, 'Terrorism and the Exclusion of Refugee Status in the UK' (2012a) 17(3) *Journal of Conflict and Security Law* 465–499.

Juss S, 'Complicity, Exclusion, and the "Unworthy" in Refugee Law' (2012b) 31(3) *Refugee Survey Quarterly* (2012) 1–39.

Kalin W, and Kunzli J, 'Article 1F(b): Freedom Fighters, Terrorists, and the Notion of Serious Non-political Crimes' (2000) 12 (Special Supplement) *International Journal of Refugee Law* 46–78.

Kapferer S, 'Exclusion Clauses in Europe – A Comparative Overview of State Practice in France, Belgium and the United Kingdom' (2000) 12 (Special Supplement) *International Journal of Refugee Law* 195–221.

Kapferer S, 'Article 14(2) of the Universal Declaration of Human Rights and Exclusion from International Refugee Protection' (2008) 27(3) *Refugee Survey Quarterly* 53–75.

Kapferer S, 'Revision of UNHCR's Guidelines on Exclusion: Update', Nordic Asylum Seminar, Bergen, Norway, 6–7 June 2013.

Kaushal A, and Dauvergne C, 'The Growing Culture of Exclusion: Trends in Canadian Refugee Exclusion' (2011) 23 *International Journal of Refugee Law* 54–92.

Klabbers J, 'Rebel with a Cause? Terrorists and Humanitarian Law' (2003) 14(2) *European Journal of International Law* 299–312.

Lambert H, 'The EU Asylum Qualification Directive, Its Impact on the Jurisprudence of the United Kingdom and International Law (2006) 55 *International and Comparative Law Quarterly* 161–192.

Lauterpacht E, and Bethlehem D, 'The Scope and Content of the Principle of *Non-refoulement*: Opinion', in Feller E, Türk V, and Nicholson F (eds) *Refugee Protection in International Law: UNHCR's Global Consultations on International Protection* (CUP, 2003) 89–177.

Lawyers Committee for Human Rights, 'Safeguarding the Rights of Refugees under the Exclusion Clauses: Summary Findings of the Project and a Lawyers Committee for Human Rights Perspective' (2000) 12 (Special Supplement) *International Journal of Refugee Law* 317–345.

Lewis C, 'UNHCR's Contribution to the Development of International Refugee Law: Its Foundations and Evolution' (2005) 17 *International Journal of Refugee Law* 67–90.

Mathew P, 'Resolution 1373 – A Call to Pre-empt Asylum Seekers?' in Jane McAdam (ed) *Forced Migration, Human Rights and Security* (Portland, 2008) 19–61.

McAdam J, 'Interpretation of the 1951 Convention', in Andreas Zimmerman (ed) *The 1951 Convention Relating to the Status of Refugees and Its 1967 Protocol: A Commentary* (OUP, 2011) 75–116.

Messari N, and van der Klaauw J, 'Counter-Terrorism Measures and Refugee Protection in North America (2011) 29 (4) *Refugee Survey Quarterly* 83–103.

Michigan Guidelines on the Exclusion of International Criminals, Sixth Colloquium on Challenges in Refugee Law, University of Michigan, 22–24 March 2013.

Nyinah MK, 'Exclusion under Article 1F: Some Reflections on Context, Principles and Practice' (2000) 12(Special Supplement) *International Journal of Refugee Law* 295–316.

Orakhelashvili A, 'Restrictive Interpretation of Human Rights Treaties in the Recent Jurisprudence of the European Court of Human Rights' (2003) 14 *European Journal of International Law* 529–568.

Pejic Z, 'Article 1F(a): The Notion of International Crimes (2000) 12 (Special Supplement) *International Journal of Refugee Law* 11–45.

Rikhof J, 'Complicity in International Criminal Law and Canadian Refugee Law' (2006) 4 *Journal of International Criminal Justice* 702–722.

Rikhof J, 'War Criminals Not Welcome; How Common Law Countries Approach the Phenomenon of International Crimes in the Immigration and Refugee Context' (2009) 21(3) *International Journal of Refugee Law* 453–507.

Roscini M, 'The United Nations Security Council and the Enforcement of International Humanitarian Law' (2010) 43 *Israel Law Review* 330–359.

Roscini M, 'Threats of Armed Force and Contemporary International Law' (2007) 54 *Netherlands International Law Review* 229–277.

Rountable of the Future of Refugee Convention Supervision, Summary Conclusions, Downing College, University of Cambridge, 28–29 September 2012.

Saul B, 'The Legal Response of the League of Nations to Terrorism' (2006) 4(1) *Journal of International Criminal Justice* 78–102.

Saul B, 'Protecting Refugees in the Global "War on Terror"' (2008) University of Sydney, Legal Studies Research Paper No. 08/130.

Saul B, 'The Special Tribunal for Lebanon and Terrorism as an International Crime: Reflections on the Judicial Function', in William A. Schabas, Yvonne McDermott, and Niamh Hayes (eds), *The Ashgate Research Companion to International Criminal Law: Critical Perspectives* (Ashgate Publishing Company, 2013).

Shah P, 'Activism in the European Court of Justice and Changing Options for Turkish Citizen Migrants in the United Kingdom', in: Kay Hailbronner, Bilgin Tiryakioglu, Esin Kucuk, and Katja Schneider (eds) *Vatandaşlık, Göç, Mültecive Yabancılar Hukukundaki Güncel Gelişmeler (Current Developments in Citizenship, Immigration, Refugee Law and Law of Foreigners)* (Union of Turkish Bar Associations, 2009) 299–326.

Simeon JC, 'Complicity and Culpability and the Exclusion of Terrorists from Convention Refugee Status Post 9/11' 29(4) *Refugee Survey Quarterly* 104–137.

Singer S, 'Exclusion from Refugee Status and Terrorist Related Offences: The Case of AH (Algeria)' (2012a) 26(4) *Journal of Immigration Asylum and Nationality Law* 337–348.

Singer S, 'Exclusion from Refugee Status: Asylum Seekers and Terrorism in the UK' (2012b) 1 *Centre for Criminal Justice and Human Rights Working Papers Series* 2–16.

Singh S, 'Will Acceptance of a "Universally Approved Definition" of Terrorism Make Article 1F of the 1951 Refugee Convention More Effective in Excluding Terrorists?' (2006) 2(3) *Journal of Migration & Refugee Issues* 91–119.

Sivakumaran S, 'Exclusion from Refugee Status: The Purposes and Principles of the United Nations and Article 1F(c) of the Refugee Convention' (2014) 26(3) *International Journal of Refugee Law* 350–381.

Sloan J, 'The Application of Article 1F of the 1951 Convention in Canada and the United States' (2000) 12(Special Supplement) *International Journal of Refugee Law* 222–248.

Storey H, 'EU Qualification Directive: A Brave New World?' (2008) 20 *International Journal of Refugee Law* 1–49.

Symes M, 'The Refugee Qualification Directive' (2006) *Electronic Immigration Network*.

Symonds S, 'The Special Immigration Status' (2008) 22 *Journal of Immigration Asylum and Nationality Law* 333–349.

Turk V, 'Forced Migration and Security' (2003) 15(1) *International Journal of Refugee Law* 113–125.

United Nations High Commissioner for Refugees, *Asylum in the European Union: A Study of the Implementation of the Qualification Directive*, November 2007.

Zard M, 'Exclusion, Terrorism and the Refugee Convention' (2002) 13 *Forced Migration Review* 32–34.

Zimmermann A, and Wennholz P, 'Article 1F 1951 Convention', in Andreas Zimmerman (ed) *The 1951 Convention Relating to the Status of Refugees and Its 1967 Protocol: A Commentary* (OUP, 2011a) 579–610.

Zimmermann A, and Wennholz P, 'Article 33, Para 2', in Andreas Zimmerman (ed) *The 1951 Convention Relating to the Status of Refugees and Its 1967 Protocol: A Commentary* (OUP, 2011b) 1397–1423.

Index

www.ingramcontent.com/pod-product-compliance
Lightning Source LLC
LaVergne TN
LVHW010625300926
849162LV00001B/66